Political Order
and the
Plural Structure of Society

Emory University
Studies in Law and Religion

General Editor
John Witte, Jr.

Number 2

Political Order and the Plural Structure of Society

edited by
James W. Skillen
Rockne M. McCarthy

Political Order
and the
Plural Structure of Society

edited by
James W. Skillen
Rockne M. McCarthy

SCHOLARS PRESS
Atlanta, Georgia

EMORY UNIVERSITY
STUDIES IN LAW AND RELIGION

Political Order
and the
Plural Structure of Society

edited by
James W. Skillen
Rockne M. McCarthy

© 1991
Emory University

Cover art by Shelley Lowell

Library of Congress Cataloging in Publication Data

Political order and the plural structure of society / edited by James
    W. Skillen, Rockne M. McCarthy.
    p. cm. — (Emory University studies in law and religion ; no.
    2)
    Includes bibliographical references.
    ISBN 1-55540-640-8. — ISBN 1-55540-641-6 (pbk.)
    1. Pluralism (Social sciences) 2. Individualism.
3. Collectivism. 4. State, The. 5. Political science—Philosophy.
I. Skillen, James W. II. McCarthy, Rockne M. III. Series.
JC541.P65 1991
323.1—dc20   91-29754
                                              CIP

Published by Scholars Press
for
Emory University

T he Emory University Studies in Law and Religion is an
occasional series of monographs, anthologies, text-
books, and translations of classic texts in the field of law and
religion. The series has been established by the Law and
Religion Program at Emory University to foster further exploration of the religious dimensions of law, the legal dimensions
of religion, and the interaction of legal and religious ideas,
institutions, and methods. The volumes published in this series
will help meet the growing demand for literature in the
burgeoning interdisciplinary field of law and religion.

Send inquiries to:
Emory University Studies in Law and Religion
Gambrell Hall
Emory School of Law
Atlanta, Georgia 30322

For

Glenn Andreas

and

John Hulst

PREFACE

This project began more than a decade ago when we confronted the need in both academic and political circles for a book like this. The Dordt College Studies Institute in Sioux Center, Iowa provided the launching pad. From 1979 to 1982, when both of us were teaching and doing research there, the plan was conceived and work began both to collect readings and to write introductions to them in order to produce a volume that would acquaint students with recent traditions of thought that are largely unknown in North American circles.

From the mid-1970s to the present time, we have also been working together in various capacities for the Association for Public Justice and the Center for Public Justice in Washington, D.C. to nurture Christian political responsibility in the United States. Here we have confronted the need for a social/political perspective that is lacking in the circles of mainstream American pragmatism and individualism.

Our hope is that this volume will contribute to both the academic and the public policy debates now in progress by helping to frame some of the questions about a just society in a fresh way. For that to become possible, many students in colleges and graduate schools may first have to study the traditions introduced here.

Those who have helped us in one way or another with this volume are beyond counting and remembering. We owe a deep debt of gratitude to Dordt College, and especially to its president, John Hulst, for encouraging and supporting our work. For ten years, Dr. Hulst also chaired the board of the Association for Public Jusitce. We also wish to express special thanks to Glenn Andreas who has labored for more than forty years in several countries to encourage the Christian reformation of scholarship and who has contributed generously to the Center for Public Justice from its inception.

We are very grateful for the translation help of Harry der Nederlander, Gordon Spykman, Harry Van Dyke, and Donald Morton, and for hours of discussion with McKendree Langley who helped in the early stages as we made reading selections and began to write the introductions. John Witte, Jr., a Fellow of the Center for Public Justice as well as director of the Law and Religion Program at Emory University, has done yeoman's service in bringing this volume to editorial completion, making many excellent suggestions along the way to make it a better book than it could have been without him. Our thanks also to others who helped with so many hours of typing, editing, and/or proofreading: Amy Brogdon, Eliza Ellison, Jay Todd Hahn, Amy Snider, and Marie Warren. To the living authors who allowed us to use selections from their publications, and the publishers who gave approval to reprint selections, we express our sincerest thanks.

To our wives and children who sustained us with the love and encouragement necessary to allow for concentration on this extensive undertaking we can only say, "We love you."

James W. Skillen
Annapolis, Maryland

Rockne M. McCarthy
Sioux Center, Iowa

May 1991

PART TWO
*Subsidiarity, Natural Law,
and the Common Good*

PART THREE
*Sphere Sovereignty, Creation Order,
and Public Justice*

CONTENTS

PART FOUR
Three Views of Social Pluralism:
A Critical Evaluation

ACKNOWLEDGMENTS

The editors wish to thank the following parties for permission to reprint copyrighted material herein:

Augsburg Fortress Publishers, for excerpts from José Míguez Bonino, *Doing Theology in a Revolutionary Situation* (Philadelphia, 1975).

Cambridge University Press and Professor Antony Black for excerpts from Otto von Gierke, *Community in Historical Perspective,* trans. Mary Fisher, selected and edited by Antony Black (Cambridge, 1990), pp. 9-12, 111-114, 118-123, 161-163.

Doubleday, a division of Bantam Doubleday Dell Publishing Group, Inc. for excerpts from Etienne Gilson, ed., *The Church Speaks to the Modern World: The Social Teachings of Leo XIII* (Garden City, NY: 1954) and for excerpts from Terence P. McLaughlin, ed., *The Church and the Reconstruction of the Modern World: The Social Encyclicals of Pope Pius XI* (Garden City, NY: 1957).

National Conference of Catholic Bishops, for excerpts from *Economic Justice for All: Pastoral Letter on Catholic Social Teaching and the U.S. Economy* (Washington, D.C.: 1986).

The University of Chicago Press, for excerpts from Jacques Maritain, *Man and the State* (Chicago, 1951).

Dr. H. Evan Runner, for revised excerpts from H. Evan Runner, *Scriptural Religion and Political Task* (Toronto, Wedge Publishing Co., 1974).

INTRODUCTION:
THE QUESTION OF PLURALISM

The collapse of communist governments in Eastern Europe beginning in 1989 represents a popular judgment that more than four decades of Soviet-dominated, Marxist-Leninist practice has failed. The drive is now on to reconstitute the states and societies of that region in ways that will allow political, economic, religious, and cultural life to flourish. Whether those countries will be reconstructed so that democracy, social freedom, and greater prosperity can become standard practice remains to be seen. But at least for the moment the rejection of centralized collectivism as a social model seems to be complete.

Many officials and experts in the West believe, of course, that the solutions to the problems in Eastern Europe can be found in the systems and practices of Western Europe and North America. The West's difficulties suddenly appear minor compared to those of Eastern Europe, and the West's virtues and successes now seem to stand out in the minds of many.

However, this celebration of the West's comparative advantage may become less confident and boisterous in the decades ahead as the dramatic events of 1989 recede into the background. The reason is that the West faces its own critical problems. In fact, some of the West's difficulties are closely related, at root, to those which brought Eastern European societies into fundamental crisis. For example, both the collectivist ideology of Marxist-Leninist-Stalinism as well as the ideology of autonomous individual freedom that dominates much of Western liberalism share a common root in the Enlightenment ideals of human self-sufficiency and world mastery. Faith in scientific reasoning, technological development, economic growth, and self-governance as the means of progress toward complete human autonomy is a faith that has sustained both communist and liberal alike. For decades now in the West, many scholars and social critics have been calling attention to the multiple crises of this Enlightenment faith as it has developed along individualist lines.[1] Thus the question for us today, it would seem, should not be narrowly whether the Eastern Europeans (including the Soviet Union) can become healthy like the West. Rather, our question should be whether countries throughout the world, including those in the West, can reform themselves in ways that will overcome the variety of defects that plague them—including the defects evident in the development of Enlightenment humanism. Much of the West may, indeed, have enjoyed a relative advantage during most of the twentieth century because it was *not* so singularly dominated by totalitarian governments imposing a materialist dogma with conformist social ideals. Perhaps Eastern Europe's disadvantage has been due chiefly to its subjection to totalitarian party control that forced upon it an anti-historical alienation from older and more diverse European traditions. Whatever the relative advantages of the West, however, the fact remains that it is not without its own contemporary crises.

To evaluate the historical development of human societies is not a simple task, to be sure. We do not want to suggest by these opening comments that such an evaluation will be completed in this volume. What we do intend to offer, however, is an introduction to a *pluralist* view of state and society. Pluralism has developed over the past two centuries in critical response to both individualism and collectivism under the conviction that the structural diversity of human social life cannot be explained away philosophically by reference to either individual autonomy or collectivist unity. There are significant differences among the pluralist perspectives presented in the three parts below, and each requires critical evaluation. But our interest in assessing this variety of pluralist arguments in a single text arises because together they stand out as different from (and critical of) modern individualist and collectivist points of view. And we believe that a properly conceived pluralism has much to offer contemporary states and societies throughout the world as they struggle with social and political reform.

Defining Terms

First, a few comments are in order about our use of the terms "collectivism," "individualism," and "pluralism."

The popular term "collectivism" depends on an essentially universalist conception of human society in which every person and institution is considered to be a functional part of a larger, unitary whole. A social or political unity is thought to be prior in principle, giving identity to all its parts. For collectivism, justice is defined as that which is good for the whole, since only the whole has an independent identity and is competent to make law. Families, schools, churches, universities, the media, industries, and individual persons are recognized by collectivists not as irreducible realities in their own right but merely as dependent parts of a larger organizable society or world community.

"Individualism," by contrast, is the foundation stone of modern liberal thought. The only irreducible reality, from this viewpoint, is the individual person. Every kind of institution or social formation is either a mere legal fiction or a behavioral manifestation of contracts and agreements among individuals. Society and social institutions are, ultimately, nothing more than collections of individuals—patterns of organized individual behavior. Justice is realized by protecting the rights of individuals and the contracts into which free individuals enter. From an individualist perspective, the collectivist makes the mistake of imagining that collections of people are real things in their own right. Every form of collectivism puts an imaginary "whole" before its supposedly dependent "parts" and then tries mentally to reduce the latter to the former. But reality is just the reverse, say the individualists. Individuals (and thus their rights and freedoms) are prior to everything that they organize and coordinate. Only individuals are competent to make binding laws; only individuals are real.

"Pluralism" is more complex and ambiguous than either collectivism or individualism, in large measure because it does not seek a radical reduction of human social life to either the individual or a single collective. Kenneth D. McRae has pointed out that genuinely pluralist theories of society are notable chiefly by their absence from the modern Western tradition.[2] There is evidence to suggest that pluralist thinking emerged more in protest against the reductionistic extremes of modern individualism and collectivism than as a clearly intended alternative view of society. Consequently, the term "pluralism" today means many things to many people.

For example, when David Nicholls set out to distinguish the different meanings of pluralism, he concluded that there are at least three varieties.[3] One variety was developed by the so-called English pluralists at the start of the twentieth century. A second is connected with the interest-group politics of the American experience. A third is associated with the structure of some former colonial, less developed societies. Look, for a moment, at the first two varieties.

At the beginning of the twentieth century, many politicians in England and on the Continent were making extreme claims for the modern state. In France the government was trying to establish a secular society in which the rights of institutions such as churches and trade unions would be denied. "There are, and there can be no rights except the right of the State," wrote Premier M. Emile Combes (1902-1905), "and there are, and there can be no other authority than the authority of the Republic."[4] Although few British political leaders would have made such an extreme statement at the time, one group of intellectuals—the English pluralists—had become distressed by the ease with which many British citizens and politicians were beginning to accept the idea of state absolutism. The climate of opinion in Great Britain at the turn of the century constituted a serious threat, they feared, to the rights of diverse corporations.

The English pluralists took their inspiration from Lord Acton and F.W. Maitland. Their leading lights were John Neville Figgis, Harold Laski, and G. D. H. Cole, who all saw in the reality of "groups" a bulwark of liberty against the dangers of an all-powerful state. Groups, as they understood them, had their own identities and even "personalities." Groups were not merely a sum of their individual members. The pluralists used the word "group" to refer to many associations and institutions in society, both voluntary and involuntary, such as families, schools, labor unions, and the church.[5] Many of the English pluralists followed the great German historian and legal theorist Otto von Gierke who argued that groups have a personality of their own and an existence not derived from individual will or the state. Figgis, for example, helped Maitland to translate part of Gierke's massive work *The German Law of Associations* which was published in 1900 as *Political Theories of the Middle Ages*.[6] Gierke's idea of "group personality" became an important part of the English pluralists' social philosophy.

A second use of the term "pluralism" is associated with the development of behavioral social science in the United States and particularly with the names of Arthur Fisher Bentley, David Truman, and Robert A. Dahl. Quite in contrast to the English pluralists, these American writers have considered groups to be collections of individuals who share a common political interest or purpose. In *The Government Process* (1908), for example, Bentley described politics as the process of inter-group conflict in which each group tries to gain or maintain some particular interest of its members.[7] The government's role, according to Bentley, is to establish an equilibrium or balance between the many competing groups or interests. While the government may be controlled for a time by one group or set of groups, the tide will turn and another group or set of groups will then have its turn. For Bentley, the term "pluralism" refers to a political process of interaction among many competing groups who may alternate or rise and fall in the control of power. Truman and Dahl followed in Bentley's footsteps adding sophistication to theories of group conflict and competition.[8]

The understanding of groups among American behavioralists is actually grounded in the individualist tradition. Groups are functional organizations of individual interests. There is little if anything in the writings of these scholars that points to a pluralist philosophy of institutional and associational differences derived from qualities and characteristics unique to each entity. Group behavior theory is an attempt to provide an empirical explanation of political interest-group activity; it is not a philosophy of social pluralism. From an English pluralist point of view this should not even be called pluralism. Taken as a whole, the work of Bentley, Truman, and Dahl shows an additional sharp contrast between the American and English pluralists. In England, Figgis and others thought of pluralism as a normative guide to the way society *ought* to be structured. They were propounding a social philosophy that defined justice as the recognition of both group rights and individual rights. Bentley, Truman, and Dahl, however, used pluralism simply to describe certain power-balancing functions performed in a liberal society. The primary concern of the American behavioralists has been to explain how the political process works. From this point of view, as Nicholls explains, "there is no right other than might, 'justice' is but a term cynically employed by the combatants to camouflage self-interest, 'legitimacy' means that which is accepted by the powerful."[9] Politics is essentially an amoral struggle among contending groups of individuals, each acting in its own self-interest.

While it may be true that the word "pluralism" can be used to describe movements as diverse as European corporatism and American behavioralism, in this volume we are using the term in a more restrictive fashion. Here we are examining views that are closer to the English pluralists than to the American behavioralists. Our interest is in those who are struggling for words and concepts to categorize the structural differences among the diverse institutions and associations of society.

By dismissing the interest-group pluralists of American behavioralism we are not, however, expressing a lack of interest in American society and politics. To the contrary, this book is written primarily with an American audience in mind. Thus, before going on to introduce the readings, let us consider briefly the American context in which the debate over social pluralism is being, and needs to be, conducted. That context is a large one covering everything from urgent public policy debates to fundamental ethical and philosophical disputes. Consequently, our contextual introduction will have something of an impressionistic character. Nevertheless, it can help to set the stage for a more detailed consideration of the pluralist perspectives that follow.

Freedom, Progress, and History

Writing in the decade following World War II, social philosopher Robert A. Nisbet began to raise serious questions about the American liberal ideals of human autonomy and inevitable human progress. From a standpoint in the 1990s, many may be inclined to look back to the 1950s with nostalgia as a time of peace, prosperity, and happiness. But Nisbet was aware then of a deeper current of doubt and pessimism running through Western societies. After all, two world wars and at least two versions of ideological fanaticism had produced unprecedented human destruction in a supposedly enlightened Europe. Western liberalism, Nisbet concluded, with its confident assumption "that history is a more or less continuous emancipation of men from despotism and evil" could offer no satisfactory account of evil on such a grand scale.[10] Belief in the inevitable progress of history is a mythical faith—a new faith emerging from the Enlightenment of the late eighteenth and early nineteenth centuries.

The Enlightenment myth of the progress of freedom, according to Nisbet, holds that as individuals become liberated from the past constraints of aristocratic and ecclesiastical bondage, they will become ever more independent, happy, and self-determining. This faith leads its adherents to reject much of what is good about traditional associations and community life. A chief consequence is that these supposedly liberated individuals fall prey to bureaucratic and even totalitarian states which make them less free in many cases than their ancestors had been. "The conception of society as an aggregate of morally autonomous, psychologically free, individuals, rather than as a collection of groups, is, in sum, closely related to a conception of society in which all legitimate authority has been abstracted from the primary communities and vested in the single sphere of the State."[11]

The actual consequence of the Enlightenment conception of liberated individuals has *not*, in fact, been the realization of full autonomy for everyone but rather a new enslavement—a new kind of powerlessness, insecurity, and loss of social meaning on a mass scale. "The inadequacy of individualism as a theory of freedom," Nisbet wrote, in 1953,

> lies plainly written in the conditions we see spreading in the Western world to-day: on the one hand, enlarging masses of socially "free," insecure, individuals; on the other, the constant increase in the custodial powers of a State that looms ever larger as the only significant refuge for individuals who insist upon escaping from the moral consequences of individualism.[12]

If one consequence of individualistic idealism is the emergence of a massive custodial state, then a consequence of the growing custodial state, as it has emerged in the United States, is the nearly overwhelming influence of interest-group politics. Theodore J. Lowi analyzes this problem in his book *The End of Liberalism*.[13] American citizens, he says, have turned increasingly to the state to secure the protection and benefits of their freedom. In the process, they have become organized more and more as political interest groups. Yet they hide from or deny the expansion of government which this movement helps to create. They try to maintain the conviction that government is simply an extension of their own freedom and self-governance. But that is an illusion. According to Lowi, interest-group liberalism in America

> helps create the sense that power need not be power at all, control need not be control, and government need not be coercive. If sovereignty is parcelled out among groups, then who is out anything? As a major *Fortune* editor enthusiastically put it, government power, group power, and individual power may go up simultaneously. If the groups to be controlled control the controls, then "to administer does not always mean to rule."[14]

What was set in motion beginning around the time of the Great Depression was an expanding process of interest-group competition. Under the pressure of that interest-group scramble for power and influence, government's authority to decide what is just and unjust—what is good policy and bad—has seriously declined. Interest-group liberalism, according to Lowi, seeks a form of government "in which there is no formal specification of means or of ends." In a government so divided, "there is, therefore, no substance. Neither is there procedure. There is only process."[15]

The epitome of interest-group liberalism's achievements, in Lowi's view, was American federal legislation produced by the War on Poverty initiated in 1964 with the omnibus Economic Opportunity Act. "Delegation of power is the order of the day in this statute. Operative standards are almost impossible to find anywhere in it."[16] In place of firm standards and clear procedures stand mere sentiments and goals, according to Lowi.

> The act is, especially in its most important and most novel titles, completely process-oriented nonlaw. It speaks of reaching the causes of poverty, but this is almost entirely rhetorical, for there is nothing in these clauses of the statute and official records that even the most legal-minded bureaucrat had to feel guided by. There is no guidance because all the apparent guidance is suggestive and permissive.[17]

The more ubiquitous and intrusive government has become, the more undefined and lacking in authority it becomes. Interest-group politics corrupts democratic government because it gives the impression that people are represented in government merely because they have been given access to the interest-group process. This kind of liberalism actually helps to render government impotent, because the latter's power is delegated out to a process without standards or limits. Both citizens and government officials become demoralized even as they become increasingly entrapped, because this kind of government cannot achieve justice. According to Lowi,

> No matter what definition of justice is used, liberal governments cannot achieve justice because their policies lack the *sine qua non* of justice—that quality without which a consideration of justice cannot even be initiated. Considerations of justice in, or achieved by, an action cannot be made unless a deliberate and conscious attempt was made to derive the action from a preexisting general rule or moral principle governing a class of actions. Therefore, any governing regime that makes a virtue of avoiding such rules puts itself outside the context of justice.[18]

By the 1970s, not only was it evident that the War on Poverty had not been won, but other critical problems in the American liberal tradition were becoming more and more evident. Peter Berger and Richard John Neuhaus, among others, turned against the ideal of autonomous individuals pursuing self-government outside a context of acknowledged social boundaries and moral standards.[19] They faulted government welfare programs for ignoring the "mediating structures" of society where genuine and original community exists. They sought to redirect policy making back toward the empowerment of families, churches, neighborhoods, and voluntary associations and away from government programs that spawned new bureaucracies founded on the delegation of power to interest groups. This neo-conservatism angered many liberals who were still seeking by every means possible to put government on the side of individual freedom and society-wide equality.

In 1983, Michael Walzer entered the growing debate over the purpose and limits of government in America with his book *Spheres of Justice*.[20] Equality, he argues, is a legitimate standard pointing toward "a society free from domination."[21] But liberty and equality do not have simple, singular meanings in a complex, differentiated society. Subtly, Walzer develops an argument from history to the effect that government in a complex society should not try to become the sole distributor of all social goods, and it certainly should not try to do so simply by means of interest-group politics. If a central authority seeks to make all individuals free and equal in all respects, it will inevitably become tyrannical by invading other spheres of social life in which different kinds of goods ought to be distributed according to other legitimate principles.

Echoing some of the critical judgments of Nisbet, Berger, Neuhaus, and Lowi, Walzer contends that distributive justice must take into account a diversity of social spheres. To overcome the inadequacies of both individualist and collectivist logic, Walzer argues for the recognition of "complex equality."

> The regime of complex equality is the opposite of tyranny. It establishes a set of relationships such that domination is impossible. In formal terms, complex equality means that no citizen's standing in one sphere or with regard to one social good can be undercut by his standing in some other sphere, with regard to some other good. Thus, citizen X may be chosen over citizen Y for political office, and then the two of them will be unequal in the sphere of politics. But they will not be unequal generally so long as X's office gives him no advantages over Y in any other sphere—superior medical care, access to better schools for his children, entrepreneurial opportunities, and so on.[22]

Walzer, in effect, accepts society's historical differentiation into multiple spheres as one of the essential protections against tyranny—whether that be the tyranny of a totalitarian dictator or of an indiscriminate majority that tries to level all social boundaries in an attempt to secure a simple kind of equality for every individual.

> Tyranny is always specific in character: a particular boundary crossing, a particular violation of social meaning. Complex equality requires the defense of boundaries; it works by differentiating goods just as hierarchy works by differentiating people. But we can only talk of a *régime* of complex equality when there are many boundaries to defend; and what the right number is cannot be specified.[23]

In different ways, what Nisbet, Lowi, Walzer, and others have done over the past four decades is to call into question the simplistic ideals of individual autonomy, liberation from all traditional authorities, and an egalitarian society of individuals maintained through a process of interest-group politics. They point, in essence, to the emptiness of a freedom ideal that promises to

liberate individuals from all social obligations except the universal and ubiquitous democratic ones. They affirm the importance of a limited state that is
constrained in part by its recognition of the boundaries of other social spheres
and by clear standards of justice. Furthermore, they are suspicious of faith in
perpetual historical progress.

But what is the source of the norms or standards that these thinkers use?
By what authority do they argue for complex equality, or for the recovery of
genuine community, or for a just government that will not succumb to interest-group politics? For the most part, Nisbet, Lowi, and Walzer appeal to
history and historical experience for the legitimacy of what they judge to be
right. As Walzer says in defense of a differentiated society whose spheres are
marked off with proper fences:

> We never know exactly where to put the fences; they have no natural location.
> The goods they distinguish are artifacts; as they were made, so they can be re-
> made. Boundaries, then, are vulnerable to shifts in social meaning, and we have
> no choice but to live with the continual probes and incursions through which
> these shifts are worked out. . . . The social world will one day look different
> from the way it does today, and distributive justice will take on a different char-
> acter than it has for us.[24]

Walzer does not look for principles that transcend history, though he expects
"distributive justice" to remain a fixed norm over time even as its character
changes. But whence comes distributive justice? If it is not natural or divine,
then what kind of standard is it? If all social spheres are merely human artifacts, then what are the boundaries and limits of human artifice and of distributive justice? Or are there none? May social meanings shift without limits
and still remain good for human beings?

What we have here is an introduction to some of the key questions and
concerns that will arise in our consideration of three pluralist views below—
especially the views of those whose writings are included in Part I. If individualism and collectivism are inadequate ideologies, is there any principled basis (in contrast to a merely reactionary one) for accepting a pluralist view of
society? If social systems and spheres arise entirely from historical artifice,
why should we accept what Nisbet, or Lowi, or Walzer finds valuable in history rather than what Rousseau, or Marx, or Hitler, or Stalin tried to create in
history? Why should we oppose tyranny? Is there a non-individualist view of
human nature that can justify that stance? Do the multiple spheres of human
association in society have any deeper grounding in natural or divine order
than is suggested by Nisbet, Lowi, and Walzer? Have these men really gone
beyond Enlightenment humanism, or are they merely looking for ways to

hold on to its original aims? We must look for answers to these questions if we are to discover an adequate foundation for a pluralist view of society.

Reason, Community, and the Common Good

Partly in response to the apparent relativism of historically grounded criticisms of liberalism, another line of moral argument is developing in the contemporary American context. It focuses on the internal contradictions of liberalism's practical reasoning about justice and society. Alasdair MacIntyre, for example, contends that Enlightenment liberalism aimed to create a "social order in which individuals could emancipate themselves from the contingency and particularity of tradition by appealing to genuinely universal, tradition-independent norms. . . ."[25] In fact, those who give themselves to this project have not managed to transcend tradition but have simply become caught in a new, more problematic tradition of their own making. What "began as an appeal to alleged principles of shared rationality against what was felt to be the tyranny of tradition, has itself been transformed into a tradition whose continuities are partly defined by the interminability of the debate over such principles."[26]

Nisbet, Lowi, and Walzer illustrate perfectly the "interminability" of the debates in our liberal context, MacIntyre would say. Each raises criticisms of the existing social order and urges the adoption of other values so that justice can be done to individuals and groups in our open society. But each one continues to assume that his argument appeals to universal principles of practical reasoning. The truth is, however, that conceptions of both justice and practical rationality differ depending on the fundamental preconceptions people have about reality, and those preconceptions are grounded in the actual social/political contexts in which people live.

The structure of modern, liberal societies is such that even as individuals confidently appeal to universal principles, they undermine any hope for achieving genuinely common or universal agreement about justice and rationality. Liberalism's view of the "common good," according to MacIntyre, is that every individual should be free to express his or her preferences in a variety of ways. Practical rationality, under these conditions, turns out to be a method of justifying individual preferences and setting constraints on the bargaining process among self-asserting, competitive individuals. The kind of reasoning and bargaining that Lowi criticizes as interest-group politics is precisely what one should expect to see emerge from liberalism. Thus the centrifugal tendencies of this individualizing and relativistic liberalism contradict its claim to being the manifestation of a universal rationality.

The very indeterminacy of social "spheres" that Walzer condones when he says that they are artifacts without any "natural" boundaries, manifests a defect in the underpinnings of modern society that MacIntyre criticizes. Liberalism cannot foster a mode of practical reasoning that proceeds from and moves toward a genuine *common good* of justice. That is because liberalism does not accept the idea of a common *natural* social order that precedes individual claims to autonomy. Under liberalism, individual preferences multiply to create a diverse range of goods and groups, each compartmentalized in its own sphere. The heterogeneity of this type of society means, therefore, that "no overall ordering of goods is possible. And to be educated into the culture of a liberal social order is, therefore, characteristically to become the kind of person to whom it appears normal that a variety of goods should be pursued, each appropriate to its own sphere, with no overall good supplying any overall unity to life."[27]

MacIntyre believes that in order to reach agreement about the demands of justice for a structurally complex society, we need more than an argument that defends the historical emergence of different social spheres each of which expresses different individual preferences. Walzer and Lowi will find themselves in a never-ending argument about their diverse valuations of historically relative preferences. What is needed is a mode of practical reasoning that develops within the context of a community that recognizes justice and other standards as natural or transcendent. Practical reasoning can truly succeed only in a community that agrees on the moral virtues appropriate to the different social roles performed by its members. The liberal tradition provides no such context in which to reason.

> In Aristotelian practical reasoning it is the individual *qua* citizen who reasons; in Thomistic practical reasoning it is the individual *qua* enquirer into his or her good and the good of his or her community; in Humean practical reasoning it is the individual *qua* propertied or unpropertied participant in a society of a particular kind of mutuality and reciprocity; but in the practical reasoning of liberal modernity it is the individual *qua* individual who reasons.[28]

MacIntyre believes that the Aristotelian-Thomistic tradition may lay claim to an authority and validity greater than that to which the liberal tradition lays claim because, among other things, it has recognized itself as a tradition of practical rationality within a particular context of order and meaning. Since diverse ethical and social traditions do, in fact, exist, the strongest kind of practical rationality will be one that recognizes itself as grounded in a tradition of virtues within an overall, integrated view of a just society.[29] In turning to Aristotle and Thomas for a normative view of justice and practical rationality, MacIntyre indicates his commitment to an ordered natural (or natural/ supernatural) hierarchy within which reasoning can find its mooring and proceed coherently. He aims to go beyond the limits of liberal individualism not by reaching for an illusory rationality that can transcend all past communities and traditions. Rather, he wants to take his stand in the best tradition of thought that is both conscious of itself as a tradition and able to direct practical reasoning toward truth and justice—the truth and justice of human community.

Jeffrey Stout appreciates MacIntyre's criticism of philosophical individualism and his quest for rational community, but he fears that MacIntyre runs the danger of throwing out the baby with the bath water.

> MacIntyre sees our society as an expression of Enlightenment philosophical ideas gone wrong. If he is right, and the Enlightenment project was bound to fail, then our way of life was bound to fail too, and we should not be surprised to find it in ruin. On MacIntyre's view, our society is as radically individualistic and unconcerned with the common good as liberal philosophers have always wanted it to be, and this is the clue to its moral downfall.[30]

But, says Stout, our social order is not purely the expression of an individualist philosophy. Despite the impact of liberalism, American society is not yet in ruin; it does display degrees of social agreement about the nature of the common good and about the virtues needed in diverse spheres of social life. Those elements of agreement are themselves the fruit of our long Western tradition in which earlier disagreements, especially those expressed through religious warfare, were overcome by decisions to limit the political order to an arena in which we would all have certain rights while enjoying the freedom to disagree peacefully and to pursue a diverse range of goods.[31]

Modern liberal societies, therefore, are not as individualistic and relativistic as MacIntyre imagines. They reveal a particular kind of practical rationality at work that produces meaningful if not completely integral political communities. By tracking the inner logic of actual social differentiation and institutional formation, says Stout, we can still work to achieve levels of rational agreement higher than MacIntyre thinks possible. Such agreement will not be exhaustive with respect to a comprehensive understanding of the common good. But it can be sufficient for building both a "thin" conception of the common political good as well as an appreciation of the protected freedom we all require in order to carry on diverse activities in other spheres of social life.

Much like Walzer, Stout sees a "thin" agreement about the nature of the common good as a manifestation of our practical Western agreement not to try to achieve complete social community through politics. Room is then made for "complex equality"—a rich complexity of life in many social spheres where people can continue to nurture virtues proper to each sphere—schooling, church, health care, family, and more. This does not mean that Stout is sanguine about the health of liberal society as if all the diverse spheres of contemporary social life manifest virtuous development.

> The idea that liberal society lacks any shared conception of the good is false, but this doesn't mean that all is well. It could still be the case that politics, as the social practice of self-governance directed toward the common good, has begun to give way to merely bureaucratic management of competition for external goods. . . . The social practice of politics is, of course, always being threatened in some such way. All genuine republics, not just our kind, are fragile, susceptible to corruption by external goods and unjust acts. So there is no permanent, utopian solution to be sought.[32]

Note carefully what Stout is doing in his response to MacIntyre and to other communitarian critics of individualism. He is advancing what he calls a "stereoscopic" view of society in which the *political* common good is understood as an agreement to protect both individual freedoms as well as the integrity of diverse spheres of social life. The inherent threat to such a society comes not so much from the intellectual conflict between different traditions of practical moral reasoning, but more from the propensity people have to act without giving sufficient attention to the different virtues that are appropriate to different social spheres. Thus, for example, they end up trying to impose "external" values from the marketplace and bureaucracies on all spheres of life.

> Moral discourse in pluralistic society is not threatened, then, by disagreement among its members about the good. Neither is it threatened by the confusion of tongues manifested in its various moral languages. It is threatened by the acids of injustice, which eat away at the moral fibre of privileged and victimized alike, and by the possibility of nuclear war, which would destroy much more than the prospects for rational moral debate. And it is also threatened by the corruption our lives have already suffered from idolizing external goods and the erosion of our most valuable practices by habits of mind and heart appropriate to the marketplace and the bureaucracies.[33]

Stout's vision here is clearly one that seeks to comprehend the whole of society as a complex, just, and balanced order of justice, not as a simple collective unity. His vision is not Aristotelian or Thomistic, though he wants to use some of MacIntyre's and Walzer's language of multiple virtues appropriate to distinct social spheres. His vision is not individualistic, though it includes a liberal conception of individual rights and a limited government; he wants an open public order that will not demand "deep" civic agreement about a comprehensive common good. His vision is not socialist, but it is critical of the power of marketplace values to overwhelm non-market forms of community.

Stout identifies his mode of reasoning as a form of pragmatic social criticism with both eyes open. And yet he conducts a moral argument for principles and practices that he believes transcend his personal preferences. "The languages of morals in our discourse are many, and they have remarkably diverse historical origins," he writes, "but they do not float in free air, and their name is not chaos. They are embedded in specific social practices and institutions—religious, political, artistic, scientific, athletic, economic, and so on."[34]

But how does this statement answer the questions posed by MacIntyre? On what basis, other than our own self-assertive preferences, should we approve the diversity of historically differentiated social practices and institutions that Stout approves? Living face to face with a wide range of religious, political, artistic, scientific, medical, and economic institutions, do we not need to articulate the norms or standards by which we believe each should be judged good or bad, healthy or unhealthy? And in order to do that, don't we need to propound arguments as to the very nature of this reality? If this complex array does not "float in free air" or go by the name of "chaos," then what order of nature or divine creation allows human life to take this complex shape? Is there any philosophical (ontological) grounding that Stout can provide for his stereoscopic view of society that lies deeper than historical development and personal preference?

Michael Novak takes a somewhat different approach to these questions while remaining closer than either Stout or Walzer to liberal individualism. Novak agrees that thinking about the common good should not be totalistic or undifferentiated. Precisely by means of societal differentiation and the opening of free economic markets, individuals have been able to realize their potential both as persons and as members of diverse communities. The conception of the common good to be adopted, therefore, should be one that presupposes and reinforces the free initiative of individuals to shape community life, to argue rationally, and to seek multiple forms of the common good. The extent to which Novak retains any comprehensive idea of social order is to be found almost entirely in his understanding of a dynamic, historical teleology of human existence. "The *formal* concept of the common good," he says, "is dynamic, and is always driving toward the full and ultimate development of human beings. Its aim is the highest stage of development in the personality of each, and in the most fully developed community of which they are capable."[35] This is not so much a stereoscopic view of complex equality as an open ended "vision of *liberty* and *progress.*"[36]

Novak drops hints of a hierarchical order of institutions while using phrases from the liberal tradition. The ultimate, eschatological common good is the kingdom of God, according to Novak, who is committed to the Christian faith, but that common good can never be achieved in history. So it remains always out of reach as a historical goal. Short of that goal, human beings seek an upward moral mobility toward fulfillment. "At each level of achievement—in person, family, city, state, and humankind as a whole—the concept of the common good recognizes both an end achieved, and a new inward impulsion toward a further achievement, upon a larger and more complex plane."[37]

But what rational meaning has Novak retained in this concept of common good? Diverse persons, families, and organizations have different identities, so one would think that the good peculiar to each must surely reveal a distinctive qualification. Otherwise, how can we differentiate between a family and a state, or between a school and a business enterprise. Moreover, schools, families, churches, and businesses do not *as such* share something in common. Thus, the common good, as Aristotle or Aquinas or MacIntyre uses the term, is still not applicable to anything Novak has identified until we consider the state or society as a whole.

Precisely at this point, however, Novak is most uncomfortable about using the words "common good" in referring to any substantive condition or aim of practical reason. In order to protect individual responsibility against the danger of totalitarianism, Novak is reluctant to allow the possibility that citizens as citizens, or individuals as individuals, can legitimately envision together a substantive common good to be legislated and enforced by government for the good of the whole community. Rather, he identifies common good in its grandest sense with the unreachable kingdom of God, and in its reachable sense with a diversity of individual and organizational initiatives. He also identifies the common good with an inner potentiality that controls the whole movement of history toward freedom. "Thus, the common good is the inner dynamo of human progress, rooted in the human's capacity to *reflect* upon his or her own actions, to grasp their deficiencies and incompletenesses, and to *choose* to press onward toward the full development of the entire range of human possibilities."[38] A public or political common good, in the more traditional sense, cannot be achieved by direct intention, according to Novak, but must be allowed to arise as a more or less indirect consequence of freedom expressed in a variety of human communities.

"In sum," Novak writes, "the new concept of the common good pushes us beyond a simple reliance upon authority that defines for all the substantive good, and turns us instead toward achieving the rules that make an open society possible."[39] Despite his talk of common good and diverse communities, Novak returns in the end to something very close to liberalism with its emphasis on individual freedom and public rules of due process and democracy. Apart from affirming the importance of "mediating institutions" between the individual and the state, Novak offers little of substance with regard to an ontological conception of the pluralistic structure of society. While Stout and Walzer try to give a historical account of the reality of multiple social spheres, and while MacIntyre tries to reconceptualize an integral, complex social order of justice, Novak reaches for theological language to back up both his teleological orientation and his belief in the universal validity of the principles of liberty and justice.

> Liberty and justice are "transcendent" principles in the sense that they can never be perfectly fulfilled at any point in history, but keep driving a pilgrim race ever forward in their pursuit. In every generation, there are always further steps in pursuit of justice and of liberty to be taken, amid the vicissitudes of historical circumstances, social necessity, and human fallibility. . . . In any case, "We the People of the United States" stand expressly under God's judgment, and are expressly committed to the pursuit of transcendent ideals of liberty and justice for every member of the community. We invite planetary criticism in that light.[40]

From MacIntyre's point of view, Novak is trying to offer a universal rational argument to justify the superiority of liberalism over other traditions. Precisely because Novak's critics either hold to other liberal preferences, or because they stand in other traditions in which his mode of practical reasoning makes no sense, the consequence is that Novak, too, cannot escape the confusion of tongues rampant in our contemporary world. Novak is trying to synthesize every tradition into the liberal tradition, but, from MacIntyre's point of view, that project cannot succeed.

What we have received, then, from MacIntyre, Stout, and Novak is a further introduction to some of the key questions that will confront us in considering a pluralist view of society. In this case, their arguments lead us most directly into the readings of Part II below. In particular, we can now understand more clearly the urgency of the question about how to comprehend society's diversity in relation to some kind of integral unity or coherence. MacIntyre argues that liberal individualism makes such an attempt at comprehension impossible. Stout believes that society is actually more integrated than the ideology of liberal individualism allows us to recognize, so we need to concentrate on deciphering the reality behind the ideologically blinding dogmas. And Novak is convinced that liberalism is part of the progressive solution to the problem of building the "common good" since it helps to scrape away false (especially totalitarian) attempts to create integral societies while freeing individuals to pursue a vast plurality of common goods.

But have we received from these writers a convincing normative argument that can guide action toward the shaping of a coherent and pluralistic society? Must we return to Thomas Aquinas or to Aristotle for a philosophy that escapes the historicizing and relativizing tendencies of modern, pragmatic liberalism? Or must we give up hope of finding a normative social philosophy that can do justice both to the diversity of social spheres and to the integrality of a common public order?

Divine Law, Differentiated Societies, and Political Order

If, as Stout argues, the reality of contemporary American society, both in its differentiated complexity and in its relative coherence, consists of more than liberal individualism can account for, then what does account for it? If the complexity of our society requires a stereoscopic viewpoint to comprehend it, then how do we explain the emergence of that complexity if the supposedly autonomous activity of individuals is not sufficient to explain it? Moreover, if individualism and collectivism are inadequate ideologies or theories, why have they arisen in the first place and how have they managed to maintain such a strong hold on the modern mind?

These questions take us to a new level of reflection. Apparently we cannot account for very much of the structure and complexity of modern society simply by referring back to human freedom as its source. Even if one hypothesizes that contracts among autonomous individuals are the source of all human organizations and relationships (including the state), one has not explained the nature of the differences between political, educational, scientific, athletic, musical, medical, familial, and ecclesiastical organizations. If each of these different spheres requires distinct sorts of virtues for its realization, then the deeper question is, What is human nature? Why do human beings exhibit these diverse kinds of talents and interests? Why do they form these kinds of associations and not others? And if Stout and Walzer are correct that we err both mentally and practically if we ignore the diverse complexity of social reality, then what is it about the structure of that reality that imposes such limitations on human freedom? Why shouldn't human beings seek perpetually to level all historic, institutional confinements and express their autonomy afresh day after day? Why shouldn't we conclude that Stout and Walzer are simply expressing their preferences and that their judgments may not lay claim to universal validity?

With these questions we enter the very heart of the debate about the character and origin of modernity itself. The authors above have already raised some of the key issues here, and their judgments vary widely from full support for the progress of individual freedom to a denunciation of the materialistic and individualistic reduction of human experience. Their judgments range from an approval of the societal differentiation process to criticisms of its fracturing effects on integral human community. Yet, generally speaking, both the champions and the critics of modernization assume that the "modern world" represents a new era in history marked by its break (for better or for worse) from a medieval past. The key category here is "secularization." The modern world is a secular world even if religion still thrives here and there; it is no longer a religious world that embraces subordinate secular pursuits.

But does "modernity" really constitute a new and different era? If so, what are its defining characteristics? Why should we accept the Enlightenment's self-assertion that autonomous human initiatives through science and free action have inaugurated a new era? What if that self-assertion is mistaken or at best merely one among many relative claims people have made in the course of the ongoing differentiation of society? Are human beings actually free and autonomous simply because they have declared their independence from God, the church, and the old aristocracy? Has the world actually been secularized or merely declared to be so by a temporarily dominant though mistaken stream of thought?

The debate over these questions still rages across many fronts today, and it bears directly on the issue of society's pluralistic structure. Contrary to Enlightenment dogma, many find the origin of the so-called modern world not in the Enlightenment's self-assertion of human autonomy but in Christianity. Max Weber was not the first, though he may be the best known scholar to argue that the spirit of modern capitalism finds its source in Calvinism.[41] Many historians of science have argued that the development of natural science is a fruit of the Christian view of the world.[42] Harold Berman and others locate the foundations of the Western legal tradition in the eleventh-century papal revolution.[43] Many attribute the pluralizing differentiation of society over the past five centuries—at least in large measure—to the impact of the Protestant Reformation.[44] And some go so far as to say that the full range of secularizing humanist influences does not stand on its own foundation at all, as modernists claim, but is a religious or idealistic displacement (a secularized form) of Christianity.[45]

We could enter the contemporary American debate over these issues at any number of points, but we will consider only one additional author to help us bring into focus some of the questions that will come to the fore in the readings that follow—especially in Part III. Ralph C. Hancock's *Calvin and the Foundations of Modern Politics*[46] heightens the tension of the debate over the nature and origin of the modern world as he engages Michael Walzer, Leo Strauss, Karl Löwith, Eric Voegelin, and Hans Blumenberg in discussion. In essence, Hancock's argument is that Calvin's reinterpretation of the Christian faith led to a strong refocusing of attention on human responsibility in this world. If, as many others beside Hancock have argued, early Christianity de-divinized the world by recognizing it as God's creation rather than as part of God, then Calvin took this conviction a step further. He so emphasized the transcendence of God that he undermined the Thomist-Aristotelian synthesis that grounded human rationality in a great chain of being which ascends to God himself. For Calvin, human reason cannot ascend to God; rather the sovereign God stoops to reveal himself to finite and sinful human creatures. According to Hancock,

> it was characteristic of premodern philosophic conceptions of order or cosmos to differentiate higher, rational kinds of being from lower, irrational kinds. This applied both to the big order, or world, and to the little order, the human soul. On this view, the soul can claim to be a microcosm because it participates intelligently in the order of the cosmos, by virtue of the rule of its rational part. Reason is capable of asserting its rule in order to constitute a hierarchy in the soul analogous to the natural hierarchy.

> For Calvin, however, there is no place for reason to assert its rule, since the desires were given all the rule they needed directly from God; the self-assertion of reason is not in accord with the order of creation but is indeed the cause of the fall of the creation into disorder and alienation from God. The very fact that this section [Bk. V, Ch. I, 51-52 of Calvin's *Institutes*] on man the microcosm forms part of a chapter in which man is treated as subject (along with the rest of "this most vast and beautiful system of the universe") to the "continuing government" of a God whose "essence is incomprehensible" (V.I; 51-52) immediately indicates a departure from the philosophic idea of order. According to that idea, man's reason gave him a claim to comprehend the ruling goodness of nature and therefore to rise above the material system of the universe, to rule a little world in his own right. But Calvin insists on the total and uniform subordination of the entire creation to its creator: man can in no sense be his own world, for there is only one God; his essence is incomprehensible to man; and to him alone belongs the government of the whole universal system.[47]

For human beings to be completely dependent on God rather than on reason means, therefore, that they now have only to concentrate on obeying the divine command to love God and one another *in this world*. If Calvin radically emphasized God's transcendence above this world, he also radically focused attention on the meaning and value of this world as God's creation—a world in which God's creatures are called to fulfill their responsibilities here and now. *This world* is what matters in God's sight—not some imaginary mystical or intelligible world behind the world at hand. "Indeed," writes Hancock,

> my analysis suggests that Calvinism—in particular the "uncorrupted" Calvinism of its founder—represents not at all a repudiation of this world but an intensification of worldly activity understood as redounding not only to the benefit of God's innocent natural creation but especially to the glory of God. . . . Calvin's hostility to the flesh was not a hostility to the body but a hostility to hierarchy, to human rule according to the purposes of human reason—precisely, one might say, a hostility to Aristotle.[48]

As Hancock sees it, there is, consequently, a much closer connection between Calvin and modern rationalism (with its practical, pragmatic, this-worldly focus) than there is between Calvin and the rationality of Aristotle or Thomas Aquinas. Calvin's was not a secularizing mode of thought in the sense of claiming autonomy for human reason in a closed world of nature. To the contrary, Calvin understood human beings and the whole of creation to be completely and radically dependent on God. Nevertheless, in the world of practical ethics as well as in the sciences the impact of Calvinism was to drive human beings to explore and to act on the creation. This did have a secularizing impact in the sense of undermining the Catholic Church's claim to being the chief and highest mediator between God and the world. Calvin emphasized the creation's direct dependence on God in all its dimensions. Not only is every believer a priest before God, but every office of authority is directly accountable to God rather than mediated through a church hierarchy. Under the impact of Calvinism human social life could become more radically differentiated and free from ecclesiastical control. For Calvin, of course, this kind of secularization had nothing to do with the autonomy claims of modern humanists. The independence of social spheres from church control simply implied that human creatures should become more fully and directly obedient to God in each sphere of life. Societal differentiation for Calvin is part and parcel of religious intensification.

"Since Calvin denies the possibility of a hierarchical ordering of the goods of the present life," says Hancock, "he must believe that each earthly delight contains its own principle of moderation within itself, that each can rule itself without reference to any superior good."[49] Human duty is to glorify God through love and service in every sphere of life.

> The glory of God is exhibited in the outward actions of men, provided they are done for the glory of God and not in view of any human good. Thus Calvin's

absolute rejection of works righteousness yields a new kind of attention to works. Although Calvin denies that human works can in any way be even a partial source of salvation, he teaches that the works God does through us may indeed be considered as signs of salvation.[50]

This is the ground of the historical activism of Calvinism, says Hancock.

From a Calvinist viewpoint, therefore, what makes possible the differentiation of society as well as its integral ordering is neither a natural hierarchy under church supervision nor the autonomous shaping of a formless void by human beings claiming to be self-sufficient. Rather, what makes earthly life possible in all of its differentiating complexity and integrality is *the very order of God's creation*—the law of God calling human beings to the creative fulfillment of their earthly responsibilities. The creative, energetic attention to life in this world inspired by Calvin's love for and fear of the transcendent Creator-Redeemer is what gave a new boost to science, political constitutionalism, economic development, and much more.[51]

If there is any truth to Hancock's interpretation of Calvin, then the debate over the shape and character of the modern world requires that we also direct our attention to the question about "religious motives." Clearly Calvin's vision and motivation were thoroughly and comprehensively religious in the sense of calling for the reform of all of life in obedience to God and for his glory. Equally as clear is the anti-Christian motive inherent in much of modern humanism, symbolized by the French revolutionaries' cry, "Neither God nor master." Two contrary motives are at work here—one calling for human obedience to God, the other calling for human independence from God. But which motive is closer to the truth about human nature, history, and social order?

In Hancock's debate about the nature of modernity with Walzer, Strauss, Löwith, Voegelin, and Blumenberg, he says that in Calvinism "I detect a religious motive for a certain secular rationalism. . . ."[52] It is just possible that Calvinism disposed "its adherents to ways of life compatible with modern trends in politics and economics but that these trends had sources and foundations distinct from Calvinism or from any religious belief."[53] On Hancock's own terms, however, the very words "religious," "secular," and "modern" are up for question because their meaning is different if used by an Enlightenment rationalist or by a Calvinist. Different religious motives matter a great deal. We could as easily say that in Calvinism there is a religious motive driving believers to act with such awe before God that they develop new and creative uses of their rational capacities in his creation. That motive may be the most important one that helped to produce great achievements in the fields of politics, economics, and science, only to be displaced later by a more dominant religious motive of human pride leading to human declarations of self-sufficiency and independence from God. Adherents to the new humanistic motive may have become partially disposed to certain trends in economics and politics set in motion by Calvinism even though the humanistic motive contradicts the very reality of the creation's complete dependence on God.

People operating with both Christian and anti-Christian motives have, of course, contributed to the development of science, democracy, capitalism, and so forth. The conflict between basic driving motives should not be ignored as if it is inconsequential. Different basic motives do, to some degree, control both the interpretation of reality and the shaping of its institutions. If the source of modern society's complex diversity and scientific achievements is the autonomous power of free persons, who really have nothing to do with God and his creation order, then everything appears in one light. But if the deepest ground of modern institutions and human achievements is actually the providential stability of God's good creation order to which human beings ought to submit, both in scientific exploration and in the practical development of many different social potentialities, then everything about history and humanity appears in quite a different light.

If Hancock's thesis about Calvinism and modernity is tenable, then the questions about societal pluralism become even more complicated. We must now consider *both* the deepest motives of human life *as well as* the underlying ontological structure of reality that either undergirds or contradicts those motives. If Walzer is correct that society really is a complex of different spheres, then perhaps there are some important boundaries and heteronomous norms in the creation that make possible that differentiated reality. Walzer may have stumbled upon important insights into the creation's order without having come up with a correct account of why that is so. The same might be said about Stout. If we do in fact need a stereoscopic view of society in order to interpret it correctly, this could be due to the reality of the creation order—an order that human beings are not free to ignore or distort without ending up with false, reductionistic theories and practical failures. If this is true, then all humanistic claims to autonomy are fundamentally flawed and misdirected even if the good creation order keeps those who make such claims from experiencing the full consequences of their motives or intentions.

MacIntyre may be correct, therefore, in his critical assessment of the internal contradictions and antinomies of liberal individualism, but he may be mistaken in believing that Thomas or Aristotle is best able to provide an adequate framework for interpreting the integral order of our contemporary, complex, differentiating societies. There may be another standpoint from which to discern the norms for the various virtues required in different spheres of social life, including the norms for an integral political order that is neither totalitarian nor anarchic. That other way might be found by following the Calvinist path of heeding the dynamic law-order of God's creation in the light of what the Bible says about sin and redemption. We need to consider the possibility, in other words, that the conflicts among religious motives— modern humanist, classical humanist, Thomist, Calvinist—are fundamental in the sense that people with basically different views of life, living out of contrary religious motives, have the greatest difficulty penetrating to the root of their differences with one another. They simply talk past one another. But MacIntyre may be too quick in accepting the ultimate historical relativity of this "tower of Babel." One religious motive and fundamental world view may be closer to the universal truth while others are farther from it. In which case, the aim of different philosophers and social reformers should be to contend for the truth from out of their positions of commitment rather than to retreat into their traditions as if each tradition is merely one among many. The con- temporary crisis of liberalism to which we referred at the outset may, at this very moment, be displaying the evidence of liberalism's imminent collapse just as the collapse of communist governments in Eastern Europe provided convincing evidence of the failure of Marxist-Leninism as an adequate ac- count of history and modern society. If so, then what truth will remain standing? The challenge we face in explaining and shaping contemporary so- ciety is that we must struggle to give a truthful, evaluative account of its health and deformities as well as to articulate the correct norms for our prac- tical shaping of it. And if it is true that the ontological basis for all societal differentiation and integration is God's creation order, then every account of contemporary society will fail to some extent if it does not acknowledge and deal with that reality from out of a commitment to its truth. That means, therefore, that a Christian motive would drive one closer to the truth than a motive that drives one to deny God and to ignore the heteronomous norms or principles of God's creation order.

With this we complete our introductory exploration of the American context in which the following readings should be considered. In each of the three parts that follow, we will first introduce the general themes of the sec- tion and then provide a brief introduction to each reading. At the conclusion of the book we return to each part for a critical, comparative assessment. Our overall objective is to present and assess arguments for a pluralist view of so- ciety, as distinguished from individualism and collectivism. The questions to be addressed include those highlighted above about the weight of history in contrast to revolutionary designs, about tradition in relation to freedom, about nature and reason, divine law and human creativity, individual and society, society and state, the differentiation of society and competing religious motives. And intermingled with all of these is the question about modernity itself.

NOTES

1 See, for example, Harold J. Berman, *Law and Revolution: The Formation of the Western Legal Tradition* (Cambridge: Harvard University Press, 1983), esp. 1-45, 520-558; Eric Voegelin, *The New Science of Politics* (Chicago: University of Chicago Press, 1952); Eric Voegelin, *From Enlightenment to Revolution*, ed. J. Hallowell, (Durham, N.C.: Duke University Press, 1975); Christopher Dawson, *The Gods of Revolution: An Analysis of the French Revolution* (New York: Minerva Press, 1972), esp. 3-65, 155-166; Herman Dooyeweerd, *Roots of Western Culture: Pagan, Secular, and Christian Options*, trans. J. Kraay; eds. M. VanderVennan and B. Zylstra (Toronto: Wedge Publishing Foundation, 1979), esp. 145-218; George Grant, *Technology and Empire: Perspectives on North America* (Toronto: House of Anansi, 1969); Thomas A. Spragens, Jr., *The Irony of Liberal Reason* (Chicago: University of Chicago Press, 1981); Lesslie Newbigin, *Foolishness to the Greeks: The Gospel and Western Culture* (Grand Rapids: Eerdmans, 1986); Michael Sandel, *Liberalism and the Limits of Justice* (Cambridge: Cambridge University Press, 1982); Robert N. Bellah, et al., *Habits of the Heart: Individualism and Commitment in American Life* (New York: Harper Perennial Library, 1985); Bob Goudzwaard, *Capitalism and Progress: A Diagnosis of Western Society*, trans. J. Zylstra (Toronto: Wedge Publishing Foundation, and Grand Rapids: Eerdmans, 1979).

2 Kenneth McRae, "The Plural Society and the Western Political Tradition," *Canadian Journal of Political Science* 12, no.4 (1979): 676ff. See also K. McRae, ed., *Consociational Democracy: Political Accommodation in Segmented Societies* (Toronto: McClelland and Stewart, 1974).

3 David Nicholls, *Three Varieties of Pluralism* (New York: St. Martin's Press, 1974). A year later, Nicholls published a longer introduction to the English pluralists titled *The Pluralist State* (London: Macmillan, 1975).

4 Quoted in J.N. Figgis, *Churches in the Modern State* (New York: Russell and Russell, 1973 [1913]), 56.

5 A valuable collection of readings from G.D.H. Cole, J.N. Figgis, and Harold J. Laski, with a fine introduction by the editor, is Paul Q. Hirst, ed., *The Pluralist Theory of the State* (New York: Routledge, 1989).

6 Gierke's original is *Das Deutsche Genossenschaftsrecht*, 4 vols. (Berlin: Weidmann, 1868-1913). A recent paperback republication of Maitland's translation of one section of Gierke's study is *Political Theories of the Middle Ages* (Cambridge: Cambridge University Press, 1988 [1900]).

7 A.F. Bentley, *The Process of Government*, newly edited by Peter H. Odegaard (Cambridge: Harvard University Press, 1967 [1908]).

8 See David B. Truman, *The Governmental Process* (New York: Knopf, 1951) and Robert A. Dahl, *A Preface to Democratic Theory* (New Haven: Yale University Press, 1956).

9 Nicholls, *Three Varieties*, 2.

10 Robert A. Nisbet, *The Quest for Community* (New York: Oxford University Press, 1953), 214.

11 *Ibid.*, 228.

[12] Ibid., 245; see also Robert A. Nisbet's *The Social Philosophers: Community and Conflict in Western Thought* (New York: Thomas Y. Crowell Co., 1973), 93-160.

[13] Theodore J. Lowi, *The End of Liberalism: The Second Republic of the United States*, 2d ed. (New York: W. W. Norton, 1979).

[14] Ibid., 55.

[15] Ibid., 63.

[16] Ibid., 213.

[17] Ibid., 214.

[18] Ibid., 296.

[19] See, for example, Peter L. Berger and Richard John Neuhaus, *To Empower People: The Role of Mediating Structures in Public Policy* (Washington, D.C.: American Enterprise Institute, 1977).

[20] Michael Walzer, *Spheres of Justice: A Defense of Pluralism and Equality* (New York: Basic Books, 1983).

[21] Ibid., xiii.

[22] Ibid., 19.

[23] Ibid., 28.

[24] Ibid., 319.

[25] Alasdair MacIntyre, *Whose Justice? Which Rationality?* (Notre Dame: University of Notre Dame Press, 1988), 335.

[26] Ibid.

[27] Ibid., 337.

[28] Ibid., 339.

[29] Ibid., 402-3.

[30] Jeffrey Stout, *Ethics After Babel: The Languages of Morals and Their Discontents* (Boston: Beacon Press, 1988), 220.

[31] Ibid., 224-228, 236.

[32] Ibid., 291.

[33] Ibid., 287.

[34] Ibid., 291.

[35] Michael Novak, *Free Persons and the Common Good* (Lanham, MD: Madison Books, 1989), 177.

[36] Ibid.

[37] Ibid., 187.

[38] Ibid.

[39] Ibid., 142.

[40] Ibid., 188.

[41] Max Weber, *The Protestant Ethic and the Spirit of Capitalism*, trans. T. Parsons (New York: Scribner's, 1958). Literature continuing the debate of Weber's thesis is massive. A recent valuable contribution comes from Bob Goudzwaard, *Capitalism and Progress: A Diagnosis of Western Society*. Two selections from Goudzwaard's other writings are included in Part III below.

[42] R. Hooykaas, *Religion and the Rise of Modern Science* (Grand Rapids: Eerdmans, 1972). Compare John Dillenberger, *Protestant Thought and Natural Science* (Notre Dame: University of Notre Dame Press, 1960).

[43] Berman, *Law and Revolution.*

44 See, for example, J.N. Figgis' 1907 classic *Political Thought from Gerson to Grotius: 1414-1625* (New York: Harper and Row, 1960) from which we have excerpted a selection for Part I below. For background see Menna Prestwich, ed. *International Calvinism: 1541-1715* (Oxford: The Clarendon Press, 1985).

45 See Eric Voegelin, *The New Science of Politics* and Voegelin, *From Enlightenment*; Karl Löwith, *Meaning in History* (Chicago: University of Chicago Press, 1949); and Dooyeweerd, *Roots*.

46 Ralph C. Hancock, *Calvin and the Foundations of Modern Politics* (Ithaca, N.Y.: Cornell University Press, 1989). Hancock is arguing primarily with Quentin Skinner, *The Foundations of Modern Political Thought*, vol. 2, *The Age of Reformation* (Cambridge: Cambridge University Press, 1978) and Michael Walzer, *The Revolution of the Saints: A Study in the Origins of Radical Politics* (Cambridge: Harvard University Press, 1965). Cf. William J. Bouwsma, *John Calvin: A Sixteenth Century Portrait* (New York: Oxford University Press, 1988), and W. Fred Graham, *The Constructive Revolutionary: John Calvin and his Socio-Economic Impact* (Richmond: John Knox Press, 1971).

47 Hancock, *Calvin*, 148-149.

48 *Ibid.*, 166.

49 *Ibid.*, 98.

50 *Ibid.*, 134.

51 Hancock does not sufficiently see or stress the relation of redemption to creation in Calvin's thought, and often this obscures his interpretation of Calvin's teaching about sin. For example, he says of the Holy Spirit's work that "the Spirit progressively restores to man the image of God, or returns him to the relation with God that obtained before the fall; the Spirit restores the right order of creation. But we have seen that the image of God is precisely man's recognition of his own nothingness and acknowledgement of God's power active within him, his consciousness of the continuous energy of the Spirit. Order is not a perfected condition of intelligible being but a consciousness of perpetual becoming. . . . Man becomes like God when God's Spirit in him shines through the nothingness of his own nature." *Calvin*, 161.

For Calvin, human creatures—the image of God—are not *by creation* nothingness. The creation, including human beings, is good and rich in content and identity. Humans are the very image of God—which is not nothing, though they are not anything in themselves apart from God. Human beings as *fallen* creatures are depraved because of their disobedience and puffed up pride. The sanctifying work of the Spirit of Christ is indeed to restore the right order of creation, which includes turning sinners to a proper estimate of themselves (which is, in their sin, as nothingness before a righteous God) to new life in Christ (which is truly something as restored images *in Christ*). Human beings are part of the good creation; they are not nothingness. God's glory is revealed through his redemptive work in Christ who, by the power of the Spirit, restores humanity to its God-honoring service and identity as the image of God.

Hancock's confusion here, which seems to come in part because of his own dependence on an Aristotelian view of reality, affects his interpretation throughout. See for example his discussion of human works (pp. 41-42); of God's transcendence (pp. 61); of the law of love and human virtue (pp. 89-91); of worldly goods and the gifts of God (pp. 96-8); of the person and work of Christ (pp. 123ff.); of the image of God (pp. 141ff.); and of God as power (pp. 162-3).

52 *Ibid.*, 165.

53 *Ibid.*

I

HISTORY, THE UNFOLDING
OF SOCIETY, AND HUMAN
FULFILLMENT

ONE

✕✕✕✕✕✕✕✕✕✕✕

THE WEIGHT OF HISTORY: AN INTRODUCTION TO THE READINGS

N ear the end of the eighteenth century a new type of argument began to be heard in European and North American circles defending the plural structure of society. We might call it simply the argument from history. Many of those who began to make such an argument maintained aspects of older arguments in support of a society's diversified structure—arguments based on natural law or divine will or hierarchical order under ecclesiastical authority. But something new was beginning to emerge.

To understand the argument from history, we must recognize the importance of the French Revolution and reactions to it. Prior to the Revolution, most of those who made the most radical claims about human self-sufficiency and rational autonomy were writers, intellectuals, and scientists, not those who gained control of political power. Of course, many debates and open conflicts proceeded apace between Catholics and Protestants and between those seeking to maintain the existing order of society and those seeking to change it. But from the Renaissance through the Reformation and up to the late 1700s, actual social, economic, and political change had occurred somewhat gradually or through events of only piecemeal suddenness.

The French Revolution exploded as something new. It rocked Europe and the world because it seemed to bring together all the streams of radical human pretension and galvanize them into concrete actions that inaugurated a new era. By act of pure will—by straightforward rational design—a revolutionary band decided it would try to rebuild society in all its parts. This was not simply the exaggerated rhetoric of a few pamphleteers. It became the declared intention of those who actually managed to gain control of power and to overthrow the French monarchy. Compared to the French Revolution, the American Revolution was no revolution at all.

According to Eric Voegelin, the sense of historical change in Europe at the time was of epochal significance.

> While the eighteenth-century's consciousness of epoch is a continuation of the movement that started in the thirteenth century, it is distinguished from the earlier phases of this process by its increased intensity, by a comprehensiveness which embraces all aspects of human existence, above all, by its broad social effectiveness which results in the final disruption of the medieval sentiments of the Western community and paves the way for new types of schismatic political movements.[1]

Suddenly and in a new way, many who had taken for granted the weight of history and the relatively slow pace of social change awakened with either joy or horror to the French Revolution and all that it portended. The reaction of many writers and intellectuals who were horrified by revolutionary pretensions became an argument *against* the French Revolution and *for* the wisdom, naturalness, and validity of tradition. The conservative reaction that developed in the early nineteenth century took aim particularly at the abstract, individualistic character of Enlightenment rationalism. "The Rights of Man," they said, amounted to a declaration of independence for disconnected, unhistorical individuals who do not in fact exist. Many who developed arguments from history idealized the seemingly organic, well-ordered, many-sided, communal character of pre-revolutionary society.

For example, Joseph de Maistre, Louis de Bonald, and François René de Chateaubriand—three French Catholics who had been scattered abroad by the French Revolution—led an ideological counterattack against revolutionary thinking in defense of the traditional order. Their writings represent a significant critique of the abstract rationalism and materialism of the revolutionaries.[2] Other romantic critics of the French Revolution began to laud the unique characteristics of French, Dutch, German, English, and other national cultures—each the fruit of a long historical process of differentiation that could not have been created overnight by an act of revolutionary will. These critics believed that the colorless, abstract, anti-historical spirit of the French Revolution and of liberalism, which began spreading throughout Europe, would eventually level and destroy their historically unique nations.[3] Of course, many different kinds of historical argument emerged. Some merely stressed the historical unfolding process; others absolutized it. Some saw history as the stage for creative individual achievements that ought not to be discarded; others saw history as an organic social process where various institutions, communities, and cultural characteristics flowered together as expressions of unique national spirits. Some romantic reactionaries were self-conscious Christians looking to divine authority in history; others were engaged in explaining away the original meaning of Christianity.

Furthermore, it is especially important for our purposes to emphasize that arguments from history have not remained the monopoly of those who look backward through time. In our day, new schools of thought, some influenced by Christian motives, have focused attention on the future. Coming primarily from Europe and Latin America, these more recent arguments start with hope, expectancy, and longing for a better society that will arise in the historical future, but they still turn out to be arguments from history.

In Jürgen Moltmann's "theology of hope" or Gustavo Gutiérrez's "theology of liberation," for example, history is viewed as a process of unfolding by which people continue to be liberated from past and present bondage.[4] When these authors invoke divine providence and authority, they do so with the conviction that God acts in the continuity of history and not simply in a transcendent spiritual realm or through ecclesiastical mediation that claims to reach beyond history. In contrast to the abstract notions of individual freedom and universal rationality held by many Enlightenment revolutionaries and liberals, these contemporary futurists have an organic sense of human community and historical development.

The selected readings that follow offer a sampling of five "arguments from history" on behalf of a plural social order. Edmund Burke (1729-1797) is the well-known, Irish-born, British statesmen and author who wrote the first and perhaps most famous critique of the French Revolution. His influence remains strong in conservative circles to the present day.

Guillaume Groen van Prinsterer (1801-1876) is a little-known Dutch historian and statesman who had an immense influence in his own country. His opposition to the spirit of revolution and to liberalism is fired by a more explicit and historically progressive Christian confession than that of Burke.

Otto von Gierke (1841-1921) is the German legal and political scholar who developed an extended historical argument in support of the real personality of groups. He criticized individualist conceptions of society in which groups are thought to be merely "fictitious persons." Gierke's historical writings had a considerable impact on the English pluralists, especially F. W. Maitland, J. N. Figgis, and Ernest Barker.

John Neville Figgis (1866-1919) is one of the "English pluralists" influenced by Gierke. An Anglican cleric and a professor at Cambridge, Figgis experienced firsthand many legal and political battles between those, on the one side, who sought to advance the power and prestige of the state and those like himself, on the other side, who championed the independent rights of multiple institutions and associations.

Finally, we consider the work of José Míguez Bonino (b. 1924) who writes within the context of twentieth-century liberation theology in Latin America. Míguez Bonino is from Argentina, and the fact that he is a Protestant serves to indicate that liberation theology is not simply a Roman Catholic phenomenon.

NOTES

[1] Eric Voegelin, *From Enlightenment to Revolution*, ed. J. Hallowell, (Durham, NC: Duke University Press, 1975), 3-4. See also Christopher Dawson, *The Gods of Revolution: An Analysis of the French Revolution* (New York: Minerva Press, 1972), esp. 3-31, 146-154.

[2] In 1796 de Maistre published the first tract of French reaction to the Revolution, *Considérations sur la France*, English translation by Richard A. Lebrun, *Considerations on France* (Montreal: McGill-Queen's University Press, 1974). One year later Bonald published his *Théorie du pouvoir politique et religieux*, and it was followed by Chateaubriand's *Essai historique, politique, et moral sur la Révolution*. For an excellent introduction to Catholic political thought and primary documents see Bela Menczer, ed., *Catholic Political Thought, 1789-1848* (Notre Dame: University of Notre Dame Press, 1962). See also Richard A. Lebrun, *Joseph de Maistre: An Intellectual Militant* (Montreal: McGill-Queens University Press, 1989) and Hans Maier, *Revolution and Church: The Early History of Christian Democracy, 1789-1901*, trans. E. Schossberger (Notre Dame: University of Notre Dame Press, 1969), 1-177.

[3] For an introduction to the romantic reaction see Ernst Cassirer, *The Myth of the State* (New Haven: Yale University Press, 1946), 176-186, and Maier, *Revolution and Church*, 142-177. The following statement from Cassirer captures the essence of the contrast between the eighteenth-century Enlightenment's view of history and the nineteenth-century romantic view:

> The romantics love the past for the past's sake. To them the past is not only a fact but also one of the highest ideals. This idealization and spiritualization of the past is one of the most distinctive characteristics of romantic thought. Everything becomes understandable, justifiable, legitimated as soon as we can trace it back to its origin. This frame of mind was entirely alien to the thinkers of the eighteenth century. If they looked back to the past they did so because they wanted to prepare a better future. The future of mankind, the rise of a new political and social order, was their great theme and real concern. For this purpose the study of HISTORY is necessary, but it is not an end in itself. History may teach us many things but it can only teach us what has been, not what

ought to be. To accept its verdict as infallible and definitive would be a crime against the majesty of reason. *Ibid.,* 181.

See also Herman Dooyeweerd, *Roots of Western Culture: Pagan, Secular, and Christian Options*, trans. J. Kraay; eds. M. Vander Vennen and B. Zylstra (Toronto: Wedge Publishing Foundation, 1979), 61-87, 175-188; and Dawson, *The Gods of Revolution*, 130-154.

[4] See Gustavo Gutiérrez, *A Theology of Liberation* (Maryknoll, NY: Orbis Books, 1973) and Jürgen Moltmann, *Theology of Hope* (New York: Harper and Row, 1967).

Two

✕✕✕✕✕✕✕✕✕✕✕✕

REFLECTIONS ON THE REVOLUTION IN FRANCE[1]
by Edmund Burke

Edmund Burke

When Edmund Burke (1729-1797), in his famous *Reflections on the Revolution in France* (1790),[2] expresses his strongest objections, he does so in large measure with an argument from history. The revolutionaries in France were engaged in eliminating the monarchy, the aristocracy, and most of the influence of the Roman Catholic Church. Treating French society as if it were a collection of building blocks that could be knocked down and built up again at will, the revolutionaries were going about their work ignorant of the power and meaning of history. As Burke argues, they foolishly and mistakenly imagined that they were free to start from scratch to construct a new government and social order solely on the basis of abstract reason.

Burke illustrates the revolutionaries' commitment to the imposition of rationalist abstractions on French society by pointing to the destruction of the diversity of the ancient communes, guilds, corporations, states, ecclesiastical districts, and provinces. In place of the traditional French provinces, for example, totally new political units were established through new laws specifically enacted by the revolutionary legislators. In this new political order the city of Paris became the focal point of the entire rationalized and centralized system. From Burke's point of view:

It is impossible not to observe that, in the spirit of this geometrical distribution and arithmetical arrangement, these pretended citizens treat France exactly like a country of conquest. Acting as conquerors, they have imitated the policy of the harshest of that harsh race. The policy of such barbarous victors, who contemn a subdued people and insult their feelings, has ever been, as much as in them lay, to destroy all vestiges of the ancient country, in religion, in policy, in laws, and in manners. . . . They have made France free in the manner in which those sincere friends to the rights of mankind, the Romans, freed Greece, Macedon, and other nations. They destroyed the bonds of their union under color of providing for the independence of each of their cities.[3]

Burke thinks that the very idea of fabricating a new government out of thin air is something that should fill the British with "disgust and horror."[4] Disgust and horror express well the deep feeling of many in his day. The highly regarded English Revolution of 1688 stood for something quite different from what the French revolutionaries were trying to achieve. We wished in 1688, and do now wish, Burke writes,

to derive all we possess as *an inheritance from our forefathers*. . . . All the reformations we have hitherto made have proceeded upon the principle of reverence to antiquity; and I hope, nay, I am persuaded, that all those which possibly may be made hereafter will be carefully formed upon analogical precedent, authority, and example.[5]

In Burke's view, change based upon "analogical precedent, authority, and example" is important not simply because it provides continuity and stability, but because it is essential to the very nature of humanity. Human creatures should not discard what God in his wise providence has built up through the actions of wise leaders in the past. "We know," says Burke, "and what is better, we feel inwardly, that religion is the basis of civil society and the source of all good and of all comfort."[6] The growth of society is not the result of arbitrary human whims. Social structures interlaced in a civil society have emerged gradually through history as human beings have acted under divine providence. Thus the uniform and common religious sense of mankind should be expressed through an established church which can consecrate the commonwealth. By means of such an establishment, "we continue to act on the early received and uniformly continued sense of mankind," namely, that "a wise architect" builds up and preserves the structure of society "from profanation and ruin," gradually purging from it "all the impurities of fraud and violence and injustice and tyranny . . . ."[7] In condemning the motives and concrete implications of the French Revolution, Burke argues from history.

In his *Reflections* and other writings, Burke does not set forth a systematic theory of society and politics. Nevertheless, his thinking is cast pervasively in unchanging categories. Since he distrusts metaphysics and *a priori* reasoning, he constantly emphasizes that politics is a matter of prescription, presumption, and prejudice. "Prescription" refers to rights or privileges established and recognized in the political culture of a people. "Presumption" has to do with the tendency to see established tradition and institutions as legitimate and beneficial to society. "Prejudice," which for Burke is not a pejorative term, entails a favorable judgment or opinion held in regard to something. Each of these concepts reflects Burke's appeal to history in support of the established order.[8]

True political wisdom, according to Burke, builds up and improves old institutions rather than destroying them. "Profound reflection," he says at one point, is "the happy effect of following nature, which is wisdom without reflection, and above it."[9] To try to uproot the many corporate bodies in society is the height of folly—something unwise and unnatural. In making this point, he employs the following argument that elsewhere he refers to as the "spirit of philosophic analogy":

> The perennial existence of bodies corporate and their fortunes are things particularly suited to a man who has long views; who meditates designs that require time in fashioning, and which propose duration when they are accomplished. . . . To destroy any power growing wild from the rank productive force of the human mind is almost tantamount, in the moral world, to the destruction of the apparently active properties of bodies in the material. It would be like the attempt to destroy (if it were in our competence to destroy) the expansive force of fixed air in nitre, or the power of steam, or of electricity, or of magnetism.[10]

But what, precisely, is the type of social order that Burke wants to defend? What had tradition established in the British Isles? As part of their inheritance the British had adopted "our fundamental laws into the bosom of our family affections, keeping inseparable and cherishing with the warmth of all their combined and mutually reflected charities our state, our hearths, our sepulchers, and our altars."[11] Burke wants to hold onto all those institutions not simply to preserve the privileges of the few, but also to maintain the variety of associations, institutions, rights, and freedoms that had achieved public recognition and protection over the years. With regard to church and state, for example, though it had taken centuries to achieve, the people of England had come to a balanced recognition of ecclesiastical privilege in society without "turning their independent clergy into ecclesiastical pensioners of state."[12]

Burke lived in fear of the destructive leveling tendencies of the French Revolution—a revolution that promised freedom and equality for individuals but had no ground for freedom and equality apart from abstract reason, revolutionary violence, and governmental power. All the traditional institutions of society were leveled or placed at the mercy of those claiming political authority on the basis of autonomous rationality.

Burke insists that he stands for the "real rights of man" as opposed to the abstract rights praised so highly by the revolutionaries.[13] For Burke, justice means the maintenance of stability and order among the variety of recognized institutions, authorities, and individual rights. It certainly does not mean that political leaders are free to clear away as mere rubbish whatever they find and, like ornamental gardeners, to reshape everything according to a preconceived geometric design. Burke is convinced that history had brought forth a relatively wise and healthy flowering of human potential in Great Britain and in parts of continental Europe up to the time of the French Revolution. English law recognizes a wide variety of individual and institutional rights, freedoms, and privileges in the context of a traditional and aristocratic society. Those fruits of history should be preserved, he believes, because they are the outgrowth of reasonable influences that had been at work for centuries.

Burke is open to change and reform, but he insists that it be based upon "analogical precedent, authority, and example." He does not argue that every existing institution is good, but he places the burden of proof on the present generation's proposals for change. The "objects of society are of the greatest possible complexity," and thus "no simple disposition or direction of power can be suitable either to man's nature or to the quality of his affairs."[14] "When ancient opinions and rules of life are taken away, the loss cannot possibly be estimated. From that moment we have no compass to govern us; nor can we know distinctly to what port we steer."[15]

REFLECTIONS ON THE REVOLUTION
IN FRANCE

[The English Revolution of 1688]

The [English] Revolution [of 1688] was made to preserve our *ancient*, indisputable laws and liberties and that *ancient* constitution of government which is our only security for law and liberty. If you are desirous of knowing the spirit of our constitution and the policy which predominated in that great period which has secured it to this hour, pray look for both in our histories, in our records, in our acts of parliament, and journals of parliament, and not in the sermons of the Old Jewry and the after-dinner toasts of the Revolution Society. In the former you will find other ideas and another language. Such a claim is as ill-suited to our temper and wishes as it is unsupported by any appearance of authority. The very idea of the fabrication of a new government is enough to fill us with disgust and horror. We wished at the period of the Revolution, and do now wish, to derive all we possess as *an inheritance from our forefathers.* Upon that body and stock of inheritance we have taken care not to inoculate any scion alien to the nature of the original plant. All the reformations we have hitherto made have proceeded upon the principle of reverence to antiquity; and I hope, nay, I am persuaded, that all those which possibly may be made hereafter will be carefully formed upon analogical precedent, authority, and example.

Our oldest reformation is that of Magna Charta. You will see that Sir Edward Coke, that great oracle of our law, and indeed all the great men who follow him, to Blackstone, are industrious to prove the pedigree of our liberties. They endeavor to prove that the ancient charter, the Magna Charta of King John, was connected with another positive charter from Henry I and that both the one and the other were nothing more than a reaffirmance of the still more ancient standing law of the kingdom. In the matter of fact, for the greater part these authors appear to be in the right; perhaps not always; but if the lawyers mistake in some particulars, it proves my position still the more strongly, because it demonstrates the powerful prepossession toward antiquity, with which the minds of all our lawyers and legislators, and of all the people whom they wish to influence, have been always filled, and the stationary policy of this kingdom in considering their most sacred rights and franchises as an *inheritance.* . . .

You will observe that from Magna Charta to the Declaration of Right it has been the uniform policy of our constitution to claim and assert our liberties as an *entailed inheritance* derived to us from our forefathers, and to be transmitted to our posterity—as an estate specially belonging to the people of this kingdom, without any reference whatever to any other more general or prior right. By this means our constitution preserves a unity in so great a diversity of its parts. We have an inheritable crown, an inheritable peerage, and a House of Commons and a people inheriting privileges, franchises, and liberties from a long line of ancestors.

This policy appears to me to be the result of profound reflection, or rather the happy effect of following nature, which is wisdom without reflection, and above it. A spirit of innovation is generally the result of a selfish temper and confined views. People will not look forward to posterity, who never look backward to their ancestors. Besides, the people of England well know that the idea of inheritance furnishes a sure principle of conservation and a sure principle of transmission, without at all excluding a principle of improvement. It leaves acquisition free, but it secures what it acquires. Whatever advantages are obtained by a state proceeding on these maxims are locked fast as in a sort of family settlement, grasped as in a kind of mortmain forever. By a constitutional policy, working after the pattern of nature, we receive, we hold, we transmit our government and our privileges in the same manner in which we enjoy and transmit our property and our lives. The institutions of policy, the goods of fortune, the gifts of providence are handed down to us, and from us, in the same course and order. Our political system is placed in a just correspondence and symmetry with the order of the world as with the mode of existence decreed to a permanent body composed of transitory parts, wherein, by the disposition of a stupendous wisdom, molding together the great mysterious incorporation of the human race, the whole, at one time, is never old or middle-aged or young, but, in a condition of unchangeable constancy, moves on through the varied tenor of perpetual decay, fall, renovation, and progression. Thus, by preserving the method of nature in the conduct of the state, in what we improve we are never wholly new; in what we retain we are never wholly obsolete. By adhering in this manner and on those principles to our forefathers, we are guided not by the superstition of antiquarians, but by the spirit of philosophic analogy. In this choice of inheritance we have given to our frame of polity the image of a relation in blood, binding up the constitution of our country with our dearest domestic ties, adopting our fundamental laws into the bosom of our family affections, keeping inseparable and cherishing with the warmth of all their combined and mutually reflected charities our state, our hearths, our sepulchres, and our altars.

Through the same plan of a conformity to nature in our artificial institutions, and by calling in the aid of her unerring and powerful instincts to fortify the fallible and feeble contrivances of our reason, we have derived several other, and those no small, benefits from considering our liberties in the light of an inheritance. Always acting as if in the presence of canonized forefathers, the spirit of freedom, leading in itself to misrule and excess, is tempered with an awful gravity. This idea of a liberal descent inspires us with a sense of habitual native dignity which prevents that upstart insolence almost inevitably adhering to and disgracing those who are the first acquirers of any distinction. By this means our liberty becomes a noble freedom. It carries an imposing and majestic aspect. It has a pedigree and illustrating ancestors. It has its bearings and its ensigns armorial. It has its gallery of portraits, its monumental inscriptions, its records, evidences, and titles. We procure reverence to our civil institutions on the principle upon which nature teaches us to revere individual men: on account of their age and on account of those from whom they are descended. All your sophisters cannot produce anything better adapted to preserve a rational and manly freedom than the course that we have pursued, who have chosen our nature rather than our speculations, our breasts rather than our inventions, for the great conservatories and magazines of our rights and privileges. . . .

The Erroneous Concept of the Rights of Men

[Those in England who look with favor on the French Revolution] look abroad with an eager and passionate enthusiasm. Whilst they are possessed by these notions, it is vain to talk to them of the practice of their ancestors, the fundamental laws of their country, the fixed form of a constitution whose merits are confirmed by the solid test of long experience and an increasing public strength and national prosperity. They despise experience as the wisdom of unlettered men; and as for the rest, they have wrought underground a mine that will blow up, at one grand explosion, all examples of antiquity, all precedents, charters, and acts of parliament. They have "the rights of men." Against these there can be no prescription, against these no agreement is binding; these admit no temperament and no compromise; anything withheld from their full demand is so much of fraud and injustice. Against these their rights of men let no government look for security in the length of its continuance, or in the justice and lenity of its administration. The objections of these speculatists, if its forms do not quadrate with their theories, are as valid against such an old and beneficent government as against the most violent tyranny or the greenest usurpation. They are always at issue with governments, not on a question of abuse, but a question of competency and a question of title. I have nothing to say to the clumsy subtilty of their political metaphysics. . . . But let them not break prison to burst like a *Levanter* [a strong easterly wind peculiar to the Mediterranean], to sweep the earth with their hurricane and to break up the fountains of the great deep to overwhelm us.

The True Concept of the Rights of Men

Far am I from denying in theory, full as far is my heart from withholding in practice (if I were of power to give or to withhold) the *real* rights of men. In denying their false claims of right, I do not mean to injure those which are real, and are such as their pretended rights would totally destroy. If civil society be made for the advantage of man, all the advantages for which it is made become his right. It is an institution of beneficence; and law itself is only beneficence acting by a rule. Men have a right to live by that rule; they have a right to do justice, as between their fellows, whether their fellows are in public function or in ordinary occupation. They have a right to the fruits of their industry and to the means of making their industry fruitful. They have a right to the acquisitions of their parents, to the nourishment and improvement of their offspring, to instruction in life, and to consolation in death. Whatever each man can separately do, without trespassing upon others, he has a right to do for himself; and he has a right to a fair portion of all which society, with all its combinations of skill and force, can do in his favor. In this partnership all men have equal rights, but not to equal things. He that has but five shillings in the partnership has as good a right to it as he that has five hundred pounds has to his larger proportion. But he has not a right to an equal dividend in the product of the joint stock; and as to the share of power, authority, and direction which each individual ought to have in the management of the state, that I must deny to be amongst the direct original rights of man in civil society, for I have in my contemplation the civil social man, and no other. It is a thing to be settled by convention.

If civil society be the offspring of convention, that convention must be its law. That convention must limit and modify all the descriptions of constitution which are formed under it. Every sort of legislative, judicial, or executory power are its creatures. They can have no being in any other state of things; and how can any man claim under the conventions of civil society rights which do not so much as suppose its existence—rights which are absolutely repugnant to it? One of the first motives to civil society, and which becomes one of its fundamental rules, is *that no man should be judge in his own cause.* By this each person has at once divested himself of the first fundamental right of uncovenanted man, that is, to judge for himself and to assert his own cause. He abdicates all right to be his own governor. He inclusively, in a great measure, abandons the right of self-defense, the first law of nature. Men cannot enjoy the rights of an uncivil and of a civil state together. That he may obtain justice, he gives up his right of determining what it is in points the most essential to him. That he may secure some liberty, he makes a surrender in trust of the whole of it.

The True Nature of Government

Government is not made in virtue of natural rights, which may and do exist in total independence of it, and exist in much greater clearness and in a much greater degree of abstract perfection; but their abstract perfection is their practical defect. By having a right to everything they want everything. Government is a contrivance of human wisdom to provide for human *wants.* Men have a right that these wants should be provided for by this wisdom. Among these wants is to be reckoned the want, out of civil society, of a sufficient restraint upon their passions. Society requires not only that the passions of individuals should be subjected, but that even in the mass and body, as well as in the individuals, the inclinations of men should frequently be thwarted, their will controlled, and their passions brought into subjection. This can only be done *by a power out of themselves,* and not, in the exercise of its function, subject to that will and to those passions which it is its office to bridle and subdue. In this sense the restraints on men, as well as their liberties, are to be reckoned among their rights. But as the liberties and the restrictions vary with times and circumstances and admit to infinite modifications, they cannot be settled upon any abstract rule; and nothing is so foolish as to discuss them upon that principle.

The moment you abate anything from the full rights of men, each to govern himself, and suffer any artificial, positive limitation upon those rights, from that moment the whole organization of government becomes a consideration of convenience. This it is which makes the constitution of a state and the due distribution of its powers a matter of the most delicate and complicated skill. It requires a deep knowledge of human nature and human necessities, and of the things which facilitate or obstruct the various ends which are to be pursued by the mechanism of civil institutions. The state is to have recruits to its strength, and remedies to its distempers. What is the use of discussing a man's abstract right to food or medicine? The question is upon the method of procuring and administering them. In that deliberation I shall always advise to call in the aid of the farmer and the physician rather than the professor of metaphysics.

The science of constructing a commonwealth, or renovating it, or reforming it, is, like every other experimental science, not to be taught *a priori*. Nor is it a short experience that can instruct us in that practical science, because the real effects of moral causes are not always immediate; but that which in the first instance is prejudicial may be excellent in its remoter operation, and its excellence may arise even from the ill effects it produces in the beginning. The reverse also happens: and very plausible schemes, with very pleasing commencements, have often shameful and lamentable conclusions. In states there are often some obscure and almost latent causes, things which appear at first view of little moment, on which a very great part of its prosperity or adversity may most essentially depend. The science of government being therefore so practical in itself and intended for such practical purposes—a matter which requires experience, and even more experience than any person can gain in his whole life, however sagacious and observing he may be—it is with infinite caution that any man ought to venture upon pulling down an edifice which has answered in any tolerable degree for ages the common purposes of society, or on building it up again without having models and patterns of approved utility before his eyes.

The Principle of the Law of Nature
Not Applicable to a Complex Society

These metaphysic rights entering into common life, like rays of light which pierce into a dense medium, are by the laws of nature refracted from their straight line. Indeed, in the gross and complicated mass of human passions and concerns the primitive rights of men undergo such a variety of refractions and reflections that it becomes absurd to talk of them as if they continued in the simplicity of their original direction. The nature of man is intricate; the objects of society are of the greatest possible complexity; and, therefore, no simple disposition or direction of power can be suitable either to man's nature or to the quality of his affairs. When I hear the simplicity of contrivance aimed at and boasted of in any new political constitutions, I am at no loss to decide that the artificers are grossly ignorant of their trade or totally negligent of their duty. The simple governments are fundamentally defective, to say no worse of them. If you were to contemplate society in but one point of view, all these simple modes of polity are infinitely captivating. In effect each would answer its single end much more perfectly than the more complex is able to attain all its complex purposes. But it is better that the whole should be imperfectly and anomalously answered than that, while some parts are provided for with great exactness, others might be totally neglected or perhaps materially injured by the overcare of a favorite member.

The pretended rights of these theorists are all extremes; and in proportion as they are metaphysically true, they are morally and politically false. The rights of men are in a sort of *middle*, incapable of definition, but not impossible to be discerned. The rights of men in governments are their advantages; and these are often in balances between differences of good, in compromises sometimes between good and evil, and sometimes between evil and evil. Political reason is a computing principle: adding, subtracting, multiplying, and dividing, morally and not metaphysically, or mathematically, true moral denominations.

By these theorists the right of the people is almost always sophistically confounded with their power. The body of the community, whenever it can come to act, can meet with no effectual resistance; but till power and right are the same, the whole body of them has no right inconsistent with virtue, and the first of all virtues, prudence. Men have no right to what is not reasonable and to what is not for their benefit; for though a pleasant writer said, *Liceat perire poetis* ["Let poets have the right to perish if they wish"], when one of them, in cold blood, is said to have leaped into the flames of a volcanic revolution, *Ardentem frigidus Aetnam insiluit* ["He jumped in cold blood into burning Etna"], I consider such a frolic rather as an unjustifiable poetic license than as one of the franchises of Parnassus [liberties given to poets]; and whether he was a poet, or divine, or politician that chose to exercise this kind of right, I think that more wise, because more charitable, thoughts would urge me rather to save the man than to preserve his brazen slippers as the monuments of his folly.

The kind of anniversary sermons to which a great part of what I write refers, if men are not shamed out of their present course in commemorating the fact, will cheat many out of the principles, and deprive them of the benefits, of the revolution they commemorate. I confess to you, Sir, I never liked this continual talk of resistance and revolution, or the practice of making the extreme medicine of the constitution its daily bread. It renders the habit of society dangerously valetudinary; it is taking periodical doses of mercury sublimate and swallowing down repeated provocatives of cantharides to our love of liberty. . .

Society is a Permanent Contract

Society is indeed a contract. Subordinate contracts for objects of mere occasional interest may be dissolved at pleasure—but the state ought not to be considered as nothing better than a partnership agreement in a trade of pepper and coffee, calico, or tobacco, or some other such low concern, to be taken up for a little temporary interest, and to be dissolved by the fancy of the parties. It is to be looked on with other reverence, because it is not a partnership in things subservient only to the gross animal existence of a temporary and perishable nature. It is a partnership in all science; a partnership in all art; a partnership in every virtue and in all perfection. As the ends of such a partnership cannot be obtained in many generations, it becomes a partnership not only between those who are living, but between those who are living, those who are dead, and those who are to be born. Each contract of each particular state is but a clause in the great primeval contract of eternal society, linking the lower with the higher natures, connecting the visible and invisible world, according to a fixed compact sanctioned by the inviolable oath which holds all physical and all moral natures, each in their appointed place. This law is not subject to the will of those who by an obligation above them, and infinitely superior, are bound to submit their will to that law. The municipal corporations of that universal kingdom are not morally at liberty at their pleasure, and on their speculations of a contingent improvement, wholly to separate and tear asunder the bands of their subordinate community and to dissolve it into an unsocial, uncivil, unconnected chaos of elementary principles. It is the first and supreme necessity only, a necessity that is not chosen but chooses, a necessity paramount to deliberation, that admits no discussion and demands no evidence, which alone can justify a resort to anarchy. This necessity is no exception to the rule, because the necessity itself is a part, too, of that moral and physical disposition of things to which man must be obedient by consent or force; but if that which is only submission to necessity should be made the object of choice, the law is broken, nature is disobeyed, and the rebellious are outlawed, cast forth, and exiled from this world of reason, and order, and peace, and virtue, and fruitful penitence, into the antagonist world of madness, discord, vice, confusion, and unavailing sorrow.

State and Church are Inseparable

These, my dear Sir, are, were, and, I think, long will be the sentiments of not the least learned and reflecting part of this kingdom. They who are included in this description form their opinions on such grounds as such persons ought to form them. The less inquiring receive them from an authority which those whom Providence dooms to live on trust need not be ashamed to rely on. These two sorts of men move in the same direction, though in a different place. They both move with the order of the universe. They all know or feel this great ancient truth: *Quod illi principi et praepotenti Deo qui omnem hunc mundum regit, nihil eorum quae quidem fiant in terris acceptius quam concilia et coetus hominum jure sociati quae civitates appellantur* ["That nothing, indeed, of the events which occur on earth is more pleasing to that supreme and prepotent God who rules this entire universe than these societies and associations of men, cemented by law, which are called states"]. They take this tenet of the head and heart, not from the great name which it immediately bears, nor from the greater from whence it is derived, but from that which alone can give true weight and sanction to any learned opinion, the common nature and common relation of men. Persuaded that all things ought to be done with reference, and referring all to the point of reference to which all should be directed, they think themselves bound, not only as individuals in the sanctuary of the heart or as congregated in that personal capacity, to renew the memory of their high origin and cast, but also in their corporate character to perform their national homage to the institutor and author and protector of civil society, without which civil society man could not by any possibility arrive at the perfection of which his nature is capable, nor even make a remote and faint approach to it. They conceive that He who gave our nature to be perfected by our virtue willed also the necessary means of its perfection: He willed therefore the state—He willed its connection with the source and original archetype of all perfection. They who are convinced of this His will, which is the law of laws and the sovereign of sovereigns, cannot think it reprehensible that this our corporate fealty and homage, that this our recognition of a seigniory paramount [authority of a feudal lord], I had almost said this oblation of the state itself as a worthy offering on the high altar of universal praise, should be performed as all public, solemn acts are performed, in buildings, in music, in decoration, in speech, in the dignity of persons, according to the customs of mankind taught by their nature—this is, with modest splendor and unassuming state, with mild majesty and sober pomp. For those purposes they think some part of the wealth of the country is as usefully employed as it can be in fomenting the luxury of individuals. It is the public ornament. It is the public consolation. It nourishes the public hope. The poorest man finds his own importance and dignity in it, whilst the wealth and pride of individuals at every moment makes the man of humble rank and fortune sensible of his inferiority and degrades and vilifies his condition. It is for the man in humble life, and to raise his nature and to put him in mind of a state in which the privileges of opulence will cease, when he will be equal by nature, and may be more than equal by virtue, that this portion of the general wealth of his country is employed and sanctified.

I assure you I do not aim at singularity. I give you opinions which have been accepted amongst us, from very early times to this moment, with a continued and general approbation, and which indeed are worked into my mind that I am unable to distinguish what I have learned from others from the results of my own meditation.

It is on some such principles that the majority of the people of England, far from thinking a religious national establishment unlawful, hardly think it lawful to be without one. In France you are wholly mistaken if you do not believe us above all other things attached to it, and beyond all other nations; and when this people has acted unwisely and unjustifiably in its favor (as in some instances they have done most certainly), in their very errors you will at least discover their zeal.

This principle runs through the whole system of their polity. They do not consider their church establishment as convenient, but as essential to their state, not as a thing heterogeneous and separable, something added for accommodation, what they may either keep or lay aside according to their temporary ideas of convenience. They consider it as the foundation of their whole constitution, with which, and with every part of which, it holds an indissoluble union. Church and state are ideas inseparable in their minds, and scarcely is the one ever mentioned without mentioning the other.

Education is Founded on Tradition and Closely Affiliated with the Church

Our education is so formed as to confirm and fix this impression. Our education is in a manner wholly in the hands of ecclesiastics, and in all stages from infancy to manhood. Even when our youth, leaving schools and universities, enter that most important period of life which begins to link experience and study together, and when with that view they visit other countries, instead of old domestics whom we have seen as governors to principal men from other parts, three-fourths of those who go abroad with our young nobility and gentlemen are ecclesiastics, not as austere masters, nor as mere followers, but as friends and companions of a graver character, and not seldom persons as well-born as themselves. With them, as relations, they most constantly keep a close connection through life. By this connection we conceive that we attach our gentlemen to the church, and we liberalize the church by an intercourse with the leading characters of the country.

So tenacious are we of the old ecclesiastical modes and fashions of institution that very little alteration has been made in them since the fourteenth or fifteenth century—adhering in this particular, as in all things else, to our old settled maxim, never entirely nor at once to depart from antiquity. We found these old institutions, on the whole, favorable to morality and discipline, and we thought they were susceptible of amendment without altering the ground. We thought that they were capable of receiving and meliorating, and above all of preserving, the accessions of science and literature, as the order of Providence should successively produce them. And after all, with this Gothic and monkish education (for such it is in the groundwork) we may put in our claim to as ample and as early a share in all the improvements in science, in arts, and in literature which have illuminated and adorned the modern world, as any other nation in Europe. We think one main cause of this improvement was our not despising the patrimony of knowledge which was left us by our forefathers.

It is from our attachment to a church establishment that the English nation did not think it wise to entrust that great, fundamental interest of the whole to what they trust no part of their civil or military public service, that is, to the unsteady and precarious contribution of individuals. They go further. They certainly never have suffered, and never will suffer, the fixed estate of the church to be converted into a pension, to depend on the treasury and to be delayed, withheld, or perhaps to be extinguished by fiscal difficulties, which difficulties may sometimes be pretended for political purposes, and are in fact often brought on by the extravagance, negligence, and rapacity of politicians. The people of England think that they have constitutional motives, as well as religious, against any project of turning their independent clergy into ecclesiastical pensioners of state. They tremble for their liberty, from the influence of a clergy dependent on the crown; they tremble for the public tranquillity from the disorders of a factious clergy, if it were made to depend upon any other than the crown. They therefore made their church, like their king and their nobility, independent.

From the united considerations of religion and constitutional policy, from their opinion of a duty to make sure provision for the consolation of the feeble and the instruction of the ignorant, they have incorporated and identified the estate of the church with the mass of *private property*, of which the state is not the proprietor, either for use or dominion, but the guardian only and the regulator. They have ordained that the provision of this establishment might be as stable as the earth on which it stands, and should not fluctuate with the Euripus of funds and actions.

NOTES

1 Selections taken from Chapters II, IV, and VII of *Reflections on the Revolution in France*, edited with an introduction by T. Mahoney (New York: The Liberal Arts Press, 1955). *Reflections* was Edmund Burke's answer to a sermon delivered to the members of the Revolution Society in London which praised the principles of the French Revolution. The Revolution Society was an organization formed to honor the Glorious Revolution of 1688 in England.

2 *Ibid.*

3 *Ibid.*, 213-14.

4 *Ibid.*, 35.

5 *Ibid.*, 35-36.

6 *Ibid.*, 102.

7 *Ibid.*, 104-105.

8 Dante Germino, *Machiavelli to Marx: Modern Western Political Thought* (Chicago: The University of Chicago Press, 1972), 224-225.

9 Burke, *Reflections*, 37.

10 *Ibid.*, 182.

11 *Ibid.*, 38.

12 *Ibid.*, 115. See also 181ff. and 196ff.

13 *Ibid.*, 55-76.

14 *Ibid.*, 70.

15 *Ibid.*, 89.

THREE

XXXXXXXXXXXXXX

UNBELIEF AND REVOLUTION[1]
by G. Groen van Prinsterer

G. Groen van Prinsterer

In the nineteenth-century Netherlands, Guillaume Groen van Prinsterer (1801-1876) also directed a sharp attack against the French Revolution. Groen lived through a time when his country was experiencing massive change. From 1795 to 1813, the Low Countries were forcibly occupied by the French, first being turned into the Batavian Republic (one of the "sister republics" of the revolutionary regime established in Paris) and then incorporated as part of the Napoleonic Empire. The smaller revolutions of 1830 and 1848 in Paris sent out further aftershocks, like those of an earthquake, that kept the Dutch populace unsettled.

Groen van Prinsterer (or Groen) was a member of a wealthy and aristocratic family. He attended the finest schools, and on a single day in 1823 he defended two dissertations on law and on literature before faculties of the famed University of Leiden. The milieu in which he reached maturity could best be described as moderately religious and liberal.[2] He felt at home in the lukewarm Protestant culture of his day. In 1827 he was appointed secretary of the Royal Cabinet. The position was not a demanding job, and it gave him time to pursue his real interest in historical studies. In 1831 the King put him in charge of the royal archives.[3]

Between 1827 when he married and 1833 when he became seriously ill, Groen experienced a profound spiritual rebirth and intellectual revitalization. Early in the 1830s, he came under the influence of leading figures in the evangelical awakening that touched many Europeans in the early nineteenth century. After recovering from his illness, and with the inspiration of renewed Christian faith, Groen entered active politics. Between 1840 and 1865, he served in the Second Chamber of Parliament.

Groen is one of the first post-Revolution Protestants on the Continent to publish a serious reflection on the meaning of human power to shape history. He concludes that pious Protestants are mistaken to think of themselves as having an eternal destiny that entails little responsibility for shaping the affairs of this world. That false dichotomy between spiritual destiny and earthly responsibility was part of the problem inherent in the lukewarm Protestantism of his day. The revival of faith during the Reformation, writes Groen, had gradually expired in dead orthodoxy or hypocrisy and moral decline, creating a vacuum for unbelief to spread in. That unbelief brought about the French Revolution.[4] "What had become of the warmth and fervor of the evangelical persuasion, which earlier had borne so much fruit in deeds of faith?" Groen asks. "In its stead we find the spectacle of either narrow superstition, or intolerant hypocrisy, or fondness from mere tradition for articles of doctrine."[5]

Christians really ought to see themselves as the people whom God has called to make history according to his will, Groen believes.[6] Only with such an attitude will Christianity truly flourish. As Groen gains insight into this simple truth, he begins to recognize that competing spirits—conflicting religious motives—are at work in the shaping of history. The spirit of the French Revolution, he discerns, is at odds with the Spirit of Christ in all areas of life.[7] The Christian cause cannot be carried on simply by preserving an orthodox church in a secularized world, but must be carried on in politics and education, in journalism and science.

Groen urges fellow Christians to reread the Scriptures in order to understand the responsibility they have to shape the history of this world to the glory of God. Groen wants to heed the normative admonitions of the gospel which denounce the evils and injustices of the existing order. The foundation of justice, he writes, "lies in the law and the ordinances of God."[8] Just as a declining and corrupt church in the Middle Ages occasioned the Reformation, so the shock of the Revolution was one ingredient that should inspire the revival of Calvinism in the Netherlands in the nineteenth century.

Though Groen appeals to the Bible and the church, much of his argument is "from history." The type of differentiated social order that developed in The Netherlands during the centuries prior to the French Revolution was threatened by revolutionary fanaticism and liberal individualism. Groen does not want to return to an old order entirely, but neither does he want to destroy the providential work of God in history. To follow the Bible in reforming zeal requires the maintenance of what God has already done in history. Thus, Groen calls himself an anti-revolutionary,[9] opposing the revolutionaries and the liberals who have no interest in obeying God or in respecting God's historical providence. Groen begins to feel his way toward a progressive social pluralism based on the Bible and history.

In his most important publication, *Unbelief and Revolution* (1847), Groen points clearly to the antithesis that exists between the spirit of the Revolution and the will of God.

> The Revolution ought to be viewed in the context of world history. Its significance for Christendom equals that of the Reformation, but then in reverse. The Reformation rescued Europe from superstition; the Revolution has flung the civilized world into an abyss of unbelief. Like the Reformation, the Revolution touches every field of action and learning. In the days of the Reformation the principle was submission to God; in these days it is a revolt against God.[10]

Groen was an aristocrat who nonetheless dared to take his distance from aristocratic reactionaries of his day in order to continue with the work of the Reformation in his time.[11] In Parliament he frequently stood alone—a "general without on army" as he was often called—in order to point the way toward a Christian-historical as well as an antirevolutionary movement.

According to Groen, the first watchword for Christians should be: "It is written!" "Unconditional submission to the Word of God has always been the guarantee both of dutiful obedience and of dutiful resistance, of order and of freedom."[12] The second watchword should be: "It has come to pass! History provides "an uninterrupted refutation of Revolution maxims."[13] "Everything that leads to genuine knowledge of Revelation and of History," Groen writes, "is anti-revolutionary in nature and serves as an antidote to the magic power of the intoxicating drink."[14] selfishness of Liberalism

Groen does not refer to a rational, hierarchical world order as the normative framework by which to measure the justice and injustice of social structures. He is a Calvinist who does not, for the most part, think within the framework of older Thomism and the subsidiarity of smaller societal units under state and church. Groen's argument from history is an affirmation that the diversified structures of society, including the limited powers of government itself, have been established and recognized in The Netherlands in the process of a somewhat organic growth of Dutch history especially since the time of the Reformation.

Groen was influenced at an early stage by Edmund Burke and by the German conservative Karl von Haller; later he was influenced by the historicism of F. J. Stahl who stressed the organic character of every societal order. The work of Félicité de Lamennais can also be seen as a shaping influence in his growing understanding of a radical antithesis between belief and unbelief.[15] But these influences are not sufficient to account for Groen's view of society.

In the early part of *Unbelief and Revolution* Groen shows why he objects to the revolutionary rejection of the principle of divine right of kings. His objection is not one of simple conservatism in order to defend the authority of any king to rule in any fashion. Rather, he criticizes the revolutionaries for throwing out the baby with the bath water. There have, indeed, been acts of oppression by monarchs in the past—acts violating principles of justice that should not be condoned. Legitimate rule is lawful rule, and lawfulness refers beyond human authority to God's authority. Without the norm of divine authority there can be no salutary and just government. The revolutionaries were reacting against abuse without having anything substantial to put in the place of God's authority which they discarded.[16]

In the same context Groen discusses other criticisms leveled by the revolutionaries against the old order. He agrees with these criticisms without drawing the same conclusions. He admits, for example, that there had been exaggerated respect for historical rights in the pre-revolutionary period, and this led to injustice. He admits, as well, that past struggles to centralize state authority violated some of the freedoms of institutions and individuals. And he shows how a forced connection between church and state did grievous harm. But in each case Groen responds by saying that the objection to abuses does not provide a sufficient cause for rejecting entirely the historically acquired rights. Abuses do not justify the rejection of properly qualified state authority or a constructive relationship between state and church.[17]

The growth of liberalism following the French Revolution constituted a genuine threat to social pluralism in the Netherlands. Unbelief must be exposed and opposed by a vital Christian-historical witness, Groen argues, because the fruits of unbelief will lead in history to further oppression of the people by unjust governments. Groen's careful and appreciative study of history is guided by his confidence that the Word of God will expose just and unjust societal structures in history and that God's revelation points the way to a just future. If people in Holland will turn to heed the Word of God and read the truth of history, they will be able to continue the gradual and constructive differentiation and reformation of society.

UNBELIEF AND REVOLUTION

My aim in these lectures will be to demonstrate that the cause of the events that have taken place *since the rise of the Revolution ideas* lies in the natural development of these disastrous notions.

It is only fair that I explain to you, esteemed friends (1) the choice, (2) the nature, (3) the usefulness, and (4) the organization of this comprehensive subject.

The Choice of Subject

The choice of subject came to me as I was working on the last part of my *Handbook of Dutch History.* In reflecting upon what has happened in the Netherlands from 1795 till the present, I became keenly aware of our national humiliation and decline. . . . Whence this regression, this confusion, this general decline?

Do you blame the forms of government for it? We have had all kinds: democracy, aristocracy, monarchy, despotism, constitutional government—the whole storehouse of revolutionary governments has served us.

Do you blame the circumstances? They have not always been unfavorable.

Do you blame the degeneration of the people? They never fell so deep that they could not be lifted up again.

Have we lacked men of ability and energy? There have been statesmen whom I for one would not deny talent or character, nor, for that matter, good intentions; so that we are all the more pressed to search for the reason why even their wisdom was deceived and their energy paralyzed.

Everything points to a *general cause,* to which the political forms, the circumstances, the national character, and the acting personages have been subordinate. This cause must be sought in the *ideas* which have predominated. I agree with Lamennais where he remarks that "everything proceeds from doctrines: manners, literature, constitutions, laws, the happiness of nations and their misfortunes, culture, barbarism, and those terrible crises which carry the nations away or which renew them, depending on their level of vitality."[18]

Historical events are the contours and configurations that reveal the sustained action of the spirit of an age. This is what I propose to demonstrate to

you in the succession of the revolutionary phases, in our country and elsewhere. The history of Europe for more than half a century has been the inevitable result of the errors which have made themselves master of the predominant mode of thinking.

Nature of the Subject

In order to bring out the nature of this subject, it is necessary to explain
what I mean by *Revolution* and by *Revolution ideas*.

By *Revolution* I do not mean one of the many events whereby a government is overthrown. Nor do I mean by it just the storm of upheaval that has
raged in France. Rather, by Revolution I mean that overturning of the general
spirit and mode of thinking which is manifest throughout Christendom.[19]

By *Revolution ideas* I mean the basic maxims of liberty and equality,
popular sovereignty, social contract, the artificial reconstruction of society—
notions which today are venerated as the cornerstones of constitutional law
and the political order.

It is my conviction that it is this wisdom—together with its source: the
rejection of the Gospel—that has given birth to the manifold disasters experienced by our fathers and by our generation. This conviction was reinforced in
me by a fresh examination of the train of events. Once again I saw clearly that
wherever these theories gain a foothold people are led about in a vicious circle of misery.

. . . A strict, consistent application of the Revolution doctrine will bring
men to the most excessive absurdities and the worst atrocities. However,
when men become terrified by the revolutionary development (which they
regard as exaggeration) and in reaction insist on moderation in practice
though without abandoning the principle, then the only course open to them,
since they shrink back from the consequences of their own convictions, is a
shilly-shally, capricious behavior which has no guide save in the succession
and pressure of circumstances. Even today this course of action is made out
to be the height of political wisdom: I mean the method of consultation of the
doctrinaires; the policy which under the name of *juste-mileu* or the middle-of-
the-road is dominant at present; the theory of the *conservatives*; and the practice, or if I must speak the truth, the *routine*, the languor and lethargy, the rut
which prevails also in our own country.

The consequences of the Revolution ideas cannot be combatted with any
success unless one places himself outside their influence, on the ground of
the antirevolutionary principles. This ground is beyond reach, however, so
long as one refuses to acknowledge that the foundation of justice lies in the

law and ordinance of God. Bonald has expressed this truth in the concise and pregnant words, "The Revolution began with the declaration of the rights of man; it will end only with the declaration of the rights of God."[20]

Usefulness of the Subject

The usefulness of our subject is obvious. It strikes at the heart of current controversies in religion and politics. The revolution doctrine is unbelief applied to politics. A life and death struggle exists between the Gospel and this practical atheism. To contemplate a rapprochement between the two would be nonsense. It is a battle which embraces everything we cherish and hold sacred and everything that is beneficial and indispensable to church and state. . . .

. . . If it is with eyes of patriotic love that we have surveyed the condition of our fatherland, we will ask ourselves, painfully aware of our present plight, what we ought to do. Would it be advisable to immerse ourselves in reflection on a multiplicity of details, perhaps on reforms of the Constitution? Ought we to throw ourselves into the political fray in order to try to call a halt to the observance of opinions we deem harmful? This may indeed, now or in the future, be the useful and mandatory thing to do. But what we should do above all is try to gain insight not only into the full extent of the evil but especially into its *root* and *ramifications*. For only in this way can we obtain from the reliable results of a believing science the firmness we need to remain immovable in the face of diverse winds of doctrine. Otherwise, in defending the truth, we may ourselves be guilty of that uncertain sound on the trumpet which often renders even a truthful testimony powerless because the witnesses themselves are only half convinced. The best intentioned efforts are fruitless so long as the kinship between the present ailments of the state and the ruinous theories has not become clear. Without respect for those principles which human self-conceit disdains, every attempt at reform is tantamount to the whitewashing of sepulchers.

For us as citizens, but also as Christians, it is important that we not be ignorant of the nature and tenor of the political philosophy of our time.

One thing—I know and confess it—one thing only is needful for us all. It is not as statesmen or as scholars but as sinners that we seek to be saved. There is but one way, one truth. I find rest and peace for my soul in the good news that by free grace there is forgiveness and salvation in the atoning sacrifice of the Savior for all who believe. In no wise do I desire to escape the shame of this confession. A general statement of "Christian principles" is vague enough to evoke no substantial opposition. To speak of such principles in connection with history and politics involves little risk of being accused or suspected of narrow-mindedness so long as one abstains from clearly defining his conviction. For this very reason I wish to repeat here, in the introduction to these lectures, that I mean by Christian principles the truths recorded in Holy Scripture and imprinted by the Holy Spirit upon the heart of the simplest Christian.

Holding fast to the truth entails also holding fast to the duties imposed by one's station and occupation. Thus, to the extent that we have any influence, directly or indirectly, through action or conversation, on the course of politics or on the minds of men, it is our duty, my friends, with gratitude for the light shed by God's Word, to penetrate the inner recesses of science and the maze of historical events in order to adore and revere the Lord even here, in these His works, and in this way too to be messengers of a Gospel that brings healing to every sphere of life.

One thing is needful; but when we possess that one thing, the fruits of it should be manifest in everything. With respect to the saving of souls we are determined to know nothing but Christ and Him crucified; but if we know this, then the knowledge of the love of Christ should move and constrain us to seek the glory of God wherever He may be glorified. Every person to whom the Gospel has been made known is called to proclaim it, for proclaiming the Gospel to every creature can be done in many different ways. No means may be neglected that opens doors to minds and hearts.

To be sure, it is possible without a change of heart to wax lyrical about God's marvels in the creation and sustenance of nature, in the processes and outcomes of His governance of the world, and if we do that—God forbid!—it would serve to increase our guilt. But if we know the Lord in the Kingdom of His grace, it is doubly irresponsible to disregard Him in the ways of His providence and with cool indifference to ignore there the signs of His omnipotence and love, the wonders of His blessings and judgments.

The heavens declare the glory of God. Would it not likewise be a declaration of God's glory if the history of the Revolution era showed that to forsake the Word of God is enough to plunge apostate man, who lacks neither intelligence and ingenuity nor favorable circumstances, into an abyss of misery? Would it not prepare the philosopher of our time to bow his proud head before the beneficent Gospel if the darkness of his enlightenment and the foolishness of his wisdom were to be exhibited to him in the narrative sequence of indisputable facts? This kind of witness too may be called confessing the Gospel; this too may be called proclamation of the Good News.

The Christian would be wrong to imagine that, having the guidance of Scripture, he could do without learning. To be able to work at his appointed task diligently and conscientiously, the Christian too needs to have precise knowledge of the nature and function of his particular task. The fear of the Lord is the beginning of knowledge, but the beginning is not the whole of the matter; the whole of knowledge also embraces the other elements which embody the starting principle. The truth of the Gospel is the leaven, but to obtain nourishing and tasty bread there must be dough along with the leaven—if one appreciates solid substance. . . .

In a reverse way, the Revolution is for world history what the Reformation was for Christendom. As the latter rescued Europe from superstition, so the Revolution has plunged the civilized world into the abyss of unbelief. Like the Reformation, the Revolution touches every field of action and learning. In the days of the Reformation the principle was submission to God; in these days it is revolt against God.[21] That is why there is again today one universal war in church, state, and the world of learning, one holy battle over the supreme question: to submit unconditionally to the law of God, or not. To understand our age requires, now more urgently than ever before, a study of the Revolution precisely from this point of view.

Organization of the Subject

A few words yet concerning the organization of these lectures.

The Age of Revolution, with its vicissitudes and calamities, is the *fruit of the Revolution ideas*. That is my thesis.

The first part of my presentation will be negative. . . . I shall argue that neither the *principles* that underlay the old order, nor the *forms* that developed from these basic truths, nor yet the *abuses* which indeed crept in, can explain the enigma of the permanently revolutionary situation that we find ourselves in today.

The positive arguments for my case are drawn from both theory and history. First, I shall set forth the *doctrine* of the Revolution in its origin and development, in order to convince you from the Revolution's guiding principle that the course it actually took was inevitable. Next, I shall turn to the *history* of the Revolution, to show you from the fortunes of various countries that its ideas work themselves out in practice according to the dictates of logic. As the fruit is known by the tree, so shall the tree be known by its fruit.

In essence my whole argument will be historical. It will be the story of what was taught and consequently came to pass. To invalidate and refute the theories I combat, all I need do is describe them in their nature and action by bringing to light the *facts*—which includes whatever transpires in the spiritual world: the *ideas* and *principles*, themselves facts of the highest order, from which flows all the rest. "Our mind," says Guizot, "works with facts; facts are its only material, and when it discovers the general laws that control them, then these laws themselves are facts which the mind ascertains. . . . The facts one studies can so overwhelm the mind that they debase, shrink, materialize it, until the mind believes there are no other facts than those observed at first glance, facts that hit one in the eye, that fall, as they say, under the senses. This is a great and gross error. There are facts remote, immense, obscure, sublime, facts very difficult to reach, to observe, to describe, which are facts nonetheless, and which man is no less obliged to study and to know. And if he ignores or forgets them, his thinking will be enormously debased, and all his thoughts will bear the imprint of this debasement."[22]

May I add to this what I desire of you? A rich measure of indulgence, together with kindly contradiction and correction for me, your fellow-student. History alone will be our instructor. To be taught by history is good for anyone, at any time.

Let us all, insofar as we have put our trust in Christ, continue to be mindful of what is required of *Christians*. The marks of our prevailing mood today are uncertainty and doubt, pessimism, apathy, indifference, and resignation. The Christian knows a principle which gives steadiness to our knowledge and which, if followed, would be sufficient to restore our tottering political structures upon unshakable foundations. Nor is the Christian permitted to slacken in the defense of justice and truth just because his personal interests are not in jeopardy. Heavy are the duties which the darkness and the corruption of the times impose on those who are called the light of the world and the salt of the earth. . . . Indeed, we live in an oppressive atmosphere. Nevertheless, it is the Christian's privilege, as he observes the signs of the times, to ascend on the wings of faith to a higher sphere. Let this be our privilege. Looking to him who gives wisdom and strength, let us be aware of the expanse of God's benefits and be mindful of the extent of our responsibility! . . .

Before I proceed with my outline, an appeal to our covenant with previous generations would not be amiss in the face of the arrogance of our day. . . . Through all the centuries, thoughtful science testifies against the political doctrine of the Revolution. . . . The anti-revolutionary or christian-historical position finds unequivocal confirmation in the unanimous witness of former times.

I call your attention to (1) the Bible, (2) History, and (3) Political Writers Ancient and Modern.

The Bible

The Bible is the book of books, also and especially in the anti-revolutionary library. The newer wisdom, even where it does not reject Revelation outright, is of the opinion that any higher pronouncements are out of place in the area of political theory. We, on the other hand, without looking for an encyclopedia in it, as some have done, hold the view that Scripture indicates also for nations and governments the foundations of justice and morality, of freedom and authority. The Bible is the infallible touchstone. Unconditional submission to the Word of God has always been the guarantee of dutiful obedience and of dutiful resistance. No doctrine of prideful self-perfection or wanton libertinism can exist alongside the pronouncements of Revelation. *It is written.* This is the ax that cuts off every root of revolutionary misgrowth.

Naturally, the pronouncements of the Bible are reflected not only in the actions but also in the writings of those who take Scripture as their guide while surrendering their own wisdom. Consider the Reformers. Many a page from the works of Luther and Calvin proves what their lives confirmed: when it came to the authority of the magistrates and the duties of the princes, they "got understanding from the precepts of God and hated every false way."[23] As a result one generally finds striking evidence of this in the simple words of the Christian creeds. . . .

History

Just as the Revolution theories are directed against Revelation, so they are directed against History. On this score Renan has made a telling observation: "What the men of 1789 lacked was a knowledge of history."[24]

And yet—you will object—the theoreticians of Revolution did appeal to history. Indeed they did, and seemingly not without grounds. The superficiality with which they treated history was very helpful to all who were seeking support for their absurd doctrines. Just as in fog or at dusk the imagination gives shape to indistinct contours almost at will, so too it enjoyed freer play in the reconstruction of history in proportion to its being less inhibited by a precise knowledge of the facts. The torch of the newer wisdom was readily used to illuminate the whole field of history. And so they fell into what Montesquieu rightly calls the most fertile source of historical errors (though he himself continually lapses into it): they projected into peoples and periods ideas that were wholly foreign to them. And just as dreams reflect what has engaged the mind during the day, so it is not strange that the features which the revolutionaries had firmly committed to memory and heart turned up again in the illusions which they peddled as historical truths. History became a false witness, and this false witness became yet another powerful means of driving public opinion into the harness of the revolutionary school. History became a museum lined with revolutionary specimens, an arsenal filled with revolutionary weapons for murdering the truth.

Such was the situation once; it is no longer so today, at least not without vigorous rebuttal. History does indeed get discolored when looked at through the revolutionary prism; but at last the deceptive glass drops from the hand and the true conduct of events comes to light. This is a privilege of our times. Especially salutary has been the publication of so many historical sources in which life itself, as it were, cries out in protest against its betrayals and distortions. From numerous investigations it has become abundantly clear that there is in world history not a steady affirmation—far from it—but an uninterrupted refutation of the Revolution maxims. Even men who are reluctant to acknowledge the worthlessness of those maxims, for example Guizot,[25] have assisted with very instructive writings in banishing false analogies. Today we can add the testimony of history, in its full purity and weight, into the scales of judgment. Thus we run much less risk than before of being confounded by the arrogant demeanor of a doctrine which had wrapped itself in an ill-befitting garb of time-honored experience. . . .

Everything that leads to genuine knowledge of Revelation and of History is anti-revolutionary in nature and serves as an antidote to the magic power of the intoxicating drink. In support of this general statement I refer to all those political writers of ancient and modern times who are in agreement with us. . . .

[There follow brief discussions of Plato, Aristotle, Cicero, Grotius, Leibniz, Gentz, Burke, Bonald, Maistre, Lamennais, Haller, and Bilderdijk. In the next chapter, entitled "Anti-Revolutionary Principles," Groen offers a rebuttal of four points of critique commonly leveled against his position, namely, that he (1) has an exaggerated respect for historical rights, (2) gives too much independence to corporate bodies within the state, (3) holds an outdated conception of divine right of government, and (4) confuses church and state. The second and third points are addressed as follows.]

Corporate Bodies in the State

"No state within the State!" A useful warning, if it means that in a well-ordered kingdom or commonwealth nobody possesses complete independence, that every inhabitant is a subject, that either alone or in union with others he is to some degree subordinate to the authorities in everything that falls under the jurisdiction of the state. But the warning turns into a dangerous dogma if men use it to demand passivity for subordination, to mistake autonomy for independence, to regard free activity as rebellion, in every respect to subject everything found within the state's territory to the arbitrary will of the state, to oppose on principle any self-government of private persons or corporations and thus, under the guise of maintaining law and order, to destroy all self-determination and all genuine liberties. Our fathers believed and acted otherwise. In their day, every family head, every corporation, every estate was entitled, within the sphere of its competence, to dispose of person and property, to make rules for its subordinates, to regulate its affairs as it pleased; in short, to exercise a form of government that differs from sovereign authority only in this respect that it lacks independence, which is the distinguishing mark of sovereignty. They believed that general prosperity was inseparable from the free development of the orders, of the estates composing the state, whose rights were held to be sacred until the Revolution came, when they were called scandalous.

Behind the rebuke you recognize the bias for *centralization*. We shall have to come back to that many times. Centralization always begins by destroying the rights of provinces and municipalities and, if forced to be consistent, ends by tolerating in fact no right or activity or existence except under its supervision and control, as a benign favour. It has no place for autonomy, for independence within one's own sphere.[26]

So, again, we glory in the rebuke. Let the supreme power be free and unchecked in the execution of its rights, precisely for the good of the people. But remove the checks referred to above, and you have lost the only means to call a halt to state omnipotence and the only means to resist a political theory that would prefer to see the "masses" passive and the state machinery irresistible than to defend self-help and organic vitality.[27]

The Divine Right of Governments

. . . The divine right of government is now almost universally denounced as an antiquated misconception from the Dark Ages; as a nonsensical fabrication of princely cunning and priestly self-interest; as a fabric of injustice, tied to a multitude of fallacies and absurdities. Just a few years ago, to stand up as a defender of divine right was a daring venture if one prized the honor of men more than the honor of God; it was to place oneself voluntarily among the ranks of the most backward fanatics. And although there has perhaps been a shift of opinion, now that every other foundation of government has proved unstable, yet from a large number of people one can still expect only indignation or pity.

All this will not keep me from affirming the excellence of the assailed doctrine. I shall do this by calling to your attention (1) the deformation, (2) the meaning, and (3) the consequences of this doctrine, which more than any other truth is worthy to be called a *principle*, inasmuch as the fear of the Lord is the *principium* of knowledge.

1. The Deformation of Divine Right.

Here too we must first dispel the clouds, for victory is certain if we but contend in the full light of day.

How foolish and how wrong (it is said) to pay men an homage which belongs only to God; to exalt rulers to a category of superhuman beings stamped indelibly with a mark of sacredness; to look upon the Jewish theocracy, exceptional in Scripture itself, as a model for all states; to adhere with bigoted partiality to the autocratic form of government; to wrap worldly-minded intentions in a cloak of authority borrowed from Heaven; to smuggle into the hands of government a form of systemic violence which allows the sovereign every injustice, denies the subject every resistance, and sacrifices to this new idol every liberty!

Woe to us if we affirm or intend what we are charged with here! But what if I fail to recognize in this series of caricatures a single true image? I do not dispute that history provides us with examples in abundance of every abuse I have just recited. But I do dispute that the defense of a doctrine obliges one likewise to defend its many deformations. We do not identify the will of any sovereign with the will of God, as some peoples are reported to have done. We do not erect altars for any government, as the Romans did under the Emperors. We do not desire any improper transfer of customs and precepts borrowed from the unique character of the Israelite dispensation. We do not dream of any sacred dynasties, with hereditary rights like the House of David. We do not wish to restrict the application of a universal truth for the exclusive benefit of the monarchical form of government, as if we were inclined to rave with James I of England about the absolute power of a king, or with Napoleon make the appeal to God serve to *sanction* and not at the same time to *regulate* and *bridle* the supreme power. We do not wish to exempt sovereignty from restraints but are convinced, rather, that the subordination of rulers and subjects to the Supreme Power above the earth is alone sufficient restraint, and that it provides the best guarantee for the observance of mutual obligations.

2. *The Meaning of Divine Right.*

Although we could also appeal to classical antiquity, the simple and plain truth is found in Scripture: "Let every soul be subject unto the higher powers. For there is no power but of God; the powers that be are ordained of God" (Romans 13:1).

All power is ordained of God: It is not permissible, whenever something seems too strong to us, to water it down with some saltless interpretation that conforms to what we consider acceptable. Therefore, we may in no way try to evade the intention of these words, for example by pointing to the care of Providence which brings forth good out of the evil that it tolerates. The powers that be are not just tolerated. They are willed, instituted, sanctified by God himself. This is the only plausible meaning of *ordained.*

We must be equally on our guard against a twisting of Scripture to which we are seduced by misunderstanding or base design. *All power* must be understood as referring to every kind of *legitimate* power, in the sound sense demanded in the context by the reminder of God's righteousness and holiness. Power is not synonymous with might or force. To be sure, I realize that when Paul wrote this, Nero was in power; I also admit that the Christian is not always called to enter into disputes concerning the legitimacy of existing powers; and I am quite willing to allow that the expression "also to the froward" (I Peter 2:18), used in connection with masters over slaves, also applies, by analogy, to the injustices of civil authorities. Nevertheless, I will not subscribe to any interpretation that would oblige us to be obedient to the villain who holds a dagger under our nose, or to hail today as a power ordained of God the crowned robber who yesterday banished our legitimate prince.

Furthermore, it is plain that the nature of the submission required of us depends upon the nature of the power granted by God. In The Hague I am not obliged to submit to the type of authority that is lawfully exercised in Constantinople or St. Petersburg. Similarly, as a Netherlander I am not entitled to the liberties and privileges enjoyed by the subjects and citizens of London or Paris.

Divine right is not the trademark of Monarchy: it belongs to every kind of lawful power and all forms of government. . . . All power is of God. A ruler is both God's *lieutenant* and God's *minister*. In this twofold relationship—directed both upwards and downwards—lies the whole theory of divine right. *We* are to obey the higher power for the Lord's sake; *he* is to be obedient to God. "For he is the minister of God to thee for good," writes the apostle (Romans 13:4). The supreme power is a gift of God which must be employed in His service, for the benefit of others, and to His honor.

But (someone will object) this is true of every gift of God. To be a lieutenant, minister, and steward of God is the calling of everybody, each in his own sphere. In every rank, in every relation, man has been given a talent, which is at his free disposal; God will call him to account for its use. A sovereign bears God's image on earth, but—thus runs the objection—so does a father with respect to his child, and a judge with respect to the accused. In fact, so does the owner of any goods and talents whatsoever, since each talent is a *gift* and every possession a *loan*. All men, therefore, are to walk in the Name and after the commandment of God in the good works which He has ordained for us.[28] The principle is the same for all, in the rights it confers, in the duties it imposes, and in the norm it implies. Wherein, then, lies that strange and exceptional position which as a rule is so pompously ascribed to government?

I welcome this objection. Its very simplicity reveals its incontestability. Far from being strange or exceptional, divine right is the more firmly grounded in the measure that it embodies the natural application of a universal truth. The objection raises the very point that has been such a fatal source of misunderstanding: those who appealed to divine right from self-interest considered it an exceptional right, those who opposed it out of resentment regarded it as an odious privilege. Away with this arbitrary restriction! The truth that a violation of justice is a violation of divine law holds for no one or it holds for all. This is what gives stability to the entire structure of society. The promise, "War to the castles, peace to the huts,"[29] always has a deceptive ring. The same reasoning which demolishes the palace of the prince will not spare the office of the merchant or the humble roof of the peasant or the lowly hut of the day-laborer. Ours, however, is a doctrine which protects at once both the throne and the property of the least of subjects. . . .

3. The Consequences of Divine Right.

The consequences of this doctrine will have become apparent to you by now. This mark of authority is a safeguard against every false criterion that one might wish to put in its place. Responsible to no one but to God, the sovereign knows he is accountable to God. Master in the sphere of his own rights, he knows he is charged with respecting the rights of others. The rights and liberties of the people cannot be disregarded without undermining the rights of the sovereign. The subjects do not obey with eyeservice, as menpleasers, but for God's sake, as servants of the eternal King who reigns over the kings of the earth.[30] That which seems to humiliate, actually exalts.

Obedience born of submission to God is regulated and delimited in accordance with the laws of God. It does not entail surrendering one's own rights and liberties. It is founded on the word, "Render unto Caesar the things which are Caesar's"; from which it does not follow: "Render unto Caesar also the things which are not Caesar's"; it is grounded, much rather, in the commandment, "Render unto God the things which are God's."[31] It does not exclude passive resistance, which can exhaust any despotism; nor does it exclude the right to modest private judgment, or even the right of firm refusal or fearless opposition—although such opposition is not unlimited and injustice in itself is no warrant for breaking a sacred relationship. It was this knowledge that led our God-fearing fathers not to take up arms until forty years of patience and suffering had passed, and then only hesitantly and in self-defense. They were prepared to sacrifice all, short of God's Word, in order to remain loyal to a lord even such as Philip was.[32]

What more shall I say about this foundation of political wisdom? Authority is confirmed, arbitrariness bridled, obedience ennobled, liberty safeguarded, and the main truth proclaimed which, in a plurality of applications, is the cement of the state edifice. "All true legislation emanates from God, Who is the eternal principle of order and the universal power ruling the society of intelligent beings. Depart from this, and I see only arbitrariness and the degrading rule of force; I see only people insolently lording it over other people; I see only slaves and tyrants."[33] The thesis that seemed to contain a legion of pernicious errors is the fountain from which issues a stream of salutary truths. "Thus all truths concerning society flow from this first and great truth, that *all power comes from God*."[34]

The Revolutionary Principle

[In his analysis of the French Revolution and the liberalism of his day, Groen was particularly interested in exposing the leveling effect and totalitarian tendencies inherent in the new revolutionary doctrines. The following extract is taken from Lecture X.]

A continuous thread runs through all the turns and transformations of the Revolution principle. The great point of similarity I find in the enduring *despotism of the revolutionary state.*

You will recall Hobbes' *Leviathan* and Rousseau's *Social Contract*. There is liberty and equality, a social compact, a state whose unity and strength rests in the omnipotence of the general will. How is that will formed and ascertained? The good pleasure of the individual citizens is channelled from the bottom up, by means of the vote, to a central point, from which point the sovereign state, embodying the sovereignty of the people in legislative power as well as executive government, imposes its omnipotent authority, in the name of the people, upon the people, while crushing every opposition.

Hence the state is *omnipotent*. To its right every other right must yield.

The state is also *indivisible*. The differences of its component parts are dissolved and melted into the whole. There is no independent status over against the state. The glorification of the state lies in the passivity of its 'departments'—mere electoral districts, mere subdivisions for facilitating the administration.

The state is *all-inclusive*. There is no subject-matter which does not fall within the province of the general will, no concern which is not also a government concern. The state wields its sceptre even over matters of conscience. Church and school are state institutions. The citizen belongs to the state with body and soul and cannot lay claim to any independence whatsoever except insofar as this is granted to him temporarily and conditionally by the state.

The state, therefore, is *autocratic*. It is sole master of life and property. As Odillon Barrot stated openly in the early days of 1830: "The Revolution may demand the last man and the last farthing."

The state is *absolute*. The state, which gives the law, is itself above the Law.

The state is *atheistic*. Within certain limits religion may sometimes be tolerated and protected as useful and indispensable, but the state itself is not subject to its authority. The expression *la loi est athée*, the law is atheistical, is the slogan of public authority.

There is, therefore, in theory and no less in practice, *idolatry* with respect to the state. For, if the state so demands, even the most sacred and cherished things are to be sacrificed to the interest of the state, known variously as the common good, the People's well-being, the happiness of the Nation. The General Welfare is supreme! One must obey men rather than God; the right to obey God is unabridged, provided His will is not in conflict with the precepts of the State.

Such is the nature of the revolutionary state and its authority. . . .

. . . Even the best of political forms depends always upon the principles that activate and animate them. Men talk of the sovereignty of the people, but what becomes of it? The existing order is turned upside down, right is trampled underfoot, society is dismantled, a state machine is organized with a rigging of pipes and funnels to channel the General Will upwards to the centre; but this is not done from unanimous conviction: it is forced through with superior power and brute force. The first concern, under the pressures of the moment, is to rally behind those who claim to be the spokesmen, defenders and executors of the General Will. And so the relationship is quickly reversed. No one has any rights before the right that emanates from all. The sovereignty of the people resides by turns with every faction that has the power to elevate itself above the sovereign people. The Government does not inquire but announces what the General Will is. That will, instead of being communicated upwards to the centre, is dispensed from the top down. Centralized power, instead of being the organ of liberty, is an iron network spread out over the whole population, a thousandfold fabric of strings reaching down to every citizen, to make each honourable member of the sovereign people trot and dance in the great puppet show to the beat of the Central Government. . . .

Such is the nourishing and fragrant fruit that grows on the tree of liberty. But allow me, when discussing a subject so important for the proper understanding and appreciation also of our own time, to further outline this despotism of the doctrine of liberty, this *state absolutism*, under the following headings:

a. It destroys civil liberty.

b. It destroys political liberty.

c. It knows no limits.

d. It is contrary to the interests of country and nation.

e. It is indestructible so long as the Revolution doctrine is not eradicated.

a. The revolutionary state destroys *civil liberty*—by rights because of the accepted principle. The civil association itself, as formed by the false philosophy, is its grave. The state has unconditional command over the whole man. Everything he possesses is a loan; property and life are conditional grants. There may be enjoyment of freedom, but a right to freedom does not exist; it may please the master to lighten the weight of the chains, but there is a legalized condition of slavery.

To see vividly how the destruction of liberty is inherent in the liberal theory, take a closer look at the proclamation that summarizes the major principles of all revolutionary politics, that compendium and catechism of the Enlightenment, the *Declaration of the Rights of Man and the Citizen*. Notice that in every article of this fundamental law of fundamental laws, the strength of each promise is vitiated by the very manner in which it is formulated. . . . A man who was acquainted at close range with the French revolution [Jeremy Bentham] will demonstrate to you, with regard to equality, liberty, property, freedom of the press, and freedom of religion, how the Declaration in the very proclamation of each right eliminated the force and significance of that right.

Such is the fate of the "imprescriptible, inviolable, sacred Rights."
Supposedly beyond the reach of government, they are the toy of every regime
that is in power.[35] What the one hand gives, the other takes away. The liberties are exhibited, not conferred. Everything is allowed, with one fatal pro-
viso: everything *insofar as* the state, the collective despot, is pleased to grant. I
would not be misunderstood. That the rights are restricted does not offend
me; this is inherent in every right. The cause of my complaint is that whereas
rights used to be circumscribed and confirmed by the unchangeable laws and
ordinances of God, they are now made to depend on the good pleasure of the
State, that is to say, on the will of changeable men, and for that reason must,
by definition, perish. The revolutionary state affords liberty, insofar as it is
possible, useful, desirable; insofar as the interest of the state allows; insofar as
it is considered compatible with the circumstances; insofar as it is in keeping
with the interests and demands and desires and whims and fancies of those
placed over you. Liberty, complete liberty, unrestricted liberty is the promise,
and in the end not liberty but the restrictions are unrestricted. Perfect liberty
there is, with one restriction—one only, but one which revokes everything
just granted: perfect liberty, subject to perfect slavery.

Later authors, like Benjamin Constant and Guizot, have looked for a
safeguard in the "doctrine of individualism," arguing that there are rights so
weighty, so sacred, so intimately intertwined with the nature and destiny of
man, that they ought to be withdrawn from the supreme power of the state.
Altogether true; unfortunately they have not shown as well how those rights
can possibly be wrested from the state once it has taken them over. . . .

Nor is the separation of powers a safeguard for liberty against the lethal
weapon of the omnicompetent sovereignty of the people. Freedom is destroyed under whatever form the revolutionary principle holds sway. I agree
with Benjamin Constant when he writes: "Where it is established that the
sovereignty of the people is unlimited there a degree of power is injected into
society which as such is far too great and which will always be an evil, be it
entrusted to monarchy, aristocracy, democracy, mixed government or the
representative system. The degree of power, not its depository, will be at fault.
No political organization can remove the danger. In vain do you separate the
powers: if the sum total of power is unlimited these powers have only to form
a coalition and despotism is beyond remedy. It is not enough that the agents
of the executive need the authorization of the legislator; what is needed is that
the legislator cannot authorize their action except within their legitimate
sphere of competence. It means little that the executive may not act unless
empowered by a law if no boundaries are set to the makers of the law."[36]

b. Will the loss of civil liberty perhaps be compensated by a gain in *political liberty*?

I doubt whether the compensation is adequate, or even real. Any state that ensures civil liberties is preferable, I think, to a situation that abounds in political rights while free life in other spheres is not allowed. But relative worth aside, let us examine the value of this political liberty somewhat more closely.

Every citizen is a co-regent, an integral part of the popular sovereignty. This is quite an honour, but whenever one belongs to the minority the privilege is small. It is an odd sort of liberty that consists in submitting oneself to the despotism of the *majority*. And yet this is inescapable. The general will is not the will of all. It is inconceivable that there will be a perfect and permanent consensus. The motor of the government will be the will of the majority. Will that be a cause of contentment and a guarantee of happiness for the minority? Benjamin Constant is right again when he writes: "The assent of the majority does not by any means always suffice to legitimize its acts: there are acts which nothing can sanction. When any government commits such acts, it matters little from what source it claims to draw its authority, nor whether it consists of an individual or a nation. If it consisted of the entire nation minus the citizen oppressed, it would be no more legitimate. . . ."[37]

c. This despotism knows *no limits*.

Under the old order the supreme power was limited by corporations and estates, by the limitation of its own resources, by the impossibility, in the long run, of demanding inordinate sacrifices from the subjects. In the revolutionary state every such restriction vanishes. Tocqueville has observed that "we have destroyed the independent powers which each on its own could wrestle with tyranny, and it is the Government that has inherited all the prerogatives wrested from families, corporations and individual persons."[38] Regular resistance is gone. Oftentimes even a short-lived, weak and shaky regime, for as long as it stays on its feet, possesses incalculable strength as a result of the destruction of the historic fabric of society. Everything is rent asunder or razed to the ground which formerly, by its prominence or stability, provided a fulcrum and focus for the dutiful defence of lawful rights and liberties.

Unlike the legitimate power, the revolutionary state has a plenitude of means at hand. After all, it has free disposal of the entire people, of persons and property. The state is centralized; it is concentrated in the Government, whoever is in power. A revolutionary Government can truly say, *L'Etat c'est moi*, since nothing that falls within its reach or power will be reckoned as having any independent status, or right, or liberty, or will of its own. . . .

d. This despotism is contrary to every interest of *country* and *nation*. . . .

The words nation and country remain in constant use. But what is meant by nation, by country, when the ties are destroyed that were created between ancestors and offspring by a common history, religion, morals, customs and principles? It does not help to give the name of 'patriotic' and 'national' to revolutionary principles, revolutionary interests, revolutionary liberties, revolutionary public spirit. It will be called a "national enlightenment" when religion recedes to the background and twilight fills the minds, darkness the hearts. In name only will the people be referred to as the original sovereign and will homage be paid to public opinion, the voice of the people, popular demand. All things considered, now that society has disintegrated what is the nation? A certain number of souls. What is the country? A certain number of square miles. And what, ultimately, is the state? It is the *pays légal*, the narrow circle of those who have the vote. The foundation of bourgeois society is the franchise, and its only cement, now that higher relations have disappeared, is money. The population will be divided into voters and non-voters, rich and poor, well-to-do and proletarians. The very appellation "the masses" will be indicative of haughty contempt—though the title is not incorrect: ranks and classes are a society's framework and if this be torn down what else would there be left but a lifeless lump, a mass, a levy of taxpayers and conscripts for the supply of the Government?

e. This despotism, finally, is *indestructible* so long as there is no return to the supremacy of God, wherein alone lies the guarantee of liberty. . . . A radical revolution requires a radical restoration. And this will be unthinkable unless it begins by acknowledging the sovereignty of God.

NOTES

[1] Selections from Lectures I, II, III, and X of Groen van Prinsterer, *Ongeloof en Revolutie* (Amsterdam: H. Hoveker, 1868 [1847]). Translated and edited from the second edition by Harry Van Dyke in collaboration with Donald Morton and Gordon Spykman.

[2] For an account of Groen's early life, education, and perspective on history, see Harry Van Dyke, *Groen van Prinsterer's Lectures on Unbelief and Revolution* (Jordan Station, Ontario: Wedge Publishing Foundation, 1989), 39-83; and Jantje Lubbegiena van Essen "Guillaume Groen van Prinsterer and his Conception of History," translated, with additional notes by Donald Morton, *Westminster Theological Journal* 44 (1982): 205-249, and reprinted in J. L. van Essen and H. Donald Morton, *G. Groen van Prinsterer: Selected Studies* (Jordan Station, Ontario: Wedge Publishing Foundation, 1990), 15-54.

[3] In 1833 Groen resigned as secretary of the Royal Cabinet, but retained his appointment as head of the royal archives. It was during the period of 1833-1849 that he published eight volumes of papers from the archives. Also during this time (1847) he published *Unbelief and Revolution*.

[4] See Groen, *Unbelief and Revolution*, Lectures VII-IX, in Van Dyke, *Groen van Prinsterer's Lectures on Unbelief and Revolution*. Van Dyke's abridged translation of Groen's text retains its own page numbers coordinating several editions of the original; the translated text appears following p. 292 of Van Dyke's historical introduction. The Dutch edition to which we refer is *Ongeloof en Revolutie*, newly edited by H. Smitskamp (Franeker: T. Wever, 1952). Page citations to the English translation will be to Groen's text in Van Dyke's aforementioned volume.

[5] Groen, *Unbelief and Revolution*, 185.

[6] *Ibid.*, 395ff., 406-408, 414-28.

[7] *Ibid.*, 199-200.

[8] *Ibid.*, 7.

[9] In the Netherlands the term "anti-revolutionary" came to stand for a progressive attitude that was opposed to the spirit of liberalism and revolution; it was not simply reactionary. The term "counter-revolutionary" or "contra-revolutionary" came to be used for the reactionary conservative attitude that the anti-revolutionaries opposed.

[10] Groen, *Unbelief and Revolution*, 24.

[11] Groen's distance from reactionary conservatives is evident in the following quotations taken from his *Handbook of the History of the Fatherland* 3rd ed. (1865). Groen wrote of the Enlightenment and the Revolution:

> One may not ignore the many good things that were achieved during this period. The efforts for reform and renewal were not unfruitful. There was remarkable material and intellectual progress and development. To a degree that would not have been thought possible, the forces of nature were made serviceable to human ingenuity. Many social improvements were brought about. And in the basic features of the [new] political forms lay the germ of civil and political liberty.
>
> Even so, the progress that was made in the areas of law and morality is to be attributed largely to the work of the Gospel. The history of Europe and especially of the Netherlands in the days of the Reformation had shown experimentally the power of saving truth for emancipation and civilization. And although this power was afterwards assigned to obscurity through the powerlessness of a

dead orthodoxy, the improvements realized even then prove that only the Gospel contains the true principle of liberty, equality and fraternization, of philanthropy and efficacious humanitarianism. . . .

The ideas that made [eighteenth-century] philosophy so attractive were of Christian origin; they were wholesome insofar as they were gotten from the Gospel, baneful insofar as they were torn loose from it.

In Christian love lies true humanity: recognition of the rights of man, even of the humblest, without distinction of race or colour or birth or class. From this follow (as the eighteenth century took to heart with commendable zeal) the abolition of slavery, of serfdom and of the rack; toleration in religion; the extension of political rights to the lower classes; numerous philanthropies; and the intent to secure an adequate standard of living for all.

Harry Van Dyke and Donald Morton, *Lectures Eight and Nine from Unbelief and Revolution* (Amsterdam: The Groen van Prinsterer Fund, 1975), Appendix A, 31-32.

[12] Groen, *Unbelief and Revolution*, 23.

[13] *Ibid.*, 24.

[14] *Ibid.*, 25.

[15] On the sources of Groen's thought, see Van Dyke, *Groen van Prinsterer's Lectures on Unbelief and Revolution*, 113-138.

[16] Groen, *Unbelief and Revolution*, 50-56.

[17] *Ibid.*, 57-65.

[18] Félicité de Lamennais, *Essai sur l'indifférence en matière de religion* 4 vols. (Paris, 1817-23), chap. 1. Eng. trans. by Lord Stanley of Alderley, *Essay on Indifference in Matters of Religion* (London, 1895).

[19] "As I [Groen] wrote in my *Grondwetherziening en Eensgezindheid* (The Hague, 1848), p. 363: *The* Revolution is the development of a wholesale skepticism, in which God's Word and Law have been brushed aside."

[20] [Louis de Bonald, *Législation primitive considérée dans les derniers temps par les seules lumières de la raison*, 2 vols. (Paris, 1802), 1: 16.] Stahl says: "The Revolution in Europe can only be stopped by Christianity and the Christian state and the Christian school." [Friedrich Julius Stahl, *Parlamentarische Reden* (Berlin, 1856), 89.]

[21] "There is much talk of the analogies between the Revolution and the Reformation; let us try to summarize them. The Revolution takes for its point of departure the sovereignty of man, the Reformation the sovereignty of God. The one has Revelation judged by reason, the other submits reason to revealed truths. The one unleashes individual opinions, the other brings the unity of faith. The one loosens the bonds of society, including those of marriage and family, the other strengthens and sanctifies them. The latter triumphs through its martyrs, the former maintains itself through massacres. The one ascends out of the bottomless pit, the other comes down out of heaven." *Archives ou Correspondance inédite de la Maison d'Orange-Nassau*, ed. G. Groen van Prinsterer (Leiden, 1847), 1: 117.

[22] François Guizot, *Histoire de la civilisation en France* (Brussels, 1835), 1: 31.

[23] Psalm 119:104.

[24] [*Revue des deux mondes*, 1 August 1858, 684.]

[25] Only after 1848 did Guizot take a positive stand against the fundamental error of the Revolution.

[26] No state can do without a centralized government, but administrative centralization is a bane to any people.

[27] I see where [Alexis de] Tocqueville in his book of 1856, *L'Ancien Régime et la Révolution*, 49, adduces evidence that administrative centralization was not a product of the Revo-

lution but of the Old Regime. Only, if this form of centralization did occur it was a *degeneration* of the constitutional law of Europe (compare England), whereas the Revolution adopted it on *principle*, as part of its *programme*.

28 [Cf. Ephesians 2:10.]

29 The slogan of the French Revolutionary armies.

30 [Ephesians 6:6.]

31 [Matthew 22:21.]

32 [This is a reference to the Dutch Revolt against Philip II, king of Spain and lord of the Low Countries (1555-98), who sought to establish absolute rule, and to suppress Protestantism by means of the Inquisition.]

33 Lamennais, *Essai sur l'indifférence*, chap. 10.

34 *Ibid.*

35 "Principles, by which they flatter the people with the possession of the theoretical rights of man, all of which they vitiate and violate in practice." (William Pitt [the Younger, *Speeches in the House of Commons*, II, 61; 20 June 1794].)

36 Constant, *Cours de politique constitutionnelle*, 1: 164.

37 *Ibid.*, 1: 167.

38 Tocqueville, *Democracy in America*, Introduction.

FOUR

※※※※※※※※※※※

COMMUNITY IN HISTORICAL PERSPECTIVE[1]
by Otto von Gierke

Otto von Gierke

Born in Prussia, Otto von Gierke (1841-1921) obtained his university education in Berlin, and then, following military service in Bismarck's wars of 1866 and 1870-71, began teaching, first at Breslau then at Heidelberg. In 1887 he returned to Berlin where he succeeded to the university chair that had been held by his teacher Georg Beseler. He remained there until his death teaching jurisprudence and political theory.

Gierke wrestled throughout his life as a philosopher and political theorist with the "crises of modern society."[2] His writings, which are as broad in scope as those of John Stuart Mill and Karl Marx, "worked up elements of the German socio-political tradition and romantic and quasi-Hegelian philosophy"[3] in an attempt to provide a solid theory of human community.

The key legal and political concepts for Gierke are ①"fellowship" or "association" (*Genossenschaft*) and ②"corporate group personality" (*Gesammtpersönlichkeit*). Since the latter concept "reflected the central role of associations in a normal social life and ensured their moral independence from the state," Gierke regards it "as the cornerstone of a just constitution and legal system. . . ."[4] Human life, in other words, is constituted essentially, and not merely accidentally, by groups. These groups themselves have moral and legal personalities—essential identities—not reducible to the individuals that compose them. "For Gierke the ultimate truth about human society was this 'real personality' of groups. Gierke saw the development of group personality as a moral goal alongside the development of individual personality."[5]

In addition to the four volumes of *Das deutsche Genossenschaftsrecht* (*The German Law of Associations*) and a number of important essays, Gierke also published a two-volume work on the history of the German concept of corporation, an influential study of Johannes Althusius and the development of natural-law political theories, and a three-volume handbook on German private law.[6]

Gierke was the leading Germanist of the historical school of philosophy and jurisprudence. As Anthony Black explains,

> Gierke believed that a correct understanding of authority and association lay embedded in the history and popular consciousness of the Germanic peoples; to reach such an understanding, therefore, one had to delve into the history of institutions and social movements. For the idea of justice (*Recht*) is inherent, not in the cosmos as natural-law theory held, but in humanity; and humanity is not a mere universal, but evolves through specific, historically developing communities with their changing and progressing social forms and ethical ideas. "Positive" legislation ought to conform to and reflect this evolution, and is invalid if it departs fundamentally from the moral insights thus built up.[7]

The first part of the reading that follows is Chapter I of the first volume of Gierke's four-volume work *The German Law of Associations*. In it, Gierke outlines the five periods of European history, as he sees them, unfolding from a patriarchal period prior to 800 A.D. up to the fifth and current period (beginning early in the nineteenth century) "from which we expect the reconciliation of the age-old opposites in the ideas of general state citizenship and the representative state."[8] The "real creative principle" of this period, Gierke believes "is, and will be, the *free association* in its modern form."[9]

The German people (or nation) is, in his interpretation, central to the ultimate historical realization of a reconciliation between social plurality and unity, between individual freedom and political authority, as these tensions worked their way out in the course of European history. Gierke's romantic nationalism is fundamental to his presuppositions here. In his Introduction to Volume I, for example, Gierke writes that

> the Germanic people have a gift other peoples lack, by means of which they have given the idea of freedom a special substance and the idea of unity a more secure foundation—they have the gift of forming fellowships [*Genossenschaften*]. The people of antiquity recognised, as do the non-Germanic people of today, the existence, between the highest generality and the individual, of many

gradations of natural and arbitrary associations. But their love of the corporate life, their sense of "family, community and nation, their ability and enthusiasm for free association, cannot even remotely be compared with that inexhaustible Germanic spirit of association, which alone is able to guarantee an independent existence to all the lesser conformations within the state, while maintaining sufficient power to create from the still uncommitted energy within the people a vast profusion of lively, active fellowships, inspired not from above but from within, for the most general as well as the most isolated purposes of human existence.[10]

In Gierke's view, according to Black, the German contribution to world history and human civilization is "the idea and practice of fellowship in a multiplicity of human groups; and also the synthesis of fellowship and lordship in the modern constitutional state."[11]

Following Gierke's outline of the periods of European history, the next part of the reading illustrates Gierke's explanation of the dynamics of the formation of the "sovereign state" during the fourth period (roughly the seventeenth and eighteenth centuries). During this period the anti-associational polarization between the absolute state and absolute individuality reaches its height. This tension nonetheless opens the possibility for equality of all citizens and even greater freedom for individuals to associate together. The climax of this period is reached in the French Revolution.

Out of the crisis of the French Revolution and its destructive effect on the old order, the building blocks of the fifth period begin to emerge. This is the time during which Gierke expects the modern association movement to reach its height. In contrast to older forms of less differentiated groups, modern associations or fellowships, Gierke explains,

are formed more and more for single purposes; so that finally, in contrast to the medieval tendency to extend each group of fellows over the whole person and simply make it into a community [Gemeinschaft], the opposite tendency has prevailed: The purposes of each individual association are precisely defined, and its organisation adapted and its significance limited accordingly. Even the highest association—the state—has its purposes, and therefore the limits of its scope prescribed by this modern trend.[12]

Though the German people were slower than the English and the Netherlandic peoples to begin developing modern free associations, in the latter half of the nineteenth century this movement in Germany has awakened "to an almost miraculous vigour,"[13] writes Gierke.

The significance for human society of this inclination to develop a multitude of free associations is obviously great with respect to the kinds and numbers of fellowships created. But the significance also extends to the very character of the modern state. The final part of our selection from Gierke below concerns the nature of the modern constitutional state—the *Rechtsstaat*. The representative constitutional state displays, in Gierke's view, a reconciliation "of the ancient idea of fellowship and the ancient idea of lordship. Both of these have validity within their own sphere; but the hostile opposition of the two is to find its resolution in a higher unity."[14]

Though Gierke's writing is often dense and academic, the following selections provide a relatively clear introduction to his understanding of history, human fellowships, the real personality of groups, and the modern constitutional state.

COMMUNITY IN HISTORICAL PERSPECTIVE

The Five Periods of European History

True history is a current which flows ceaselessly and admits of no division. With ours more than with any other people, local and temporal variations have determined the variety of activity in the sphere of Right [justice], often producing entirely divergent developments or, at the very least, often displacing the boundaries of old and new by centuries. In Germany, to a greater extent than elsewhere, the products of older philosophies have persisted in full vigor alongside the products of what is by and large the dominant idea of the epoch, while at the same time the seeds of the principle destined to dominate the future have already been developing in profusion. None the less, if one examines the development of German law in its entirety with regard to the form of human association which predominates in it, periods naturally suggest themselves, which, despite their arbitrariness and imperfection, are indispensable (if artificial) tools of historical study and indicate the main turning-points of the German system of fellowship. And so periods emerge, each of which was dominated by its own characteristic constitutional principle and therefore developed its own peculiar social structure which became the characteristic one of the age in specific spheres of activity, as well as in more general ones up to and including the state.

There are five such periods. The first of these extends from the earliest history until the imperial coronation of Charles the Great (800). Although the circumstances at the beginning and end of this millennium have little in common, it can be summed up as the time when the Germanic concept of Right came to reside in a predominantly *partriarchal* perception of all human associations. At the end of the period the principle of the basic *freedom of the people* is still, at least in theory, the foundation of public life, although the opposing principle of *lordship and service* has of course already become the sole source of creative development. And so throughout this whole period the basic form of all society [*Verbindung*] is that which corresponds to the patriarchal concept of the freedom of the people—the *free fellowship of the old law*; which, since it rests on a union for upholding peace and law based on *natural* affinity, transfers all right to the collectivity. But, from the beginning, it is confronted by the opposite forms of human community, in which one individual is the bond of all—the *lordship group* in its patriarchal, personal form; and the irresistible development of this principle increasingly pushes the other back. The conflict between lordship and fellowship intersects with the conflict between the old idea of personality and the new idea of the material character [*Dinglichkeit*] of all groups: the fellowships become property-based communities, the lordship groups become territorial lordships and at the end of this period the patriarchal concept of the constitution is on the point of yielding to the patrimonial concept of law and the state.

In the second period, which extends until 1200, comes the definitive victory of lordship over fellowship and material over personal conceptions. The *patrimonial and feudal* principle of organisation dominates the life of the nation. A powerful edifice of lords and servants towers up within the church and Empire, extending up to heaven itself, but each relationship between lord and servant has become real [sc. material: *dinglich*] and therefore patrimonial. The old free fellowship only survives to any great extent in a subordinate position and in those areas which are cut off from the main movement of the age. Yet the corporate idea [*korperativer Gedanke*] is so deeply seated in the German spirit that it penetrates the lordship groups themselves, first restructuring them and then dissolving them. And so a new form of association arises, which is characteristic of this second period: the *dependent or lordship-based fellowship*. This develops its own collective Right around and beneath the lords, who represent the original unity of the group. But towards the end of the period a newer and more powerful principle is already emerging, the principle which finally reduces the feudal state to ruins. This is the principle of free association [*Vereinigung*]-union [*Einung*]. In place of the old fellowships which were based on purely natural association, it produces voluntary [*gewillkürte*] fellowships, but in the towns it combines the freely chosen union with the natural base and so simultaneously produces the first local community and the first state on German soil.

In the third period (which ends with the close of the Middle Ages), while the feudal state and hierarchical structure collapse irretrievably, the principle of *union* creates the most magnificent organisations from below by means of *freely chosen* [gekorenen] *fellowships*. Fellowships, and communities [*Gemein-wesen*] based on them, unite in *confederations* to encompass even greater areas; they prepare the way for the emancipation of personality from its base in the land, without conversely invalidating the independence of the law of property which had been achieved. They lead to the separation of public and private law, give birth to the concept of the ideal personality of the group [*ideale Gesammtpersönlichkeit*] as state, local community and corporation: and, by means of free association from below, they *almost* succeed in creating a German state. But not quite! For the system of fellowship in this period does not have the strength to complete its task. Incapable of breaking through the barriers of the system of estates which it has, on the contrary, made more rigid, and above all incapable of drawing the peasantry into the movement, it finally begins to atrophy in its established forms and is unable to resist a new force which is working towards the levelling of the estates, the fusing of town and country, and a greater and more focussed unity within the state. This force is territorial independence [*Landeschoheit*], and it succeeds in trans-forming lordship over land into the territorial state and in making itself sole representative of the modern concept of state.

The fourth period—until 1806—sees the definitive victory of territorial independence, and with it of the principle of *sovereignty* [*Obrigkeit*], which it had developed by taking over Roman law. The sovereign-state idea develops, and with it the supervisory and tutelary state [*Polizei- und Bevormun-dungstaat*]. The fellowship structure is toppled and replaced by a system of privileged corporations which establish themselves exclusively on a basis of private law and thereby give up any further participation in public Right. In the face of these corporations, which no longer perceive themselves as part of the generality but as privileged exceptions, yet are unwilling to undertake the duties corresponding to their privileges, the power of a unified state which can bend or break them is a necessity. To begin with, this naturally meant the destruction of the earlier freedom and autonomy. The state moves away from and above the people; whatever wishes to be recognised in public law can only continue to exist as a function of the state, while the *dependent corporations based on private law*—the characteristic type of association in this period—cannot revive their extinguished public significance. Absolute state and absolute individuality become the emblems of the age. However, with the dissolution of all the old associations, territorial independence also destroys the privileges and inequalities of public Right and brings the idea of the equality of all before the law and—for the first time in history—the idea of individual freedom for all within the grasp of its subjects. Although it has little at first to do with civic freedom, although a German's rights to political freedom were mercilessly destroyed, the transitional period is indispensable in order to prepare the ground for the civic freedom of *all* men, which in our century replaces the freedom of the estates.

We are now at the beginning of the fifth period, from which we expect the reconciliation of the age-old opposites in the ideas of general state citizenship and the representative state. Despite the short duration of this period up to now, we can say that the real creative principle is, and will be, the *free association* in its modern form. In this epoch German fellowship, reawoken after a death-like sleep to more vigorous life, has reached fulfilment. No longer bound by the chains of the estates, not limited by exclusiveness, infinitely flexible and divisible in its form, equally suitable for the noblest and humblest ends, for the most comprehensive and most isolated purposes, enriched by many of the merits of the Roman concept of Right, but long since ridiculing the narrow Roman mould itself (into which theory and practice still attempt to force it)—this is the ancient German idea of fellowship newborn, bringing forth an incalculable wealth of new forms of community and giving new substance to the old. It is taking part in the transformation of the German *community* [*Gemeinde*] and state, which have only achieved progress in the past and will only advance in the future by means of a return to the root of fellowship. This alone is creator of a free form of association, becoming involved in and transforming all areas of public and private life; and, although it has already achieved great things, it will achieve even more in the near and distant future.

The Modern State and Modern Associations

[The fourth period of history, according to Gierke, runs from the Reformation to the dissolution of the Holy Roman Empire in 1806. This is the time in which "privileged corporations" are established by title or concession of governing authorities. The "sovereign state" emerges "as something apart from the people" with all public power concentrated in an authority that becomes highly "supervisory." This authoritarian state is, then, also a "tutelary state" inclining "towards bureaucratic over-government, centralisation and standardisation."]

From such basic principles it follows that the relationship of the sovereign power to the system of fellowships is one of total antagonism. Of course, the sovereign state is as little able to do without articulation into lesser associations as the system of fellowship, nor is it able entirely to suppress associations which are outwith the state. But, while the free system of association in German law recognises the lesser associations of its citizens as

communities homogeneous with the greater whole, and allows them independent life even while it uses them as building blocks for the overall structure, sovereignty endeavours with steely single-mindedness to reach a twofold goal: first, to absorb all the public significance of communities [*Gemeinden*] and fellowships into the concept of state, and secondly to reduce
whatever remains in these groups of innate importance to the level of a state-
owned capacity. All corporations, therefore, in so far as their nature is based
on public law, are to be considered *components of the state*—whether as divisions of the state territory or as its subjects, as administrative districts or as
state institutions . . . [Otherwise] they are to be *private associations*, which, as
a result of a specific state charter, have the right to be regarded within certain
confines as unitary subjects of private rights. In this way, the autonomy, jurisdiction and self-administration of associations of fellows are annulled;
whatever remains of these things *de facto* is either assumed to relate to private
law, or explained as originating from a special commission of the authorities
and accordingly treated as a right which derives from outside the group. Even
in the law of property the corporation must pay for its legal personality with
the utmost dependence. Its existence is tolerated and standardised from
above; and its standing is far behind that of the individual, for it is not even
regarded as having reached its majority in private. . . .

The dissipation of all local communities and fellowships into the concept
of state on one hand, and into the concept of the individual on the other, is
only a symptom of a more universal tendency which aimed also to achieve,
alongside the absolute state, *absolute individuality*.[15] This tendency, which
begins with the slow emancipation of the individual, in all spheres of life,
from the Middle Ages onwards, but has only been consciously active since the
second half of the last century, sets as its ultimate goal a condition in which
apart from the state there are only individuals. Hence there are no intermediate
links of any kind between the supreme universality of the all-caring state and
the sum total of single individuals, comprising the people [*Volk*]. Such connecting bodies as there are count only as local manifestations of the state, or
as themselves individuals. This last goal, which came close to being realised
in France by means of the Revolution, was never achieved in Germany, least
of all in practice. . . .

Since the authoritarian state, single-mindedly pursuing its own ends,
worked against all particularities which stood between it and the individual, it
achieved for all its subjects *individual freedom and equality under the law*; this
has been almost perfected today.[16] *Individual freedom* was bound to result if
the state destroyed the lordship associations contained within it, as it had the
fellowships, and annulled any indirect or private subjection which was in-

compatible with direct subjection to the state. Not until relatively late did the absolute state perceive this great and fruitful consequence of its basic principle. But it did—and thereby accomplished one of the greatest deeds of history. The liberation of the peasantry at the end of the [eighteenth] century and the beginning of this, atoning for the injustice of centuries, produced for the first time states in which there were only free men. Hand in hand with universal freedom went the legal *equality* of all. For the political and legal equality of subjects was the beneficial consequence of the destruction of the medieval corporations and lordship associations, based on the estates, and of the final levelling of the estates themselves.

This represented an immense step forward from the medieval gild-state. For in spite, or rather because, of the equality established between those most closely associated, the gild-state was based on the utmost inequality under public law, since, alongside the full members, there were lesser associates and protected members . . . Even if in the Middle Ages the high regard for the unconditional correspondence of Right and duty counterbalanced this inequality before the law, it held within it the seed of the downfall of the old fellowship system. There was, on the other hand, from the very beginning a tendency inherent in the idea of sovereignty to subject all members of the state to the same authority, the same law and the same courts; and to afford them all the same measure of protection, representation and care for their welfare. The realisation of this idea came late, and even today has not been fully implemented.

Yet the freedom and equality aspired to by the absolute state were only the freedom and equality of *subjects*. The content, therefore, was exclusively negative and the participation passive. A further development, by which the *freedom of state citizenship* was added to individual freedom and the equality of subjects was increased by equal participation in active political rights, could not be accomplished on the basis of the sovereign-state concept. It was initiated by the new political philosophy of our century, which transferred the state back to the people. This one-sided tendency to place state absolutism and absolute individuality alongside one another, without any intermediaries, can be overcome in the same way. Necessary as this is for political unity and equality, it is the death-knell of all true freedom, since its ultimate consequences are *centralisation of government and fragmentation of the people*. In Germany, we were protected from such a danger, the scale of which could be seen in France, by our sense of fellowship. This had never completely died, and with the awakening of the nation's vigour [*Volkskraft*] it became more powerful than ever. . . .

The victory in principle of the concept of the absolute state and of individualism was determined when the storms of the French Revolution were carried over into Germany, when, following the dissolution of the Empire, territorial dominion was transformed into sovereignty, and the revolutionary legislation completely or partly adopted. From then till now it has been a question of slow progress towards the realisation of both principles in detail, which today is almost complete. The idea of the absolute state has more and more asserted itself in a state unity carried virtually to the point of centralisation, in the formation of modern administrative organisations, and in a levelling-out of local differences in public law, verging on standardisation. On the other hand, the barriers which separated the individual from direct contact with the state, and produced inequality in public Right were increasingly disposed of: privileges and exemptions, the estates' prerogatives, patrimonial powers, differences occasioned by religious creed, trade and business monopolies, and the inequality of public impositions, were increasingly abolished. At the same time, the old associations which fettered the individual in agriculture, trade and status were broken up or robbed of their binding power.

If, in all these areas, modern developments appear to be solely the result of ideas which had for centuries been determining the direction of the sovereign state, and whose realisation is brought nearer, consciously or unconsciously, by each step forward, in our century quite a different principle is at work. It works partly in association with older ideas and partly alongside them. The value of our modern upheavals would in fact be very questionable if they were influenced solely by that power which used its positive creative energy only in favour of unconditional state unity, and whose effect on all other organisms was only to negate and dissolve them; and if their inevitable result was a one-sided culmination in a centralised and mechanistic state and an atomised people. We owe the fact that such is not the case, and never will be, to the reawakened *spirit of association*. By endeavouring to fill all public associations from below with an independent communal life and by building together the particles, into which the nation had threatened to disintegrate, into countless new combinations, organic in structure and containing inherent vigour, this is the real positive principle which shapes the new epoch for the development of the German law and constitution in our century. It, above all others, gives us a firm guarantee that the epoch will not represent the old age of the German people, but rather the full bloom of its manly vigour.

The *modern association movement* is still so much in its early stages that its nature can scarcely be defined and it has no proper history of its own. It

ought to be clear, therefore, that it is in essence a new and distinctive phenomenon and that its development will be ever upwards.

The essence of the modern association movement clearly brings it much
closer to the medieval union movement than to the privileged corporation
system of later days. In most points it is the direct opposite of the latter; while
in relation to the medieval system of union, it is but a higher stage of development of the same principle. Thus the modern system of association offers
many analogies with the medieval system of union. It too comes from within
the people and builds upwards from below. It too is an expression of the
awakening national consciousness and the vigour of the people [*Volksbe-
wusstsein . . . Volkskraft*] with quite free self-help creating forms of the self-
determination and self-management they have longed for. As the medieval
union was set against the idea of lordship and service, so the modern
association sets its face against the idea of a sovereign standing above and
beyond the whole. Likewise, it is combated, restricted and prohibited by representatives of the old principle, who cannot however quite succeed in
smothering the new idea. Modern association, like union, is rooted in freedom; and it too tries to build ever wider spheres onto narrow ones. The privileged corporation's corporative separateness, exclusivity, rigidity of form and
privitisation of public rights is no less alien to it.

In contrast to the pronounced corporate forms of the intervening period,
the modern association, like the medieval union, has an air of constant flux—
the essential mark of a time of strong growth. Hence it is rich in transitional
forms and intermediate structures, in short-lived phenomena which exist only
to pave the way for a fuller legal structure, in a wealth of intersections and
combinations which it is difficult to systematise. To an even greater extent
than in the Middle Ages, countless forms of community [*Gemeinschaft*]
emerge from the modern association. These almost fill the gulf between the
conceptual opposites of a personal society (or proprietorial community) and a
fellowship endowed with an independent legal personality (or living community). Just as, lastly, union had the dual effect of remodelling fellowships
based on necessity and recreating fellowships based on will, so that no clear
boundary could be drawn here, so too the modern system of association operates in both areas with no clear demarcation.

There are, however, alongside these analogies, fundamental points of
difference between the modern phase of the fellowship system and its medieval manifestation. The higher development of public and private life on the
one hand, and the more precise definition of legal terminology on the other,
along with the multiplication of forms, has brought about a division of the
fellowship system into many branches. Although there are links between

these, they are much more sharply distinct from each other than were the medieval forms of community. In the first instance, groups with their own legal personality emerge in distinction to mere communities and societies. Among the former, groups comprising states, whose existence is independent of free will, are much more distinct than before from freely formed associations. Of the utmost importance is the fact that public and private law have separated out, so that groups with importance in the public sphere are put together and organised on principles of public law, and private-law corporations on principles of private law. The danger of their being transformed into privileged corporations thereby disappears.

But the most important difference between the modern and the medieval is that, through the continued splitting-up of group life, fellowships are formed more and more for single purposes; so that finally, in contrast to the medieval tendency to extend each group of fellows over the whole person and simply make it into a community [*Gemeinschaft*], the opposite tendency has prevailed: *the purposes of each individual association are precisely defined*, and its organisation adapted and its significance limited accordingly. Even the highest association—the state—has its purposes, and therefore the limits of its scope prescribed by this modern trend. The purposes of local communities [*Gemeinden*] of higher or lesser degree are defined even more precisely; indeed in many cases special groups resembling *Gemeinden* are set up for specific purposes. The same goes for the church and other public bodies. It is, in short, the general rule today that freely formed associations are confined to single specialised purposes.[17] Corporate fellowships are brought into existence solely for one stated purpose related to the law of property, solely for one specified spiritual or moral purpose; indeed today it is chiefly for specific purposes that people group themselves together. The composition and organisation of each particular corporation is bound up with this specification of purposes; for example, fellowships based on property are exclusive and constructed according to the law of property, whereas a fellowship based on labour for economic purposes or a political association is non-exclusive and constructed on a personal basis, and so on.

This is further related to the precise delimitation of the amount of individuality which the individual gives up to the fellowship, or, to put it differently, the relationship between unity and plurality. Even for the state there is an attempt, articulated in the demand for so-called basic rights, to express in a precise formula which sides of the individual personality could be independent even of the supreme universality [*höchste Allgemeinheit*], and which individual rights should be inviolable. It is even more expressly stated how much individuality a person should relinquish to other compulsory groups.

In the area of association by free choice, it is possible to belong to one group of fellows or another with one's individuality as one wishes, sometimes with a precisely proportionate sum of personal rights and obligations, sometimes with a precisely defined share of capital, without the individual having to forego his own personality. If the individual as citizen helps form a state, province, district, and local community, and perhaps a range of special groups to look after the poor, or a school, or to maintain roadways, dikes and waterways; if as fellow-believer he helps form a church, or if, as a member of a specific vocational group, he helps form a corporation [*Innung*]; if, as a personally active member, he helps form any number of political, social, charitable or recreational groups, or again as a shareholder he helps to form however many business companies at home or abroad—in all of this in terms of law his individuality is so little used up that the possibility of helping to call new fellowships [into] being, for these or other purposes in life, appears quite limitless. Thus, while the corporation system ultimately fetters the individual, the modern association is compatible with the greatest conceivable personal freedom.

But, at the same time, there emerged in place of the fixed order of medieval fellowships encircling one another, a system of groups of varying importance intersecting one another at many points: hence the class [*standisch*] foundation was overcome, and the danger of a new separation based on class was avoided. The old system of corporations united the *fellows* as closely as possible, in order to distinguish the fellow*ships* all the more clearly from one another; the modern association forces the fellows to unite only so far as is requisite for one quite specific purpose, so as finally to construct one collective unity out of single groups interlocking with one another in a hundred different ways. Here there is no longer any division according to class [*Klasse*] or estate [*Stand*].

The modern association, therefore, although it started in the towns, does not exclude the rural population but draws the whole nation into its circle. Lastly, the modern system of fellowship is exempt also from the danger of raising the particular above the universal, and thus ultimately of creating states within the state. It is opposed by a strong unitary state which had developed before it. Furthermore, it has the tendency to prevent state centralism without weakening the idea of the state, achieved after centuries. For it recognises the latter's value, and willingly finds the measure and limit of its own sphere over against this powerful phenomenon. Up to now the real effectiveness of the new concept of association, which did not question the unitary state and free individuality resulting from the idea of sovereignty, but encompassed these in higher forms, emerged chiefly in two ways. First, it had a modifying effect on those groups whose existence was independent of their members' will. By aiming to provide these with an inner life conditioned and determined by the collective will, and an organisational structure to facilitate this—that is, the form of the fellowship—it has produced a series of radical transformations in public law which in many cases has breathed a new life into the old lifeless bodies.

Above all it has begun to relocate the state itself within the people. For, through a representative constitution, public control of the administration, the participation of the people in law-making and the restoration of traditional [volksthümlich] criminal adjudication, it has given expression to the idea that the state is nothing other than the organised people. It has built up the state under sovereign leadership but on the basis of a fellowship of citizens.

The reorganisation of lesser public associations too, along the lines of independent communities of fellowship, has in certain respects been begun by taking at least the first steps towards the autonomy, self-management and comradely [genossenschaftlich] organisation of communes, districts and provinces, of special commune-like associations, and of other corporations based on public law. In the church too the concept of the institution has already been forced to give some ground to the notion of religious fellowships.

Secondly, the concept of association has produced effects in its own right by its free activity, by calling into being a great number of free fellowships of the most varied kinds, for all conceivable ends. In a relatively very short time, the system of free groups has become a great power in private as in public law, in associations based on capital as well as on labour, in morality, social life and economics. An endlessly lively, independent common life pulses in these groups of comrades [Genossenverbände]; a sense of community and self-functioning is generated. As small universalities over their members, they none the less willingly submitted to being members of a greater universality. Today the life of the nation and of individuals has already been enriched and strengthened by this in ways which can scarcely be comprehended.

The effectiveness of the concept of association appears all the more considerable if one considers how little time it has yet had in which to develop freely. Its beginnings must be fixed in the eighteenth century. But while in England and the Netherlands (where there was almost unbroken continuity with the medieval system of corporations) it was already flourishing in much splendour, in Germany it was still confined to a few pitiful structures, and these based chiefly on private law. With the resurgence of the might of the German people brought forth by the oppression of foreign rule, the stirrings of the new idea gained power. But, until 1848, in the majority of German states it was often opposed by authority; and, even if not, as with enterprises of capital, societies for intellectual interests etc., in this period the association manifested only limited creative power. Its full efficacy . . . belongs only to the last twenty years, when restrictions from above declined, and from below the ancient power of German association awoke to an almost miraculous vigour.

The Representative, Constitutional State

[In Gierke's day, the fifth period of history is still taking shape. Popular representation in government is leading to equal citizenship of all. The spirit of the German people is reviving, and with it "the demand that the state be given back to the people." A new association movement is growing, and the plurality of free associations grows hand in hand with demand for the unity of the people with the state.]

Implicit in the demand for unity of state and people, is the further demand for the unity of state and legal justice [Recht]. In contrast to the ancient and Roman state, and also to the interventionist state [Polizeistaat] briefly implemented amongst us, the modern Germanic state is to be a state based on legal justice [Rechtsstaat]. This is not to say that the ancient Germanic conditions, in which the state was absorbed by Right, when it only existed for the sake of Right and consequently stood under the law [Recht], will ever return; but equally the state must not be above the law or itself absorb the law. Rather, the state is to be based on justice [Recht], since its organism itself is legal justice; since, in other words, public law [öffentliches Recht] is recognised and defended as being truly law. The constitutional state [Verfassungsstaat] can only move freely inside the sphere of its positive life within the constitution; and the law can only move freely in respect of individual details. The state, in so far as it comes into contact with any other sphere of existence, of an individual, a smaller universality or one of its members, is bound by legal justice. Conversely, public law—that is, the legal justice which regulates the relations between the state as a universality and the lesser universalities or the individual citizens as members of that highest universality, and therefore determines the organism of the state—is bound by the state. Since, therefore, in public law freedom retreats in the face of necessity, the state must, conversely, recognise legal justice as an insurmountable barrier to its freedom of movement.

Administration, therefore, which forms the content of the positive life of the state, finds in legal justice its boundary. It is true that, for both the state and the individual, the definition of their positive [sphere of] activity follows

from considerations of expediency. But it is equally true that neither the state
nor the individual may infringe legal justice for considerations of expediency:
for legal justice reconciles differing interests and, in the last analysis, the general interests and the interests of individuals. The principle 'salus publica
suprema lex esto' (let public safety be the supreme law) is, therefore, turned on
its head in the constitutional state [Rechtsstaat]. The public good is, of course,
the positive content of the state's function; but statute [Gesetz] draws the
boundaries between the pursuit of the public good and of particular goods. If
the law [Recht] becomes inadequate for the needs of the state, it must be
changed by constitutional means through the legislative agencies. If the law is
in doubt or in dispute, then the judicial agencies, the courts, must declare
what the law is. The idea of the constitutional state culminates in the demand,
still nearly everywhere denied, for the protection of public law through the
courts by means of positive statutes. . . .

Let us, finally, ask how the modern idea of the state, which aims to replace the authoritarian state with the unity of state and people, and the administrative state with the constitutional state, is related to the idea of fellowship. We find that, although the alterations which have occurred or begun to
occur, in the internal and external nature of the state, have originated in the
idea of fellowship, that idea does not claim to determine the modern idea of
the state exclusively, nor to be identical with it; rather, it is contained in it
only as part of it. When [Otto] Bähr, in his work on the constitutional state[18],
claims to regard the state in all its manifestations simply as the supreme, most
comprehensive 'fellowship', this is based on a wider linguistic usage, since by
fellowship he understands every human association. Even with this modification, Bähr's principle is correct only in so far as the state can be conceived of
and organised in the form of an association (Verein); it is incorrect in so far as
it relates to any historical manifestations of the state. For many nations the
state has been, and is, far more an institution [Anstalt] than an association.
Even the German state, at the time when public life was dead, was anything
but a civic society [bürgerliche Gesellschaft]; rather, it was an institution
[Institution] standing utterly above and beyond society, a personality transcending the people. If the modern trend, in harmony with the basic
Germanic view which it has rejuvenated, endeavors to turn the state, in theory and in practice, back into a civic society, and to create a state personality
immanent within the people, then in the spirit of this aspiration the modern
German state is indeed, as Bähr argues, nothing other than the supreme, most
comprehensive human association.

Divested of its mystical character and traced back to the natural process
of growth (instead of supernatural origins), such a state is not generically

different from the lesser public-law associations contained within it—the communities and corporations. Its relation to them is only that of the more complete to the less complete state of development. It is the product of the same power which we still see on a small scale daily, constructing universalities of a more limited kind over particularities. It is, therefore, homologous with the communities and fellowships. The multitude of consequences which follow from this one difference are of course overwhelming: the state, as the highest universality, has no more universalities above it, and is sovereign, so that, while all other groups are still determined by something external and are ultimately regulated by something outside themselves, the state is wholly determined by itself alone and contains its own regulating principle within itself. However, the philosophy which deduces from this that the state has an absolute, unique political personality, while allowing to all the smaller universalities only at most a fragment of political personality, derived from the state personality, is incompatible with the modern idea of the state.

But even if the state actually, according to our contemporary idea of it, stands for the supreme and most universal association, it still does not follow that it is a pure fellowship, or nothing but a fellowship. Even if one were willing to define the idea of fellowship so widely as to include an association whose existence is based on necessity and whose form alone lies in the domain of free will, an association (furthermore) for which a territory as well as a plurality of persons is an essential prerequisite, then even the *organisation* of the state, as it has historically developed, has only half of a fellowship-like nature. For, granted that the idea of a fellowship-like association of the folk collectivity—that is, a fellowship of citizens in which the fully and equally enfranchised independent citizens are collectively the active citizens—forms the *foundation* of the modern constitutional state, none the less its *summit* [*Spitze*] has emerged from lordship (transformed into princely sovereignty). Indeed, to organise the state on a constitutional basis is to attempt to fuse the elements of lordship and fellowship together into a harmonious unity. The modern idea of the state, therefore, embodies the reconciliation of the ancient idea of fellowship and the ancient idea of lordship. Both of these have validity within their own sphere; but the hostile opposition of the two is to find its resolution in a higher unity.

The representative constitutional state, therefore, is neither a pure fellowship, like the earliest patriarchal state, nor a pure lordship, like the feudal state; nor again is it purely a community based on fellowship, like the medieval town, a dual entity made up of an independent lordship and an independent fellowship, like the medieval territorial state, a purely sovereignty-based system, like the modern states of territorial lords. It is, rather, a community which organically brings together the foundation of fellowship (the fellowship of citizens) and the sovereign peak (the monarchy), uniting them not as an aggregate but as a new living unity.

NOTES

[1] Excerpts from Gierke's *Community in Historical Perspective*, trans. Mary Fischer, selected and edited by Antony Black (Cambridge: Cambridge University Press, 1990). This volume consists almost entirely of selections from vol. I of Gierke's four-volume *Das deutsche Genossenschaftsrecht* (Berlin: 1868-1913).

[2] "Editor's Introduction," to Otto von Gierke, *Community in Historical Perspective*, xiv.

[3] *Ibid.*

[4] *Ibid.*

[5] *Ibid.*, xviii.

[6] Gierke's major works, publication dates, and translations are listed in *Ibid.*, xii-xiii.

[7] *Ibid.*, xvi.

[8] *Ibid.*, 12.

[9] *Ibid.*

[10] *Ibid.*, 4.

[11] *Ibid.*, xxiv. Paul Hirst offers this summary judgment about Gierke while explaining the use made of him by Maitland and Figgis: "Gierke's views are complex and Maitland and Figgis each adapted them to their own purposes, subjecting them to a definite 'reading'. In particular Gierke did not reject the theory of state sovereignty and was a patriot for the new German empire. What Gierke offered was twofold: first, a history of political thought before the advent of the modern theory of the state, showing the possibility of thinking about politics in terms other than those of Machiavelli and Hobbes; and second, a view of associations as corporate personalities, as real bodies with a life of their own which were not mere legal 'fictions'." "Introduction," to Paul Hirst, ed., *The Pluralist Theory of the State* (New York: Routledge, 1989), 18.

[12] Gierke, *Community*, 120.

[13] *Ibid.*, 123.

[14] *Ibid.*, 163.

[15] Cf. Otto von Gierke, *Das deutsche Genossenschaftsrecht*, vol. 3, translated by F.W. Maitland as *Political Theories of the Middle Age* (Cambridge: Cambridge University Press, 1900), 100.

[16] A similar view is expressed by Alexis de Tocqueville, *Democracy in America*, vol. I, author's introduction; and Alexis de Tocqueville, *The Ancien Régime and the French Revolution*, part 2, ch. 8.

[17] Cf. de Tocqueville, *Democracy*, 2: bk. 2, ch. 5.

[18] Otto Bähr, *Der Rechtsstaat: eine publicistische Skizze* (Cassel and Gottingen, 1864); translated into Italian in 1891.

FIVE

POLITICAL THOUGHT FROM GERSON TO GROTIUS[1]

by John Neville Figgis

John Neville Figgis

J.N. Figgis (1866-1919), one of the leading English pluralists of the late nineteenth and early twentieth centuries, was particularly concerned to discover the origins of state absolutism. The aim of his historical research and writing is to show the dangers and inferiority of that ideal compared with the progress of social pluralism since the end of the Middle Ages. Unlike Groen who focused his attention on the conflict of spirits (or religious motives) between Reformation and Revolution, and unlike Burke who criticized the destructive, leveling tendency of the Revolution's ideal of abstract individualism, Figgis targets the *collectivist* consequences of modern humanism which were becoming more and more evident in his day. The English pluralists turned their critical attention to the constitutional and social-structural consequences of the unlimited state.

In nineteenth-century England, for example, famed legal philosopher John Austin further developed the idea of state absolutism which had its roots in the work of Jean Bodin and Thomas Hobbes. Figgis pits his historical analysis, indebted as he is to Gierke, against Austin's more abstract philosophical defense of state sovereignty to show that individuals and institutions such as the church do not owe their existence to the modern state. Certain prior

rights and identities, therefore, ought to be recognized and preserved in public law. One of Figgis' chief slogans is a "free Church in a free State," and he
uses it as the title of the first chapter in his book *Churches in the Modern
State*.[2] The freedom and independence of the church is not the only concern
of Figgis. That is simply a key point of focus for all questions of political philosophy. "The question concerns not merely ecclesiastical privilege, but the
whole complex structure of any society and the nature of political union."[3]

Drawing on the work of Gierke, Figgis argues that a correct understanding of the character of non-state institutions and their relation to the state requires the rejection of two widely held theories—the "fiction" and the
"concession" theories. The fiction theory assumes that the individual is a real
person in law, but that all institutions and corporations are only aritifical
"persons" and therefore fictional. The concession theory says that legal rights
accorded to "fictitious" bodies are concessions from the state. In other words,
corporate bodies have "no right to exist, except on concession, expressed or
implied, and no power of action beyond what the State (in theory) delegates
to them."[4]

Both of these theories have ancient roots, so they may not be criticized as
if they are recent outgrowths of the French Revolution or of modern humanist thinking in general. Figgis traces them back to the *damnosa hereditas* of
Roman law and the claims of Imperial Rome.[5] He also shows that they had
been baptized and incorporated by the medieval Church. Thus, even though
Roman law was never accepted in England, the fiction and concession theories were carried there through the influence of English chancellors trained in
canon law and through the general development of state absolutist theory in
the sixteenth and seventeenth centuries.[6]

With the spread of Enlightenment faith in human reason in the eighteenth century and the growth of romantic nationalism in the nineteenth
century, the fiction and concession theories of institutional identity were easily incorporated into modern political thought. On the one hand, the fiction
theory fit well with an individualist theory of society, while, on the other
hand, the growth of national, centralizing states allowed for the concession
theory to take on modern legal forms. From his study of Western political
thought, Figgis notices the same phenomenon that Robert Nisbet later criticizes, namely, the repeated oscillation between an "unreal individualism" and
a "wildly impossible socialistic ideal."[7] Rejecting both individualism and collectivism, Figgis goes in search of historical foundations for a pluralist alternative.

In his classic study of the transition from medieval to modern eras,
Political Thought from Gerson to Grotius: 1414-1625, Figgis looks for the influ-

ences that prompted or promoted the differentiation of society.[8] His search takes him from Gerson in 1414 to Grotius in 1625. "In the Middle Ages," Figgis concludes, "the Church was not a State, it was the State; the State or rather the civil authority (for a separate society was not recognized) was merely the police department of the Church."[9] That began to change with the conciliar movement within the Church, of which Gerson is a leading representative. While the conciliar movement aimed to preserve the unity of a weakening Roman Catholic Church in the fifteenth century, it wanted to do so by making a federal, representative church council the supreme authority and by imposing checks on the absolute authority of the Popes.

The conciliar movement was one of the steps toward modern constitutionalism and the further differentiation of society, as Figgis sees it. It was followed by the disintegrating influences of Machiavelli and Luther, and then by the rise of state absolutist doctrines. In the vacuum left by the collapse of the Church's universal "police" authority, a number of states each stepped in to claim absolute sovereignty over a limited territory. Opposed to absolutism were the "monarchomachi"— those with roots in the Calvinist Reformation who argued and fought for the right of revolt against unjust rulers and who thus made a further contribution to societal differentiation and constitutionalism. Responding to the monarchomachi, the Jesuits arose as the most formidable representatives of the Catholic counter-Reformation, symbolized most dramatically in the Spanish aggression.

Figgis covers all this ground in following a course that leads him to a concluding study of the Netherlands revolt against Spain. It is from this final chapter that we have drawn the excerpts below. The resistance of the Netherlands to Spanish aggression "gathered up the various tendencies against absolutism, made them effectual as a practical force and operative in the future," Figgis writes.[10] Had it not been for that resistance, "it is almost certain that European liberty would have succumbed to the universal aggression of Spain."[11] The best representative interpreter of what the Low Countries achieved, according to Figgis, is Johannes Althusius who summed up "the whole thought of the day."[12] Althusius (1557-1638) is the German Calvinist whom Gierke uncovered in his nineteenth-century research. Althusius had been forgotten until Gierke recovered him, and Figgis is one of the first to bring Althusius to the attention of the English-speaking world.

POLITICAL THOUGHT FROM
GERSON TO GROTIUS

The Netherlands Revolt

William The Silent is the triumphant figure of the latter half of the sixteenth century. The assured independence of the Netherlands is a greater achievement than the defeat of the Armada or the Battle of Ivry or the deposition of Mary Stuart. Henri IV sacrificed half of the principles for which he stood in order to secure success. William the Silent sacrificed only his life. In spite even of the religious intolerance of the Synod of Dort and persecution he would never have approved, the Netherlands were to the seventeenth what the England of the Revolution was to the eighteenth and early nineteenth centuries, a working model of free institutions, and the centre of light for the rest of Europe. Laud complains of the way in which books which he disliked got themselves printed in Amsterdam. In the struggle between liberty and authority the possession of a hostile printing press becomes of capital importance. It is not in any novelty of ideas, so much as in their practical accomplishment, that the influence of the Netherlands was so important. Hitherto we have spoken of movements like the Conciliar or the Huguenot, which ultimately failed, however fertile in ideas; or the Jesuits whose early excursions into popular politics were forgotten by the age which connected them entirely with the *ancien régime*. These movements had all their influence, and were not merely heralds but makers of our modern world of thought. But it was the Netherlands that gave them the leverage which rendered them effectual—until that was done even more powerfully by England. The Dutch revolt gathered up the various tendencies against absolutism, made them effectual as a practical force and operative in the future. Its success enabled them to crystallize and take philosophical shape, just as the success of Henri IV made the same process possible for the theory of royalism, and was the condition *sine quâ non* for such writers as Pierre Grégoire of Toulouse or Barclay. Dr Cunningham has taught us to look to the Dutch as the source of our commercial improvements in the seventeenth century. That "conscious imitation" of them of which he wrote is no less conspicuous in regard to politics. For they appeared to have solved the problem which others were discussing. They had shown how to combine liberty with order in a modern State, they had secured control over their own government, too much control as was afterwards apparent. During the early years of their revolution, the ideas of toleration had found deliberate expression. Even if these were afterwards deserted, the example of William the Silent remained. They had paved the way for federalism. Their existence rested on the principle of nationality, no less than on that of the right of resistance to tyranny. The status of their leader was that of a small sovereign prince, and prepared the way for the recognition of the "equality before the Law" of all States, while their position in regard to the Emperor, like that of the Swiss, served still further to emphasize the passing away of the old European order. Their government was rather a limited monarchy than a republic. Ideas, which might otherwise have been buried for all time, could influence future developments because there was now a modern place where they could be seen actually at work—not the relict of two Empires like Venice, nor the cast-off clothes of feudalism like Poland, but a living, growing community consciously occupied with modern problems, and shaping its destinies in accordance with principles destined after long obscuration to become generally recognized. . . .

If ever there was an instance of the superiority of intellect to force in human concerns, it is to be found in the success of the Dutch. It was not, as the oleographic theory of history teaches, because Philip was a monster of wickedness that he lost the Netherlands, but because like most kings, *e.g.*, Louis XIV and George III, who have been thoroughly representative of their peoples, he was stupid, and typified the Spanish character in its least tactful elements. He was opposed by a man who, whatever his faults, was above all things quick and adroit at using opportunities. The Dutch were placed "in the very Thermopylae of the universe." But for their resistance it is almost certain that European liberty would have succumbed to the universal aggression of Spain. Even England would have been endangered. In the days of their triumph the Netherlands became the University of Europe. If we remove from the first half of the seventeenth century the thinkers, publicists, theologians, men of science, artists, and gardeners who were Dutch, and take away their influence upon other nations, the record would be barren instead of fertile, despite the great name of Bacon. They form a natural conclusion to this series of lectures, for they carry on the tradition to the seventeenth century. Further, they exhibit the beginning of the gradual disentanglement of political from theocratic arguments, which was completed only at the close of the age. Stained at times with intolerance, which even the spectacle of their sufferings should not lead us to ignore, with leaders clever but opportunist, of whom it is well said that "only the extravagance of partisanship can make him a hero," exhibiting already some of those faults of obstinacy, avarice, and slowness, which a century later ruined them as a great power at the close of their most victorious war, with a fanaticism equal to the ultramontanes and a "provincialism" in itself as ignoble as that of Castile, they remain the pioneers of liberty in modern as distinct from medieval Europe, the one oasis in the desert of absolutism, the great source of intellectual and moral enlightenment. . . . Their supreme object was their own independence of the foreigner, and the preservation of their own religion and of local rights. The first object had nothing to do with political liberty proper, for it is secured equally well and often more effectively under a national absolutism. The second in no way meant the toleration of other forms of faith, and even in their hours of direst distress, the Prince of Orange had the utmost difficulty in securing decent treatment for the Catholics. The third, indeed, had a connection with liberty and may have been the main cause which prevented a thorough absolutism. Certainly it helped towards a theory of federalism. But the real importance of the Netherlands lay in their success. In an age when all the tendencies were the other way, and the Counter-Reformation had at least half conquered even in France, the Dutch were there—a people who had united themselves, had chosen their own head, had resisted at once their own sovereign and the cause of universal monarchy, had proclaimed, if not tolerance, at any rate bounds to the progress of the Counter-Reformation. On the one hand this fact helped to inspire the princes in the Thirty Years' War, the last great effort at once of the Counter-Reformation, and of Imperial authority—in other words the last attempt to restore the old order temporal as well as spiritual. On the other hand over England their influence was enormous. There is no doubt that the Puritans feared that the movement led by Charles I and Laud was merely a part of the Counter-Reformation. The mere provision of the Netherlands as a place of refuge for malcontents was alone important, while the Dutch influence in hindering the attempt of James II to produce a Counter-Reformation here is too obvious to need pointing out. What does need pointing out, is that our Revolution was partly the culminating triumph of the Dutch mind; that it was the final achievement of forces that had been at work for a century; that England owed at least a few peerages and pensions to the representatives of the nation, which had by both example and precept prepared her for constitutional liberty. It was not the defeat of the Armada but William of Orange who finally conquered Philip II. The House of Orange may be regarded as the educators of England. When Holland had trained this country to keep alight the torch of liberty and enlightenment, the historical mission was over, and she sank into a second-rate power. To estimate our debt to Holland is hard; to over-estimate it is harder. The supreme fact is that it was a free State in a world rapidly tending to a uniformity of absolutism, a Calvinist Teutonic federalism, unlike anything else—for Geneva was a Latin

city-state, and its influence in France was over until the days of Voltaire and
Rousseau. . . .

[Johannes Althusius (1557-1638)]

By the close of the sixteenth century the independence of the
Netherlands was practically assured. It remained for the Dutch to consolidate
their victory and to crystallize into systematic treatises the principles of the
movement. For our purpose we may confine ourselves to two writers, who on
different sides expressed these principles—Althusius and Grotius. The former
was not himself a Netherlander, but he came to reside within the territory,
was clearly influenced by the facts he found before him at Herborn and may
be regarded as the representative publicist. His work *Politica Methodice
Digesta* is, with the exception of Bodin's treatise, the most important of all
works for the scientific student. Dr Gierke in a work, compared with which
everything else on the subject is but prattle, has demonstrated the value of the
book and traced its influence backwards and forwards. Perhaps, indeed,
Treumann is right in saying that he rather exaggerates the importance of the
book. There seems to be no proof forthcoming that it directly influenced
Rousseau—although the likeness of ideas is so great as to render that a highly
probable conjecture. M. Dreyfus-Brisac, who quotes the relevant passages in
his edition of *Le Contrat Social*, appears to think not proven the charge of pla-
giarism. Althusius writes as a professor not a pamphleteer. His book is emphatically not a *livre de circonstance*, and is perhaps for that reason charged
(and I think justly) by Dr Gierke with a certain insipidity of tone. It has not
the eloquence or the appeal of the *Vindiciae contra Tyrannos* and is less
readable.

More, however, than any other writer does Althusius sum up the whole
thought of the day. Like Albericus Gentilis he both quotes and knows the
words of all previous publicists, and he appears to have been considerably influenced in the structure of his work by the dull and flat lucubration of
Lambertus Daneus. He makes considerable use of Gregory of Toulouse,
Salamonius and of Patricius of Siena, a renaissance scholar who wrote a
book—*De Republica*—with reference to the Italian city-states. He criticises
Bodin, but he is indebted to him. In this as in other ways he prepared the way
for Rousseau, who combined with the royalist conceptions of legal omnipotence popular theories of the origin of power.

This is what Althusius does. If he does not accept quite *ex animo* the legal
theory of sovereignty he is far nearer to it than are the Huguenots or the
Whigs, who always—as we have seen—endeavour to deny the existence of

any power in the State above the law, whether royal or parliamentary. The reason of this is that for them contract is a bond between governor and governed, which settles the relations of each and is therefore above legal review.

To Althusius, however, the contract is social, it is the mutual agreement of all to live in an ordered society. His view is not essentially dissimilar from that of Suarez or Molina. There may indeed be another contract between whatever ruler the people, which is now a single power, may agree to set up, and themselves. In this he is different from Rousseau, who allows only a single contract—the social; but the practical result is very similar. In both cases the rights of sovereignty belong not to the ruler, whether one, many, or few, but to the members of the association. The sovereignty of the people becomes the foundation of the State. Althusius does not display the profundity of the deeper thinking Jesuits, like Suarez and Molina, who evolve sovereign power from a community by the mere fact of its existence without any deliberate pact, thus preparing the way for the true theory of corporations, in which authority and self-dependence are inherent essentially, and not dependent on any agreement, since they arise from the nature of the case. But his doctrine of a social contract is less artificial than that of the original contract, as ordinarily propounded. It escapes the logical absurdity which made Whigs even as great as Locke or Hoadly the legitimate sport of writers, like Filmer and Leslie, who were never weary of pointing out that law-makers must have existed before laws, and that the conception of the constitution of a State as unalterable is not possible. On Althusius' theory it was quite possible, as indeed on that of Rousseau, to assert the limited nature of all actual governmental authority, without making the formal error of declaring that laws could not be altered even by the legislature.

By another conception Althusius' system was preserved from the great practical danger of that of Rousseau, the enunciation of the sovereignty of the people in so violent a form, that there is nothing to check the tyranny of the majority or even a plebiscitary despotism. This defect was inherent in Rousseau's system, and appears in every modification of it, owing to the absolutely unitary conception of the State, entertained alike by Rousseau and by royalists, which is a legacy of the Roman Empire through the Papacy. Alike under the theory of Hobbes and that of Rousseau, or (in regard to the Church) under that of the Canonists or the Jesuits all power is ultimately concentrated at a single centre, and every form of right or liberty is of the nature of a privilege, tacitly or expressly granted by the central authority, which may be king, nobles or people.

The last three centuries have witnessed the victory of the principle that, so far as individuals are concerned, some rights or liberties shall always be practically, even if not theoretically, recognized by the modern State—though even here the liberties of the subject are less fully assured than often seems the case. The struggles in England, and still more the declaration of the rights of man, proclaim these liberties as the universal limit upon the practical exercise of the legal omnipotence of the central power. But owing partly to the very sharpness of the idea of a legal sovereign, partly to the long struggle to destroy illegitimate immunities, and to the arrogance of the Churches, partly to the influence of theories originally derived from city-states, partly even to the very recognition of those individual rights above mentioned, there is nothing like the same recognition of the reality of corporate communities apart from the fiat of the State.

In other words, in spite of all actual Parliamentary institutions, the modern unitary State is still conceived as a *Herrschaftsverband* rather than a *Genossenschaft*. The controversy over the right and the nature of Trades Unions, the Associations' Law in France, the ecclesiastical difficulty in Scotland, and even certain aspects of the education question all alike turn at bottom on the question whether the State creates or whether it only recognizes the inherent rights of communities; whether in the Jesuit phrase there may not be a *societas perfecta* besides the more obvious one of the State; or whether in modern German phrase the corporate union be not a real rather than a fictitious personality, *i.e.*, possessing its own inherent life and powers that may be checked, but cannot in the nature of things be destroyed. This position is rendered the more important by the growth of federalism real in the United States, Switzerland and Germany, and quasi in this country. A conception of law and sovereignty which may fairly fit the facts in a unitary State becomes increasingly difficult of practical application to any developed federal community, and ceases to have any but a paper value. It may indeed be argued that the victory of the North in 1866 was really a victory for that idea, for it decided that the rights of the States were not ultimate, and went a step towards abolishing them except as delegations of the supreme power. But it may be replied that just as individuals may have rights recognized by a State, which yet crushes a rebellion, so may societies.

But the point to notice here is that this federalistic idea is to be found in Althusius and through him connects itself with the medieval theory of community life. There is not much difference between that idea of the *communitas communitatum* which the Middle Ages meant by the commons, and Althusius' notion of the State as above all else a *consociato consociationum*. He definitely protests against those who refuse to consider the smaller associations such as the family as anything but economic. The novelty in him is his view of the State as entirely built up on the principle of associations. Indeed the change of the connotation of commons from the view delineated above to the modern one of the mass of common people is significant of the whole development of thought from medieval to modern times, a development which in part will have to be retraced in face of the actual facts. In other words the *Selbständigkeit* of the individual, as against an omnipotent State, has been the battleground of liberty for three centuries; this has now given place to that of the *Selbständigkeit* of societies. What the issue will be or when it will be decided it may not be possible for a historian to say before nineteen hundred has become three thousand. What these lectures have endeavoured to point out is that, as a matter of fact, this achievement of individual liberty was never attained and except for the short period of the Benthamite movement never sought merely for its own sake. Its achievement became feasible only because it was connected with the recognition of the right to exist of some society usually religious, which the civil magistrate did not desire to exist. It is often agreed that religious differences are the ground of modern liberty. It is a mistake to suppose, as we have shown, that this is because as a rule any or all religious bodies cared about such liberty. What they desired was the right to be, what they denied was the right of the State to suppress them as societies, and in standing up against State omnipotence they secured individual liberty in spite of themselves. Indeed they secured it so well that we have forgotten how it was secured and have to learn once more the lesson, that the State is something more than a mass of individuals. What is needed nowadays is that as against an abstract and unreal theory of State omnipotence on the one hand, and an atomistic and artificial view of individual independence on the other, the facts of the world with its innumerable bonds of association and the naturalness of social authority should be generally recognized and become the basis of our laws, as it is of our life.

Now, if Gierke at all exaggerates the importance of Althusius, the reason is doubtless because he is nearer than anyone else to those ideas of "realism," so dear to the great jurist's heart. Here, as in other matters, Holland led the way. Its government was federal. The rights of each province and even each town were recognized as inalienable. Hence, we find that Althusius starts, not, like some writers on politics, from the top, but from the bottom; the unit of civil life is for him not the individual but the family, and he rises by a series of concentric circles from the family to the town, to the province, and the State. His State is a true *Genossenschaft*, a fellowship of all the heads of families, and he takes care to prevent the absorption of local and provincial powers into the central administration. It is not merely that he allows rights to families and provinces; but he regards these rights as anterior to the State, as the foundation of it, and as subsisting always within it. He would no more deny or absorb them than a hive of bees would squash all the cells into a pulp. Only, be it remembered, it is not separate and equal cells, but differing and organic limbs of the body politic which he contemplates. He admits indeed the need of a central organ. This is to the whole like soul to body. It is significant that the old symbol of the relation of ecclesiastical to civil power is used to signify the relation of government to society.

Into his doctrine of the influence of ephors, who are to prevent excesses of government, we need hardly go, as there is nothing here but what is paralleled elsewhere. The dependence of the theory on the peculiar facts of the Netherlands and on the nature of the struggle with Spain is fairly evident. The strength of the communal burgher element; the federalistic tie; the deliberate agreement to throw off the Spanish yoke; the choice of the House of Orange—all had their influence in shaping the theory, and in influencing future generations. How far American federalism was developed from these sources it would be hard to say. But the close connection of Puritanism with Dutch Calvinism must have prepared the ground. In England a pamphlet of 1642 in praise of the Dutch system quotes almost verbatim the words of Boucher in favour of the rights of subjects.

Even in his theory of contract Althusius, as we have seen, combines elements that are found commonly opposed in the sixteenth century; with the general conception of the State entertained by the Dutch thinkers, the same is true. But for the Netherlands it might have seemed that there was no *via media* between the exaltation of royal power, and the general attitude of suspicion of the State and denial of sovereignty which characterized the Huguenot and Ligue and English Presbyterian writers and passed by them through the Whigs to the *laisser-faire* school of Radicals.

There was also the controversy between the ideas of those who, recognizing with Luther or the *Politiques* the sanctity of the civil power, were prepared to go all lengths in establishing the claims of the prince to deal with religion, and that other view typified by Jesuits, but held also by Presbyterians, that the State itself was a mere contrivance, of purely temporal significance, needing for inspiration the guidance of the Church, or at any rate unable to compete with the superior claims of the kingdom which, though not "of this world," was so very much in it, that its behests were paramount on any question involving morals. Now, as we saw, the development of the theory of two societies was due to the peculiar circumstances of the Huguenots in France, of the Presbyterians in England and Scotland, of the Roman Church as against an encroaching State. It was by no means bound up with what is ordinarily known as Calvinism, or with the practical working of it in Geneva, which was definitely a Church State. So in the Netherlands. In spite of the toleration originally proclaimed by the Union of Utrecht, the ideal of religious uniformity eventually triumphed. Toleration was undoubtedly the ideal of William the Silent, who was essentially a *Politique*: and it was appealed to by the Arminians in the controversy of 1614. But they were allied with the party of the burgher oligarchy, and Maurice seized the opportunity of strengthening his power by making use of the Calvinist predilections of the populace. Exile and confiscation were then proclaimed against the Remonstrants. Calvinism, having thus become a conservative force, attempted, just as it did in England, to repress by the strong hand the invasion of wider and more rational views. The party of Arminians in both Holland and England was the party of liberty or at least of change as against the authority of Calvinism, which was an inspiration in the sixteenth century, in the seventeenth became a tradition, and in the eighteenth died down into a prejudice. In Althusius, despite his federalism, we have no hint of any sort of independence for the Church; it is not envisaged as a separate society. Its officers are merely a part of the general machinery of the State. The latter, indeed, is conceived as holy. The author's view of the State is thus definitely that of Luther, the Anglicans, Zwingli, Erastus, as opposed to that of Jesuits and Presbyterians, the difference being that in his case the sovereignty over religious matters is inalienably vested in the people, for the original contract of association can only disappear with the State, whereas the others as a rule vest it in "the godly Prince." The point to note is that Althusius holds a high not a low view of the State; it is something consecrated, the embodiment of justice. His most frequent tag is that from S. Augustine, *remota justitia, quid regna nisi magna latrocinia?* The rights of the State extend over all persons and all causes. There is no conception of a contract between Church and State, or an alliance between them. Even Grotius, who was imprisoned in the Arminian controversy, strongly maintained the Erastian view. In his lengthy treatise, *De Jure Regni apud Sacra*, he develops it in the ordinary way. But while it is the idea of a Christian commonwealth that rules the thoughts of both writers, it is more of the political than the theocratic side that they are thinking. The notion of a Church-State may be interpreted so as to lay emphasis on either one or the other aspect. It may become a pure theocracy, like the Anabaptist kingdom at Münster, the Puritan *régime* in England, and to some extent Laud's system; or it may be a body politic in which uniformity of religious worship and the paramount authority of the secular government are the main elements. It may fulfill the ideas of a Calvin or a Savonarola. It may express the aspirations of a Selden or a Bacon. In both Althusius and Grotius it is distinctly political. It is not a Church with civil officers that they mean by a Christian commonwealth, but a State with ecclesiastical among other ministers. In this respect again they display their kinship to other German princes. What Althusius contemplates is the ordered life of the community as a whole, consecrated to civil ends, with education, like religion, cared for, with all possible provision for leading the good life, and for correlating the smaller activities of town and provincial life with that of the State. Combining elements from both parties, in his conception of governmental activity, in his idea of the inalienability of sovereignty, in the whole notion of the wide competence of the State, Althusius is really more akin to bureaucratic statesmen of the type of Pierre Grégoire and Bacon, than he is to the enthusiasts of revolution. It is of the life of the community organized on a recognized basis of popular sovereignty that he is thinking far more than of the rights of subjects against their rulers. Hence his treatise had little or no influence on the next revolutionary movement, that of England. The Whig ideal is more individualistic, more suspicious of government, more akin to the *Vindiciae contra Tyrannos*, than it is to anything to be found in Althusius. Only with the development of American independence and the reaction of the ideas which it expressed on the Continent had Althusius (or at least his ideas) a chance in Europe. The indebtedness of Rousseau to Althusius may or may not be demonstrable. That the conceptions of the two writers *with the significant exception of federalism* are similar and in some respects identical, there can be no doubt.

[Hugo Grotius (1583-1645)]

If we turn to the final work of Grotius, we see at work principles which at first sight are the opposite of what we should expect, but nevertheless are the result of the Netherlands revolt. With the rules of International Law these lectures are not concerned, with its foundations they are. . . .

The fundamental basis of the whole system of Grotius is the claim that men are in a society bound together by a natural law which makes promises binding. This is also at the root of the doctrine of the original contract. It is the same with writers like Vasquez and Suarez and Albericus Gentilis, whose fundamental ideas are similar to those of Grotius. Albericus Gentilis in his treatment of the social nature of men and his citation of authorities lends strong support to the view of Mr. A. J. Carlyle, that the most decisive change in political thinking is that which came some time between the days of Aristotle and Cicero, and proclaimed the fundamental equality of men—a doctrine ever since asserted, until it was denied in our own day once more by Gobineau, Nietzsche and by others who are facing the problem of brown and yellow races. All these earlier works are the true anti-Machiavel. They strike at the roots of his assumption; which is that of the absolute separateness of

States, the fundamental badness of human beings, and the universal predominance of self-interest and fear. . . .

Lastly, the practical value of the work of Grotius was great. The danger of Machiavelli was not that he dissected motive and tore the decent veil of hypocrisy from statesmen, but that he said or implied that these facts were to be the only ideal of action. The service of Grotius, his forerunners and successors, is not that they produced a scientific system under which State action could be classified, but that they succeeded in placing some bounds to the unlimited predominance of "reason of state." Machiavelli's was a rough generalization from observed facts. Like all theories based on the universality of low motives, it contained a minimum of truth with a maximum of plausibility and was of great immediate practical utility. For its success it unconsciously assumes the existence of other motives, *e.g.*, the religious, whose existence as a real power the whole system denies. The object of Grotius was not to make men perfect or treat them as such, but to see whether there were not certain common duties generally felt as binding, if not always practiced, and to set forth an ideal. As Albericus Gentilis points out, he is concerned not only with what men do, but what they ought to do, and the jurist has ever to remember that *jus* is *ars aequi et boni*.

The founders of International Law did not stop, they regulated the struggle of existence. That famous pamphlet *The fight in Dame Europa's school* rests for its verisimilitude on a conception of Grotius and implies a contradiction of those of Hobbes and Machiavelli. International Law is like schoolboy honour or good form, it does not destroy selfishness or quarreling or cheating; but it proclaims that certain things are to be avoided and others are obligatory, and it unites even those most sharply divided as members in a single society. It does not solve the problem of man in society, but it recognizes it. Now the theory of Machiavelli and Hobbes at bottom is the reverse of this. It teaches that men are not in society at all except by accident and artifice. With all its superficial attractions it fails to reach the true facts; that even hatred implies a relation, and that neither States nor individuals can have differences unless there be some atmosphere which unites them.

I hope that enough has been said to point out how the intellectual no less than the practical conditions which made the work of Grotius possible and necessary were the result partly of age-long influences, partly of the peculiar effects of the religious revolution. The former explain the continued and ever-growing influence of the Civil Law, the ideal of the Holy Roman Empire, its connection with the Canon Law, which makes International Law a sort of legacy of the Middle Ages. The foundations both of International Law and modern politics are the residuum which the medieval world passed on to its

successor; and the same may largely be said of the connection between feudalism and the contractual theory of government. But it was the religious revolution alone which produced the actual conditions to which all this was
applied. On the one hand it helped in Germany and England towards that development of national unity, royal omnipotence, and administrative
universality, which was to be the common form of the continental State till
1789 and the ideal of English statesmen for a long time. On the other hand,
by the division it produced (a) between Emperor and princes, (b) between
princes and subjects, and (c) between State and State, it shattered for ever the
ancient conditions even as an ideal, and prevented the notion of international
justice taking the form of a reconstituted Empire. This process was further
assisted by the division between the two branches of the Habsburgs and the
predominance of Spain, the conditions under which the early Jesuits imbibed
their ideals. These general conditions assumed the predominance of territorial
sovereignty, the recognition of the non-religious basis of the State or at least
of the multi-religious nature of the European State-system, while the unity of
humanity, which had been taught in some way from the time of the Stoics
and impressed as an ideal on every generation from the time of Augustine to
the Renaissance, prevented the final and deliberate outward recognition of the
view that States have no duties to one another and that the international
polity is a fortuitous concourse of atoms. It was these conditions compacted
of the ancient ideas of human society and the immutable authority of the law
natural, coupled with the modern facts of State independence and self-sufficiency and religious differences, that made International Law in the form
which it took possible, i.e., it made it truly international and in the form of its
expression really law. It made it a system fundamentally secular although it
was in origin ethical and even theological. Of both the international and the
municipal commonwealth the basis was becoming though it had not become
frankly secular—and the most remarkable advance towards this end was
made in the theories of the *Politiques*. But religious divisions everywhere and
the establishment of the Dutch Republic especially helped towards this end,
while the latter, more than anything else, contributed towards the change of
the idea of political authority from a lordship into an association. This again
was assisted both by Jesuit speculations on society in general and the actual
nature and constitution of their own community.

One final truth may be noticed. The doctrine of the unity of history is
more impressively realized in a study of political thought than of any actual
constitution. Lord Acton was of opinion that here more than anywhere else a
continuous development could be demonstrated. If the pages of a writer like
Grotius, or still more Albericus Gentilis, be studied carefully, it will be seen

how to him the world was always one; that true principles in politics are to be found partly by reasoning, but still more by the distilled essence of thought ancient and modern, by something akin at least to the comparative study of institutions and by the wise selection of historical instances which as in Machiavelli are valued always for their significance as parts of a system. International Law is indeed a philosophy of history in the idea of its early exponents—just as the "law of beasts" is in that of Machiavelli, only while the latter like modern "naturalism" gives to its system the superficial clearness of an induction from a narrowed basis and an assumption of low motives, the former recognises that however imperfect its realization in fact some notion of righteousness had always regulated men's judgments of value, even if it had been belied by their actions. Alike in international relations, in popular theory, and in absolutist apology, the idea of law and right is upheld in some form, and utility merely and purely as such is repudiated by all except avowed followers of Machiavelli and Hobbes. In this indeed lies the connection of all these doctrines both with theocratic assumptions and with medieval life. The gradual supersession of these notions by that of immediate and perceptible utility took two centuries to develop, and was largely helped by the general secularisation of life which followed the destruction of religious unity and the *Aufklärung* of the eighteenth century. What is to be noted is that only through this revolution did ideas no less than facts take the shape in which they influenced the modern world.

NOTES

1 Selections from Lecture VII, "The Netherlands Revolt," of J. N. Figgis, *Political Thought from Gerson to Grotius, 1414-1625* (New York: Harper Torchbooks, 1960; first published in 1907, with a second edition in 1916). The few notes in Figgis' text have not been retained here.

2 J.N. Figgis, *Churches in the Modern State* (New York: Russell and Russell, 1973 [1913]). For more on Figgis, see Paul Q. Hirst, ed., *The Pluralist Theory of the State: Selected Writings of C.D.H. Cole, J.N. Figgis, and H.J. Laski* (New York: Routledge, 1989).

3 Figgis, *Churches*, 40.

4 *Ibid.*, 249.

5 *Ibid.*, 25, 226.

6 *Ibid.*, 62-3.

7 *Ibid.*, 225.

8 Figgis, *Political Thought.*

9 *Ibid.*, 5.

10 *Ibid.*, 219.

11 *Ibid.*, 222.

12 *Ibid.*, 230. Figgis draws heavily on Gierke at this point. On Althusius, see the abridged translation of his *Politica Methodice Digesta* in Frederick S. Carney, *The Politics of Johannes Althusius* (Boston: Beacon Press, 1964), and James W. Skillen, "The Political Theory of Johannes Althusius," *Philosophia Reformata* (Amsterdam), 39 (1974): 170-190. Gierke's work is *Johanes Althusius und die Entwicklung der natürrechtlichen Staatstheorien,* translated by B. Freyd as *The Development of Political Theory* (London: Allen and Unwin, 1939; reprinted in 1966, New York: Howard Fertig).

SIX

XXXXXXXXXXXX

DOING THEOLOGY IN A REVOLUTIONARY SITUATION[1]

by José Míguez Bonino

José Míguez Bonino

The first impression that one may receive from reading the liberation theologians of contemporary Latin America is that they stand closer to modern revolutionaries than to Edmund Burke, Groen van Prinsterer, Otto von Gierke, or J.N. Figgis. They argue for liberation from all confining traditions rather than for continuity with tradition. They are prone to emphasize injustice and dehumanization rather than God's providence in their past and present. Stating the problem of modern humanity in its broadest sense, Gustavo Gutiérrez says that human social life is now reaching its maturity.

> It is the behavior of man ever more conscious of being an active subject of history; he is ever more articulate in the face of social injustice and of all repressive forces which stand in the way of his fulfillment; he is ever more determined to participate both in the transformation of social structures and in effective political action.[2]

But liberation theology is not so much anti-historical as it is futuristic. Gutiérrez, Míguez Bonino (b. 1924), and other liberation theologians take history as seriously as did Burke and Groen. Yet they view history more in the light of its future positive goal and destiny than in the light of its past

traditions. To be sure, their study of history is guided by a critical sociopolitical analysis that is based on a synthesis of Marxist and Christian
assumptions, but some liberation theologians still want to find a "third way"
between collectivism and individualist liberalism.[3]

For many Latin Americans, liberal individualism has very negative connotations. As an imported ideology that took hold in the nineteenth century,
it did indeed help many countries to gain their independence from Spain and
Portugal. It led to the separation of church and state, aided the growth of
economic enterprises, and inspired the constitutional recognition of a number
of individual and democratic freedoms. But the positive benefits of liberalism
were enjoyed primarily by a small, educated, propertied elite and not generally by the poor peasants and Indians. Masses of Latin Americans experienced
even the liberal state as a form of state absolutism. As Enrique Dussel explains:

> From 1850 to 1929 we see the unfolding of a whole new project in Latin
> America, a project sponsored by a liberal oligarchy rather than by a conservative
> one. In general we could say that it looked to France for cultural ideals and to
> the United States for its technological ideals. It was in these places that it would
> find its concrete historical ideals, rejecting our past as a period of barbarism.[4]

Or as Míguez Bonino puts it:

> The class structure obtaining at the time of the colonies carried over into the
> new economic and political conditions. The leaders of the emancipation and
> modernization had their faces turned toward Europe and the U.S.A. and their
> backs to the interior of the countries. There, Indians and peasants were simply
> incorporated as cheap labor for production. Their condition was, if anything,
> worse than it had been before under a sometimes more or less lenient paternal-
> istic system. A free press, free trade, education, politics—all the "achievements"
> of liberalism—were the privilege of the elite.[5]

Opposition to totalitarian collectivism is also clear in the writings of
some liberation theologians who are vigorous critics of every form of oppression, imperialism, dictatorship, and dehumanization. Brazilian Archbishop
Dom Helder Camara once said, "I am a socialist. . . . But I don't see the solution in the socialist governments that exist today. . . . the Marxist record is
awful. . . . God made man in his image and likeness, so he could become his
co-creator and not a slave. My socialism is a special one which respects the
human person and turns to the gospel. My socialism is justice."[6] In 1971 the
Roman Catholic bishops of Peru formulated a statement arguing that
"Christians ought to opt for socialism." But by "socialism" they said, "We do

not mean a bureaucratic, totalitarian, or atheistic socialism; we mean a social-ism that is both humanistic and Christian."[7]

Míguez Bonino draws on the covenantal and prophetic revelation of the Bible for his vision of a healthy unfolding of societal life. That revelation is rooted in God's love for his creatures and his will for their liberation and re-newal. The background of Jesus' ministry and proclamation, he says, "is the jubilee tradition and the prophetic promise of God's ultimate peace—his shalom—a very rich expression which embraces the total welfare of the indi-vidual and the community: health, abundance, just relations, personal fulfill-ment, faithfulness to God, a just government."[8]

This understanding of diversified human experience under God is di-rectly related to Míguez Bonino's concept of "the 'corporality' of history."[9] By this he means the communal life of man that reaches fulfillment in the order of the Kingdom of God. "In the same vein, historical 'works' in all orders of life—social, economic, political—are permanent insofar as they belong to that order."[10] "Once we see divine initiative as that action of God within history and in historical terms which opens history toward the promise, we seem not only entitled but required to use the strong language of growth, realization, creation which, furthermore, is that of the prophets and apostles!"[11] Despite his dependence on Marxist social analysis, Míguez Bonino seems not to want a collectivist social order. He envisions both individual and communal di-versity as essential to social harmony and justice.

The gospel is central to Míguez Bonino's social thought. He is, however, critical of the way Christianity has lost the vision of the total transformation of the world and the advent of the Kingdom of God. When the original vision was lost it was replaced "by a spiritualized and individualistic hope for im-mortal, celestial life," so that temporal life lost its significance.[12] "The hope of the Kingdom, far from awakening an ethos to transform the world in the di-rection of that which was expected," now "worked as a deterrent for historical action."[13] But if a "dualistic" view is not intrinsic to the Christian gospel, then how can an individualist and other-worldly view of life be overcome theologi-cally and practically?

In Míguez Bonino's response to these questions he calls for the recovery of a "monistic" view of Christianity. It is a view in which

> God builds his Kingdom from and within human history in its entirety; his ac-tion is a constant call and challenge to man. Man's response is realized in the concrete arena of history with its economic, political, ideological options. Faith is not a different history but a dynamic, a motivation, and, in its eschatological horizon, a transforming invitation.[14]

Míguez Bonino confesses that for him the gospel is the power of new life from God in Christ. Therefore, the resurrection of Christ cannot be reduced to a sign of hope for spiritual life after death which leaves the profane history of this world largely untouched. The gospel will not allow us to bypass the unjust liberal and collectivist ideologies and societal structures of our present age. No, he says, the resurrection of Christ is the promise that God's Kingdom will be built, and it is a call and a challenge to unfold every dimension of earthly life.

> Resurrection, far from being the rescue of a spiritual element in human life, cleansing it from the bodily experience and identity obtained throughout life, is the total redemption of man, the true and unhindered realization of a bodily life cleansed from self-deception and self-seeking (flesh) and made perfect in transparent (glorious) singleness of purpose and experience (spiritual) and full community with God.[15]

One reason why the liberation theologians criticize tradition so much more than does Burke or Groen is that they see the results of the influence of conservatism and liberalism in Latin America over the past 200 years. Many of the consequences of the French Revolution are now part of their tradition. Many Latin American institutions, social structures, and economic and political traditions are highly inflexible and extremely unjust for large portions of the population. Míguez Bonino and others criticize liberalism and conservatism after decades of social, economic, and political developments that Groen and Burke could not have anticipated. The Word of God, which Groen wanted to obey in history, has been ignored and twisted, says Míguez Bonino. Thus, the will of God, the Kingdom of God, is not to be found by looking around among the institutions of recent history. Rather, it is a call to keep on moving toward human maturity, liberation, full responsibility, and justice for all in the promised future. He explains:

> Instead of asking, where is the Kingdom present or visible in today's history? we are moved to ask, how can I participate—not only individually but in a community of faith and in a history—in the coming world? The main problem is not noetic but, so to say, empirical. It has to do with an active response. The Kingdom is not an object to be known through adumbrations and signs that must be discovered and interpreted but a call, a convocation, a pressure that impels. History, in relation to the Kingdom, is not a riddle to be solved but a mission to be fulfilled.[16]

Just as Burke and Groen were confident that God had acted in history, and that many historical patterns of political, economic, and ecclesiastical life should be conserved because of their historical legitimacy, so Míguez Bonino is confident that God will continue to act in history, that God is calling human beings to create new social, economic, and political structures that will set people free rather than keep them enslaved. He envisions a type of societal order that does not now exist in Latin America. In this context he affirms that the Christian faith

> provides today both a stimulus and a challenge for revolutionary action when it encourages us to look and work for historical realization in the direction of the Kingdom in terms of justice, solidarity, the real possibility for men to assume responsibility, access of all men to the creation which God has given to man, freedom to create a human community through work and love, space to worship and play.[17]

Further, the Christian is "to invest his life historically in the building of a temporary and imperfect order with the certainty that neither he nor his effort is meaningless or lost."[18]

Míguez Bonino insists that the theological perspective which should inform "the sociopolitical project and the faith of the Christians committed to it" must be developed in close relationship to questions that arise out of the concrete historical situation in Latin America and elsewhere.[19] He suggests that a sound point of departure might be an exploration of the relation between what has been called "the covenant of creation" and the "covenant of redemption."

> Freely interpreted this would mean that mankind has been placed in a realm of responsibility which embraces a three-fold free relationship to fellow men, to nature (the world), and to Yahweh (the God of the covenant). The Christian dispensation will then be understood in relation to such a covenant, as God's active will to restore man's relationships and responsibility, to reinstate him in his position as partner in the covenant of creation, to put him back again on the road of his self-realization.[20]

Institutions, communities, and other manifestations of social life do emerge in the course of history. There is an undeniable historical dimension to the process of human action in bringing about societal differentiation. Edmund Burke, Groen van Prinsterer, Otto von Gierke, J.N. Figgis, and José Míguez Bonino appeal in different ways to history as they make a case for the importance of a differentiated social order. In Chapter Nineteen, we will return to some of the questions raised at the outset about the adequacy of their historical arguments for a pluralist social order.

DOING THEOLOGY IN A REVOLUTIONARY SITUATION

The Kingdom of God, Utopia, and Historical Engagement

The relation between Christian eschatology and the Marxist vision of the future has been pointed out often enough. It is interesting to note that for Engels—who devoted quite a bit of attention to the origins and development of the Christian religion—there was an even more important similarity between early Christianity and the socialist movement. "The history of early Christianity," he writes, "has notable points of resemblance with the modern working-class movement."[21] He summarizes it in four points: both are originally a movement of oppressed people; both "preach forthcoming salvation from bondage and misery"; both are persecuted, discriminated, and despised, and both "forge victoriously, irresistibly ahead." He goes so far as to say that Christianity was the form in which socialism was possible and even became dominant within the historical possibilities of the first centuries. The unavoidably religious form that the rebellion of the oppressed took at that time meant that the hope for liberation was projected to another, heavenly world. In that sense, like all religious movements, it falls under the well-known Marxist criticism of being an imaginary substitute for real liberation. On the other hand, lacking the scientific instruments of analysis, its aspirations share the imaginary and fantastic features of utopian socialism.

There is no doubt that the ardent expectation of the total transformation of the world and the advent of the Kingdom of God was soon replaced in Christianity by a spirtualized and individualistic hope for immortal, celestial life. Whether and to what extent this transformation was due to the influence of the Hellenistic culture, to the delay of the *Parousia*, to the influence of the mystery religions, to the sociologically necessary phenomenon of the institutionalization of the *ecclesia* is for us at this point a question which can remain unanswered. What matters most is to realize the importance of the conception of two worlds: this present, temporal, earthly one, which had a preparatory, contingent, and even at points negligible value, and the eternal one which is the true realm of life, fulfillment and happiness, the goal for the Christian.

The connection between these two worlds came to be seen almost exclusively in terms of the moral and religious life of the individual. Temporal, collective life has no lasting significance except as it may help or hinder the individual to achieve and/or to express the religious and moral virtues which belong to the Christian life. The hope of the Kingdom, far from awakening an ethos to transform the world in the direction of that which was expected, worked as a deterrent for historical action. The Christian and the Marxist utopias (to use this equivocal word) had, therefore, quite opposite historical consequences. The latter galvanizes for action, the former leads to accommodation to present conditions; the latter lends value and meaning to history, the former empties history of meaning and value; the latter legitimizes immediate and provisory stages and achievements, the former relativizes them and makes differences among them irrelevant. Are these consequences intrinsic to the Christian gospel? If not, how can they be overcome, both theologically and practically? This is the issue that we have to explore.

The consideration of this question seems to me to involve at least three issues: the problems of the "two worlds" or, as we shall see, of the "two histories"; the possibility of an intrinsic, substantial—and not merely formal—connection between historical action and eschatological expectation, and the determination of the necessary historical mediations. We shall try in the remainder of this chapter to suggest an initial approach to these issues.

There is scarcely a question of "two histories" in relation to the Old Testament. There, God's action takes place in history and as history. It inextricably involves human action and, conversely, there is no human action reported outside the relation with God's purpose and word. This interconnection does not mean an equation between God's sovereignty and history, as if the former would justify or sacralize everything that happens—as in the rationalist optimism of Voltaire's Pangloss, or as if history would unambiguously fulfill God's will. But the distinction is conceived *polemically*: the lordship of Yahweh is an efficacious word which becomes history and creates history by convoking and rejecting men and peoples in relation to God's purpose. Thus, Yahweh's sovereignty does not appear in history as an abstract act or an interpretation but as announcement and commandment, as an announcement which convokes, as promise and judgment demanding and inviting a response. History is, precisely, this conflict between God and his people in the midst and in relation to all peoples.

Two more points must be emphasized in this connection. The first is that any separation between the brute facts of history and their prophetic interpretation is alien to the Bible and originates in the Greek epistemological split between brute facts and *logos*. The prophetic message is for the Old Testament an act and a factor in itself. It is not primarily destined to explain but to call, to invite, to condemn. I think it is possible to show that the liturgical and the didactic word belong in this same category. Secondly, we must stress the *political* character of this history, i.e., as action and word embracing the total life of the people and of peoples as collective entities and the reality of power. Every attempt to separate the political from the religious areas in the Old Testament is completely artificial. Even the more personal manifestations—like Moses' or Isaiah's vocation, the moving episode of Ruth and Naomi, the prayers of the Psalms—are indissolubly worked into this movement of the peoples and "God's people." God polemicizes with the peoples and through them. The covenant is sealed within this conflict. In the kings and judges, laws and worship, commerce and art, internal life and external relations of this people, Yahweh conflictively asserts his sovereignty by calling and rejecting, forgiving and punishing, and thus erecting the signs and the road of his coming final victory, his Kingdom.

Nobody can fail to see that we move into a somewhat different climate as we enter the New Testament, particularly the Pauline and Johannine literature. The question is to determine what is the difference. Some of the traditional explanations of this change seem to originate in Greek intellectualism and smack of Gnostic and Marcionite heresy. These are the explanations that claim that the New Testament is more spiritual or religious than the Old. We remain in the same area of ideas when the "individualism" of the New Testament is placed over against the "collectivism" of the Old. Modern theological research has amply refuted the basis for these interpretations—although, curiously enough, many times returning to them in other forms!

It is not enough, nevertheless, to reject false explanations. Where does, in fact, the difference in "climate" lie between the expectation of God's Kingdom and the movement of history in the Old and New Testament? I advance the following thesis. In the New Testament, the history of salvation acquires a certain "density" of its own, a certain "distance" in relation to the totality of human history. It is not—let us be clear about it—that we have now a separate history: it is still the story of Herod, of Pilate, or of the merchants of Ephesus. But as a new mission emerges, which is indissolubly tied to a particular historical nucleus (the history of Israel and of Jesus Christ), which becomes dated in time, the faith of the converted "heathen" becomes related to a twofold historical reference: their own history and this other one, which now comes to be constitutive for their faith. In other words, while the salvific memory or recollection of Israel was one with their historical memory as a people, with their historical project, the memory of the converted Gentile, without losing its connection with the latter, incorporates this other, "alien" history, the story of Israel and of Jesus the Christ. To confess the Kingdom is not for us, Gentile Christians, only to enter into the heritage of our own history but at the same time to take distance from it and to become engrafted into this other one. It is to confess the exodus, the exile, Bethel and Nazareth, the Golgotha and the tomb of Joseph of Arimathea as our own—and this not merely in their significance or in their exemplariness but in their particular and unrepeatable historicity. Consequently, an inevitable duality of histories appear. We Gentiles, in distinction to Israel, cannot believe without this double historical reference and, therefore, without asking ourselves how to relate God's action to this double historical reference in which the gospel involves us.

With some few and notable exceptions, the line of solution has been dualistic. With due reserve, we can trace it back to Augustine's *City of God.* Essentially, it consists in relating the Kingdom to one of these histories, the history of faith, which thus becomes a univocal, sacred, and distinct line, and in reducing the other history to a general episodic framework devoid of eschatological significance: a mere stage. It may be debated whether Augustine himself identifies the former history—that of the *civitas dei*—with the Church, but this does not matter so much in the present context. The decisive point is that this is the history of the Kingdom—whether it be identified with the hierarchical, the pious, or the orthodox Church.

This dualistic solution suffers from unsolvable difficulties. On the one hand, the continuity Church-Kingdom is untenable in view of the all too evident failures of the Church. How are we to dodge the fact that the history of faith shares quite plainly the characteristics of secular history and proves to be, in many ways, an empirically undistinguishable parcel of it? Here theologians have introduced all the theories about an invisible Church or the different sectarian solutions. But, on the other hand, neither can a total discontinuity between Kingdom and general history be maintained in view of the witness of Scripture and our own experience of God's presence in the world. It is difficult to read the Bible and to go on saying that general history is a mere episode, unrelated to the Kingdom, and without eschatological significance. . . .

Theologians of liberation have decidedly rejected the "dualistic" position. As we have seen, they strive to maintain the integrity of "one single God-fulfilled history," as Gutiérrez puts it. "Monist" formulations are not without precedent. Origen's and Irenaeus' theological perspectives—quite different from each other—can be counted in their camp. But it is in recent theology where a systematic attempt has been made to overcome dualism, as in [Jürgen] Moltmann and [Johannes] Metz, by stressing the historical significance of the eschatological expectation as critical questioning and, in our theology, the eschatological value of present historical praxis of liberation. God builds his Kingdom from and within human history in its entirety; his action is a constant call and challenge to man. Man's response is realized in the concrete arena of history with its economic, political, ideological options. Faith is not a different history but a dynamic, a motivation, and, in its eschatological horizon, a transforming invitation.

Very few responsible theologians would openly support today a clear dualistic approach. The God of the prophets and of Jesus Christ can hardly be assimilated to a Gnostic or mystic *soter* of a sect concerned with populating his Olympus with a few souls rescued from the stormy sea of history. The biblical account is clearly incompatible with a "religious" reductionism which consigns to the limbo of irrelevance the history of persons and peoples. But we must admit that theoretical and practical problems are not automatically solved by adopting a monistic solution. In order to give to this *one* history a concrete content, one must find a transcription of the gospel which can be seen as effectively operating in general history. In other words, it is necessary "to name the Kingdom" in the language of everyday human history. There is no lack of precedents and possibilities. As we have seen, we speak of "love," "liberation," "the new man" as the signs which allow us to identify the active sovereignty of God in history, the redeeming presence of Jesus Christ, and, consequently, the call and the obedience of faith. This, we contend, is biblically and theologically legitimate. But a serious risk lurks in this option, because, as these terms are historicized in the general history of mankind, they run the risk of being uprooted, of de-historicizing themselves in the particular historical reference of faith. That is, we come to speak of a love, a new man, a liberation in which the reference to the history of Israel, of Jesus Christ, of the Apostles becomes secondary, or merely exemplary, or dispensable. If this happens we have, in Christian terms, vacated any reference to God himself. What God and whose Kingdom are we speaking about? At the extreme of this line, we would conclude by deifying man and history and it would be more honest to call a spade a spade and to avow a total immanentism. This is not, to be sure, the intention of those of us who attempt to overcome dualism. But how can a theological and practical formulation avoid this risk without falling back on dualism? This is an important task for our theologians, which we cannot avoid.

The question which is posed for us is, in simple terms, how to describe the relation between the two historical references of faith without vacating either one. Or, how do we account for the eschatological significance of general human history? Or, again, how do we return to the eschatological Christian faith the historical dynamism which it seems to have lost?

Do historical happenings, i.e., historical human action in its diverse dimensions—political, cultural, economic—have any value in terms of the

Kingdom which God prepares and will gloriously establish in the Parousia of the Lord? If there is such a relation, how shall we understand it? And what is its significance for our action? . . .

[Míguez Bonino concludes that most contemporary theological views tend to reinforce "the dualistic relativizing of historical action." He then goes on to discuss how Paul's understanding of "body" and "resurrection" overcomes dualistic thinking.[22]]

The former concept [body] allows Paul to underline at the same time the continuity and discontinuity between present and risen life, a continuity in which the recognizable identity of the two is asserted together with the transformation of our present historical life. Such a transformation is not a disfiguration or denaturalization of our bodily life but its fulfillment, its perfecting, the elimination of corruptibility and weakness. As a matter of fact, bodily life reaches its true shape, its full meaning—communication, love, praise—in the resurrection. Resurrection, far from being the rescue of a spiritual element in human life, cleansing it from the bodily experience and identity obtained throughout life, is the total redemption of man, the true and unhindered realization of a bodily life cleansed from self-deception and self-seeking (flesh) and made perfect in transparent (glorious) singleness of purpose and experience (spiritual) and full community with God.

Another Pauline concept supplements the previous one: the concept of "works." Once the passion of the polemical age is over, we can again raise the question of the eschatological significance of human works performed in this life. It seems to me that, for Paul, the works fulfilled "in the body," in everyday historical life, have a future to the extent that they belong to the new order, the order of the world of the resurrection, the order of love. They have a future, not because of some merit attributed to them but because they belong to this new order. At the same time, these are works performed within the structures of history, as master or slave, as wife or husband, or son, or authority, or even as a missionary. The decisive Pauline distinction between the works of faith and the works of the law does not refer—it seems to me—to any discrimination between sacred and profane, or merely human and Christian works, but to the relation to the new age, which becomes explicit in love. Since Christ has risen and inaugurated a new realm of life, man's existence in love bears the marks of this new age and will find lasting fulfillment when this new age will become an unresisted and total realization.

For several reasons, into which we cannot enter now, Christian theology and ethics have separated human actions from their historical context and reduced them to their individual significance. Such narrowing seems quite strange to the biblical way of thinking, cast in the conception of eons or ages in which the divine purpose is fulfilled. When we overcome this reductionism it becomes quite normal to assert both continuity and discontinuity between history and the Kingdom of God of the same order as the continuity/discontinuity between earthly body/spiritual body. The Kingdom is not the denial of history but the elimination of its corruptibility, its frustrations, weakness, ambiguity—more deeply, its sin—in order to bring to full realization the true meaning of the communal life of man. In the same vein, historical "works" in all orders of life—social, economic, political—are permanent insofar as they belong to that order. At the same time, all possibilities of confusion are eliminated because, in one case as in the other, there is the intervening fact of judgment which divides, excludes, and cleanses ("burns") that which does not belong in the new age. The Kingdom is not—here we must deepen the meaning of the apocalyptic literature—the natural denouement of history. Quite the contrary, history arrives at the Kingdom through suffering, conflict, and judgment. But the Kingdom redeems, transforms, and perfects the "corporality" of history and the dynamics of love that has operated in it.

If these observations are true, any language which confines the relation between history and the Kingdom to the realm of image-reality remains inadequate. The Kingdom is not merely adumbrated, reflected, foreshadowed, or analogically hinted at in the individual and collective realizations of love in history, but actually present, operative, authentically—however imperfectly and partially—realized. The objections against expressions like "building" the Kingdom are legitimate protest against naive optimism or at times justified protection of the primacy of divine initiative. But they are usually cast in a quite unbiblical concept of God as a kind of machine programmed to produce certain facts (the incarnation, the Parousia) irrespective of the movement of history. Once we see divine initiative as that action of God within history and in historical terms which opens history toward the promise, we seem not only entitled but required to use the strong language of growth, realization, creation which, furthermore, is that of the prophets and apostles!

When this perspective is adopted, the main question which recent theology has been asking must also be shifted. Instead of asking, where is the Kingdom present or visible in today's history? we are moved to ask, how can I participate—not only individually but in a community of faith and in a history—in the coming world? The main problem is not noetic but, so to say, empirical. It has to do with an active response. The Kingdom is not an object to be known through adumbrations and signs that must be discovered and interpreted but a call, a convocation, a pressure that impels. History, in relation to the Kingdom, is not a riddle to be solved but a mission to be fulfilled. That mission, one must hasten to add, is not a mere accumulation of unrelated actions, but a new reality, a new life which is communicated in Christ, in the power of the Spirit. How can we participate, act out, *produce* the quality of personal and corporate existence which has a future, which possesses eschatological reality, which concentrates the true history? We face the question of historical mediations for our participation in the building of the Kingdom.

When we ask the question as to how to participate in the Kingdom in our historical action we are, to some extent, thrown back to the tension of the twofold reference of our faith, because the kind of action which corresponds to the Kingdom, has a permanent future, must be one which *names* this future and *corresponds to its quality*. It is therefore impossible to reduce proclamation to the efficacious action of love or vice-versa. Recent ecumenical discussion has frequently been quite agitated on this point. There have been advocates of proclamation and advocates of action. But it seems that much of this discussion is seriously misleading insofar as the two things are seen as either reconcilable through some sort of balance or the one subordinate to the other. Rather, we should see that both action and announcement are eschatologically significant, while their unity is not in our hands. The tension cannot therefore be overcome this side of the full realization of God's Kingdom. Only at that point will all proclamation and all action of love be rescued from their ambiguity, reunited, and perfectly manifested, in the biblical sense of this word. This eschatological unity of that which is named and that which is done is what is intended in the numerous biblical references to the surprising inversions at the Last Judgment. But we live in the tension of this double reference, which is one in Jesus Christ and at the end but never totally one in our experience.

To the extent that this last assertion is true, we have to qualify and correct the emphasis on "one single history." We may even have to ask whether this formulation does not suffer from the still strong influence of the Scholastic view of the relation between nature and grace in which the latter becomes a superstructure built on the basis of the former, with the corresponding danger of mystic absorption of the human into a divine order. Once we take notice of this criticism and accept the tension of the "double historical reference" of our faith, still we have to look at the ethical understanding of this twofoldness. At this point one of the main divergences between Latin American and European/North American theologians seems to surface. For the latter, it seems, the specific "Christ-reference" relativizes the "present" historical reference of our faith and action. . . .

[Míguez Bonino proceeds to show both his admiration for and the shortcomings of Moltmann's perspective. He points out that although Moltmann saw "a 'political theology of the cross' in opposition to the classical political theologies which glorified and sacralized power," he failed "to grasp the basic challenge of Latin American theological thought" and remained, therefore, "within the circle of European political theology." Moltmann's position is inadequate, according to Míguez Bonino, because he did not see the need for "a coherent and all-embracing method of sociopolitical analysis." Thus he never really identifies with the poor and dispossessed as members of an oppressed "class" of people, and never fully appreciates the fact that only "revolutionary action" will be able to bring true liberation. Rather, like other spokespersons of European theology, Moltmann attempts "to remain above right and left, ideologically neutral, independent of a structural analysis of reality."[23] Míguez Bonino asks, Why does this happen?]

We are told that this is the only way to avoid sacralizing a particular ideology or power structure. I think this is a crucial point, to which we must respond in two ways. On the one hand, it is indeed necessary to reject as strongly as possible any sacralization of ideology and system. In this respect, even such expressions as "materializations of God's presence" or "sacrament" seem to me to run the risk of mystical identifications; there must be no room for theocratic dreams of any sort either from right or from left. But it is important to stress that such a secularization of politics is to be attained not through a new idealism of Christian theology, but through a clear and coherent recognition of historical, analytical, and ideological mediations. There is no *divine* politics or economics. But this means that we must resolutely use the best *human* politics and economics at our disposal.

This brings us to the final point in the discussion. In order to carry through the process of de-sacralizing, of a true secularization of politics, we believe that the European theologians must de-sacralize their conception of "critical freedom" and recognize the human, ideological contents that it carries. When they conceive critical freedom as the form in which God's eschatological Kingdom impinges on the political realm, they are simply opting for *one* particular ideology, that of liberalism. This follows very clearly, for instance, from Metz's description of the process of freedom in the modern world, or from Moltmann's own sketch of "the liberations" (he himself stresses the plural) from the demonic circles. What emerges is one form of the liberal social-democratic project which progressive European theologians seem to cherish particularly. They may be totally justified in this choice. The only point is that it should not be camouflaged as "the critical freedom of the gospel" but analytically and ideologically presented and justified in human political terms in the same way as our own option for socialism and a Marxist analysis.

We must bring together and summarize several points and arguments developed in this chapter concerning the relation of God's Kingdom and our concrete engagement in a particular historical project and course of action. This summary is, to be sure, only a tentative one, offered for further dialogue, but at the same time it is offered as theses related to our own Christian existence in Latin America today.

1. The positive relation between God's Kingdom and man's historical undertaking justifies us in understanding the former as a call to engage ourselves actively in the latter. The gospel invites and drives us to make concrete historical options and assures them eschatological permanence insofar as they represent the quality of human existence which corresponds to the Kingdom. We can, therefore, within human history, engage with other men in action which is significant in terms of God's redemptive purpose, of his announced and promised future Kingdom.

2. God's judgment encompasses the totality of our human achievements. But this is not meant to deter us from participating in the human enterprise but to liberate us for it, because we know that within and through this enterprise he will rescue what is significant and destroy what is negative. There is, therefore, also a critical and polemical dimension in the Christian witness which consists in bringing to judgment the human situation and assuming its conflicts and contradictions in terms of the realization of God's announced purpose.

3. Such a polemical and engaged participation necessarily implies a judgment between historical alternatives. This judgment rests both on an understanding of the direction of God's redemptive will and an analytical and projective judgment of the present historical conditions. As to the former, although it is not possible to derive from the Scriptures any set of laws or principles for society, it is indeed possible and necessary to underline a *continuum*, a direction and a purpose in God's historical action as portrayed and interpreted in the Scriptures, which is conveyed through such expressions and symbols as "justice," "peace," "redemption" in their concrete biblical "illustrations." At the same time, it is equally necessary to stress the fact that such insights cannot be operative except in terms of historical projects which must incorporate, and indeed always do incorporate, an analytical and ideological human, secular, verifiable dimension.

4. The relation between the direction which we discover in God's witness in Scripture and tradition, the ideological projection which mobilizes man and gives a coherent project for action, and the analysis which guides and defines action is neither one-directional nor static. Science develops when

it sets for itself human goals. These, in turn, can only be envisaged as science discloses the nature of the historical and natural process. New human possibilities lead us to enlarge our understanding of the biblical witness—indeed, in evangelical terms, the Spirit discloses Jesus Christ to us as we engage in the concrete witness to his redeeming love. But also the love which belongs to God's Kingdom suggests further horizons for human life which act as magnetic poles or horizons of hope for kindling man's analytical and ideological imagination.

5. This action of faith in kindling imagination is what has been called "the utopian function" of Christian eschatology. The name is not correct to the extent that the Kingdom is not *utopian*: it has a place both in history and in God's eschatological time. Moreover, the mobilizing visions of the future are also not utopian in the sense that they define projectively (both negatively and positively) the possibility for which we work in the present. But, with these cautions, it can be said that the Christian faith provides today both a stimulus and a challenge for revolutionary action when it encourages us to look and work for historical realizations in the direction of the Kingdom in terms of justice, solidarity, the real possibility for men to assume responsibility, access of all men to the creation which God has given to man, freedom to create a human community through work and love, space to worship and play.

6. An eschatological faith makes it possible for the Christian to invest his life historically in the building of a temporary and imperfect order with the certainty that neither he nor his effort is meaningless or lost. In this context, the bold confession of the resurrection of the dead and the life everlasting is not a self-centered clinging to one's own life or a compensation for the sufferings of life or a projection of unfulfilled dreams but the confident affirmation of the triumph of God's love and solidarity with man, the witness to the enduring quality of man's responsible stewardship of creation and of his participation in love, the final justification of all fight against evil and destruction.

Church, People, and the Avant-Garde

. . . Is there an alternative theological framework? I think the question is not a purely theoretical one but a service demanded for the health of both the sociopolitical project and the faith of the Christians committed to it. We must be on our guard, at the same time, in order to avoid creating a purely artificial theological construction. The theological methodology we have defended requires that we develop theological theories in close relationship with the questions which arise out of the concrete historical praxis, and then look to the biblical and theological tradition in order that it may clarify such questions. The basic question posed for Christians politically committed is, in this respect, a certain tension, to which we have already alluded, in their relationships to a community of political engagement and to the community of Christian confession. In a very tentative and exploratory way I want to suggest a theological perspective which may help us to find our bearings in such a situation.

I think we must approach the theological tradition in terms of the relationship between the creational and the soteriological. Under the salutary influence of Karl Barth, most Protestant theology has practically buried this question under the epitaph of "natural theology." Barth's timely and needed defense of the freedom of the word does not, nevertheless, solve the problem, and he had himself to resort to notions like that of an *analogia fides*, and even *analogia relationis* to deal with the problems posed by ethics. We might ask whether we can't find a sound point of departure in the exploration of the relation between what some Reformed theologians called "the covenant of creation" and the "covenant of redemption."[24] Freely interpreted this would mean that mankind has been placed in a realm of responsibility which embraces a threefold free relationship to fellow men, to nature (the world), and to Yahweh (the God of the covenant). The Christian dispensation will then be understood in relation to such a covenant, as God's active will to restore man's relationships and responsibility, to reinstate him in his position as partner in the covenant of creation, to put him back again on the road of his self-realization.

The advantage of this approach is that it underlines the significance of the soteriological without swallowing up the creational. Christ is not seen as a mere step in man's progress as in some evolutionist visions or as a semi-Gnostic mystical principle as in some cosmic christologies. On the other hand, this approach must be carefully set within the dynamic perspective which recent biblical, particularly Old Testament, research has lifted up. If creation—and human reality within it—is seen as a static, ready-made thing, the Christian dispensation might appear as a purely restorational device (the two-story view) or as an independent supra-historical realm (the two-kingdom idea). But if we take seriously the dynamic dimension inherent in the covenant-prophetic theology, the picture is altogether different. Creation is the installation of a movement; it is an invitation and a command to man to create his own history and culture, creatively to transform the world and make it into his own house and to explore the configurations of human relationships available to him.

When the realm of creation is understood in the terms we have sketched, the soteriological notions of sin and redemption gain a new meaning. They are seen in their truly accidental but crucial importance. Jesus Christ does not come to superimpose a different, transcendent, or celestial reality on top of the realm of nature and history, but to reopen for man the will and the power to fulfill his historical vocation. He has not come to make man into a super-human being, or a religious creature, but to open to him the will and the power to be man. There is, to be sure, a certain provisionality and temporari-ness of the Christian dispensation implicit in this view. The German theolo-gian Dorothee Soelle has offered in this respect a very valuable insight in her distinction between Christ as substitute—somebody who totally and perma-nently takes the place of another in relation to some task or function—and as representative—a person who temporarily and within limitations takes the representation of another *until* he is able to take his own representation and *in order that* he may do so.[25] Jesus' freedom before God, his love for men, his power over nature are not an end in themselves, nor a merely substitutionary activity on our behalf but a truly representational function, in order that and until we ourselves may assume such relationships. Although we cannot here enter into a discussion of such christological interpretation, its New Testament ring will be easily perceived.

Faith in Christ is not, therefore, a step beyond humanity but toward it. "We are not men in order to be Christians, but Christians in order to be men."[26] In this soteriological order, the Church has a distinct but provisional and subordinate place. It is commissioned to proclaim God's salvation in Jesus Christ. This means, in traditional terms, the forgiveness of sins, namely, man's freedom in God's grace to take up again, in whatever circumstances and after whatever failure and destruction, the work committed to him in cre-ation. It means, also in traditional terms, the call to the sanctification of man, namely, the invitation to effective love and the freedom to love. The Church is itself when it witnesses to God's saving activity in Jesus Christ, that is, when it makes clear God's renewed authorization, commandment, and liber-ation to man to be human, to create his own history and culture, to love and to transform the world, to claim and exercise the glorious freedom of the children of God. The Church's distinct—and certainly scandalous—claim is that the fullness of this humanity is given in the explicit, faithful, and grateful acknowledgment of Jesus Christ.

Lest everything we have just said be misunderstood, two things must be made clear. The first is that proclamation and faith always take place in his-tory and as historically defined actions. In traditional philosophical language, we would say that there is no purely formal announcement of God's graceful invitation to man. It is always a concrete project for human existence, embodied—whether the Church is conscious of it or not—in a particular political, ideological option. It is, at the same time, an invitation to dare to be, in God's freedom, a lord or a servant, a bourgeois or a revolutionary, a man of yesterday or a man of tomorrow. And this is not merely done verbally but given in the total insertion of a Church in history, in its total praxis, in the way in which it is located and it locates itself in the power-field of contemporary historical conflicts. The question of proclamation is, therefore, always the question as to the praxis of faith of the Church, as to the historical option in which this faith is embodied. Transcendence, as we have already discussed, can only be found from within such a praxis, never as a super-added, disembodied x. The historical imprint of faith in a given human praxis—which may and should become visible—can only be recognized *by others* and *when it takes place*. It cannot be prescribed beforehand! This is—if I understand him correctly—what Bonhoeffer meant by "living before God as if God did not exist."

The second point to clarify has to do with the often debated question of the "men of good will" or the non-Christians who embrace the same liberating historical praxis. Curiously enough we have reversed the biblical concern with this problem. The service of love, the trust and goodness of the nonbeliever, is presented in the Bible not as a problem but as a sign of God's free and universal grace and as a call to repentance and conversion. Humility and praise, not confusion, is the proper response to the experience of the selflessness, generosity, and faithfulness of the nonbeliever who militates at our side. As an aside, one should add that this does not apply only to individuals and groups but to the total historical process. Why should we be concerned and bewildered when man takes into his own hands the humanization of life— physical and mental health, the regularization of nature, the future of the human race? Our only concern is for the full responsibility of man, not the vindication of some restricted sphere for God (and for ourselves as his representatives). Insofar as he really believes, the Christian is not afraid of becoming superfluous, as Jesus was not when he promised to his disciples: "He who believes in me will do the works I do, nay, he will do greater works than mine, because I go to the Father" (John 14:12). . . .

NOTES

[1] Selections from Chapters Seven and Eight of José Míguez Bonino's *Doing Theology in a Revolutionary Situation* (Philadelphia: Fortress Press, 1975).

[2] Gustavo Gutiérrez, *A Theology of Liberation*, trans. C. Inda and J. Eagleson (Maryknoll, NY: Orbis Books, 1973), 46.

[3] Míguez Bonino, *Doing Theology*, 147, 158.

[4] Enrique Dussel, *History and the Theology of Liberation*, trans. J. Drury (Maryknoll, N.Y.: Orbis Books, 1976), 104.

[5] Míguez Bonino, *Doing Theology*, 15.

[6] Quoted in *ibid.*, 46-7.

[7] Dussel, *History and Theology*, 134.

[8] José Míguez Bonino, *Christians and Marxists: The Mutual Challenge to Revolution* (Grand Rapids: Eerdmans Publishing Co., 1976), 110.

[9] Míguez Bonino, *Doing Theology*, 142.

[10] *Ibid.*

[11] *Ibid.*

[12] *Ibid.*, 133.

[13] *Ibid.*

[14] *Ibid.*, 138.

[15] *Ibid.*, 140-41.

[16] *Ibid.*, 143.

[17] *Ibid.*, 152. Enrique Dussel makes a similar comment regarding the unfolding of human life in freedom: "The mission of the Christian is not performed solely by building churches. It is carried out by participating in real-life history in its many different aspects. The kingdom of God is fashioned through these projects. If they are not carried out, the kingdom will never come. We must get rid of many of the false antinomies that still weigh down upon us." Dussel, *History*, 170.

[18] Míguez Bonino, *Doing Theology*, 152.

[19] *Ibid.*, 165.

[20] *Ibid.*

[21] The main documents here are Engels' articles "On the History of Early Christianity," published in the journal *Neue Zeit* I/1-2 (1894-1895), 4-13, 36-43. In English, *Marx and Engels on Religion* (Moscow: Foreign Language Publishing House, 1957), 313-343.

[22] Míguez Bonino develops this idea further in his "The Kingdom of God and History," in C. René Padilla, ed., *El Reino de Dios* (El Paso, TX: Junta Bautista de Publicaciones, 1974).

[23] Míguez Bonino's discussion of Moltmann is with reference to the latter's *Theology of Hope: On the Ground and Implications of a Christian Eschatology* (New York: Harper and Row, 1967), and *The Crucified God* (New York: Harper and Row, 1974).

[24] For this formulation I am particularly indebted to my colleague Lambert Schuurman. [Schuurman is a Dutch theologian living in Argentina.]

[25] Dorothee Soelle, *Christ the Representative* (London: S.P.C.K., 1969).

[26] The expression is often quoted by Lambert Schuurman.

II

SUBSIDIARITY, NATURAL LAW,
AND THE COMMON GOOD

SEVEN

THE RECENT CATHOLIC TRADITION:
AN INTRODUCTION TO THE READINGS

The response of the Roman Catholic community to individualist and collectivist ideologies that developed in the nineteenth century was quite different from the response of those pluralists who argued primarily "from history." The Catholic view of pluralism is also much older; it has roots that reach back to Greek thought as well as to the Bible.

Not all Catholics hold a uniform view of pluralism, of course. For example, Joseph de Maistre and Louis de Bonald, both Catholics, represented the so-called romantic-traditionalist movement that reacted to the French Revolution with appeals for recovery of the *ancien régime*.[1] Félicité de Lamennais was another influential Catholic who protested the radicalism of the French Revolution early in the nineteenth century. But Lamennais was not a reactionary. He was among the first to call his Church to an open acceptance of the democratic longings of the French people.[2] Yet none of these thinkers—Maistre, Bonald, or Lamennais—represented what came to be recognized as official Catholic social philosophy. To discover that perspective, we must turn to the statements of the Catholic Church and to those scholars who were most influential in developing and articulating its point of view.

In this chapter, we have selected five documents to illustrate the Catholic view of social pluralism. The documents include two papal encyclicals—

Rerum Novarum (1891) from Pope Leo XIII and *Quadragesimo Anno* (1931) from Pope Pius XI; a selection from Jacques Maritain's *Man and the State* (1951); a selection from the Pastoral Constitution promulgated by the bishops of the Second Vatican Council in Rome—*The Church in the World Today* (1965); and selections from the American Catholic Bishops' pastoral letter *Economic Justice for All* (1986).

Many of the insights and principles evident in nineteenth- and twentieth-century Catholic social philosophy are not new in the sense of being unique to the period following the French Revolution and the rise of liberalism. Two of the concepts that figure prominently in the following readings—natural law and the common good—were of central importance to Thomas Aquinas (1225–1274). In response to the challenges of secularizing liberalism and socialism, modern Catholic social thought returned with new vigor and adaptive creativity to the work of Aquinas in order to address the needs of contemporary industrializing and differentiating societies.

Natural law is one of four forms of law that Aquinas analyzed in his *Summa Theologiae* (The Sum of Theology).[3] The other three are the "eternal law," which Aquinas identifies with God's reason that governs the universe; "divine law," which represents God's Word as revealed in the Old and New Testament; and "human law," which is an ordinance of reason promulgated by one who has responsibility for a community.[4] Natural law is the medium by which eternal law imprints itself on human law. It is a reflection of divine reason in created things; it is the "participation of the eternal law in the rational creature."[5] Natural law represents, according to Aquinas, the "natural inclination" of things and persons to act properly and seek their proper end.[6]

According to St. Thomas and traditional Catholicism, human reason is capable of discovering the natural truth about the necessity of a differentiated social order. The "light of reason is placed by nature in every man, to guide him in his acts towards his end."[7] This movement toward the natural fulfillment of human life can only be achieved in human community. Thomas believed that it was "natural for man, more than for any other animal, to be a social and political animal, to live in a group."[8] Moreover, the truth about human social life is that it is pluriform, displaying many different kinds of human relationships and capabilities.

The "social nature of man" becomes obvious, for example, in the fact that the solitary person cannot procure the necessities of life. And just as this lack of self-sufficiency leads to group activity, the inability of smaller groups to be self-sufficient leads to a highly differentiated order where different groups emerge to fulfill different "natural purposes." Aquinas summarizes his view of societal differentiation this way:

Now since man must live in a group, because he is not sufficient unto himself to
procure the necessities of life were he to remain solitary, it follows that a society
will be the more perfect the more it is sufficient unto itself to procure the necessities of life. There is, to some extent, sufficiency for life in one family or one
household, namely, in so far as pertains to the natural acts of nourishment and
the begetting of offspring and other things of the kind. Self-sufficiency exists,
furthermore, in one street with regard to those things which belong to the trade
of one guild. In a city, which is the perfect community, it exists with regard to
all the necessities of life. Still more self-sufficiency is found in a province because of the need of fighting together and of mutual help against enemies.[9]

defense → fed. gov't today

Human reason is capable of discovering not only the natural necessity of
a differentiated social order but also the truth of its hierarchical structure. In
nature, human beings stand at the pinnacle of a hierarchical order of creation.

ordained by God

The *telos* (end or purpose) of the person, unlike the end or purpose of lower
animals and inanimate things, must be achieved through reason. Only humans, as rational creatures, participate in divine reason and provide deliberately for their own and others' well being. All other creatures—irrational animals and inanimate things—merely display divine reason as they move in-
stinctually or by physical necessity toward their natural *telos*. Human freedom
is displayed by the fact that the *telos* of human life can be either accepted or
denied, either pursued or rejected. Only human creatures have this freedom
of choice.

Applying the Aristotelian principle that "the whole is of necessity prior to
the part," Aquinas arrived at the conclusion that in a logical and philosophical
sense "every multitude is derived from unity."[10] Since the body politic represents the unity (whole) of the natural order, the multitude of groups within
the body politic are parts within the whole. The person is thus a social or
communal animal destined to live in an hierarchy of social groupings. The
family exists at the base of the social hierarchy which reaches its natural fullness and self-sufficiency in political community.

The philosophy of Thomas Aquinas corresponded in many respects to
the realities of life in the late Middle Ages—a social reality made up of artisans, farmers, soldiers, lords, and a diversified institutional arrangement of
families, guilds, villages, and the Church. This differentiated social order and
the diversification of human tasks was the direct result, according to Aquinas,
of the decree of providence and the laws of nature.

The diversification of men for diverse tasks is the result, primarily, of divine
providence, which details the various compartments of man's life in such a way
that nothing necessary to human existence is ever lacking; secondarily, this diversification proceeds from natural causes which bring it about that different

men are born with aptitudes and tendencies for the different functions and the various ways of living.[11]

Aquinas was also convinced, however, that since a person's deepest need and longing is for the knowledge and enjoyment of God, even the bonds of political society are not ultimately sufficient. Though political society represents the most complete human community (*societas perfecta*) in temporal reality, it is surpassed by, and subject to, a supra-temporal society, a divine community which represents the supernatural destiny of human beings. Thus Aquinas believed that the full and final end of human creatures is not natural but rather supernatural—the Kingdom of God; and the proper end of society is the virtuous life understood in its richest Christian sense.[12]

Since all creatures strive naturally for their proper end or destiny, then the proper end of temporal life coincides with the common good of society even as the proper end of eternal life is communion with God through the Church. Indeed, for Aquinas "every law [natural law included] is ordained to the common good."[13] The rights of individuals and of the various communities within the political society come to expression in the common good, which is, in a sense, the fundamental law of society. The common good is the realization and guarantee of all fundamental rights and obligations. It is the concrete expression of the moral order and it functions as an authentic ethical standard. The common good represents sociability itself, the peace of society, the balance, harmony, and stability of the many relationships in society. It truly represents the good of the whole.

Given the importance of natural law and the concept of the common good in the thought of Aquinas, it is not surprising that both have continued to play a prominent role in Catholic pluralist thinking ever since the revival of Thomism at the end of the nineteenth century. At the same time, Catholic social thought has been dynamic and adaptive. New formulations have emerged which sharpen the distinction between a Catholic understanding of a differentiated societal order and that of both individualism and collectivism. One such formulation can be found in the principle that Pope Pius XI refers to as the "subsidiary function" of society.

The principle of subsidiarity is concerned broadly with the harmonious relationship among persons and institutions (autonomous in their own peculiar spheres) in a hierarchically ordered society.[14] With respect to institutions, for example, the rational law of nature dictates, and the common good requires, that the lower or smaller societies depend on the higher or more self-sufficient societies for the ordering activities and support that they cannot provide for themselves. Although there are higher and lower institutions,

↙ discovered thru reason over history

each has its proper realm of activity and authority, its task to perform, and its
rights to be protected.

The concept of subsidiarity is thus <u>concerned with the normative rela-</u>
<u>tionship among many societal entities</u>. It is important to emphasize that the
principle of subsidiarity (which literally means supplementary, furnishing aid
or help, auxiliary) is applicable to every human and institutional relationship
in society.[15] Although the term subsidiarity was not used or explicitly defined
until Pius XI wrote *Quadragesimo Anno* in 1931, the concept goes back to
Thomas Aquinas and is present, though not by name, in Leo XIII's famous
1891 encyclical, *Rerum Novarum*.

In the readings that follow, we will see the creative development of
Catholic social teaching from the 1890s to the 1980s as it seeks to give normative guidance to the Church and society alike. Building on Thomist philosophy, Catholic teaching becomes increasingly expansive and adaptive as its
leading proponents use the principles of natural law, common good, and subsidiarity to deal with the growing democratization, urbanization, and economic interdependence of modern societies.

NOTES

[1] Romanticism was an international movement which swept Europe as a humanist
reaction to the rationalist currents of the eighteenth century. Traditionalism is a name
given to a particular philosophical and theological expression of Romanticism born in
France in response to the Revolution of 1789.

[2] Lamennais was a complex person—at different times a monarchist, an ultramontane,
a religious liberal, and a messianic revolutionary. It is clear, however, that when he
directed the daily newspaper *L'Avenir* (1830-31), he was committed to a social perspective
which embraced freedom of conscience, separation of church and state, educational
freedom, liberty of the press, the freedom to associate, the introduction of popular
suffrage, and the abolishment of state centralization. For a fuller discussion of the career
and thought of Lamennais see Peter Stearns, *Priest and Revolutionary: Lamennais and the
Dilemma of French Catholicism* (New York: Harper and Row, 1967); John Oldfield, *The
Problem of Tolerance and Social Existence in the Writings of Félicité Lamennais, 1809-1831*
(Leiden: E. J. Brill, 1973); Alec R. Vidler, *Prophecy and Papacy: A Study of Lamennais, The
Church and The Revolution* (New York: Charles Scribner's Sons, 1954); Robert A. Nisbet,
"The Politics of Social Pluralism: Some Reflections on Lamennais," *The Journal of Politics*,
10 (1948): 764-786; and Hans Maier, *Revolution and Church: The Early History of Christian
Democracy, 1789-1901* trans. E. Schossberger (Notre Dame: University of Notre Dame
Press, 1969), 165-201.

[3] Thomas Aquinas, *Summa Theologiae*, I-II, qq. 90-95. Excerpts from this section can
be found in Dino Bigongiari, ed. *The Political Ideas of St. Thomas Aquinas: Representative
Sections* (New York: Hafner Publishing Company, 1953). All references below to the writings of Aquinas are from this work unless otherwise noted.

[4] *Ibid.*, 11-16.

⁵ *Ibid.*, 13.

⁶ *Ibid.*

⁷ *Ibid.*, 175.

⁸ *Ibid.*

⁹ *Ibid.*, 178-179. This social perspective reflects Aristotelian doctrine wedded to medieval historical realities.

¹⁰ *Ibid.*, 180.

¹¹ Aquinas, *Quaestiones quodlibetales*, quoted in *ibid.*, 7.

¹² Aquinas's belief that the proper *telos* is the first and foremost principle of causality was borrowed from Aristotle who maintained that the "nature of a thing is its end." An analysis of the influence of Aristotle on Aquinas along with an evaluation of such concepts as the common good and natural law can be found in John F. Cox, *A Thomistic Analysis of the Social Order*, (Washington, D.C.: The Catholic University of America Press, 1943). See also Etienne Gilson, *The Philosophy of St. Thomas Aquinas*, trans. E. Bullough; ed. G. Elrington (New York: Arno Press, 1979 [1937]), 9-23.

¹³ Bigongiari, *Political Ideas*, 7.

¹⁴ The concept of "subsidiarity" combines two principles in Catholic social thought: autonomy and hierarchy. The latter concept emphasizes the *duty* of the higher societal entities towards lower ones and the lower to the higher; the former concept stresses the right of every person and institution to its own integrity as regards the fulfillment of its own *telos* and functions in society. In other words, "individuals and social groups have the right to achieve, undisturbed, their nature-given tasks." Cox, *A Thomistic Analysis*, 118. The idea of distinct spheres of society is intrinsic to a Catholic concept of a differentiated social order.

¹⁵ Cox defines subsidiarity and comments on the positive and negative function of the principle in the following passage:

> This principle may be stated briefly with a stress on its functional character as follows: *every social function by its nature and concept is subsidiary*. This word '*subsidiary*' is derived from the *subsidiarius*, which properly means 'of or belonging to a reserve.' The '*reserves*' in the Roman army were the auxiliary corps held in waiting on the third line of battle for the purpose of meeting possible emergencies or demands. From this original application, this Latin word and its English derivative have come to mean 'supplementary,' furnishing aid, 'auxiliary.' Both of these meanings bring out well the sense of the principle under discussion. *To be by nature and concept subsidiary* means that every social action must be a supplementary help; and that every social group must be a complementary entity, in the sense that its very reason for existence is the supplying of auxiliary aid; this aid is summoned forth, like the reserve action of the Roman Legion, not to initiate action, but *to strengthen, reinforce, and perfect that which has already begun*. The negative side of this principle implies that the social objective cannot consist in absorbing, destroying or replacing its members, for these annihilative tendencies would be incompatible with society's true role, which is help, supplementation and completion.

Cox, *A Thomistic Analysis*, 117-118.

EIGHT

✸✸✸✸✸✸✸✸✸✸

RERUM NOVARUM
(ON THE CONDITION OF WORKERS)[1]
Encyclical Letter of Pope Leo XIII

Pope Leo XIII

Throughout the nineteenth century the Catholic Church came under increasing political and intellectual attack. Never before had so many of its fundamental premises been questioned or denied. The rise of the modernist movement and the popularization of liberalism, socialism, and Darwinism came at a time when the Church was also being challenged by nationalist movements in Italy and several of the most powerful national states in the rest of Europe. In Italy, Mazzini and Cavour championed Italian nationalism and directed armies against the last remnants of the Pope's temporal rule. In France, the anti-clerical crusade of the Third Republic militantly opposed the participation of Catholics in the public life of the state. This anti-clericalism was manifested in a series of laws which converted all schools in France into extensions of the secular state. In Germany, the Church was engaged in a bitter struggle against Bismark's policy of centralization. And in England there were voices like Gladstone's which led the attack against the Church for its supposedly antidemocratic views.

Against this background, leaders of the Catholic Church took up the task of strengthening the philosophical defenses of the faith and addressing the political, social, and economic problems of the day. This new offensive was

characterized by a clear critique of the foundations of contemporary individualist and collectivist social philosophies and by the attempt to establish a pluralist alternative.

The Catholic leader who introduces a coherent and eloquent defense of
the faith and a positive program for dealing with what became known as the
"social question" is Pope Leo XIII.[2] His encyclical *Rerum Novarum* (1891) is
recognized by many to be "the Magna Charta of the Social Order."[3] This description was first applied to that letter by Pope Pius XI who recognized that
it was more than a discussion of "the relative rights and mutual duties of the
rich and of the poor, of capital and of labor."[4] Pius XI later saw in *Rerum
Novarum* a fundamental discussion of the nature and structure of society and
realized that Leo XIII's real objective was nothing less than the restoration or
re-establishment of a traditional social order. For this reason Pius XI gave the
title "On Reconstructing the Social Order" to his own encyclical *Quadragesimo Anno*, published in 1931 on the fortieth anniversary of *Rerum
Novarum*. A study of these two encyclicals provides important insight into a
Catholic understanding of societal pluralism, as it developed up to the 1930s.[5]

In *Rerum Novarum* Leo XIII clearly distinguishes a pluralist social philosophy from individualism and collectivism—the "twin rocks of shipwreck"—
as Pius XI later called them in *Quadragesimo Anno*.[6] In the case of individualism, Leo XIII points out that this false ideology has produced a situation in
which "working men have been surrendered, isolated and helpless, to the
hard-heartedness of employers and the greed of unchecked competition."[7] He
believes that an individualist social philosophy lies behind the current popu-
larity of both political liberalism and laissez-faire economic policies.
Liberalism produces a society in which the conduct of trade is concentrated
in the hands of a few individuals "so that a small number of very rich men
have been able to lay upon the teeming masses of the laboring poor a yoke
little better than that of slavery itself."[8] Of particular importance to Leo XIII is
the fact that eighteenth-century individualism had left workers "isolated and
helpless" because it had destroyed associations such as the guilds.

Both Leo XIII and Pius XI realize that while it is necessary to avoid the
Scylla of individualism it is equally important to steer clear of the Charybdis
of collectivism. In reaction to individualism, which asserts that the state has
few if any legitimate tasks to perform in such areas as economic organization
and planning, socialists want to take society in a collectivist direction, affirming the nearly universal responsibility of the state. This position, the Papacy
warns, should also be rejected. The state must not be allowed to do for individuals and other institutions what they can do for themselves. Leo XIII's
conclusion in *Rerum Novarum*, which he had stated in even more detail in his

encyclical *On The Christian Constitution of States* (*Immortale Dei*, 1885), is that although the legitimate authority of the state must be upheld, it should not be allowed to interfere with the lawful rights and tasks of other institutions such as the family. Such rights and tasks are equally derived from God and exist prior to the state.[9] "We have said that the State must not absorb the individual or the family; both should be allowed free and untrammeled action as far as is consistent with the common good and the interest of others."[10]

Pope Leo XIII has the concept of subsidiarity in mind when, following Aquinas, he differentiates the body politic from the many private societies that exist within it and discusses the proper function of the state in relationship to the private societies. The body politic exists for the common good; the private societies (family, school, labor association, and others) exist within its bosom and are called private "since their immediate purpose is the private advantage of the associates."[11]

> "Now, a private society," says St. Thomas again, "is one which is formed for the purpose of carrying out private objects; as when two or three enter into partnership with the view of trading in common." Private societies, then, although they exist within the body politic, and are severally part of the commonwealth, cannot nevertheless be absolutely, and as such, prohibited by public authority. For, to enter into a "society" of this kind is the natural right of man; and the State has for its office to protect natural rights, not to destroy them; and, if it forbid its citizens to form associations, it contradicts the very principle of its own existence, for both they and it exist in virtue of the like principle, namely, the natural tendency of man to dwell in society.[12]

Two important distinctions are evident in this passage. One distinction is between the body politic (public/political society) and the private societies that exist as parts within it. The second distinction is between the body politic and the state. The state exists within the body politic, but unlike all private societies the state has as its special concern the public interest of the whole. Once these distinctions are recognized, the principle of the subsidiarity of the state, though not by name, becomes easier to identify in the passage.[13]

One of the "subordinate groups" that the state should recognize and protect, according to Leo XIII, is the workingmen's unions—those associations "consisting either of workmen alone, or of workmen and employers together."[14] While the Pope recognizes in the guild structure of the Middle Ages a just and balanced provision for consumer and producer, and shared responsibility between master guildmen, journeymen, and apprentices, it would be a mistake to conclude that he is interested in returning to an earlier period of history. Leo XIII believes that guilds cannot be reproduced in an age increasingly dominated by large-scale industry. His concern is to find ways to incorporate what he judges to be the normative spirit and motivation of the ancient guilds into the economic structures of his day. The guilds of olden times afforded many advantages to the arts and the artisans. "Such unions should be suited to the requirements of this age—an age of wider education, of different habits, and of far more numerous requirements in daily life."[15] Leo XIII immediately goes on to argue that labor associations represent the natural impulse of persons to unite together and, therefore, they "exist of their own right."[16] They are not the creatures of the state.

The social teachings of Leo XIII provided the opening in France and in the rest of Europe for the formation of Catholic social study groups, labor unions, and, eventually, political parties.[17] By the time of Pius XI, several Christian political parties were already in full flower as Christian Democratic parties. One of their basic concerns was to see the implementation of public policies based upon the pluralist social philosophy of *Rerum Novarum* and *Quadragesimo Anno*. By means of direct political involvement of many who held such views, a particular vision of a differentiated societal order came to exercise a significant influence well beyond the confines of the Catholic community.[18]

RERUM NOVARUM
(ON THE CONDITION OF WORKERS)

1. That the spirit of revolutionary change, which has long been disturbing the nations of the world, should have passed beyond the sphere of politics and made its influence felt in the cognate sphere of practical economics is not surprising. The elements of the conflict now raging are unmistakable, in the vast expansion of industrial pursuits and the marvelous discoveries of science; in the changed relations between masters and workmen; in the enormous fortunes of some few individuals, and the utter poverty of the masses; in the increased self-reliance and closer mutual combination of the working classes; as also, finally, in the prevailing moral degeneracy. The momentous gravity of the state of things now obtaining fills every mind with painful apprehension; wise men are discussing it; practical men are proposing schemes; popular meetings, legislatures, and rulers of nations are all busied with it—actually there is no question which has taken a deeper hold on the public mind.

2. Therefore, venerable brethren, as on former occasions when it seemed opportune to refute false teaching, We have addressed you in the interests of the Church and of the common weal, and have issued letters bear-

ing on political power, human liberty, the Christian constitution of the State, and like matters, so have We thought it expedient now to speak on the condition of the working classes.[19] It is a subject on which We have already touched more than once, incidentally. But in the present letter, the responsibility of the apostolic office urges Us to treat the question of set purpose and in detail, in order that no misapprehension may exist as to the principles which truth and justice dictate for its settlement. The discussion is not easy, nor is it void of danger. It is no easy matter to define the relative rights and mutual duties of the rich and of the poor, of capital and of labor. And the danger lies in this, that crafty agitators are intent on making use of these differences of opinion to pervert men's judgments and to stir up the people to revolt.

3. In any case we clearly see, and on this there is general agreement, that some opportune remedy must be found quickly for the misery and wretchedness pressing so unjustly on the majority of the working class: for the ancient working-men's guilds were abolished in the last century, and no other protective organization took their place. Public institutions and the laws set aside the ancient religion. Hence, by degrees it has come to pass that working men have been surrendered, isolated and helpless, to the hard-heartedness of employers and the greed of unchecked competition. The mischief has been increased by rapacious usury, which, although more than once condemned by the Church, is nevertheless, under a different guise, but with like injustice, still practiced by covetous and grasping men. To this must be added that the hiring of labor and the conduct of trade are concentrated in the hands of comparatively few; so that a small number of very rich men have been able to lay upon the teeming masses of the laboring poor a yoke little better than that of slavery itself.

4. To remedy these wrongs the socialists, working on the poor man's envy of the rich, are striving to do away with private property, and contend that individual possessions should become the common property of all, to be administered by the State or by municipal bodies. They hold that by thus transferring property from private individuals to the community, the present mischievous state of things will be set to rights, inasmuch as each citizen will then get his fair share of whatever there is to enjoy. But their contentions are so clearly powerless to end the controversy that were they carried into effect the working man himself would be among the first to suffer. They are, moreover, emphatically unjust, for they would rob the lawful possessor, distort the functions of the State, and create utter confusion in the community.

5. It is surely undeniable that, when a man engages in remunerative labor, the impelling reason and motive of his work is to obtain property, and

thereafter to hold it as his very own. If one man hires out to another his strength or skill, he does so for the purpose of receiving in return what is necessary for the satisfaction of his needs; he therefore expressly intends to acquire a right full and real, not only to the remuneration, but also to the disposal of such remuneration, just as he pleases. Thus, if he lives sparingly, saves money, and, for greater security, invests his savings in land, the land, in such case, is only his wages under another form; and, consequently, a working man's little estate thus purchased should be as completely at his full disposal as are the wages he receives for his labor. But it is precisely in such power of disposal that ownership obtains, whether the property consist of land or chattels. Socialists, therefore, by endeavoring to transfer the possessions of individuals to the community at large, strike at the interests of every wage-earner, since they would deprive him of the liberty of disposing of his wages, and thereby of all hope and possibility of increasing his resources and of bettering his condition in life.

6. What is of far greater moment, however, is the fact that the remedy they propose is manifestly against justice. For, every man has by nature the right to possess property as his own. This is one of the chief points of distinction between man and the animal creation, for the brute has no power of self-direction, but is governed by two main instincts, which keep his powers on the alert, impel him to develop them in a fitting manner, and stimulate and determine him to action without any power of choice. One of these instincts is self-preservation, the other the propagation of the species. Both can attain their purpose by means of things which lie within range; beyond their verge the brute creation cannot go, for they are moved to action by their senses only, and in the special direction which these suggest. But with man it is wholly different. He possesses, on the one hand, the full perfection of the animal being, and hence enjoys at least as much as the rest of the animal kind, the fruition of things material. But animal nature, however perfect, is far from representing the human being in its completeness, and is in truth but humanity's humble handmaid, made to serve and to obey. It is the mind, or reason, which is the predominant element in us who are human creatures; it is this which renders a human being human, and distinguishes him essentially from the brute. And on this very account—that man alone among the animal creation is endowed with reason—it must be within his right to possess things not merely for temporary and momentary use, as other living things do, but to have and to hold them in stable and permanent possession; he must have not only things that perish in the use, but those also which, though they have been reduced into use, continue for further use in after time.

7. This becomes still more clearly evident if man's nature be considered a little more deeply. For man, fathoming by his faculty of reason matters without number, linking the future with the present, and being master of his own acts, guides his ways under the eternal law and the power of God, whose providence governs all things. Wherefore, it is in his power to exercise his choice not only as to matters that regard his present welfare, but also about those which he deems may be for his advantage in time yet to come. Hence, man not only should possess the fruits of the earth, but also the very soil, inasmuch as from the produce of the earth he has to lay by provision for the future. Man's needs do not die out, but forever recur; although satisfied today, they demand fresh supplies for tomorrow. Nature accordingly must have given to man a source that is stable and remaining always with him, from which he might look to draw continual supplies. And this stable condition of things he finds solely in the earth and its fruits. There is no need to bring in the State. Man precedes the State, and possesses, prior to the formation of any State, the right of providing for the sustenance of this body.

[Paragraphs 8-10 elaborate on the argument for private ownership and against those who deny this right.]

11. With reason, then, the common opinion of mankind, little affected by the few dissentients who have contended for the opposite view, has found in the careful study of nature, and in the laws of nature, the foundations of the division of property, and the practice of all ages has consecrated the principle of private ownership, as being pre-eminently in conformity with human nature, and as conducing in the most unmistakable manner to the peace and tranquility of human existence. The same principle is confirmed and enforced by the civil laws—laws which, so long as they are just, derive from the law of nature their binding force. The authority of the divine law adds its sanction, forbidding us in severest terms even to covet that which is another's: "Thou shalt not covet thy neighbor's wife; nor his house, nor his field, nor his manservant, nor his maid-servant, nor his ox, nor his ass, nor anything that is his."[20]

12. The rights here spoken of, belonging to each individual man, are seen in much stronger light when considered in relation to man's social and domestic obligations. In choosing a state of life, it is indisputable that all are at full liberty to follow the counsel of Jesus Christ as to observing virginity, or to bind themselves by the marriage tie. No human law can abolish the natural and original right of marriage, nor in any way limit the chief and principal purpose of marriage ordained by God's authority from the beginning: "Increase and multiply."[21] Hence we have the family, the "society" of a man's house—a society very small, one must admit, but none the less a true society,

and one older than any State. Consequently, it has rights and duties peculiar to itself which are quite independent of the State.

13. That right to property, therefore, which has been proved to belong naturally to individual persons, must in like wise belong to a man in his capacity of head of a family; nay, that right is all the stronger in proportion as the human person receives a wider extension in the family group. It is a most sacred law of nature that a father should provide food and all necessaries for those whom he has begotten; and, similarly, it is natural that he should wish that his children, who carry on, so to speak, and continue his personality, should be by him provided with all that is needful to enable them to keep themselves decently from want and misery amid the uncertainties of this mortal life. Now, in no other way can a father effect this except by the ownership of productive property, which he can transmit to his children by inheritance. A family, no less than a State, is, as We have said, a true society, governed by an authority peculiar to itself, that is to say, by the authority of the father. Provided, therefore, the limits which are prescribed by the very purposes for which it exists be not transgressed, the family has at least equal rights with the State in the choice and pursuit of the things needful to its preservation and its just liberty. We say, "at least equal rights"; for, inasmuch as the domestic household is antecedent, as well in idea as in fact, to the gathering of men into a community, the family must necessarily have rights and duties which are prior to those of the community, and founded more immediately in nature. If the citizens, if the families, on entering into association and fellowship, were to experience hindrance in a commonwealth instead of help, and were to find their rights attacked instead of being upheld, society would rightly be an object of detestation rather than of desire.

14. The contention, then, that the civil government should at its option intrude into and exercise intimate control over the family and the household is a great and pernicious error. True, if a family finds itself in exceeding distress, utterly deprived of the counsel of friends, and without any prospect of extricating itself, it is right that extreme necessity be met by public aid, since each family is a part of the commonwealth. In like manner, if within the precincts of the household there occur grave disturbance of mutual rights, public authority should intervene to force each party to yield to the other its proper due; for this is not to deprive citizens of their rights, but justly and properly to safeguard and strengthen them. But the rulers of the commonwealth must go no further; here, nature bids them stop. Paternal authority can be neither abolished nor absorbed by the State; for it has the same source as human life itself. "The child belongs to the father," and is, as it were, the continuation of the father's personality; and speaking strictly, the child takes

its place in civil society, not of its own right, but in its quality as member of the family in which it is born. And for the very reason that "the child belongs to the father" it is, as St. Thomas Aquinas says, "before it attains the use of free will, under the power and the charge of its parents."[22] The socialists, therefore, in setting aside the parent and setting up a State supervision, act against natural justice, and destroy the structure of the home.

15. And in addition to injustice, it is only too evident what an upset and disturbance there would be in all classes, and to how intolerable and hateful a slavery citizens would be subjected. The door would be thrown open to envy, to mutual invective, and to discord; the sources of wealth themselves would run dry, for no one would have any interest in exerting his talents or his industry; and that ideal equality about which they entertain pleasant dreams would be in reality the leveling down of all to a like condition of misery and degradation.

Hence, it is clear that the main tenet of socialism, community of goods, must be utterly rejected, since it only injures those whom it would seem meant to benefit, is directly contrary to the natural rights of mankind, and would introduce confusion and disorder into the commonweal. The first and most fundamental principle, therefore, if one would undertake to alleviate the condition of the masses, must be the inviolability of private property. This being established, we proceed to show where the remedy sought for must be found.

[In paragraphs 16-30 the argument is developed that the Church, rulers of States, employers, the wealthy, and workers all have a responsibility in solving the "social question." Before this can happen, however, the belief that there is an intrinsic struggle between classes must be rejected. This false assumption must be replaced by a clearer understanding of the mutual duties and responsibilities that individuals owe to each other. The Church has a unique power to encourage the bonds of friendship and brotherly love, and to apply the principles of the gospel to human needs and the institutional life of society. The only way society is to be healed, Leo XIII argues, is to "return to Christian life and Christian institutions."]

31. It cannot, however, be doubted that to attain the purpose we are treating of, not only the Church, but all human agencies, must concur. All who are concerned in the matter should be of one mind and according to their ability act together. It is with this, as with the providence that governs the world; the results of causes do not usually take place save where all the causes co-operate.

It is sufficient, therefore, to inquire what part the State should play in the work of remedy and relief.

32. By the State we here understand, not the particular form of government prevailing in this or that nation, but the State as rightly apprehended; that is to say, any government conformable in its institutions to right reason and natural law, and to those dictates of the divine wisdom which we have expounded in the encyclical *On the Christian Constitution of the State*. The foremost duty, therefore, of the rulers of the State should be to make sure that the laws and institutions, the general character and administration of the commonwealth, shall be such as of themselves to realize public well-being and private prosperity. This is the proper scope of wise statesmanship and is the work of the rulers. Now a State chiefly prospers and thrives through moral rule, well-regulated family life, respect for religion and justice, the moderation and fair imposing of public taxes, the progress of the arts and of trade, the abundant yield of the land—through everything, in fact, which makes the citizens better and happier. Hereby, then, it lies in the power of a ruler to benefit every class in the State, and amongst the rest to promote to the utmost the interests of the poor; and this in virtue of his office, and without being open to suspicion of undue interference—since it is the province of the commonwealth to serve the common good. And the more that is done for the benefit of the working classes by the general laws of the country, the less need will there be to seek for special means to relieve them.

33. There is another and deeper consideration which must not be lost sight of. As regards the State, the interests of all, whether high or low, are equal. The members of the working classes are citizens by nature and by the same right as the rich; they are real parts, living the life which makes up, through the family, the body of the commonwealth, and it need hardly be said that they are in every city very largely in the majority. It would be irrational to neglect one portion of the citizens and favor another, and therefore the public administration must duly and solicitously provide for the welfare and the comfort of the working classes; otherwise, that law of justice will be violated which ordains that each man shall have his due. To cite the wise words of St. Thomas Aquinas: "As the part and the whole are in a certain sense identical, so that which belongs to the whole in a sense belongs to the part."[23] Among the many and grave duties of rulers who would do their best for the people, the first and chief is to act with strict justice—with that justice which is called *distributive*—toward each and every class alike.

34. But although all citizens, without exception, can and ought to contribute to that common good in which individuals share so advantageously to themselves, yet it should not be supposed that all can contribute in the like way and to the same extent. No matter what changes may occur in forms of government, there will ever be differences and inequalities of condition in the

State. Society cannot exist or be conceived of without them. Some there must be who devote themselves to the work of the commonwealth, who make the laws or administer justice, or whose advice and authority govern the nation in times of peace, and defend it in war. Such men clearly occupy the foremost place in the State, and should be held in highest estimation, for their work concerns most nearly and effectively the general interest of the community. Those who labor at a trade or calling do not promote the general welfare in such measure as this, but they benefit the nation, if less directly, in a most important manner. We have insisted, it is true, that, since the end of society is to make men better, the chief good that society can possess is virtue. Nevertheless, it is the business of a well-constituted body politic to see to the provision of those material and external helps "the use of which is necessary to virtuous action."[24] Now, for the provision of such commodities, the labor of the working class—the exercise of their skill, and the employment of their strength, in the cultivation of the land, and in the workshops of trade—is especially responsible and quite indispensable. Indeed, their co-operation is in this respect so important that it may be truly said that it is only by the labor of working men that States grow rich. Justice, therefore, demands that the interest of the working classes should be carefully watched over by the administration, so that they who contribute so largely to the advantage of the community may themselves share in the benefits which they create—that being housed, clothed, and bodily fit, they may find their life less hard and more endurable. It follows that whatever shall appear to prove conducive to the well-being of those who work should obtain favorable consideration. There is no fear that solicitude of this kind will be harmful to any interest; on the contrary, it will be to the advantage of all, for it cannot but be good for the commonwealth to shield from misery those on whom it so largely depends for the things that it needs.

35. We have said that the State must not absorb the individual or the family; both should be allowed free and untrammeled action so far as is consistent with the common good and the interests of others. Rulers should, nevertheless, anxiously safeguard the community and all it members; the community, because the conservation thereof is so emphatically the business of the supreme power, that the safety of the commonwealth is not only the first law, but it is a government's whole reason of existence; and the members, because both philosophy and the Gospel concur in laying down that the object of the government of the State should be, not the advantage of the ruler, but the benefit of those over whom he is placed. As the power to rule comes from God, and is, as it were, a participation in His, the highest of all sovereignties,

it should be exercised as the power of God is exercised—with a fatherly solic-itude which not only guides the whole, but reaches also individuals.

36. Whenever the general interest or any particular class suffers, or is threatened with harm, which can in no other way be met or prevented, the public authority must step in to deal with it. Now, it is to the interest of the community, as well as of the individual, that peace and good order should be maintained; that all things should be carried on in accordance with God's laws and those of nature; that the discipline of family life should be observed and that religion should be obeyed; that a high standard of morality should prevail, both in public and private life; that justice should be held sacred and that no one should injure another with impunity; that the members of the commonwealth should grow up to man's estate strong and robust, and capa-ble, if need be, of guarding and defending their country. If by a strike of workers or concerted interruption of work there should be imminent danger of disturbance to the public peace; or if circumstances were such as that among the working class the ties of family life were relaxed; if religion were found to suffer through the workers not having time and opportunity afforded them to practice its duties; if in workshops and factories there were danger to morals through the mixing of the sexes or from other harmful occasions of evil; or if employers laid burdens upon their workmen which were unjust, or degraded them with conditions repugnant to their dignity as human beings; finally, if health were endangered by excessive labor, or by work unsuited to sex or age—in such cases, there can be no question but that, within certain limits, it would be right to invoke the aid and authority of the law. The limits must be determined by the nature of the occasion which calls for the law's interference—the principle being that the law must not undertake more, nor proceed further, than is required for the remedy of the evil or the removal of the mischief.

37. Rights must be religiously respected wherever they exist, and it is the duty of the public authority to prevent and to punish injury, and to pro-tect every one in the possession of his own. Still, when there is question of defending the rights of individuals, the poor and badly off have a claim to es-pecial consideration. The richer class have many ways of shielding them-selves, and stand less in need of help from the State; whereas the mass of the poor have no resources of their own to fall back upon, and must chiefly de-pend upon the assistance of the State. And it is for this reason that wage-earn-ers, since they most belong in the mass of the needy, should be specially cared for and protected by the government.

[Paragraphs 38-47 consider what the common good and justice require for working conditions, hours of employment, wages, and so forth.]

48. In the last place, employers and workmen may of themselves effect much, in the matter We are treating, by means of such associations and organizations as afford opportune aid to those who are in distress, and which draw the two classes more closely together. Among these may be enumerated societies for mutual help; various benevolent foundations established by private persons to provide for the workman, and for his widow or his orphans, in case of sudden calamity, in sickness, and in the event of death; and institutions for the welfare of boys and girls, young people, and those more advanced in years.

49. The most important of all are workingmen's unions, for these virtually include all the rest. History attests what excellent results were brought about by the artificers' guilds of olden times. They were the means of affording not only many advantages to the workmen, but in no small degree of promoting the advancement of art, as numerous monuments remain to bear witness. Such unions should be suited to the requirements of this our age—an age of wider education, of different habits, and of far more numerous requirements in daily life. It is gratifying to know that there are actually in existence not a few associations of this nature, consisting either of workmen alone, or of workmen and employers together, but it were greatly to be desired that they should become more numerous and more efficient. We have spoken of them more than once, yet it will be well to explain here how notably they are needed, to show that they exist of their own right, and what should be their organization and their mode of action.

50. The consciousness of his own weakness urges man to call in aid from without. We read in the pages of holy Writ: "It is better that two should be together than one; for they have the advantage of their society. If one fall he shall be supported by the other. Woe to him that is alone, for when he falleth he hath none to lift him up."[25] And further: "A brother that is helped by his brother is like a strong city."[26] It is this natural impulse which binds men together in civil society; and it is likewise this which leads them to join together in associations which are, it is true, lesser and not independent societies, but, nevertheless, real societies.

51. These lesser societies and the larger society differ in many respects, because their immediate purpose and aim is different. Civil society exists for the common good, and hence is concerned with the interest of all in general, albeit with individual interest also in their due place and degree. It is therefore called a *public* society, because by its agency, as St. Thomas of Aquinas says, "Men establish relations in common with one another in the setting up of a commonwealth."[27] But societies which are formed in the bosom of the commonwealth are styled *private*, and rightly so, since their immediate pur-

pose is the private advantage of the associates. "Now, a private society," says St. Thomas again, "is one which is formed for the purpose of carrying out private objects; as when two or three enter into partnership with the view of trading in common.[28] Private societies, then, although they exist within the body politic, and are severally part of the commonwealth, cannot nevertheless be absolutely, and as such, prohibited by public authority. For, to enter into a "society" of this kind is the natural right of man; and the State has for its office to protect natural rights, not to destroy them; and, if it forbid its citizens to form associations, it contradicts the very principle of its own existence, for both they and it exist in virtue of the like principle, namely, the natural tendency of man to dwell in society.

52. There are occasions, doubtless, when it is fitting that the law should intervene to prevent certain associations, as when men join together for purposes which are evidently bad, unlawful, or dangerous to the State. In such cases, public authority may justly forbid the formation of such associations, and may dissolve them if they already exist. But every precaution should be taken not to violate the rights of individuals and not to impose unreasonable regulations under pretense of public benefit. For laws only bind when they are in accordance with right reason, and, hence, with the eternal law of God.[29]

53. And here we are reminded of the confraternities, societies, and religious orders which have arisen by the Church's authority and the piety of Christian men. The annals of every nation down to our own days bear witness to what they have accomplished for the human race. It is indisputable that on grounds of reason alone such associations, being perfectly blameless in their objects, possess the sanction of the law of nature. In their religious aspect they claim rightly to be responsible to the Church alone. The rulers of the State accordingly have no rights over them, nor can they claim any share in their control; on the contrary, it is the duty of the State to respect and cherish them, and, if need be, to defend them from attack. It is notorious that a very different course has been followed, more especially in our own times. In many places the State authorities have laid violent hands on these communities, and committed manifold injustice against them; it has placed them under control of the civil law, taken away their rights as corporate bodies, and despoiled them of their property. In such property the Church had her rights, each member of the body had his or her rights, and there were also the rights of those who had founded or endowed these communities for a definite purpose, and, furthermore, of those for whose benefit and assistance they had their being. Therefore We cannot refrain from complaining of such spoliation as unjust and fraught with evil results; and with all the more reason do We complain because, at the very time when the law proclaims that association is

free to all, We see that Catholic societies, however peaceful and useful, are hampered in every way, whereas the utmost liberty is conceded to individuals whose purposes are at once hurtful to religion and dangerous to the commonwealth.

54. Associations of every kind, and especially those of working men, are now far more common than heretofore. As regards many of these there is no need at present to inquire whence they spring, what are their objects, or what the means they employ. Now, there is a good deal of evidence in favor of the opinion that many of these societies are in the hands of secret leaders, and are managed on principles ill-according with Christianity and the public well-being; and that they do their utmost to get within their grasp the whole field of labor, and force working men either to join them or to starve. Under these circumstances Christian working men must do one of two things: either join associations in which their religion will be exposed to peril, or form associations among themselves and unite their forces so as to shake off courageously the yoke of so unrighteous and intolerable an oppression. No one who does not wish to expose man's chief good to extreme risk will for a moment hesitate to say that the second alternative should by all means be adopted.

55. Those Catholics are worthy of all praise—and they are not a few—who, understanding what the times require, have striven, by various undertakings and endeavors, to better the condition of the working class by rightful means. They have taken up the cause of the working man, and have spared no efforts to better the condition both of families and individuals; to infuse a spirit of equity into the mutual relations of employers and employed; to keep before the eyes of both classes the precepts of duty and the laws of the Gospel—the Gospel which, by inculcating self-restraint, keeps men within the bounds of moderation, and tends to establish harmony among the divergent interests and the various classes which compose the body politic. It is with such ends in view that we see men of eminence, meeting together for discussion, for the promotion of concerted action, and for practical work. Others, again, strive to unite working men of various grades into associations, help them with their advice and means, and enable them to obtain fitting and profitable employment. The bishops, on their part, bestow their ready good-will and support; and with their approval and guidance many members of the clergy, both secular and regular, labor assiduously in behalf of the spiritual interests of the members of such associations. And there are not wanting Catholics blessed with affluence, who have, as it were, cast in their lot with the wage-earners, and who have spent large sums in founding and widely spreading benefit and insurance societies, by means of which the working man may without difficulty acquire through his labor not only many present

advantages, but also the certainty of honorable support in days to come. How greatly such manifold and earnest activity has benefited the community at large is too well known to require Us to dwell upon it. We find therein grounds for most cheering hope in the future, provided always that the associations We have described continue to grow and spread, and are well and wisely administered. The State should watch over these societies of citizens banded together in accordance with their rights, but it should not thrust itself into their peculiar concerns and their organization, for things move and live by the spirit inspiring them, and may be killed by the rough grasp of a hand from without.

[The encyclical concludes, in paragraphs 56-64, by detailing the nature, structure, and tasks of Catholic working-men's associations. Such associations, says Leo XIII, can be of incalculable service to society, and an effective witness of the need to re-establish Christian morals in society.]

NOTES

[1] Selections from *Rerum Novarum* (May 15, 1891) in *The Church Speaks to the Modern World: The Social Teachings of Leo XIII*, edited, annotated, and with an introduction by Etienne Gilson (Garden City, New York: Doubleday and Company, Inc., 1954). Gilson's translation is based on the translation published by the Catholic Truth Society of London. Variants found in the footnotes in Gilson's edition have been deleted. All references to *Rerum Novarum* are from this volume.

[2] With respect to "the social question," Pope Leo XIII writes: "The elements of the conflict now raging are unmistakable, in the vast expansion of industrial pursuits and the marvelous discoveries of science; in the changed relations between masters and workmen; in the enormous fortunes of some few individuals, and the utter poverty of the masses; in the increased self-reliance and closer mutual combination of the working classes; as also, finally, in the prevailing moral degeneracy." *Rerum Novarum*, 205.

[3] A year before his death in 1903, Leo XIII wrote an apostolic letter on the occasion of the twenty-fifth anniversary of his election to the Holy See. This letter indicated that nine of his social encyclicals form a doctrinal body. The first of the nine encyclicals was foundational for his entire perspective: *On Christian Philosophy* (*Aeterni Patris*, 1879). In it the Pope declared that true social reformation is possible only on the basis provided by the doctrines of Thomas Aquinas. It was to the philosophical synthesis of the Angelic Doctor—the medieval effort to reconcile Greek philosophy (reason) and Christian teaching (revelation)—that Leo XIII turned for guidance in addressing the pressing intellectual and social problems of his day. See Emmet John Hughes, *The Church and the Liberal Society* (Notre Dame: University of Notre Dame Press, 1961 [1944]); A. R. Vidler, *A Century of Social Catholicism* (London: Faber & Faber, 1964); and Hans Maier, *Revolution and Church: The Early History of Christian Democracy, 1789-1901*, trans. E. Schossberger (Notre Dame: University of Notre Dame Press, 1969), 178-289.

[4] *Rerum Novarum*, 206.

[5] For a detailed comparison and analysis of *Rerum Novarum* and *Quadragesimo Anno*, see Joseph Husslein, *The Christian Social Manifesto: An Interpretative Study of the Encycli-

cals Rerum Novarum and Quadragesimo Anno, 5th ed. (Milwaukee: The Bruce Publishing Company, 1939). An overview of the Church's social teachings can be found in Jean-Yves Calvez and Jacques Perrin, *The Church and Social Justice: The Social Teachings of the Popes from Leo XIII to Pius XII* (Chicago: Henry Regnery Co., 1961). For a more contemporary analysis of Catholic social thought see Charles E. Curran, *American Catholic Social Ethics: Twentieth Century Approaches* (Notre Dame: University of Notre Dame Press, 1982); Michael Novak, *Freedom With Justice: Catholic Social Thought and Liberal Institutions* (New York: Harper & Row, 1984).

6 Pope Pius XI, *Quadragesimo Anno*, in Terence P. McLaughlin, ed., *The Church and the Reconstruction of the Modern World: The Social Encyclicals of Pope Pius XI* (New York: Doubleday & Co., 1957), 234. All references to *Quadragesimo Anno* are from this volume.

7 *Rerum Novarum*, 206.

8 *Ibid.*, 206-207.

9 In *Rerum Novarum* Leo XIII is quite explicit concerning the rights of individuals and institutions such as the family. He declares: "Man is older than the State and he holds the right of providing for the life of his body prior to the formation of any state," and "Thus we have the family—the 'society' of a man's own household; a society limited indeed in numbers, but a true 'society,' anterior to every kind of State or nation, with rights and duties of its own, totally independent of the commonwealth." *Ibid.*, 171, 173.

10 *Ibid.*, 224.

11 *Ibid.*, 232. The Church is the only institution which stands above the whole/part relationship. This is because it is the only institution of supernatural origin. All other institutions, including the state, are of natural origin. There was no doubt, therefore, in Pope Leo's mind that of all the institutions the Church possessed "the most exalted of all authority." A full discussion of Leo XIII's understanding of Church/State relations can be found in his encyclicals *On the Christian Constitution of States* and *On Christian Citizenship*.

12 *Rerum Novarum*, 232-233.

13 The distinction between the body politic and the state is easier to recognize in the Latin language. Latin has several different words to designate what is sometimes translated into the one English word "state." For example, *civitas* means the body politic or public society while *res publica* represents the politically organized society (state) which possesses the topmost authority within the body politic. Unfortunately, since the English word "state" is used to translate both *civitas* and *res publica*, it is sometimes difficult to determine from the English text the Latin original. These terms and their usage receive special attention from Jacques Maritain in the selection from his writings below.

14 *Rerum Novarum*, 232.

15 *Ibid.*

16 *Ibid.*

17 The last of the great social encyclicals of Leo XIII is *Christian Popular Action* (*Graves de Communi*, 1901). It has generally become known throughout the English-speaking world under the title "Christian Democracy." For an excellent introduction to Christian Democratic organizational movements, see Michael P. Fogarty, *Christian Democracy in Western Europe: 1820-1953* (Westport, CT: Greenwood Press, 1974 [1957]).

18 As already noted, forty years after the promulgation of *Rerum Novarum* Pope Pius XI repeated the appeal for social justice in the encyclical *Quadragesimo Anno*. In 1967, Pope Paul VI described the new global dimension of justice in his *Populorum Progressio*. Then in 1971 he stressed that many of the original demands made in *Rerum Novarum* still, unfortunately, needed repeating. Ten years later (1981) Pope John Paul II echoed this same thought in his encyclical *On Human Work* (*Laborem Exercens*) published to celebrate the ninetieth anniversary of *Rerum Novarum*.

[19] The title sometimes given to this encyclical, *On the Condition of Workers* (or the "Working Classes"), is therefore perfectly justified. A few lines after this sentence, the Pope gives a more comprehensive definition of the subject of *Rerum Novarum*, namely, the "relative rights and mutual duties of the rich and of the poor, of capital and of labor."

[20] Deuteronomy 5:21.

[21] Genesis 1:28.

[22] Thomas Aquinas, *Summa Theologiae*, IIa-IIae, q. x, art. 12, Answer.

[23] *Ibid.*, IIa-IIae, q. lxi, art. 1, ad 2m.

[24] Thomas Aquinas, *On the Governance of Rulers*, 1, 15 (*Opera omnia*, ed. Vives, vol. 27, p. 356).

[25] Ecclesiastes 4:9-10.

[26] Proverbs 18:19.

[27] Aquinas, *Contra impugnantes Dei cultum et religionem*, Part 2, ch. 8 (*Opera omnia*, ed. Vives, vol. 29, p. 16).

[28] *Ibid.*

[29] "Human law is law only by virtue of its accordance with right reason; and thus it is manifest that it flows from the eternal law. And in so far as it deviates from right reason it is called an unjust law; in such case it is no law at all, but rather a species of violence." Aquinas, *Summa Theologiae*, Ia-IIae, q. xciii, art. 3, ad 2m.

NINE

QUADRAGESIMO ANNO
(ON RECONSTRUCTING THE SOCIAL ORDER)[1]

Encyclical Letter of Pope Pius XI

Pope Pius XI

The papal encyclical *Rerum Novarum* of Leo XIII became so important in European Catholic circles that 40 years later, in 1931, Pope Pius XI commemorated it in his own letter *Quadragesimo Anno*. World War I had radically challenged expectations of political and economic progress. Communism was growing as a challenge to all established orders in Europe. The "social question" had not yet been adequately answered by Christians. The challenge of *Rerum Novarum* to individualism and collectivism inspired Pius XI to continue the effort to advance Catholic social teaching along pluralist lines.

The influence of individualism in Europe, Pius charges, has resulted in the overthrow and near extinction of that rich social life which was once highly developed through associations of various kinds.[2] After the destruction of the many intermediate associations, nothing remains but individuals and the state. Pius XI is convinced that this development has proved disastrous, not only for workingmen, but for the entire institutional character of society. Institutions, such as the state, though not destroyed, have their identity so distorted that they can no longer fulfill their proper task in society. The state is no longer capable of establishing, preserving, and promoting the common good because "with the taking over of all the burdens which the wrecked associations once bore, the State has been overwhelmed and crushed by almost infinite tasks and duties."[3]

In response to the havoc wreaked by individualist excesses on the social order, socialism comes in to promise the reordering of community, the benefits of equality, and the end of earthly misery arising from mass poverty. The only adequate response to this false gospel is a thoroughly Christian answer that carries with it a realistic and fully developed social philosophy. Pope Leo XIII, depending on Thomas Aquinas, points us in the correct direction, and now we must continue to develop that teaching, according to Pope Pius XI.

The common good and the universal law of nature attest to the proper place of persons and institutions and to the harmony and balance among them in the social order. Throughout *Quadragesimo Anno* Pius XI grounds a differentiated social order in natural law which upholds, reinforces, and sanctions the common good. His concern for the relationship among many different entities in society is expressed in the principle of subsidiarity. The concept of subsidiarity assumes that the body politic has a hierarchical order. At the apex is a transcendent God, and all creatures and institutions are subordinated to him in a descending order, each bound to fulfill its task within society. In this view, each of the lesser and subordinate communities has privileges, rights, and duties; each exercises a certain measure of control within its own sphere; and each is a source of help to the others when necessary and/or appropriate.

In 1931, Pope Pius XI for the first time formally uses the phrase "subsidiary function," referring to it as "that most weighty principle, which cannot be set aside or changed. . . ."[4]

> Just as it is gravely wrong to take from individuals what they can accomplish by their own initiative and industry and give it to the community, so also it is an injustice and at the same time a grave evil and disturbance of right order to assign to a greater and higher association what lesser and subordinate organizations can do. For every social activity ought of its very nature to furnish help to the members of the body social [politic] and never destroy and absorb them.[5]

In the very next paragraph of *Quadragesimo Anno* Pius XI applies the general principle of subsidiarity to the specific function and task of the state in the political society.

> The supreme authority of the State ought, therefore, to let subordinate groups handle matters and concerns of lesser importance which would otherwise dissipate its efforts greatly. Thereby the State will more freely, powerfully and effectively do all those things which belong to it alone because it alone can do them: directing, watching, urging, restraining, as occasion requires and necessity demands. Therefore, those in command should be sure that the more perfectly a

graduated order is preserved among the various associations, in observance of the principle of "subsidiary function," the stronger social authority and effectiveness will be, and the happier and more prosperous the condition of the State.[6]

For Pius XI, as for Leo XIII, the state plays an important role in a political society characterized by a differentiated yet integrated order of authority, power, and dignity.

Pius XI reemphasizes Leo XIII's judgment concerning the importance of labor associations which are "a matter of private order and private right."[7] He contrasts his view of corporate organizations based on vocations with the syndicates and corporations of his day which are in fact nothing more than organs of a centralized state.[8] Mussolini, for example, had 22 Italian corporations established by law in 1934 (one for every major branch of production). They functioned directly under the sponsorship of the state as its means of bringing about "the integral, organic and unitary discipline of the productive forces."[9]

Pope Pius XI's concern to see corporations function as proper organs of society and independent of the state must be contrasted with the fascist version of a corporative regime. The corporations the Pope advocates are to be essentially autonomous, self-governing bodies, with the door opened to state intervention only in cases of unresolvable conflict between employees and employers. They should not be mere tools of a centralized state. Pius XI recognizes that the principle of corporatism can be abused. He shares the concern of those who fear that the state under Mussolini is trying to dominate rather than aid (as a subsidiary function) economic groups, and that the corporative character of the Italian state is excessively bureaucratic and political. According to Pius XI,

> We are compelled to say that to Our certain knowledge there are not wanting some who fear that the State, instead of confining itself as it ought to the furnishing of necessary and adequate assistance, is substituting itself for free activity; that the new syndical and corporative order savors too much of an involved and political system of administration; and that . . . it rather serves particular political ends than leads to the reconstruction and promotion of a better social order.[10]

There is ambiguity, however, in Pius XI's judgment concerning the Italian corporative state. In *Quadragesimo Anno* the Pope does approve the way Mussolini is able to settle industrial conflicts and suppress "socialist organizations and their activities."[11] It is understandable, then, why fascists pointed to the encyclical to justify their views. At the same time it is a mistake to identify the papal view of corporatism with that of fascist collectivism.[12] Papal concern is to see corporations function as independent entities in society, acting as buffers against every form of centralizing force.[13] A pluralist society, one based on natural law, structured according to the principle of subsidiarity, and directed to the common good, is the type of non-totalitarian society envisioned by Pius XI—a society characterized by a diversity of free institutions.

QUADRAGESIMO ANNO
(ON RECONSTRUCTING THE SOCIAL ORDER)

1. Forty years have passed since Leo XIII's peerless encyclical *Rerum novarum* first saw the light, and the whole Catholic world, filled with grateful recollection, is undertaking to commemorate it with befitting solemnity.

2. Other encyclicals of Our predecessor had in a way prepared the path for that outstanding document and proof of pastoral care: namely, those on the family and the holy sacrament of matrimony as the source of human society,[14] on the origin of civil authority[15] and its proper relations with the Church,[16] on the chief duties of Christian citizens,[17] against the tenets of Socialism,[18] against false teachings on human liberty,[19] and others of the same nature fully expressing the mind of Leo XIII. Yet the encyclical *Rerum novarum*, compared with the rest, had this special distinction that, at a time when it was most opportune to do so, it laid down for all mankind the surest rules to solve rightly that difficult problem of human relations called "the social question."

3. For toward the close of the nineteenth century, the new kind of economic life that had arisen and the new developments of industry had gone to the point in most countries that human society was clearly becoming divided more and more into two classes. One class, very small in number, was enjoying almost all the advantages which modern inventions so abundantly provided; the other, embracing the huge multitude of working people, oppressed by wretched poverty, was vainly seeking escape from the straits wherein it stood.

4. Quite agreeable, of course, was this state of things to those who, in their abundant riches, thought it the result of inevitable economic laws and accordingly, as if it were for charity to veil the violation of justice which lawmakers not only tolerated but at times sanctioned, wanted the whole care of supporting the poor committed to charity alone. The workers, on the other hand, crushed by their hard lot, were barely enduring it, and were refusing

longer to bend their necks beneath so galling a yoke; and some of them, carried away by the heat of evil counsel, were seeking the overthrow of everything, while others, whom Christian training restrained from such evil designs, stood firm in the judgment that much in this had to be wholly and speedily changed.

5. The same feeling was shared by those many Catholics, both priests and laymen, whom a truly wonderful charity had long spurred on to relieve the unmerited poverty of the non-owning workers, and who could in no way convince themselves that so enormous and unjust an inequality in the distribution of this world's goods truly conforms to the designs of the all-wise Creator.

6. Those men were without question sincerely seeking an immediate remedy for this lamentable disorganization of States and a secure safeguard against worse dangers. Yet such is the weakness of even the best of human minds that, now rejected as dangerous innovators, now hindered in the good work by their very associates advocating other courses of action and, uncertain in the face of various opinions, they were at a loss which way to turn.

7. In such a sharp conflict of minds, therefore, while the question at issue was being argued this way and that, and not always with calmness, all eyes as often before turned to the Chair of Peter, to that sacred depository of all truth whence words of salvation pour forth to all the world. And to the feet of Christ's Vicar on earth were flocking in unaccustomed numbers men well versed in social questions, employers, and workers themselves, begging him with one voice to point out finally the safe road to them.

8. The wise Pontiff long weighed all this in his mind before God; he summoned the most learned and experienced to counsel; he pondered the issues carefully and from every angle. At last, admonished "by the consciousness of His Apostolic Office,"[20] lest silence on his part might be regarded as failure in his duty,[21] he decided, in virtue of the divine teaching office entrusted to him, to address not only the whole Church of Christ but all mankind.

9. Therefore on the fifteenth of May, 1891, that long-awaited voice thundered forth; neither daunted by the arduousness of the problem, nor weakened by age, but with vigorous energy, it taught the whole human family to strike out upon new paths in the social question.

[Paragraphs 10-15 of the encyclical point out that Leo XIII's understanding and solution of the social question represented a rejection of both liberalism and socialism. Although *Rerum novarum* was openly received by many, there were those who bitterly opposed Leo's social philosophy. Thus on the fortieth anniversary of *Rerum novarum* Pius XI argues that it is time to recall the benefits of the encyclical, to defend its teachings against certain doubts, to develop Leo XIII's views on certain points, including contemporary economic issues and socialism, and to demonstrate the root cause for the existing social confusion and emphasize once again the fact that true reform requires "the Christian reform of morals." Pius XI announced that these topics would be addressed under three main headings: (1) "Benefits Which Have Come From *Rerum Novarum*" (paras. 16-40); (2) "Authority of Church In Social And Economic Matters" (paras. 41-98); (3) "Great Changes Since Leo's Time" (paras. 99-149). We continue here with paras. 76-98 dealing with the restoration of the social order.]

Social Order To Be Restored

76. What We have thus far stated regarding an equitable distribution of property and regarding just wages concerns individual persons and only indirectly touches social order, to the restoration of which, according to the sublime precepts of the law of the Gospel, Our predecessor Leo XIII devoted all his thought and care.

77. Still, in order that what he so happily initiated may be solidly established, that what remains to be done may be accomplished, and that even more copious and richer benefits may accrue to the family of mankind, two things are especially necessary: reform of institutions and correction of morals.

78. When We speak of the reform of institutions, the State comes chiefly to mind, not as if universal well-being were to be expected from its activity, but because things have come to such a pass through the evil of what We have termed "individualism" that, following upon the overthrow and near extinction of that rich social life which was once highly developed through associations of various kinds, there remain virtually only individuals and the State. This is to the great harm of the State itself; for, with a structure of social governance lost, and with the taking over of all the burdens which the wrecked associations once bore, the State has been overwhelmed and crushed by almost infinite tasks and duties.

79. As history abundantly proves, it is true that on account of changed conditions many things which were done by small associations in former times cannot be done now save by large associations. Still, that most weighty principle, which cannot be set aside or changed, remains fixed and unshaken in social philosophy: Just as it is gravely wrong to take from individuals what they can accomplish by their own initiative and industry and give it to the community, so also it is an injustice and at the same time a grave evil and dis-

turbance of right order to assign to a greater and higher association what lesser and subordinate organizations can do. For every social activity ought of its very nature to furnish help to the members of the body social and never destroy and absorb them.

80. The supreme authority of the State ought, therefore, to let subordinate groups handle matters and concerns of lesser importance which would otherwise dissipate its efforts greatly. Thereby the State will more freely, powerfully and effectively do all those things which belong to it alone because it alone can do them: directing, watching, urging, restraining, as occasion requires and necessity demands. Therefore, those in command should be sure that the more perfectly a graduated order is preserved among the various associations, in observance of the principle of "subsidiary function," the stronger social authority and effectiveness will be, and the happier and more prosperous the condition of the State.

Mutual Cooperation Of Industries And Professions

81. First and foremost, the State and every good citizen ought to look to and strive toward this end: that the conflict between the hostile classes be abolished, and harmonious cooperation of the Industries and Professions be encouraged and promoted.

82. The social policy of the State, therefore, must devote itself to the reestablishment of the Industries and Professions. In actual fact, human society now, for the reason that it is founded on classes with divergent aims and hence opposed to one another and therefore inclined to enmity and strife, continues to be in a violent condition and is unstable and uncertain.

83. Labor, as Our predecessor explained well in his encyclical,[22] is not a mere commodity. On the contrary, the worker's human dignity in it must be recognized. It therefore cannot be bought and sold like a commodity. Nevertheless, as the situation now stands, hiring and offering for hire in the so-called labor market separate men into two divisions, as into battle lines, and the contest between these divisions turns the labor market itself almost into a battlefield where, face to face, the opposing lines struggle bitterly. Everyone understands that this grave evil which is plunging all human society to destruction must be remedied as soon as possible. But complete cure will not come until this opposition has been abolished and well-ordered members of the social body—Industries and Professions—are constituted, in which men may have their place, not according to the position each has in the labor market but according to the respective social functions which each performs. For under nature's guidance it comes to pass that just as those who are joined

together by nearness of habitation establish towns, so those who follow the same industry or profession—whether in the economic or other field—form guilds or associations, so that many are wont to consider these self-governing organizations, if not essential, at least natural to civil society.

84. Because order, as St. Thomas well explains,[23] is unity arising from the harmonious arrangement of many objects, a true, genuine social order demands that the various members of a society be united together by some strong bond. This unifying force is present not only in the producing of goods or the rendering of services—in which the employers and employees of an identical Industry or Profession collaborate jointly—but also in that common good, to achieve which all Industries and Professions ought, each to the best of its ability, to cooperate amicably. And this unity will be the stronger and more effective, the more faithfully individuals and the Industries and Professions themselves strive to do their work and excel in it.

85. It is easily deduced from what has been said that the interest common to the whole Industry or Profession should hold first place in these guilds. The most important among these interests is to promote the cooperation in the highest degree of each Industry and Profession for the sake of the common good of the country. Concerning matters, however, in which particular points, involving advantage or detriment to employers or workers, may require special care and protection, the two parties, when these cases arise, can deliberate separately or, as the situation requires, reach a decision separately.

86. The teaching of Leo XIII on the form of political government, namely, that men are free to choose whatever form they please, provided that proper regard is had for the requirements of justice and of the common good, is equally applicable in due proportion, it is hardly necessary to say, to the guilds of the various industries and professions.[24]

87. Moreover, just as inhabitants of a town are wont to found associations with the widest diversity of purposes, which each is quite free to join or not, so those engaged in the same industry or profession will combine with one another into associations equally free for purposes connected in some manner with the pursuit of the calling itself. Since these associations are clearly and lucidly explained by Our predecessor of illustrious memory, We consider it enough to emphasize this one point: People are quite free not only to found such associations, which are a matter of private order and private right, but also in respect to them "freely to adopt the organization and the rules which they judge most appropriate to achieve their purpose."[25] The same freedom must be asserted for founding associations that go beyond the boundaries of individual callings. And may these free organizations, now

flourishing and rejoicing in their salutary fruits, set before themselves the task of preparing the way, in conformity with the mind of Christian social teaching, for those larger and more important guilds, Industries and Professions, which We mentioned before, and make every possible effort to bring them to realization.

The Directing Principle Of Economic Life To Be Restored

88. Attention must be given also to another matter that is closely connected with the foregoing. Just as the unity of human society cannot be founded on an opposition of classes, so also the right ordering of economic life cannot be left to a free competition of forces. For from this source, as from a poisoned spring, have originated and spread all the errors of individualist economic teaching. Destroying through forgetfulness or ignorance the social and moral character of economic life, it held that economic life must be considered and treated as altogether free from and independent of public authority, because in the market, that is in the free struggle of competitors, it would have a principle of self-direction which governs it much more perfectly than would the intervention of any created intellect. But free competition, while justified and certainly useful provided it is kept within certain limits, clearly cannot direct economic life—a truth which the outcome of the application in practice of the tenets of this evil individualistic spirit has more than sufficiently demonstrated. Therefore, it is most necessary that economic life be again subjected to and governed by a true and effective directing principle. This function is one that the economic dictatorship which has recently displaced free competition can still less perform, since it is a headstrong power and a violent energy that, to benefit people, needs to be strongly curbed and wisely ruled. But it cannot curb and rule itself. Loftier and nobler principles—social justice and social charity—must, therefore, be sought whereby this dictatorship may be governed firmly and fully. Hence, the institutions themselves of peoples and particularly those of all social life ought to be penetrated with this justice, and it is most necessary that it be truly effective, that is, establish a juridical and social order which will, as it were, give form and shape to all economic life. Social charity, moreover, ought to be as the soul of this order, an order which public authority ought to be ever ready effectively to protect and defend. It will be able to do this the more easily as it rids itself of those burdens which, as We have stated above, are not properly its own.

89. Furthermore, since the various nations largely depend on one another in economic matters and need one another's help, they should strive with a united purpose and effort to promote by wisely conceived pacts and

institutions a prosperous and happy international cooperation in economic life.

90. If the members of the body social are, as was said, reconstituted, and if the directing principle of economic-social life is restored, it will be possible to say in a certain sense even of this body what the Apostle says of the Mystical Body of Christ: "The whole body (being closely joined and knit together through every joint of the system according to the functioning in due measure of each single part) derives its increase to the building up of itself in love."[26]

91. Recently, as all know, there has been inaugurated a special system of syndicates and corporations of the various callings which in view of the theme of this encyclical it would seem necessary to describe here briefly and comment upon appropriately.

92. The civil authority itself constitutes the syndicate as a juridical personality in such a manner as to confer on it simultaneously a certain monopoly-privilege, since only such a syndicate, when thus approved, can maintain the rights (according to the type of syndicate) of workers or employers, and since it alone can arrange for the placement of labor and conclude so-termed labor agreements. Anyone is free to join a syndicate or not, and only within these limits can this kind of syndicate be called free; for syndical dues and special assessments are exacted of absolutely all members of every specified calling or profession, whether they are workers or employers; likewise all are bound by the labor agreements made by the legally recognized syndicate. Nevertheless, it has been officially stated that this legally recognized syndicate does not prevent the existence, without legal status however, of other associations made up of persons following the same calling.

93. The associations or corporations are composed of delegates from the two syndicates, that is of workers and employers, respectively of the same Industry or Profession and, as true and proper organs and institutions of the State, they direct the syndicates and coordinate their activities in matters of common interest toward one and the same end.

94. Strikes and lock-outs are forbidden; if the parties cannot settle their dispute, public authority intervenes.

95. Anyone who gives even slight attention to the matter will easily see what are the obvious advantages in the system We have thus summarily described: The various classes work together peacefully; socialist organizations and their activities are repressed; and a special magistracy exercises a governing authority. Yet lest We neglect anything in a matter of such great importance and that all points treated may be properly connected with the more general principles which We mentioned above and with those which We in-

tend shortly to add, We are compelled to say that to Our certain knowledge there are not wanting some who fear that the State, instead of confining itself as it ought to the furnishing of necessary and adequate assistance, is substituting itself for free activity; and the new syndical and corporative order savors too much of an involved and political system of administration; and that (in spite of those more general advantages mentioned above, which are of course fully admitted) it rather serves particular political ends than leads to the reconstruction and promotion of a better social order.

96. To achieve this latter lofty aim and in particular to promote the common good truly and permanently, We hold it is first and above everything wholly necessary that God bless it and, secondly, that all men of good will work with united effort toward that end. We are further convinced, as a necessary consequence, that this end will be attained the more certainly the larger the number of those ready to contribute toward it their technical, occupational, and social knowledge and experience; and also, what is more important, the greater the contribution made thereto of Catholic principles and their application, not indeed by Catholic Action (which excludes strictly syndical or political activities from its scope), but by those sons of Ours whom Catholic Action imbues with Catholic principles and trains for carrying on an apostolate under the leadership and teaching guidance of the Church, of that Church which in this field also that We have described, as in every other field where moral questions are involved and discussed, can never forget or neglect through indifference its divinely imposed mandate to be vigilant and to teach.

97. What We have taught about the reconstruction and perfection of social order can surely in no wise be brought to realization without reform of morality, as the very record of history clearly shows. For there was a social order once which, although indeed not perfect or in all respects ideal, nevertheless met in a certain measure the requirements of right reason, considering the conditions and needs of the time. If that order has long since perished, that surely did not happen because the order could not have accommodated itself to changed conditions and needs by development and by a certain expansion, but rather because men, hardened by too much love of self, refused to open the order to the increasing masses as they should have done, or because, deceived by allurements of a false freedom and other errors, they became impatient of every authority and sought to reject every form of control.

98. There remains to Us, after again calling to judgment the economic system now in force and its more bitter accuser, Socialism, and passing explicit and just sentences upon them, to search out more thoroughly the roots

of these many evils and to point out that the first and most necessary remedy is a reform of morals.

NOTES

[1] Selections from *Quadragesimo Anno* (May 15, 1931) from *The Church and the Reconstruction of the Modern World: The Social Encyclicals of Pope Pius XI*, edited, annotated, and with an introduction by Terence P. McLaughlin (Garden City, NY: Doubleday & Company, Inc., 1957). McLaughlin used the translation used by the National Catholic Welfare Conference (Washington), which is a translation from *Two Basic Encyclicals* (New York: Benziger Bros., n.d.). Variants found in the endnotes in McLaughlin's edition have been deleted and some footnotes have been shortened. All references to *Quadragesimo Anno* are to this volume.

[2] *Quadragesimo Anno*, 246. Novak argues that the papal critique of liberalism reflects more of a reaction to German interpreters of liberalism (Manchester School) than to the actual circumstances of industrialization in England or to the writings of Londoners and Scots. He thus faults the critique as being based on too limited an exposure to liberal thought. Michael Novak, *Freedom With Justice: Catholic Social Thought and Liberal Institutions* (New York, Harper & Row, 1984), 81-87.

[3] *Quadragesimo Anno*, 246.

[4] Ibid., 247.

[5] *Ibid.* John F. Cox discusses this "ascending scale of societies" and draws the following conclusion: "There must be a progressive ascent of man's personal contribution through the effective mediacy of member group upon larger group. It is only through the freedom and autonomy of each successive group—which groups should be but the corporate extension of his personality—that man can maintain his dominance over society, and make felt throughout the whole order the impact of his personal action. If these intermediate relationships, through which man's personal efforts are freighted upwards towards the common good, be extinguished or cease to function, then he is reduced, from his rightful and crucial function as a radical principle of responsibility and social participation, to the mere helplessness of a numerical unit. And so it is only through this order of subsidiarity that man will be able to assert his practical liberty and personal responsibility. *It is only in such an arrangement of social groups, where corporate initiative and responsibility are the outgrowth and manifestation of personal initiative and responsibility, that man can be said to really count, and to have his due part in the important virtue of social justice.*" John F. Cox, *A Thomistic Analysis of the Social Order*, (Washington, D.C.: The Catholic University Press of America, 1943), 123-124 (italics in the original).

[6] *Quadragesimo Anno*, 247.

[7] Ibid., 249.

[8] The term corporate is employed to describe the vocation groups because those associations were thought to be true and real organs of the social body. The vocational groups were more than the sum of the individual persons in a vocational activity—they were permanent bodies possessing rights.

[9] Quoted in Sander Griffioen, *Facing the New Corporatism* (Toronto: Christian Labour Association of Canada, 1981), 3.

[10] *Quadragesimo Anno*, 252. Pius XI is speaking of Italian corporatism as it existed in 1931. In 1928 parliamentary government was suspended and replaced by Mussolini's

Fascist Corporative State. The Lateran Treaty with the Papacy was signed a year later in 1929.

11 *Ibid.*, 252.

12 Griffioen argues that while Pius XI supported the establishment of syndical and corporative organizations, and while fascism relied heavily on corporatist arguments, "fascism was a perversion of corporatism. It never paid more than lip service to the principle of the multiplicity of authorities." Griffioen, *Facing the New Corporatism*, 3. For a detailed analysis of Papal corporatism in *Rerum Novarum* and *Quadragesimo Anno*, and a full discussion of how it differs from State corporatism, see chapter XIX, "The Church's Plan for Society: Community and Responsibility," in Jean-Yves Calvez and Jacques Perrin, *The Church and Social Justice: The Social Teachings of the Popes from Leo XIII to Pius XII* (Chicago: Henry Regnery Co., 1961). See also Richard Ares, *What is Corporative Organization?* (St. Louis: Central Bureau Press, 1939).

13 Oswald von Nell-Breuning, S. J., a professor of moral theology and canon law, was commissioned to write the original draft of *Quadragesimo Anno*. In an article published in 1981, Nell-Breuning argues that Mussolini understood the encyclical as it was intended—a critique of the fascist corporative state. He makes the point this way: "Immediately after the publication of the encyclical, Mussolini reacted with fury by closing the Catholic youth organizations in retaliation. He apparently understood the text exactly as I intended it to be understood as a *fundamental critique* of his system clothed in the language of diplomatic irony. Others who were less familiar with the curial style, interpreted this Papal exposition as praise [of fascism]." Oswald von Nell-Breuning, "50 Jaar Quadragesimo Anno," *Christen Democratische Verkenningen* (The Hague) December, 1981. See also Nell-Breuning, *Reorganization of Social Economy: The Social Encyclical Developed and Explained* (New York: Bruce Publishing Co., 1936), 222-256.

14 Leo XIII, encyclical, *Arcanum*, Feb. 10, 1880.

15 Leo XIII, encyclical, *Diuturnum*, June 20, 1881.

16 Leo XIII, encyclical, *Immortale Dei*, Nov. 1, 1885.

17 Leo XIII, encyclical, *Sapientiae Christianae*, Jan. 10, 1890.

18 Leo XIII, encyclical, *Quod Apostolici Muneris*, Dec. 28, 1878.

19 Leo XIII, encyclical, *Libertas*, June 20, 1888.

20 Leo XIII, encyclical, *Rerum Novarum*, May 15, 1891, par. 3.

21 *Ibid.*, par. 24.

22 *Ibid.*, par. 31.

23 Thomas Aquinas, *Contra Gentiles*, III, 71; cf. *Summa Theologiae*, I, Q. 65, Art. 2.

24 Leo XIII, encyclical, *Immortale Dei*, Nov. 1, 1885.

25 Cf. *Rerum Novarum*, par. 76.

26 Ephesians 4:16.

TEN

※※※※※※※※※※※※

MAN AND THE STATE[1]

by Jacques Maritain

Jacques Maritain

The philosophical and political writings of Jacques Maritain (1882-1973) brought even greater maturity to Catholic pluralist thought in the twentieth century. Early in his academic career he devoted himself to a lifelong study of St. Thomas Aquinas. "Woe to me if I do not Thomistize," he once said. Maritain's aim was to incorporate new data and to address contemporary issues within a Thomist philosophical and political framework. He became one of the most influential figures in Christian Democratic circles in the twentieth century.

Maritain was appointed to a chair of philosophy at the Institut Catholique of Paris in 1914, and that same year he published the first of more than 50 books. In the beginning, his writing dealt almost entirely with problems of metaphysics, epistemology, and the philosophy of nature. But the growing ideological and political storm prior to World War II forced on him a thorough examination of political philosophy in order to determine just what principles were consistent with the world view of Catholic doctrine and Thomist philosophy. After his first important political work in 1927, *The Things That Are Not Caesar's*,[2] he focused most of his attention on ethical, political, and social matters. In 1933 he published *Freedom in the Modern World*,[3] followed three years later by his widely acclaimed *True Humanism*.[4]

Maritain's reputation as one of the finest Thomist thinkers spread widely. He was invited to lecture in almost every part of Europe and traveled extensively in North and South America. During one of his lecture tours to major American universities in 1940, Germany occupied France, and Maritain decided to stay in North America. He taught for a time at Columbia and Princeton Universities and at the Pontifical Institute of Medieval Studies in Toronto. After the war he served as the French ambassador to the Vatican from 1945 to 1948. He then returned to Princeton where he remained until his retirement.

In 1949, Maritain gave a series of lectures under the auspices of the Charles R. Walgreen Foundation for the Study of American Institutions. The lectures were published in 1951 under the title *Man And The State*,[5] considered by many to be his most mature and important work in political theory. We have selected the first chapter of this book to illustrate his contribution to Catholic pluralist thought. In it he sorts out terms such as "community," "society," "nation," and "state." His distinction between the the terms "body politic" and "state" sheds important light on his understanding of subsidiarity, natural law, and the common good.

From Maritain's Thomist standpoint, reality consists of two irreducible orders, one higher than the other and each with its own proper end. Maritain puts it this way: "For human life has two ultimate ends, the one subordinate to the other: an ultimate end *in a given order*, which is the terrestrial common good, or the *bonum vitae civilis*; and an *absolute* ultimate end, which is the transcendent, eternal common good."[6] Maritain never questions this Thomist view of reality, a view which embraces the fundamental complementarity of nature and grace—a duality which rules the whole of his thought.[7]

In the hierarchical order of the universe, the temporal realm of nature is thus subordinate to the transcendent realm of grace. In the supra-temporal realm—the domain of grace—the Church reigns supreme. In the temporal realm—the domain of nature—the body politic or political society is "the most perfect of temporal societies" and represents "the political whole."[8] All other temporal societies are parts of this whole.

> Not only is the national community, as well as all communities of the nation, thus comprised in the superior unity of the body politic. But the body politic also contains in its superior unity the family units, whose essential rights and freedoms are anterior to itself, and a multiplicity of other particular societies which proceed from the free initiative of citizens and should be as autonomous as possible.[9]

Maritain employs the figure of a pyramid to describe the authority relationship within the body politic. The pyramid represents the body politic and
is "made up of particular and partial authorities rising in tiers above one another up to the top authority of the State."[10] "At the point of the pyramid of
all the particular structures of authority which in a democratic society should
take form in the body politic from the bottom up, the State enjoys topmost
supervising authority."[11]

Thus while the state is the superior part in the body politic, the principle
of subsidiarity dictates that the state be "concerned only with the final supervision of the achievements of institutions born out of freedom, whose free
interplay expressed the vitality of a society integrally just in its basic structures."[12] This "genuine prerogative as the topmost umpire and supervisor,
regulating these spontaneous and autonomous activities from the superior
political point of view of the common good," is the unique contribution of the
state to the body politic.[13] Maritain is clear on this point:

> The common good of the political society is the final aim of the State, and
> comes before the immediate aim of the State, which is the maintenance of the
> public order. The State has a primary duty concerning justice, which should be
> exercised only in the manner of an ultimate supervision in a body politic basi-
> cally just in its inner structures. Finally the body politic must control the State,
> which however contains the functions of government within its own fabric.[14]

Central, then, to the principle of subsidiarity, is the understanding that
within the body politic there should be as much autonomy as possible for the
many "particular and partial authorities." Indeed, for Maritain the concept of
autonomy within the whole "is the element of pluralism inherent in every
truly political society. Economic, cultural, educational, family, and religious
life matter as much as does political life to the very existence and prosperity
of the body politic.[15]

Maritain's language in this and similar passages suggests the linkage between the concept of the diversified spheres of societal reality and the principle of subsidiarity. A key to the relationship between these concepts is the
Catholic understanding that superiority does not mean sovereignty or absolutism.[16] This is true, for example, for the sphere of authority of both the
Church and the state. In both cases the very definition of superiority is limited by a recognition that a superior agent has real but limited authority in
relationship to other entities and ultimately in relation to God—the only true
Sovereign.

This means that in the realm of nature the authority of the Church extends only to the supra-temporal aspects of individuals and the sacramental

aspects of natural institutions such as marriage. The Church may not interfere with the temporal authority of the state, which permeates, from above, the entire body politic. At the same time, the authority of the state is also limited with respect to the rights and identities of other entities within the body politic. These distinctions make sense, once again, because of a particular understanding of the role of superiority in a differentiated society. Maritain summarizes it this way:

> Let us not forget what constitutes the essential sign and property of superiority. A superior agent is not confined or shut up within itself. It radiates. It stimulates the inner forces and energies of other agents—even autonomous in their own peculiar spheres—whose place is less high in the scale of being.[17]

Thus while superiority implies "a penetrating and vivifying influence," it also entails a limited influence—a limitation defined by the autonomous authority of other agents "in their own peculiar spheres."[18]

For Maritain, as for Leo XIII and Pius XI, natural law is intrinsically related to the principle of subsidiarity.[19] Natural law lays down the fundamental rights and duties of individuals and institutions in society. According to Maritain,

> it is because we are enmeshed in the universal order, in the laws and regulations of the cosmos and of the immense family of created natures (and finally in the order of creative wisdom), and it is because we have at the same time the privilege of sharing in spiritual nature, that we possess rights vis-à-vis other men and all the assemblage of creatures.[20]

Every being has its own natural law, its own "inner typical law," and thus it is possible to speak of the proper way in which every entity in the body politic should function.[21] Thus the basis for the subsidiarity principle is the existence of a universal order of nature. A pluralistically organized body politic is rooted in a natural law and the exigencies of the common good.

MAN AND THE STATE

Nation, Body Politic, and State

There is no more thankless task than trying rationally to distinguish and to circumscribe—in other words, trying to raise to a scientific or philosophical level—common notions that have arisen from the contingent practical needs of human history and are laden with social, cultural, and historical connotations as ambiguous as they are fertile, and which nevertheless envelop a core of intelligible meaning. Such concepts are nomadic, not fixed; they are shifting and fluid. Now they are used synonymously, now in opposition to one another. Everybody is the more at ease in using them as he does not know exactly what they mean. But as soon as one tries to define them and separate them from one another, hosts of problems and difficulties arise. One runs the risk of being switched onto a wrong track while attempting to bring out the truth, and to make analytical and systematic what has been conveyed to him by confused experience and concrete life.

The preceding remarks apply strikingly to the notions of *Nation, Body Politic* (or Political Society), and *State*. Yet nothing is more necessary, for a sound political philosophy, than to try to *sort out* these three notions, and clearly circumscribe the genuine meaning of each.

Often, when we speak in the current, more or less vague manner, these three concepts are used, and can be legitimately used, as synonymous with one another. But when it comes to their genuine sociological meaning and to political theory, they must be sharply distinguished. The confusion between, or the systematic identification of, *Nation* and *Political Society*—or *Political Society* and *State*—or *Nation* and *State*, has been a woe to modern history. A correct restatement of the three concepts in question is badly needed. The austerity of my analysis may perhaps be excused, therefore, on account of the importance of the principles in political philosophy it may make us aware of.

Community and Society

A preliminary distinction must be made—namely between *community* and *society*. Of course these two terms may licitly be used synonymously, and I myself have done so many times. But it is also licit—and proper—to assign them to two kinds of social groups which are actually different in nature. This distinction, though it has been misused in the most grievous manner by the theorists of the superiority of "life" over reason, is in itself an established sociological fact. Both community and society are ethico-social and truly human, not mere biological realities. But a community is more of a work of nature and more nearly related to the biological; a society is more of a work of reason, and more nearly related to the intellectual and spiritual properties of man. Their inner social essences and their characteristics, as well as their spheres of realization, do not coincide.

In order to understand this distinction, we must remember that social life as such brings men together by reason of a certain common *object*. In social relations there is always an object, either material or spiritual, around which the relations among human persons are interwoven. In a *community*, as J.T. Delos has rightly pointed out, the object is a *fact* which precedes the determinations of human intelligence and will, and which acts independently of them to create a common unconscious psyche, common feelings and psychological structures, and common mores. But in a *society* the object is a *task* to be done or an *end* to be aimed at, which depends on the determinations of human intelligence and will and is preceded by the activity—either decision, or, at least, consent—of the reason of individuals; thus, in the case of society the objective and rational element in social life explicitly emerges and takes the leading role. A business firm, a labor union, a scientific association are *societies* as much as is the body politic. Regional, ethnic, linguistic groups, social classes are *communities*. The tribe, the clan are communities that pave the way for, and foreshadow the advent of, the political society. The *community* is a product of instinct and heredity in given circumstances and historical frameworks; the *society* a product of reason and moral strength (what the Ancients called "virtue").

In the *community*, social relations proceed from given historical situations and environments: the collective patterns of feeling—or the collective unconscious psyche—have the upper hand over personal consciousness, and man appears as a product of the social group. In *society*, personal consciousness retains priority, the social group is shaped by men, and social relations proceed from a given initiative, a given idea, and the voluntary determination of human persons.

Even in *natural* societies, such as the family society and political society—that is, in societies which are both necessarily required and spontaneously rough-hewn by nature—*society* finally springs up from human freedom. Even in communities—regional communities, for instance, or vocational communities—that grow around some particular society, like an industrial or commercial establishment, *community* springs up from nature; I mean, from the reaction and adjustment of human nature to a given historical environment, or to the factual impact of the industrial or commercial society in question upon the natural conditioning of human existence. In the *community*, social pressure derives from coercion imposing patterns of conduct on man and comes into play in a deterministic mode. In *society*, social pressure derives from law or rational regulations, or from an idea of the common aim; it calls forth personal conscience and liberty, which must obey the law freely.

A society always gives rise to communities and community feelings within or around itself. Never can a community develop into a society, though it can be the natural soil from which some societal organization springs up through reason.

The Nation

Now the *Nation* is a community, not a society. The Nation is one of the most important, perhaps the most complex and complete community engendered by civilized life. Modern times have been faced with a conflicting tension between the Nation and another momentous human community, the Class; yet, as a matter of fact, the dynamism of the Nation has appeared to be the stronger—because it is more deeply rooted in nature.

The word nation originates from the Latin *nasci*, that is, from the notion of *birth*, but the nation is not something biological, like the Race. It is something ethico-social: a human community based on the fact of birth and lineage, yet with all the moral connotations of those terms: birth to the life of reason and the activities of civilization, lineage in familial traditions, social and juridical formation, cultural heritage, common conceptions and manners, historical recollections, sufferings, claims, hopes, prejudices, and resentments. An ethnic community, generally speaking, can be defined as a *community of patterns of feeling* rooted in the physical soil of the origin of the group as well as in the moral soil of history; it becomes a *nation* when this factual situation enters the sphere of self-awareness, in other words, when the ethnic group *becomes conscious* of the fact that it constitutes a community of patterns of feeling—or rather, has a common unconscious psyche—and possesses its own unity and individuality, its own will to endure in existence. A nation is a community of people who become aware of themselves as history has made them, who treasure their own past, and who love themselves as they know or imagine themselves to be, with a kind of inevitable introversion. This progressive awakening of national consciousness has been a characteristic feature of modern history. Though it is normal and good in itself, it finally became exacerbated and gave rise to the plague of Nationalism, while—and probably because—the concept of Nation and the concept of State were confused and mixed up in an unfortunate and explosive manner.

The Nation has, or had, a soil, a land—this does not mean, as for the State, a territorial area of power and administration, but a cradle of life, work, pain, and dreams. The Nation has a language—though the linguistic groups by no means always coincide with the national ones. The Nation thrives on institutions—the creation of which, however, depends more on the human person and mind, or the family, or particular groups in the society, or the body politic, than on the Nation itself. The Nation has rights, which are but the rights of human persons to participate in the peculiar human values of a national heritage. The Nation has a historic calling, which is not its *own* calling (as if there were primordial and predestined national monads each of which was possessed of a supreme mission), but which is only a historical and contingent particularization of a man's calling to the unfolding and manifestation of his own multifarious potentialities.

Yet for all of that the Nation is not a society; it does not cross the threshold of the political realm. It is a community of communities, a self-aware network of common feelings and representations that human nature and instinct have caused to swarm around a number of physical, historical and social data. Like any other community the Nation is "acephalous": it has élites and centers of influence—no head or ruling authority; structures—no rational form or juridical organization; passions and dreams—no common good; solidarity among its members, faithfulness, honor—no civic friendship; manners and mores—no formal norms and order. It does not appeal to the freedom and responsibility of personal conscience, it instils [sic] in human persons a second nature. It is a general pattern in private life, it does not know any principle of public order. Thus it is that in reality the national group cannot *transform itself* into a political society: a political society can progressively differentiate itself within a confused social life in which political functions and community activities were first commingled; the idea of the body politic can arise in the bosom of a national community; but the national community can only be a propitious soil and an occasion for that blossoming. In itself the idea of the body politic belongs to another, superior order. As soon as the body politic exists, it is something other than a national community.

The preceding analysis makes us realize how serious have been for modern history the confusion between Nation and State, the myth of the National State, and the so-called principle of nationalities understood in the sense that each national group must set itself up as a separate state. Such a confusion has wrenched both Nation and State out of shape. The trouble began in the democratic theater, during the XIXth century. It came to full madness in the anti-democratic reaction of the present century. Let us consider the result in the most acute cases.

Uprooted from its essential order, and therefore losing its natural limits in the course of an anti-natural growth, the Nation has become an earthly divinity whose absolute selfishness is sacred, and it has used political power to subvert any steady order among peoples. The State, when it has been identified with the Nation, or even with the Race, and when the fever of the instincts of the earth has thus invaded its own blood—the State has had its will to power exasperated; it has presumed to impose by force of law the so-called type and genius of the Nation, thus becoming a cultural, ideological, caesaro-papist, totalitarian State. At the same time, that totalitarian State has degenerated by losing the sense of the objective order of justice and law, and by swerving toward what is peculiar to tribal as well as to feudal community achievements. For the universal and objective ties of law and for the specific relationship between the individual person and the political body, have been substituted personal ties derived from blood, or from a particular commitment of man to man or to the clan, the party, or the chief.

I have just emphasized the distinction between that sociological reality which is a *National Community* and that other sociological reality which is a *Political Society*. It must now be added that, as I have previously remarked, the existence of a given society naturally calls forth the birth of new communities within or around that societal group. Thus, when a *political society* has been formed, especially when it has a century-old experience strengthening genuine civic friendship, it naturally gives rise, within itself, to a *national community* of a higher degree, either with regard to the self-awareness of such an already existing community, or with regard to the very formation of a new National Community in which various nationalities have been merged. Thus, to the exact contrary of the so-called principle of nationalities, the Nation here depends on the existence of the body politic, not the body politic on the existence of the Nation. The Nation does not become a State. The state causes the Nation to be. Thus it is that a multi-national *Federation of States*, as is the United States, is at the same time a multinational *Nation*. A genuine principle of nationalities would be formulated as follows: the body politic should develop both its own moral dynamism and the respect for human freedoms to such a point that the national communities which are contained within it would both have their natural rights fully recognized, and tend spontaneously to merge in a single higher and more complex National Community.

Let us compare from this point of view four significant instances: Germany, the old Austro-Hungarian Empire, France, and the United States. Germany is a complex of nations, and has been unable to bring about a gen-

uine body politic; it has made up for that frustration by an unnatural exaltation of the national feeling and an unnatural Nation-State. The Austro-
Hungarian double crown created a State but was unable to produce a Nation.
France and the United States enjoyed particularly favorable circumstances,—
as well as a sense of freedom and of the basic role of free choice or consent by
people in political life; in each case this helped to produce a single Nation
centered on the body politic—a Nation which achieved unity, as a result either of century-old trials or of a ceaseless process of self-creation. So for practical purposes we may use the expression the American Nation, the French
Nation, to denote the American or French political body. Yet such a practical
synonymity must not deceive us and make us forget the fundamental distinction between National Community and Political Society.

The Body Politic

In contradistinction to the *Nation*, both the *Body Politic* and the *State*
pertain to the order of society, even society in its highest or "perfect" form. In
our modern age the two terms are used synonymously, and the second tends
to supersede the first. Yet if we are to avoid serious misunderstandings, we
have to distinguish clearly between the State and the Body Politic. These do
not belong to two diverse categories, but they differ from each other as a part
differs from the whole. The *Body Politic* or the *Political Society* is the whole.
The *State* is a part—the topmost part—of this whole.

Political Society, required by nature and achieved by reason, is the most
perfect of temporal societies. It is a concretely and wholly human reality,
tending to a concretely and wholly human good—the common good. It is a
work of reason, born out of the obscure efforts of reason disengaged from
instinct, and implying essentially a rational order; but it is no more Pure
Reason than man himself. The body politic has flesh and blood, instincts,
passions, reflexes, unconscious psychological structures and dynamism—all
of these subjected, if necessary by legal coercion, to the command of an Idea
and rational decisions. Justice is a primary condition for the existence of the
body politic, but Friendship is its very life-giving form. It tends toward a really human and freely achieved communion. It lives on the devotion of the
human persons and their gift of themselves. They are ready to commit their
own existence, their possessions and their honor for its sake. The civic sense
is made up of this sense of devotion and mutual love as well as of the sense of
justice and law.

The entire man—though not by reason of his entire self and of all that he
is and has—is part of the political society; and thus all his community activi-

ties, as well as his personal activities, are of consequence to the political whole. As we have pointed out, a national community of a higher human degree spontaneously takes shape by virtue of the very existence of the body politic, and in turn becomes part of the substance of the latter. Nothing matters more, in the order of material causality, to the life and preservation of the body politic than the accumulated energy and historical continuity of that national community it has itself caused to exist. This means chiefly a heritage of accepted and unquestionable structures, fixed customs and deep-rooted common feelings which bring into social life itself something of the determined physical data of nature, and of the vital unconscious strength proper to vegetative organisms. It is, further, common inherited experience and the moral and intellectual instincts which constitute a kind of empirical, practical wisdom, much deeper and denser and much nearer the hidden complex dynamism of human life than any artificial construction of reason.

Not only is the national community, as well as all communities of the nation, thus comprised in the superior unity of the body politic. But the body politic also contains in its superior unity the family units, whose essential rights and freedoms are anterior to itself, and a multiplicity of other particular societies which proceed from the free initiative of citizens and should be as autonomous as possible. Such is the element of pluralism inherent in every truly political society. Family, economic, cultural, educational, religious life matter as much as does political life to the very existence and prosperity of the body politic. Every kind of law, from the spontaneous, unformulated group regulations to customary law and to law in the full sense of the term, contributes to the vital order of political society. Since in political society authority comes from below, through the people, it is normal that the whole dynamism of authority in the body politic should be made up of particular and partial authorities rising in tiers above one another, up to the top authority of the State. Finally, the public welfare and the general order of law are essential parts of the common good of the body politic, but this common good has far larger and richer, more concretely human implications, for it is by nature the good human life of the multitude and is common to both the *whole* and the *parts*, the persons into whom it flows back and who must benefit from it. The common good is not only the collection of public commodities and services which the organization of common life presupposes: a sound fiscal condition, a strong military force; the body of just laws, good customs, and wise institutions which provides the political society with its structure; the heritage of its great historical remembrances, its symbols and its glories, its living traditions and cultural treasures. The common good also includes the sociological integration of all the civic conscience, political virtues and sense of law and freedom, of all the activity, material prosperity and spiritual riches, of unconsciously operating hereditary wisdom, of moral rectitude, justice, friendship, happiness, virtue and heroism in the individual lives of the members of the body politic. To the extent to which all these things are, in a certain measure, *communicable* and revert to each member, helping him to perfect his life and liberty as a person, they all constitute the good human life of the multitude.

The State

From this enumeration of the features of the body politic, it should be evident that the body politic differs from the State. The State is only that part of the body politic especially concerned with the maintenance of law, the promotion of the common welfare and public order, and the administration of public affairs. The State is a part which *specializes* in the interests of the *whole*. It is not a man or a body of men, it is a set of institutions combined into a topmost machine: this kind of work of art has been built by man and uses human brains and energies and is nothing without man, but it constitutes a superior embodiment of reason, an impersonal, lasting superstructure, the functioning of which may be said to be rational in the second degree, insofar as the reason's activity in it, bound by law and by a system of universal regulations, is more abstract, more sifted out from the contingencies of experience and individuality, more pitiless also, than in our individual lives.

The State is not the supreme incarnation of the Idea, as Hegel believed; the State is not a kind of collective superman; the State is but an agency entitled to use power and coercion, and made up of experts or specialists in public order and welfare, an instrument in the service of man. Putting man at the service of that instrument is political perversion. The human person as an individual is for the body politic and the body politic is for the human person as a person. But man is by no means for the State. The State is for man.

When we say that the State is the superior part in the body politic, this means that it is superior to the other organs or collective parts of this body, but it does not mean that it is superior to the body politic itself. The part as such is inferior to the whole. The State is inferior to the body politic as a whole, and is at the service of the body politic as a whole. Is the State even the *head* of the body politic? Hardly, for in the human being the head is an instrument of such spiritual powers as the intellect and the will, which the whole body has to serve; whereas the functions exercised by the State are for the body politic, and not the body politic for them.

The theory which I have just summarized, and which regards the State as a part or an instrument of the body politic, subordinate to it and endowed with topmost authority not by its own right and for its own sake, but only by virtue and to the extent of the requirements of the common good, can be described as an "instrumentalist" theory, founding the genuinely *political* notion of the State. But we are confronted with quite another notion, the *despotic* notion of the State, based on a "substantialist" or "absolutist" theory. According to this theory the State is a subject of right, i.e., a moral person, and consequently a whole; as a result it is either superimposed on the body politic or made to absorb the body politic entirely, and it enjoys supreme power by virtue of its own natural, inalienable right and for its own final sake.

Of course there is for everything great and powerful an instinctive tendency—and a special temptation—to grow beyond its own limits. Power tends to increase power, the power machine tends ceaselessly to extend itself; the supreme legal and administrative machine tends toward bureaucratic self-sufficiency; it would like to consider itself an end, not a means. Those who specialize in the affairs of the whole have a propensity to take themselves for the whole; the general staffs to take themselves for the whole army, the Church authorities for the whole Church; the State for the whole body politic. By the same token, the State tends to ascribe to itself a peculiar common good—its own self-preservation and growth—distinct both from the public order and welfare which are its immediate end, and from the common good which is its final end. All these misfortunes are but instances of "natural" excess or abuse.

But there has been something much more specific and serious in the development of the *substantialist* or *absolutist* theory of the State. This development can be understood only in the perspective of modern history and as a sequel to the structures and conceptions peculiar to the Mediaeval Empire, to the absolute monarchy of the French classical age, and the absolute government of the Stuart kings in England. Remarkably enough, the very word *State* only appeared in the course of modern history; the notion of the State was implicitly involved in the ancient concept of city (*polis, civitas*) which meant essentially body politic, and still more in the Roman concept of the Empire: it was never explicitly brought out in Antiquity. According to a historical pattern unfortunately most recurrent, both the normal development of the State—which was in itself a sound and genuine progress—and the development of the spurious—absolutist—juridical and philosophical conception of the State took place at the same time.

An adequate explanation of that historical process would require a long and thorough analysis. Here I merely suggest that in the Middle Ages the au-

thority of the Emperor, and in early modern times the authority of the absolute King, descended from above on the body politic, upon which it was superimposed. For centuries, political authority was the privilege of a superior
"social race" which had a right—and believed it to be an innate or immediately God-given and inalienable right—to supreme power over, and leadership as well as moral guidance of, the body politic—made up, it was assumed,
of people under age who were able to make requests, remonstrances, or riots,
not to govern themselves. So, in the "baroque age," while the reality of the
State and the sense of the State progressively took shape as great juridical
achievements, the concept of the State emerged more or less confusedly as the
concept of a whole—sometimes identified with the person of the king—
which was superimposed on or which enveloped the body politic and enjoyed
power from above by virtue of its own natural and inalienable right,—that is
to say, which possessed sovereignty. For in the genuine sense of this word—
which depends on the historical formation of the concept of sovereignty,
prior to jurists' various definitions—sovereignty implies not only actual possession of and right to supreme power, but a right which is *natural and inalienable*, to a supreme power which is supreme *separate from* and *above* its
subjects.

At the time of the French Revolution that very concept of the State considered as a whole unto itself was preserved, but it shifted from the King to
the Nation, mistakenly identified with the body politic; hence Nation, Body
Politic and State were identified. And the very concept of sovereignty—as a
natural or *innate* and *inalienable* right to supreme *transcendent* power—was
preserved, but shifted from the King to the Nation. At the same time, by
virtue of a voluntarist theory of law and political society, which had its acme
in eighteenth-century philosophy, the State was made into a person (a so-
called moral person) and a subject of right, in such a way that the attribute of
absolute sovereignty, ascribed to the Nation, was inevitably, as a matter of
fact, to be claimed and exercised by the State.

Thus it is that in modern times the despotic or absolutist notion of the
State was largely accepted among democratic tenets by the theorists of
democracy—pending the advent of Hegel, the prophet and theologian of the
totalitarian, divinized State. In England, John Austin's theories only tended to
tame and civilize somewhat the old Hobbesian Leviathan. This process of acceptance was favored by a symbolical property which genuinely belongs to
the State, namely, the fact that, just as we say twenty head of cattle meaning
twenty animals, in the same way the topmost part in the body politic naturally *represents* the political whole. Nay more, the notion of the latter is raised
to a higher degree of abstraction and symbolization, and the consciousness of

the political society is raised to a more completely individualized idea of itself in the idea of the State. In the absolutist notion of the State, that symbol has been made a reality, has been hypostasized. According to this notion the State is a metaphysical monad, a person; it is a whole unto itself, *the* very political whole in its supreme degree of unity and individuality. So it absorbs in itself the body politic from which it emanates, as well as all the individual or particular wills which, according to Jean-Jacques Rousseau, have engendered the General Will in order mystically to die and resurge in its unity. And it enjoys absolute sovereignty as an essential property and right.

That concept of the State, enforced in human history, has forced democracies into intolerable self-contradictions, in their domestic life and above all in international life. For this concept is no part of the authentic tenets of democracy, it does not belong to the real democratic inspiration and philosophy, it belongs to a spurious ideological heritage which has preyed upon democracy like a parasite. During the reign of individualist or "liberal" democracy the State, made into an absolute, displayed a tendency to substitute itself for the people, and so to leave the people estranged from political life to a certain extent; it also was able to launch the wars between nations which disturbed the XIXth Century. Nevertheless, after the Napoleonic era the worst implications of this process of State absolutization were restrained by the democratic philosophy and political practices which then prevailed. It is with the advent of the totalitarian regimes and philosophies that those worst implications were released. The State made into an absolute revealed its true face. Our epoch has had the privilege of contemplating the State totalitarianism of Race with German Nazism, of Nation with Italian Fascism, of Economic Community with Russian Communism.

The point which needs emphasis is this. For democracies today the most urgent endeavor is to develop social justice and improve world economic management, and to defend themselves against totalitarian threats from the outside and totalitarian expansion in the world; but the pursuit of these objectives will inevitably involve the risk of having too many functions of social life controlled by the State from above, and we shall be inevitably bound to accept this risk, as long as our notion of the State has not been restated on true and genuine democratic foundations, and as long as the body politic has not renewed its own structures and consciousness, so that the people become more effectively equipped for the exercise of freedom, and the State may be made an actual instrument for the common good of all. Then only will that very topmost agency, which is made by modern civilization more and more necessary to the human person in his political, social, moral, even intellectual and scientific progress, cease to be at the same time a threat to the freedoms of the human person as well as of intelligence and science. Then only will the highest functions of the State—to ensure the law and facilitate the free development of the body politic—be restored, and the sense of the State be regained by the citizens. Then only will the State achieve its true dignity, which comes not from power and prestige, but from the exercise of justice.

Normal Growth and the Simultaneous
Process of Perversion

At this point I should like not to be misunderstood. I hope that my previous remarks have made it sufficiently clear that I by no means condemn or depreciate the State and its astonishing growth in the course of modern history. That would be as blindly unreal and futile as to condemn or reject the mechanical achievements which have transformed the world, and which could and should become instruments for the liberation of man. From the last period of the XIXth Century on, state intervention has been needed to compensate for the general disregard for justice and human solidarity that prevailed during the early phases of the industrial revolution. State legislation with regard to employment and labor is in itself a requirement of the common good. And without the power of the State—the democratic State—how could a free body politic resist the pressure or the aggression of totalitarian States? The growth of the State, in modern centuries, as a rational or juridical machine and with regard to its inner constitutive system of law and power, its unity, its discipline; the growth of the State, in the present century, as a technical machine and with regard to its law-making, supervising, and organizing functions in social and economic life, are in themselves part of normal progress.

Such progress has been entirely corrupted in totalitarian States. It remains normal progress, though subject to many risks, in democratic States, especially as regards the development of social justice.

We may dislike the State machinery; I do not like it. Yet many things we do not like are necessary, not only in fact, but by right. On the one hand, the primary reason for which men, united in a political society, need the State, is the order of justice. On the other hand, social justice is the crucial need of modern societies. As a result, the primary duty of the modern State is the enforcement of social justice.

As a matter of fact, this primary duty is inevitably performed with abnormal emphasis on the power of the State to the very extent that the latter has to make up for the deficiencies of a society whose basic structures are not sufficiently up to the mark with regard to justice. Those deficiencies are the first cause of the trouble. And thus any theoretical objections or particular claims, even justified in their own particular spheres, will inevitably be considered as but minor things in the face of the vital necessity—not only factual but moral—of meeting the long-neglected wants and rights of the human person in the deepest and largest strata of the human society.

The problem, in my opinion, is to distinguish the normal progress of the State from the false notions, connected with the concept of sovereignty, which prey upon it; and also to change the backward general conditions which, by imposing a too heavy burden upon it, make it liable to become seriously vitiated. For both those backward social conditions and those false absolutist notions give rise to a process of perversion combined with and preying upon normal growth. How to describe this process of perversion? It occurs—that is apparent from all our previous remarks—when the State mistakes itself for a whole, for the whole of the political society, and consequently takes upon itself the exercise of the functions and the performance of the tasks which normally pertain to the body politic and its various organs. Then we have what has been labelled "the paternalist State": the State not only supervising from the political point of view of the common good (which is normal), but directly organizing, controlling, or managing, to the extent which it judges the interests of public welfare to demand, all forms—economic, commercial, industrial, cultural, or dealing with scientific research as well as with relief and security—of the body politic's life.

Let us point out in this connection that what is called "nationalization," and is in reality "statization," can be opportune or necessary in certain cases, but should by nature remain exceptional—limited to those public services so immediately concerned with the very existence, order, or internal peace of the body politic that a risk of bad management is then a lesser evil than the risk of giving the upper hand to private interests. The fact remains that the State has skill and competence in administrative, legal, and political matters, but is inevitably dull and awkward—and, as a result, easily oppressive and injudicious—in all other fields. To become a boss or a manager in business or industry or a patron of art or a leading spirit in the affairs of culture, science, and philosophy is against the nature of such an impersonal topmost agency, abstract so to speak and separated from the moving peculiarities, mutual tensions, risks, and dynamism of concrete social existence. By virtue of a strange intermingling in human vocabulary, the word *nationalization* conveys a socialistic meaning, whereas the word *socialization*, on the contrary, if it were correctly understood, would have rather personalist and pluralist implications. For, taken in its genuine sense, it refers to that process of social integration through which association in a single enterprise extends not only to the capital invested, but also to labor and management, and all persons and various groups involved are made participants in some form or other of co-ownership and co-management. This process is not an attack on, but an expansion of private ownership. It depends on the search of free initiative for new economic modalities and adjustments, the more successful of which will be one day sanctioned by the law. It rises from the natural growth of the system of free enterprise, when common consciousness becomes aware of the social function of private property and of the necessity of giving organic and institutional forms to that law of the "common use" on which Thomas Aquinas has laid particular stress.

As a result I would say that if our present social structure is to evolve along normal lines, a first step, made necessary by the requirements of public welfare, would consist in having the State start and support—as has been shown possible by the outstanding example of the Tennessee Valley Authority—large scale undertakings planned and managed *not* by the State and not from the center of the country's political administration, but on the spot, by private enterprises co-ordinated with one another and by the various communities of the very people concerned, under the leadership of independent responsible appointees. Thus the State itself would launch a movement of progressive decentralization and "destatization" of social life, tending toward the advent of some new personalist and pluralist régime.

The final step would take place, in such a new régime, when prodding by the State would no longer be necessary, and all organic forms of social and economic activity, even the largest and most comprehensive ones, would start from the bottom, I mean from the free initiative of and mutual tension between the particular groups, working communities, co-operative agencies, unions, associations, federated bodies of producers and consumers, rising in tiers and institutionally recognized. Then a definitely personalist and pluralist pattern of social life would come into effect in which new societal types of private ownership and enterprise would develop. And the State would leave to the multifarious organs of the social body the autonomous initiative and management of all the activities which by nature pertain to them. Its only prerogative in this respect would be its genuine prerogative as topmost umpire and supervisor, regulating these spontaneous and autonomous activities from the superior political point of view of the common good.

So perhaps it will be possible, in a pluralistically organized body politic, to make the State into a topmost agency concerned only with the final supervision of the achievements of institutions born out of freedom, whose free interplay expressed the vitality of a society integrally just in its basic structures.

To sum up, the common good of the body politic demands a network of authority and power in political society, and therefore a special agency endowed with uppermost power, for the sake of justice and law. The State is that uppermost political agency. But the State is neither a whole nor a subject of right, or a person. It is a part of the body politic, and, as such, inferior to the body politic as a whole, subordinate to it, and at the service of its common good. The common good of the political society is the final aim of the State, and comes before the immediate aim of the State, which is the maintenance of the public order. The State has a primary duty concerning justice, which should be exercised only in the manner of an ultimate supervision in a body politic basically just in its inner structures. Finally the body politic must control the State, which however contains the functions of government within its own fabric. At the point of the pyramid of all the particular structures of authority which in a democratic society should take form in the body politic from the bottom up, the State enjoys topmost supervising authority. But this supreme authority is received by the State *from the body politic*, that is, from the people; it is not a natural right to supreme power which the State possesses of itself. As follows from a critical elucidation of the concept of sovereignty—with which the second chapter of this book is concerned—the supreme authority of the State should in no way be called sovereignty.

In the eyes of a sound political philosophy there is no sovereignty, that is, no natural and inalienable right to *transcendent* or *separate* supreme power in political society. Neither the Prince nor the King nor the Emperor were really sovereign, though they bore the sword and the attributes of sovereignty. Nor is the State sovereign; nor are even the people sovereign. God alone is sovereign.

The People

We have discussed the Nation, the Body Politic, the State. Now what about the People?

I just said that the people are not sovereign in the genuine sense of this word. For in its genuine sense the notion of sovereignty relates to a power and independence which are supreme *separately from* and *above* the whole ruled by the sovereign. And obviously the power and independence of the people are not supreme *separately from* and *above the people themselves*. Of the people as well as of the body politic we have to say, not that they are sovereign, but that they have a natural right to *full autonomy*, or to self-government.

The people exercise this right when they establish the Constitution, written or unwritten, of the body politic; or when, in a small political group, they meet together to make a law or a decision; or when they elect their representatives. And this right remains always in them. It is by virtue of it that they control the State and their own administrative officials. It is by virtue of it that they cause to pass into those who are designated to take care of the common good, the right to make laws and to govern, so that, by investing those particular men with authority, within certain fixed limits of duration · and power, the very exercise of the right of the people to self-government restricts to the same extent its further *exercise*, but does not make the *possession* of this right itself cease or lessen in any way. The administrative officials, or the Administration, that is, the human persons who are invested with executive power, are (in the strictest sense of the word "governing") the governing organ *in the State*, because the people have made them, *in the body politic*, the deputies for the very whole. All this is fully consistent with our conclusion that the most accurate expression concerning the democratic régime is not "sovereignty of the people." It is Lincoln's saying: "government of the people, by the people, for the people." This means that the people are governed by men whom they themselves have chosen and entrusted with a right to command, for functions of a determined nature and duration, and over whose management they maintain a regular control—first of all by means of their representatives and the assemblies thus constituted.

As concerns furthermore the very notion of the people, I would say that the modern concept of the people has a long history and stems from a singular diversity of meanings which have fused together. But considering only the political significance of the word, suffice it to say that the people are the multitude of human persons who, united under just laws, by mutual friendship, and for the common good of their human existence, constitute a political society or a body politic. The notion of body politic means the whole unit composed of the people. The notion of the people means the members organically united who compose the body politic. Thus what I have said concerning either Body Politic and Nation or Body Politic and State holds good for either People and Nation or People and State. Nay more, since the people are human persons who not only form a body politic, but who have each one a spiritual soul and a supratemporal destiny, the concept of the people is the highest and noblest concept among the basic concepts that we are analyzing. The people are the very substance, the living and free substance, of the body politic. The people are above the State, the people are not for the State, the State is for the people.

I should finally like to point out that the people have a special need of the State, precisely because the State is a particular agency specializing in the care of the whole, and thus has normally to defend and protect the people, their rights and the improvement of their lives against the selfishness and particularism of privileged groups or classes. In ancient France the people and the King relied upon each other, somewhat ambiguously, in their struggle against the supremacy of the great feudal lords or the nobility. In modern times it has been the same with the people and the State in regard to the struggle for social justice. Yet, as we have seen, this normal process, if it becomes corrupted by the absolutism of the totalitarian State, which raises itself to the supreme rule of good and evil, leads to the misfortune and enslavement of the people; and it is impaired and jeopardized if the people surrender themselves to a State, which, as good as it may be, has not been freed from the notion of its so-called sovereignty, as well as from the factual deficiencies of the body politic itself. In order both to maintain and make fruitful the movement for social improvement supported by the State, and to bring the State back to its true nature, it is necessary that many functions now exercised by the State should be distributed among the various autonomous organs of a pluralistically structured body politic—either after a period of State capitalism or of State socialism, or, as is to be hoped, in the very process of the present evolution. It is also necessary that the people have the will, and the means, to assert their own control over the State.

NOTES

1 Selections from Chapter One of Jacques Maritain, *Man and the State* (Chicago: The University of Chicago Press, 1951), with footnotes omitted.

2 Jacques Maritain, *The Things That Are Not Caesar's* (New York: Charles Scribner's Sons, 1930).

3 Jacques Maritain, *Freedom in the Modern World* (New York: Scribner's, 1938).

4 Jacques Maritain, *True Humanism*, trans. M. Adamson (New York: Scribner's, 1938).

5 Maritain, *Man and the State.*

6 *Ibid.*, 62.

7 Elsewhere, Maritain describes the duality in these words: "[W]e shall have to distinguish between two orders—the order of nature and the order of grace; and between two existential realms, distinct but not separate—the world, on the one hand, and the Kingdom of God, the Church, on the other." Jacques Maritain, *On the Philosophy of History*, ed. J. Evans (London: Geoffrey Bles, 1959), 29-30.

8 Maritain, *Man and the State*, 10.

9 *Ibid.*, 11.

10 *Ibid.*

11 *Ibid.*, 24.

12 *Ibid.*, 23.

13 *Ibid.*

14 *Ibid.*, 24.

15 *Ibid.*, 11.

16 Maritain rejects the political concept of sovereignty as applicable to either the state or the body politic. In his mind, sovereignty and absolutism are one and the same thing. Since sovereignty implies supreme independence and power, such qualities can never reside within temporal reality. For Maritain, God alone is sovereign. For a full discussion of the concepts of sovereignty and absolutism ("forged together on the same anvil"), see Chapter Two of *Man and the State*, "The Concept of Sovereignty."

17 *Ibid.*, 164.

18 *Ibid.*

19 Maritain develops the argument concerning the relationship of natural law to the societal order in Chapter Four of *Man and the State*. See also Jacques Maritain, *The Rights of Man and Natural Law* (New York: Charles Scribner's Sons, 1943).

20 Maritain, *Man and the State*, 95.

21 *Ibid.*, 86. An example of extending Maritain's philosophy of groups to current American legal processes is Larry May, *The Morality of Groups: Collective Responsibility, Group-Based Harm, and Corporate Rights* (Notre Dame: University of Notre Dame Press, 1987).

ELEVEN

⊠⊠⊠⊠⊠⊠⊠⊠⊠⊠

THE POLITICAL COMMUNITY[1]
from The Second Vatican Council

Bishops of the Second Vatican Council

From Jacques Maritain's theoretical analysis, we turn to the work of the Bishops of the Second Vatican Council in order to understand more fully the relationship of pluralist thought to issues of our contemporary society. The agenda of the Council was intimately related to the character and thought of Pope John XXIII who stood opposed to all world-denial and world-flight. He was deeply convinced that the responsibility of the Church is not limited to the salvation of souls. In his encyclical *Mater et Magistra* (dated May 15, 1961, commemorating the 70th anniversary of *Rerum Novarum*) he stresses the relevance of the gospel to the "increasing needs of mankind and for the cares and burdens of this mortal life."[2]

Vatican Council II was convened in 1962 neither to combat heresies nor to attack the enemies of the Church. It was rather a major effort to renew the Church and to engage in an ecumenical dialogue with those referred to as the "separated brethren" who find themselves in "ecclesial communities" outside Catholicism. With respect to religious freedom in the political order, the Vatican documents show how far the Catholic Church had traveled from the time of Leo XIII to that of John XXIII in coming to accept state policies of confessional pluralism. This development was due in part to a more fully developed understanding of the concept of the common good.

The last of the 16 documents promulgated by the Council was The Pastoral Constitution *Guadium et Spes*—on *The Church in the World Today*.[3] It consists of two parts. The first part is foundational in setting forth the doctrinal basis for "the dignity of the human person and his individual and social role in the universe."[4] In the second part the Council applies the doctrine to many of the urgent issues of contemporary society—issues of marriage, family, and culture, of economics, society, and politics of war, peace, and international relations.

The selection below, "The Life of the Political Community," comes from the end of the second part of this Pastoral Constitution. In it the words "political community" should be read as "state." "Political community" should not be confused with the terms "political society," "civil community" ("society"), or "body politic." Each of the latter three terms represents the whole of society, while the state or "political community" designates the topmost part of the whole. These distinctions, as well as the purpose of political communities (states), are made clear in the following statement by the Council:

> Individuals, families, and the various groups which make up the civil community, are aware of their inability to achieve a truly human life by their own unaided efforts; they see the need for a wider community where each one will make a specific contribution to an even broader implementation of the common good. For this reason they set up various forms of political communities. The political community, then, exists for the common good; this is its full justification and meaning and the source of its specific and basic right to exist. The common good embraces the sum total of all those conditions of social life which enable individuals, families, and organizations to achieve complete and efficacious fulfillment.[5]

It is clear that, since the days of Leo XIII the subsidiarity principle has been used to deal with the relationships between both (1) the body politic and individuals, and (2) the body politic and all lesser societies or institutions that make up the body politic. The Bishops of the Vatican Council understand this twofold concern of the subsidiarity principle, and they believe that a system of law should reflect it.

> The rights of all individuals, families, and organizations and their practical implementation must be acknowledged, protected, and fostered, together with the public duties binding on all citizens. . . . Governments should take care not to put obstacles in the way of family, cultural or social groups, or of organizations and intermediate institutions, nor to hinder their lawful and constructive activity; rather, they should eagerly seek to promote such orderly activity. Citizens, on the other hand, either individually or in association, should take care not to

vest too much power in the hands of public authority nor to make untimely and exaggerated demands for favors and subsidies, lessening in this way the responsible role of individuals, families, and social groups.[6]

The Bishops are here attempting to achieve a sense of balance and harmony with respect to the rights and activities of individuals, intermediate institutions, and the state within the body politic. The question of the proper role of the state within society, was the question Pope Leo XIII first addressed in *Rerum Novarum*. Given the perspective of liberalism, which denies to the state any positive role in economic and social issues, one of Leo XIII's main objectives was to justify and strengthen the state. Forty years later the situation had changed dramatically. For Pope Pius XI in *Quadragesimo Anno*, it was rather a matter of preventing the power of the state from dominating all of social life. In Pius XI's day socialism and communism, not liberalism, were the most immediate threats to a diversified social order. One of the contributions of the Bishops of the Second Vatican Council is the application of the principle of subsidiarity to the issues of their day. Once again they make the case for "how authority can be reconciled with freedom, personal initiative and with the solidarity and the needs of the whole social framework, and the advantages of unity with profitable diversity."[7]

THE POLITICAL COMMUNITY

Modern Public Life

In our times profound transformations are to be noticed in the structure and institutions of peoples; they are the accompaniment of cultural, economic, and social development. These transformations exercise a deep influence on political life, particularly as regards the rights and duties of the individual in the exercise of civil liberty and in the achievement of the common good; and they affect the organization of the relations of citizens with each other and of their position vis-à-vis the state.

A keener awareness of human dignity has given rise in various parts of the world to an eagerness to establish a politico-juridical order in which the rights of the human person in public life will be better protected—for example, the right of free assembly and association, the right to express one's opinions and to profess one's religion privately and publicly. The guarantee of the rights of the person is, indeed, a necessary condition for citizens, individually and collectively, to play an active part in public life and administration.

Linked with cultural, economic, and social progress there is a growing desire among many to assume greater responsibilities in the organization of political life. Many people are becoming more eager to ensure that the rights of minority groups in their country be safeguarded, without overlooking the duties of these minorities towards the political community; there is also an increase in tolerance for others who differ in opinion and religion; at the same time wider cooperation is taking place to enable all citizens, and not only a few privileged individuals, to exercise their rights effectively as persons.

Men are repudiating political systems, still prevailing in some parts of the world, which hinder civil and religious liberty or victimize their citizens through avarice and political crimes, or distort the use of authority from being at the service of the common good to benefiting the convenience of political parties or of the governing classes.

There is no better way to establish political life on a truly human basis than by encouraging an inward sense of justice, of good will, and of service to the common good, and by consolidating the basic convictions of men as to the true nature of the political community and the aim, proper exercise, and the limits of public authority.

Nature and Purpose of the Political Community

Individuals, families, and the various groups which make up the civil community, are aware of their inability to achieve a truly human life by their own unaided efforts; they see the need for a wider community where each one will make a specific contribution to an even broader implementation of the common good.[8] For this reason they set up various forms of political communities. The political community, then, exists for the common good: this is its full justification and meaning and the source of its specific and basic right to exist. The common good embraces the sum total of all those conditions of social life which enable individuals, families, and organizations to achieve complete and efficacious fulfilment.[9]

The persons who go to make up the political community are many and varied; quite rightly, then, they may veer towards widely differing points of view. Therefore, lest the political community be ruined while everyone follows his own opinion, an authority is needed to guide the energies of all towards the common good—not mechanically or despotically, but by acting above all as a moral force based on freedom and a sense of responsibility. It is clear that the political community and public authority are based on human nature, and therefore that they need belong to an order established by God;

nevertheless, the choice of the political régime and the appointment of rulers are left to the free decision of the citizens.[10]

It follows that political authority, either within the political community as such or through organizations representing the state, must be exercised within the limits of the moral order and directed toward the common good (understood in the dynamic sense of the term) according to the juridical order legitimately established or due to be established. Citizens, then, are bound in conscience to obey.[11] Accordingly, the responsibility, the dignity, and the importance of state rulers is clear.

When citizens are under the oppression of a public authority which oversteps its competence, they should still not refuse to give or to do whatever is objectively demanded of them by the common good; but it is legitimate for them to defend their own rights and those of their fellow citizens against abuses of this authority within the limits of the natural law and the law of the Gospel.

see Romans

The concrete forms of structure and organization of public authority adopted in any political community may vary according to the character of various peoples and their historical development; but their aim should always be the formation of a human person who is cultured, peace-loving, and well disposed towards his fellow men with a view, to the benefit of the whole human race.

Participation by All in Public Life

It is fully consonant with human nature that there should be politico-juridical structures providing all citizens without any distinction with ever improving and effective opportunities to play an active part in the establishment of the juridical foundations of the political community, in the administration of public affairs, in determining the aims and the terms of reference of public bodies, and in the election of political leaders.[12] Every citizen ought to be mindful of his right and his duty to promote the common good by using his vote. The Church praises and esteems those who devote themselves to the public good for the service of men and take upon themselves the burdens of public office.

If the citizens' cooperation and their sense of responsibility are to produce the favourable results expected of them in the normal course of public life, a system of positive law is required providing for a suitable division of the functions and organs of public authority and an effective and independent protection of citizens' rights. The rights of all individuals, families, and organizations and their practical implementation must be acknowledged, protected, and fostered,[13] together with the public duties binding on all citizens. Among these duties it is worth mentioning the obligation of rendering to the state whatever material and personal services are required for the common good. Governments should take care not to put obstacles in the way of family, cultural or social groups, or of organizations and intermediate institutions, nor to hinder their lawful and constructive activity; rather, they should eagerly seek to promote such orderly activity. Citizens, on the other hand, either individually or in association, should take care not to vest too much power in the hands of public authority nor to make untimely and exaggerated demands for favors and subsidies, lessening in this way the responsible role of individuals, families, and social groups.

The growing complexity of modern situations makes it necessary for public authority to intervene more often in social, cultural and economic matters in order to bring about more favorable conditions to enable citizens and groups to pursue freely and effectively the achievement of man's well-being in its totality. The understanding of the relationship between socialization[14] and personal autonomy and progress will vary according to different areas and the development of peoples. However, if restrictions are imposed temporarily for the common good on the exercise of human rights, these restrictions are to be lifted as soon as possible after the situation has changed. In any case it is inhuman for public authority to fall back on totalitarian methods or dictatorship which violate the rights of persons or social groups.

Citizens should cultivate a generous and loyal spirit of patriotism, but without narrow-mindedness, so that they will always keep in mind the welfare of the whole human family which is formed into one by various kinds of links between races, peoples, and nations.

Christians must be conscious of their specific and proper role in the political community: they should be a shining example by their sense of responsibility and their dedication to the common good; they should show in practice how authority can be reconciled with freedom, personal initiative with the solidarity and the needs of the whole social framework, and the advantages of unity with profitable diversity. They should recognize the legitimacy of differing points of view about the organization of worldly affairs and show respect for their fellow citizens, who even in association defend their opinions by legitimate means. Political parties, for their part, must support whatever in their opinion is conducive to the common good, but must never put their own interests before the common good.

So that all citizens will be able to play their part in political affairs, civil and political education is vitally necessary for the population as a whole and for young people in particular, and must be diligently attended to. Those with talent for the difficult yet noble art of politics,[15] or whose talents in this matter can be developed, should prepare themselves for it, and, forgetting their own convenience and material interests, they should engage in political activity. They must combat injustice and oppression, arbitrary domination and intolerance by individuals or political parties, and they must do so with integrity and wisdom. They must dedicate themselves to the welfare of all in a spirit of sincerity and fairness, of love and of the courage demanded by political life.

The Political Community and the Church

It is of supreme importance, especially in a pluralistic society, to work out a proper vision of the relationship between the political community and the Church, and to distinguish clearly between the activities of Christians, acting individually or collectively in their own name as citizens guided by the dictates of a Christian conscience, and their activity acting along with their pastors in the name of the Church.

The Church, by reason of her role and competence, is not identified with any political community nor bound by ties to any political system. It is at once the sign and the safeguard of the transcendental dimension of the human person.

The political community and the Church are autonomous and independent of each other in their own fields. Nevertheless, both are devoted to the personal vocation of man, though under different titles. This service will redound the more effectively to the welfare of all insofar as both institutions practice better cooperation according to the local and prevailing situation. For man's horizons are not bounded only by the temporal order; living on the level of human history he preserves the integrity of his eternal destiny. The Church, for its part, being founded in the love of the Redeemer, contributes towards the spread of justice and charity among nations and within the borders of the nations themselves. By preaching the truths of the Gospel and clarifying all sectors of human activity through its teaching and the witness of its members, the Church respects and encourages the political freedom and responsibility of the citizen.

Since the apostles, their successors and all who help them have been given the task of announcing Christ, Saviour of the world, to man, they rely in their apostolate on the power of God, who often shows forth the force of the Gospel in the weakness of its witnesses. If anyone wishes to devote himself to the ministry of God's Word, let him use the ways and means proper to the Gospel, which differ in many respects from those obtaining in the earthly city.

Nevertheless, there are close links between the things of earth and those things in man's condition which transcend the world, and the Church utilizes temporal realities as often as its mission requires it. But it never places its hopes in any privileges accorded to it by civil authority; indeed, it will give up the exercise of certain legitimate rights whenever it becomes clear that their use will compromise the sincerity of its witness, or whenever new circumstances call for a revised approach. But at all times and in all places the Church should have true freedom to preach the faith, to proclaim its teaching about society, to carry out its task among men without hindrance, and to pass moral judgments even in matters relating to politics, whenever the fundamental rights of man or the salvation of souls requires it. The means, the only means, it may use are those which are in accord with the Gospel and the welfare of all men according to the diversity of times and circumstances.

With loyalty to the Gospel in the fulfillment of its mission in the world, the Church, whose duty it is to foster and elevate all that is true, all that is good, and all that is beautiful in the human community,[16] consolidates peace among men for the glory of God.[17]

NOTES

1 Selections from *Gaudium et Spes* (Pastoral Constitution on the Church in the Modern World), Part II, ch. 4, "The Political Community," *Vatican Council II: The Conciliar and Post Conciliar Documents*, study edition, ed. Austin Flannery (Northport, New York: Costello Publishing Company, 1975, 1986). The English translation by Ronan Lennon and Senan Crowe is based on the official Latin text prepared by the General Secretariat of the Second Vatican Council and published in 1966 under the title: *Sacrosanctum Oecumenicum Concilium Vaticanum II: Constitutiones, Decreta, Declarationes.*

2 John XXIII, *Mater et Magistra*, eds. D. Champion and E. Culhane (New York: The American Press, 1961). Though the bull was dated May 15, it was actually issued July 15, 1961. In the encyclical the pope deals extensively with the principle of subsidiarity.

3 *Guadium et Spes.*

4 *Ibid.*, 948.

5 *Ibid.*, 980-981.

6 *Ibid.*, 982-983.

7 *Ibid.*, 983.

8 Cf. John XXIII, Litt. Encycl. *Mater et Magistra: AAS* 53 (1961), 417.

9 Cf. John XXIII, *ibid.*

10 Cf. Rom. 13:1-5.

11 Cf. Rom. 13:5.

12 Cf. Pius XII, *Christmas Message* 1942: *AAS* 35 (1043), 9-24; *Christmas Message* 1944: *AAS* 37 (1945), 11-17; John XXIII, Litt. Encycl. *Pacem in Terris: AAS* 55 (1963), 263, 271, 277, 278.

13 Cf. Pius XII, *radio message*, 1 June 1941: *AAS* 33 (1941), 200; John XXIII, Litt. Encycl. *Pacem in Terris: AAS* 55 (1963), 273, 274.

14 Cf. John XXIII, Litt. Encycl., *Mater et Magistra: AAS* 53 (1961), 415-418.

15 Cf. Pius XI, *Allocution to the Directors of the Catholic University Federation: Discorsi di Pio XI*, ed. Bertetto, Torino, vol. 1 (1960), 743.

16 Cf. Vatican Council II, Dogmatic Constitution *Lumen Gentium*, n. 13: *ASS* 57 (1965), 17.

17 Cf. Luke 2:14.

TWELVE

✦✦✦✦✦✦✦✦✦✦

ECONOMIC JUSTICE FOR ALL[1]
from the National (U. S.) Conference of Catholic Bishops

The American Catholic Bishops

In the early 1980s, nearly two decades after U.S. President Lyndon Johnson had launched his War on Poverty, Americans were aware that poverty was becoming more, not less severe among its lowest classes. Moreover, growing Third-World poverty was agonizingly evident across much of Africa, Asia, and Latin America, especially in the expanding urban areas.

With a sense of alarm about such poverty in and around the world's richest country, the American Catholic Bishops felt compelled to address questions of economic justice in a new way. The first draft of their pastoral letter on the U.S. economy was released in 1984 and the final draft in 1986.[2] This was not the first time the American Bishops had addressed the Church together with the wider American public on economic issues. Beginning at the end of World War I with their "Program of Social Reconstruction," and moving up through statements during the Depression era and the civil-rights era, to a brief 1975 comment on the human dimensions of unemployment, the Bishops had returned again and again to questions that had been framed by Pope Leo XIII in 1891.[3]

This time, from 1984 to 1986, the American Bishops decided to make the very process of drafting their letter a cause for public discussion, and they aimed for a more comprehensive message. They succeeded on both counts. Their letter, *Economic Justice for All*, breathes the air of the Second Vatican Council when they say that "Followers of Christ must avoid a tragic separation between faith and everyday life."[4] They "write as heirs of the biblical prophets who summon us 'to do the right, and to love goodness, and to walk humbly with your God' (Mi 6:8)."[5] They write as pastors to a people whom they fear are becoming used to living with much wealth in the midst of much poverty. They write to urge reform of both U.S. and world economies so that justice might be done. Several drafts of the letter were written "in public," so to speak, with countless hearings and much press attention.

The Bishops are aware that American Catholics themselves are not sufficiently conscious of the long tradition of Catholic social teaching that reaches back to Pope Leo XIII. But it is not just the *recent* Catholic tradition of which Christians are ignorant; ignorance of Christian history reaching all the way back to the Bible is a mark of the modern secular world. So the American Bishops write as "heirs of a long tradition of thought and action on the moral dimensions of economic activity," beginning with the "life and words of Jesus and the teaching of his Church. . . ."[6]

At the beginning of the letter the Bishops clearly delineate their basic themes. Their pastoral message is intended *not* as "a blueprint for the American economy" but as a moral message stressing the "standards we must meet."[7] Six "moral principles" constitute the primary themes of the letter:

1. Every economic decision and institution must be judged in the light of whether it protects or undermines the dignity of the human person.

2. Human dignity can be realized and protected only in community.

3. All people have a right to participate in the economic life of society.

4. All members of society have a special obligation to the poor and vulnerable.

5. Human rights are the minimum conditions for life in community.

6. Society as a whole, acting through public and private institutions, has the moral responsibility to enhance human dignity and protect human rights.[8]

These principles reflect many currents of twentieth-century Catholic thought and experience, ranging from the special concern for the poor that is stressed particularly by Latin American liberation theologians to the long-standing stress on community and the emphasis on the responsibility of "society as a whole" to meet human needs.

The selections below come entirely from the second chapter of *Economic Justice for All*—titled "The Christian Vision of Economic Life." Here the Bishops set forth ethical norms and discuss the responsibilities of diverse institutions for economic justice. These excerpts follow directly after an extended summary of "biblical perspectives" in the full text of the letter. Chapter Three then takes up the issues of employment, poverty, food and agriculture, and development in the world's poor countries. Chapter Four calls for a "new American experiment" of partnership among different institutions and regions "for the public good." The last chapter looks to the future of the Christian vocation in the world.

Ch 2
ch 1
Ch 3
Ch 4
Ch 5

The reader will see many lines of continuity running from *Rerum Novarum* and *Quadragesimo Anno* through the documents of the Second Vatican Council to the American Bishops' pastoral letter. The common good, the principle of subsidiarity, and the natural character of a socially differentiated human community all stand out in this regard. In the letter as a whole, references to biblical justice, to human rights, and to the urgent plight of the poor reflect more contemporary emphases in Catholic thought since the time of the Second Vatican Council.

common themes w/ 2nd Vatican

The American Bishops say that their letter is intended not only for American Catholics but also for the wider public, including "many who do not share Christian religious convictions."[9] They count on the fact that "Human understanding and religious belief are complementary, not contradictory."[10] To be sure, many of the policy prescriptions of the letter are either held or rejected by both Catholics and non-Catholics. But the pastoral letter's stress on the distinctive features of a Christian approach should not be overlooked. To believe that human beings are created in the image of God and that they have as their proper destiny (their final *telos*) communion with God through Jesus Christ is to hold a radical and uniquely Christian vision.

Although the Bishops do not stress the idea of a "third way" in American public life in the same way that some Christian Democrats in Europe or Latin America might do, there can be no doubt that their vision of human persons, of community, of the common good, of economic justice, and of the ultimate purpose of human life is neither individualistic nor collectivistic. They write from out of a distinctive tradition which "insists that human dignity, realized in community with others and with the whole of God's creation, is the norm against which every social institution must be measured."[11] "We want to make the legacy of Christian social thought a living, growing resource that can inspire hope and help shape the future."[12]

ECONOMIC JUSTICE FOR ALL

The Responsibilities of Social Living

63. Human life is life in community. Catholic social teaching proposes several complementary perspectives that show how moral responsibilities and duties in the economic sphere are rooted in this call to community.

Love and Solidarity

64. *The commandments to love God with all one's heart and to love one's neighbor as oneself are the heart and soul of Christian morality.* Jesus offers himself as the model of this all-inclusive love: ". . . love one another as I have loved you" (Jn 15:21). These commands point out the path toward true human fulfillment and happiness. They are not arbitrary restrictions on human freedom. Only active love of God and neighbor makes the fullness of community happen. Christians look forward in hope to a true communion among all persons with each other and with God. The Spirit of Christ labors in history to build up the bonds of solidarity among all persons until that day on which their union is brought to perfection in the Kingdom of God.[13] Indeed Christian theological reflection on the very reality of God as a trinitarian unity of persons—Father, Son, and Holy Spirit—shows that being a person means being united to other persons in mutual love.[14]

65. What the Bible and Christian tradition teach, human wisdom confirms. Centuries before Christ, the Greeks and Romans spoke of the human person as a "social animal" made for friendship, community, and public life. These insights show that human beings achieve self-realization not in isolation, but in interaction with others.[15]

66. The virtues of citizenship are an expression of Christian love more crucial in today's interdependent world than ever before. These virtues grow out of a lively sense of one's dependence on the commonweal and obligations to it. This civic commitment must also guide the economic institutions of society. In the absence of a vital sense of citizenship among the businesses, corporations, labor unions, and other groups that shape economic life, society as a whole is endangered. Solidarity is another name for this social friendship and civic commitment that make human moral and economic life possible.

67. The Christian tradition recognizes, of course, that the fullness of love and community will be achieved only when God's work in Christ comes to completion in the kingdom of God. This kingdom has been inaugurated among us, but God's redeeming and transforming work is not yet complete. Within history, knowledge of how to achieve the goal of social unity is limited. Human sin continues to wound the lives of both individuals and larger social bodies and places obstacles in the path toward greater social solidarity. If efforts to protect human dignity are to be effective, they must take these limits on knowledge and love into account. Nevertheless, sober realism should not be confused with resigned or cynical pessimism. It is a challenge to develop a courageous hope that can sustain efforts that will sometimes be arduous and protracted.

Justice and Participation

68. Biblical justice is the goal we strive for. This rich biblical understanding portrays a just society as one marked by the fullness of love, compassion, holiness, and peace. On their path through history, however, sinful human beings need more specific guidance on how to move toward the realization of this great vision of God's Kingdom. This guidance is contained in the norms of basic or minimal justice. These norms state the *minimum* levels of mutual care and respect that all persons owe to each other in an imperfect world.[16] Catholic social teaching, like much philosophical reflection, distinguishes three dimensions of basic justice: commutative justice, distributive justice, and social justice.[17]

69. *Commutative justice calls for fundamental fairness in all agreements and exchanges between individuals or private social groups.* It demands respect *contracts* for the equal human dignity of all persons in economic transactions, contracts, or promises. For example, workers owe their employers diligent work in exchange for their wages. Employers are obligated to treat their employees as persons, paying them fair wages in exchange for the work done and establishing conditions and patterns of work that are truly human.[18]

70. *Distributive justice requires that the allocation of income, wealth, and power in society be evaluated in light of its effects on persons whose basic charity material needs are unmet.* The Second Vatican Council stated: "The right to have a share of earthly goods sufficient for oneself and one's family belongs to everyone. The fathers and doctors of the Church held this view, teaching that we are obligated to come to the relief of the poor and to do so not merely out of our superfluous goods."[19] Minimum material resources are an absolute necessity for human life. If persons are to be recognized as members of the

human community, then the community has an obligation to help fulfill these basic needs unless an absolute scarcity of resources makes this strictly impossible. No such scarcity exists in the United States today.

71. Justice also has implications for the way the larger social, economic, and political institutions of society are organized. *Social justice implies that persons have an obligation to be active and productive participants in the life of society and that society has a duty to enable them to participate in this way.* This form of justice can also be called "contributive," for it stresses the duty of all who are able to help create the goods, services, and other nonmaterial or spiritual values necessary for the welfare of the whole community. In the words of Pius XI, "It is of the very essence of social justice to demand from each individual all that is necessary for the community good."[20] Productivity is essential if the community is to have the resources to serve the well-being of all. Productivity, however, cannot be measured solely by its output in goods and services. Patterns of production must also be measured in light of their impact on the fulfillment of basic needs, employment levels, patterns of discrimination, environmental quality, and sense of community.

72. The meaning of social justice also includes a duty to organize economic and social institutions so that people can contribute to society in ways that respect their freedom and the dignity of their labor. Work should enable the working person to become "more a human being," more capable of acting intelligently, freely, and in ways that lead to self-realization.[21]

73. Economic conditions that leave large numbers of able people unemployed, underemployed, or employed in dehumanizing conditions fail to meet the converging demands of these three forms of basic justice. Work with adequate pay for all who seek it is the primary means for achieving basic justice in our society. Discrimination in job opportunities or income levels on the basis of race, sex, or other arbitrary standards can never be justified.[22] It is a scandal that such discrimination continues in the United States today. Where the effects of past discrimination persist, society has the obligation to take positive steps to overcome the legacy of injustice. Judiciously administered affirmative action programs in education and employment can be important expressions of the drive for solidarity and participation that is at the heart of true justice. Social harm calls for social relief.

74. Basic justice also calls for the establishment of a floor of material well-being on which all can stand. This is a duty of the whole of society and it creates particular obligations for those with greater resources. This duty calls into question extreme inequalities of income and consumption when so many lack basic necessities. Catholic social teaching does not maintain that a flat, arithmetical equality of income and wealth is a demand of justice, but it does

challenge economic arrangements that leave large numbers of people impoverished. Further, it sees extreme inequality as a threat to the solidarity of the human community, for great disparities lead to deep social divisions and conflict.[23]

75. This means that all of us must examine our way of living in light of the needs of the poor. Christian faith and the norms of justice impose distinct limits on what we consume and how we view material goods. The great wealth of the United States can easily blind us to the poverty that exists in this nation and the destitution of hundreds of millions of people in other parts of the world. Americans are challenged today as never before to develop the inner freedom to resist the temptation constantly to seek more. Only in this way will the nation avoid what Paul VI called "the most evident form of moral underdevelopment," namely greed.[24]

wealth can to blind us needs of others

76. These duties call not only for individual charitable giving but also for a more systematic approach by businesses, labor unions, and the many other groups that shape economic life—as well as government. The concentration of privilege that exists today results far more from institutional relationships that distribute power and wealth inequitably than from differences in talent or lack of desire to work. These institutional patterns must be examined and revised if we are to meet the demands of basic justice. For example, a system of taxation based on assessment according to ability to pay[25] is a prime necessity for the fulfillment of these social obligations. . . .

Human Rights: The Minimum Conditions for Life in Community

79. Catholic social teaching spells out the basic demands of justice in greater detail in the human rights of every person. These fundamental rights are prerequisites for a dignified life in community. The Bible vigorously affirms the sacredness of every person as a creature in the image and likeness of God. The biblical emphasis on covenant and community also shows that human dignity can only be realized and protected in solidarity with others. In Catholic social thought, therefore, respect for human rights and a strong sense of both personal and community responsibility are linked, not opposed. Vatican II described the common good as "the sum of those conditions of social life which allow social groups and their individual members relatively thorough and ready access to their own fulfillment."[26] These conditions include the rights to fulfillment of material needs, a guarantee of fundamental freedoms, and the protection of relationships that are essential to participation in the life of society.[27] These rights are bestowed on human beings by

God and grounded in the nature and dignity of human persons. They are not created by society. Indeed society has a duty to secure and protect them.[28]

80. The full range of human rights has been systematically outlined by John XXIII in his encyclical *Peace on Earth*. His discussion echoes the United Nations Universal Declaration of Human Rights and implies that internationally accepted human rights standards are strongly supported by Catholic teaching. These rights include the civil and political rights to freedom of speech, worship, and assembly. A number of human rights also concern human welfare and are of a specifically economic nature. First among these are the rights to life, food, clothing, shelter, rest, medical care, and basic education. These are indispensable to the protection of human dignity. In order to ensure these necessities, all persons have a right to earn a living, which for most people in our economy is through remunerative employment. All persons also have a right to security in the event of sickness, unemployment, and old age. Participation in the life of the community calls for the protection of this same right to employment, as well as the right to healthful working conditions, to wages, and other benefits sufficient to provide individuals and their families with a standard of living in keeping with human dignity, and to the possibility of property ownership.[29] These fundamental personal rights— civil and political as well as social and economic—state the minimum conditions for social institutions that respect human dignity, social solidarity, and justice. They are all essential to human dignity and to the integral development of both individuals and society, and are thus moral issues.[30] Any denial of these rights harms persons and wounds the human community. Their serious and sustained denial violates individuals and destroys solidarity among persons.

81. Social and economic rights call for a mode of implementation different from that required to secure civil and political rights. Freedom of worship and of speech imply immunity from interference on the part of both other persons and the government. The rights to education, employment, and social security, for example, are empowerments that call for positive action by individuals and society at large.

82. However, both kinds of rights call for positive action to create social and political institutions that enable all persons to become active members of society. Civil and political rights allow persons to participate freely in the public life of the community, for example, through free speech, assembly, and the vote. In democratic countries these rights have been secured through a long and vigorous history of creating the institutions of constitutional government. In seeking to secure the full range of social and economic rights today, a similar effort to shape new economic arrangements will be necessary.

83. The first step in such an effort is the development of a new cultural consensus that the basic economic conditions of human welfare are essential to human dignity and are due persons by right. Second, the securing of these rights will make demands on *all* members of society, on all private sector institutions, and on government. A concerted effort on all levels in our society is needed to meet these basic demands of justice and solidarity. Indeed political democracy and a commitment to secure economic rights are mutually reinforcing.

84. Securing economic rights for all will be an arduous task. There are a number of precedents in U.S. history, however, which show that the work has already begun.[31] The country needs a serious dialogue about the appropriate levels of private and public sector involvement that are needed to move forward. There is certainly room for diversity of opinion in the Church and in U.S. society on *how* to protect the human dignity and economic rights of all our brothers and sisters.[32] In our view, however, there can be no legitimate disagreement on the basic moral objectives. . . .

Working for Greater Justice: Persons and Institutions

96. The economy of this nation has been built by the labor of human hands and minds. Its future will be forged by the ways persons direct all this work toward greater justice. The economy is not a machine that operates according to its own inexorable laws, and persons are not mere objects tossed about by economic forces. Pope John Paul II has stated that "human work is a key, probably the essential key, to the whole social question."[33] The Pope's understanding of work includes virtually all forms of productive human activity: agriculture, entrepreneurship, industry, the care of children, the sustaining of family life, politics, medical care, and scientific research. Leisure, prayer, celebration, and the arts are also central to the realization of human dignity and to the development of a rich cultural life. It is in their daily work, however, that persons become the subjects and creators of the economic life of the nation.[34] Thus, it is primarily through their daily labor that people make their most important contributions to economic justice.

97. All work has a threefold moral significance. First, it is a principal way that people exercise the distinctive human capacity for self-expression and self-realization. Second, it is the ordinary way for human beings to fulfill their material needs. Finally, work enables people to contribute to the well-being of the larger community. Work is not only for one's self. It is for one's family, for the nation, and indeed for the benefit of the entire human family.[35]

98. These three moral concerns should be visible in the work of all, no matter what their role in the economy: blue collar workers, managers, home-makers, politicians, and others. They should also govern the activities of the many different, overlapping communities and institutions that make up society: families, neighborhoods, small businesses, giant corporations, trade unions, the various levels of government, international organizations, and a host of other human associations including communities of faith.

99. Catholic social teaching calls for respect for the full richness of social life. The need for vital contributions from different human associations—ranging in size from the family to government—has been classically expressed in Catholic social teaching in the "principle of subsidiarity":

> Just as it is gravely wrong to take from individuals what they can accomplish by their own initiative and industry and give it to the community, so also it is an injustice and at the same time a grave evil and disturbance of right order to assign to a greater and higher association what lesser and subordinate organizations can do. For every social activity ought of its very nature to furnish help (*subsidium*) to the members of the body social, and never destroy and absorb them.[36]

100. This principle guarantees institutional pluralism. It provides space for freedom, initiative, and creativity on the part of many social agents. At the same time, it insists that *all* these agents should work in ways that help build up the social body. Therefore, in all their activities these groups should be working in ways that express their distinctive capacities for action, that help meet human needs, and that make true contributions to the common good of the human community. The task of creating a more just U.S. economy is the vocation of all and depends on strengthening the virtues of public service and responsible citizenship in personal life and on all levels of institutional life.[37]

101. Without attempting to describe the tasks of all the different groups that make up society, we want to point to the specific rights and duties of some of the persons and institutions whose work for justice will be particularly important to the future of the United States economy. These rights and duties are among the concrete implications of the principle of subsidiarity. Further implications will be discussed in Chapter IV of this letter ["A New American Experiment: Partnership for the Public Good"].

Working People and Labor Unions

102. Though John Paul II's understanding of work is a very inclusive one, it fully applies to those customarily called "workers" or "labor" in the

United States. Labor has great dignity, so great that all who are able to work are obligated to do so. The duty to work derives both from God's command and from a responsibility to one's own humanity and to the common good.[38] The virtue of industriousness is also an expression of a person's dignity and solidarity with others. All working people are called to contribute to the common good by seeking excellence in production and service.

103. Because work is this important, people have a right to employment. In return for their labor, workers have a right to wages and other benefits sufficient to sustain life in dignity. As Pope Leo XIII stated, every working person has "the right of securing things to sustain life."[39] The way power is distributed in a free market economy frequently gives employers greater bargaining power than employees in the negotiation of labor contracts. Such unequal power may press workers into a choice between an inadequate wage and no wage at all. But justice, not charity, demands certain minimum guarantees. The provision of wages and other benefits sufficient to support a family in dignity is a basic necessity to prevent this exploitation of workers. The dignity of workers also requires adequate health care, security for old age or disability, unemployment compensation, healthful working conditions, weekly rest, periodic holidays for recreation and leisure, and reasonable security against arbitrary dismissal.[40] These provisions are all essential if workers are to be treated as persons rather than simply as a "factor of production."

104. The Church fully supports the right of workers to form unions or other associations to secure their rights to fair wages and working conditions. This is a specific application of the more general right to associate. In the words of Pope John Paul II, "The experience of history teaches that organizations of this type are an indispensable element of social life, especially in modern industrialized societies."[41] Unions may also legitimately resort to strikes where this is the only available means to the justice owed to workers.[42] No one may deny the right to organize without attacking human dignity itself. Therefore, we firmly oppose organized efforts, such as those regrettably now seen in this country, to break existing unions and prevent workers from organizing. Migrant agricultural workers today are particularly in need of the protection, including the right to organize and bargain collectively. U.S. labor law reform is needed to meet these problems as well as to provide more timely and effective remedies for unfair labor practices.

105. Denial of the right to organize has been pursued ruthlessly in many countries beyond our borders. We vehemently oppose violations of the freedom to associate, wherever they occur, for they are an intolerable attack on social solidarity.

106. Along with the rights of workers and unions go a number of important responsibilities. Individual workers have obligations to their employers, and trade unions also have duties to society as a whole. Union management in particular carries a strong responsibility for the good name of the entire union movement. Workers must use their collective power to contribute to the well-being of the whole community and should avoid pressing demands whose fulfillment would damage the common good and the rights of more vulnerable members of society.[43] It should be noted, however, that wages paid to workers are but one of the factors affecting the competitiveness of industries. Thus, it is unfair to expect unions to make concessions if managers and shareholders do not make at least equal sacrifices.

107. Many U.S. unions have exercised leadership in the struggle for justice for minorities and women. Racial and sexual discrimination, however, have blotted the record of some unions. Organized labor has a responsibility to work positively toward eliminating the injustice this discrimination has caused.

108. Perhaps the greatest challenge facing United States workers and unions today is that of developing a new vision of their role in the United States economy of the future. The labor movement in the United States stands at a crucial moment. The dynamism of the unions that led to their rapid growth in the middle decades of this century has been replaced by a decrease in the percentage of U.S. workers who are organized. American workers are under heavy pressures today that threaten their jobs. The restrictions on the right to organize in many countries abroad make labor costs lower there, threaten American workers and their jobs, and lead to the exploitation of workers in these countries. In these difficult circumstances, guaranteeing the rights of U.S. workers calls for imaginative vision and creative new steps, not reactive or simply defensive strategies. For example, organized labor can play a very important role in helping to provide the education and training needed to help keep workers employable. Unions can also help both their own members and workers in developing countries by increasing their international efforts. A vital labor movement will be one that looks to the future with a deepened sense of global interdependence.

109. There are many signs that these challenges are being discussed by creative labor leaders today. Deeper and broader discussions of this sort are needed. This does not mean that only organized labor faces these new problems. All other sectors and institutions in the U.S. economy need similar vision and imagination. Indeed new forms of cooperation among labor, management, government, and other social groups are essential, and will be discussed in Chapter IV of this letter.

Owners and Managers

110. The economy's success in fulfilling the demands of justice will depend on how its vast resources and wealth are managed. Property owners, managers, and investors of financial capital must all contribute to creating a more just society. Securing economic justice depends heavily on the leadership of men and women in business and on wise investments by private enterprises. Pope John Paul II has pointed out, "The degree of well-being which society today enjoys would be unthinkable without the dynamic figure of the business person, whose function consists of organizing human labor and the means of production so as to give rise to the goods and services necessary for the prosperity and progress of the community."[44] The freedom of entrepreneurship, business, and finance should be protected, but the accountability of this freedom to the common good and the norms of justice must be assured.

rec. of cap.

111. Persons in management face many hard choices each day, choices on which the well-being of many others depends. Commitment to the public good and not simply the private good of their firms is at the heart of what it means to call their work a vocation and not simply a career or a job. We believe that the norms and priorities discussed in this letter can be of help as they pursue their important tasks. The duties of individuals in the business world, however, do not exhaust the ethical dimensions of business and finance. The size of a firm or bank is in many cases an indicator of relative power. Large corporations and large financial institutions have considerable power to help shape economic institutions within the United States and throughout the world. With this power goes responsibility and the need for those who manage it to be held to moral and institutional accountability.

112. Business and finance have the duty to be faithful trustees of the resources at their disposal. No one can ever own capital resources absolutely or control their use without regard for others and society as a whole.[45] This applies first of all to land and natural resources. Short-term profits reaped at the cost of depletion of natural resources or the pollution of the environment violate this trust.

113. Resources created by human industry are also held in trust. Owners and managers have not created this capital on their own. They have benefited from the work of many others and from the local communities that support their endeavors.[46] They are accountable to these workers and communities when making decisions. For example, reinvestment in technological innovation is often crucial for the long-term viability of a firm. The use of financial resources solely in pursuit of short-term profits can stunt the production of

needed goods and services; a broader vision of managerial responsibility is needed.

114. The Catholic tradition has long defended the right to private ownership of productive property.[47] This right is an important element in a just economic policy. It enlarges our capacity for creativity and initiative.[48] Small and medium-sized farms, businesses, and entrepreneurial enterprises are among the most creative and efficient of our economy. They should be highly valued by the people of the United States, as are land ownership and home ownership. Widespread distribution of property can help avoid excessive concentration of economic and political power. For these reasons ownership should be made possible for a broad sector of our population.[49]

115. The common good may sometimes demand that the right to own be limited by public involvement in the planning or ownership of certain sectors of the economy. Support of private ownership does not mean that anyone has the right to unlimited accumulation of wealth. "Private property does not constitute for anyone an absolute or unconditioned right. No one is justified in keeping for his exclusive use what he does not need, when others lack necessities."[50] Pope John Paul II has referred to limits placed on ownership by the duty to serve the common good as a "social mortgage" on private property.[51] For example, these limits are the basis of society's exercise of eminent domain over privately owned land needed for roads or other essential public goods. The Church's teaching opposes collectivist and statist economic approaches. But it also rejects the notion that a free market automatically produces justice. Therefore, as Pope John Paul II has argued, "One cannot exclude the socialization, in suitable conditions, of certain means of production."[52] The determination of when such conditions exist must be made on a case by case basis in light of the demands of the common good.

116. United States business and financial enterprises can also help determine the justice or injustice of the world economy. They are not all-powerful, but their real power is unquestionable. Transnational corporations and financial institutions can make positive contributions to development and global solidarity. Pope John Paul II has pointed out, however, that the desire to maximize profits and reduce the cost of natural resources and labor has often tempted these transnational enterprises to behavior that increases inequality and decreases the stability of the international order.[53] By collaborating with those national governments that serve their citizens justly and with intergovernmental agencies, these corporations can contribute to overcoming the desperate plight of many persons throughout the world.

117. Business people, managers, investors, and financiers follow a vital Christian vocation when they act responsibly and seek the common good. We

encourage and support a renewed sense of vocation in the business community. We also recognize that the way business people serve society is governed and limited by the incentives which flow from tax policies, the availability of credit, and other public policies.

118. Businesses have a right to an institutional framework that does not penalize enterprises that act responsibly. Governments must provide regulations and a system of taxation which encourage firms to preserve the environment, employ disadvantaged workers, and create jobs in depressed areas. Managers and stockholders should not be torn between their responsibilities to their organizations and their responsibilities toward society as a whole.

Citizens and Government

119. In addition to rights and duties related to specific roles in the economy, everyone has obligations based simply on membership in the social community. By fulfilling these duties, we create a true commonwealth. Volunteering time, talent, and money to work for greater justice is a fundamental expression of Christian love and social solidarity. All who have more than they need must come to the aid of the poor. People with professional or technical skills needed to enhance the lives of others have a duty to share them. And the poor have similar obligations: to work together as individuals and families to build up their communities by acts of social solidarity and justice. These voluntary efforts to overcome injustice are part of the Christian vocation.

120. Every citizen also has the responsibility to work to secure justice and human rights through an organized social response. In the words of Pius XI, "Charity will never be true charity unless it takes justice into account. . . . Let no one attempt with small gifts of charity to exempt himself from the great duties imposed by justice."[54] The guaranteeing of basic justice for all is not an optional expression of largesse but an inescapable duty for the whole of society.

121. The traditional distinction between society and the state in Catholic social teaching provides the basic framework for such organized public efforts. The Church opposes all statist and totalitarian approaches to socioeconomic questions. Social life is richer than governmental power can encompass. All groups that compose society have responsibilities to respond to the demands of justice. We have just outlined some of the duties of labor unions and business and financial enterprises. These must be supplemented by initiatives by local community groups, professional associations, educational insti-

tutions, churches, and synagogues. All the groups that give life to this society have important roles to play in the pursuit of economic justice.

122. For this reason, it is all the more significant that the teachings of the Church insist that *government has a moral function protecting human rights and securing basic justice for all members of the commonwealth.*[55] Society as a whole and in all its diversity is responsible for building up the common good. But it is government's role to guarantee the minimum conditions that make this rich social activity possible, namely, human rights and justice.[56] This obligation also falls on individual citizens as they choose their representatives and participate in shaping public opinion.

123. More specifically, it is the responsibility of all citizens, acting through their government, to assist and empower the poor, the disadvantaged, the handicapped, and the unemployed. Government should assume a positive role in generating employment and establishing fair labor practices, in guaranteeing the provision and maintenance of the economy's infrastructure, such as roads, bridges, harbors, public means of communication, and transport. It should regulate trade and commerce in the interest of fairness.[57] Government may levy the taxes necessary to meet these responsibilities, and citizens have a moral obligation to pay those taxes. The way society responds to the needs of the poor through its public policies is the litmus test of its justice or injustice. The political debate about these policies is the indispensable forum for dealing with the conflicts and trade-offs that will always be present in the pursuit of a more just economy.

124. The primary norm for determining the scope and limits of governmental intervention is the "principle of subsidiarity" cited above. This principle states that, in order to protect basic justice, government should undertake only those initiatives which exceed the capacity of individuals or private groups acting independently. Government should not replace or destroy smaller communities and individual initiative. Rather it should help them to contribute more effectively to social well-being and supplement their activity when the demands of justice exceed their capacities. This does not mean, however, that the government that governs least governs best. Rather it defines good government intervention as that which truly "helps" other social groups contribute to the common good by directing, urging, restraining, and regulating economic activity as "the occasion requires and necessity demands."[58] This calls for cooperation and consensus-building among the diverse agents in our economic life, including government. The precise form of government involvement in this process cannot be determined in the abstract. It will depend on an assessment of specific needs and the most effective ways to address them.

NOTES

1 Selections from Chapter II, "The Christian Vision of Economic Life," of the U. S. Catholic Bishops, *Economic Justice for All: Pastoral Letter on Catholic Social Teaching and the U.S. Economy* (Washington, D.C.: National Conference of Catholic Bishops, 1986).

2 *Economic Justice for All.*

3 All the U.S. Bishops's statements related to economic justice are collected in David M. Byers, ed., *Justice in the Marketplace: Collected Statements of the Vatican and the U.S. Catholic Bishops on Economic Policy, 1891-1984* (Washington, D.C.: U.S. Catholic Conference, 1985).

4 *Economic Justice for All*, vi.

5 *Ibid.*

6 *Ibid.*, vii.

7 *Ibid.*, ix.

8 *Ibid.*, ix-xi. All of the statements are emphasized in the original.

9 *Ibid.*, 32 par. 61.

10 *Ibid.*

11 *Ibid.*, 12, par. 25.

12 *Ibid.*, 13, par. 26.

13 Pope Paul VI, *On Evangelization in the Modern World* (*Evangelii Nuntiandi*), December 8, 1975, par. 24.

14 Vatican Council II, *The Pastoral Constitution on the Church in the Modern World* (*Gaudium et Spes*), December 7, 1965, par. 32. Subsequent references will be to *The Pastoral Constitution.*

15 *Ibid.*, par. 25.

16 The idea of minimal justice is developed in par. 39 of the letter as well as in paras. 79-84 included below.

17 Josef Pieper, *The Four Cardinal Virtues* (Notre Dame: University of Notre Dame Press, 1966), 43-116; David Hollenbach, "Modern Catholic Teachings Concerning Justice," in John C. Haughey ed., *The Faith That Does Justice* (New York: Paulist Press, 1977), 207-231.

18 Jon P. Gunnemann, "Capitalism and Commutative Justice," presented at the 1985 meeting of the Society of Christian Ethics, forthcoming in *The Annual of the Society of Christian Ethics.*

19 *The Pastoral Constitution*, par. 69.

20 Pope Pius XI, *Divini Redemptoris*, March 19, 1937, par. 51. See John A. Ryan, *Distributive Justice*, 3d ed. (New York: Macmillan, 1942), 188. The term "social justice" has been used in several different but related ways in the Catholic ethical tradition. See William Ferree, "The Act of Social Justice," *Philosophical Studies*, vol. 72 (Washington, D.C.: The Catholic University of America Press, 1943).

21 Pope John Paul II, *On Human Work* (*Laborem Exercens*), September 14, 1981, paras. 6, 9.

22 *The Pastoral Constitution*, par. 29.

23 *Ibid.* Paras. 180-182 (not included here) develop this point further.

24 Pope Paul VI, *On Promoting the Development of Peoples* (*Populorum Progressio*), March 26, 1967, par. 19.

[25] Pope John XXIII, *On Christianity and Social Progress* (*Mater et Magistra*), May 15, 1961, par. 132.

[26] *The Pastoral Constitution*, par. 26.

[27] Pope John Paul II, Address at the General Assembly of the United Nations (October 2, 1979), paras. 13, 14.

[28] See Pope Pius XII, 1941 Pentecost Address, in V. Yzermans, *The Major Addresses of Pope Pius XII*, vol. I (St. Paul: North Central, 1961), paras. 32-33.

[29] Pope John XXIII, *Peace on Earth* (*Pacem in Terris*), April 11, 1963, paras. 8-27. See *On Human Work*, paras. 18-19. *Peace on Earth* and other modern papal statements refer explicitly to the "right to work" as one of the fundamental economic rights. Because of the ambiguous meaning of the phrase in the United States, and also because the ordinary way people earn their living in our society is through paid employment, the NCCB has affirmed previously that the protection of human dignity demands that the right to useful employment be secured for all who are able and willing to work. See NCCB, *The Economy: Human Dimensions* (November 20, 1975), par. 5, in NCCB, *Justice in the Marketplace*, 470-1. See also Congregation for the Doctrine of the Faith, *Instruction on Christian Freedom and Liberation*, par. 85.

[30] *On Promoting the Development of Peoples*, par. 14.

[31] Martha H. Good, "Freedom from Want: The Failure of United States Courts to Protect Subsistence Rights," *Human Rights Quarterly*, 6 (1984): 335-365.

[32] *The Pastoral Constitution*, par. 43.

[33] *On Human Work*, par. 3.

[34] *Ibid.*, paras. 5, 6.

[35] *Ibid.*, paras. 6, 10.

[36] Pope Pius XI, *On Reconstructing the Social Order* (*Quadragesimo Anno*), May 15, 1931, par. 79. The meaning of this principle is not always accurately understood. For studies of its interpretation in Catholic teaching see: Calvez and Perrin in John F. Cronin, *Catholic Social Principles* (Milwaukee: Bruce, 1950), 328-342; Johannes Messner, "Freedom as a Principle of Social Order: An Essay in the Substance of Subsidiary Function," *Modern Schoolman*, 28 (1951): 97-110; Richard E. Mulcahy, "Subsidiarity," *New Catholic Encyclopedia*, 13 (New York: McGraw-Hill, 1966): 762; Franz H. Mueller, "The Principle of Subsidiarity in Christian Tradition," *American Catholic Sociological Review*, 4 (October, 1943): 144-157; Oswald von Nell-Breuning, "Zur Sozialreform, Erwagungen zum Subsidiaritatsprinzip," *Stimmen der Zeit*, 157, Bd. 81 (1955-1956): 1-11; id., "Subsidiarity," *Sacramentum Mundi* (New York: Herder and Herder, 1970): 6, 114-116; Arthur Fridolin Utz, *Formen und Grenzen des Subsidiaritatsprinzips* (Heidelberg: F.H. Kerle Verlag, 1956); id., "The Principle of Subsidiarity and Contemporary Natural Law," *Natural Law Forum*, 3 (1958): 170-183; id., *Grundsätze der Sozialpolitik: Solidaritat und Subsidiaritat in der Alterversicherung* (Stuttgart: Sewald Verlag, 1969).

[37] *The Pastoral Constitution*, par. 31.

[38] *On Human Work*, par. 16.

[39] Pope Leo XIII, *On the Condition of Workers* (*Rerum Novarum*), May 15, 1891, par. 62; see also par. 9.

[40] *On Human Work*, par. 19.

[41] *Ibid.*, par. 20.

[42] *Ibid.*

[43] *Ibid.*

[44] Pope John Paul II, Address to Business Men and Economic Managers (Milan, May 22, 1983) in *L'Osservatore Romano*, weekly edition in English (June 20, 1983), 9:1.

45 Thomas Aquinas, *Summa Theologiae*, IIa, IIae, q. 66.

46 As Pope John Paul II has stated: "This gigantic and powerful instrument—the whole collection of the means of production that in a sense are considered synonymous with 'capital'—is the result of work and bears the signs of human labor." *On Human Work*, par. 12.

47 *Rerum Novarum*, paras. 10, 15, 36.

48 *Mater et Magistra*, par. 109.

49 *Rerum Novarum*, paras. 65, 66; *Mater et Magistra*, par. 115.

50 *On Promoting the Development of Peoples*, par. 23.

51 Pope John Paul II, Opening Address at the Puebla Conference (Puebla, Mexico, January 28, 1979) in John Eagleson and Philip Scharper, eds., *Puebla and Beyond* (Mary Knoll: Orbis Books, 1979), 67.

52 *On Human Work*, par. 14.

53 *Ibid.*, par. 17.

54 *Divini Redemptoris*, par. 49.

55 *Peace on Earth*, paras. 60-62.

56 Vatican Council II, *Declaration on Religious Freedom (Dignitatis Humanae)*, par. 6. See John Courtney Murray, *The Problem of Religious Freedom*, Woodstock Papers, no. 7 (Westminster, Md.: Newman Press, 1965).

57 *Peace on Earth*, paras. 63-64. Quadragesimo Anno, par. 80. In *Rerum Novarum* Pope Leo XIII set down the basic norm that determines when government intervention is called for: "If, therefore, any injury has been done to or threatens either the common good or the interests of individual groups, which injury cannot in any other way be repaired or prevented, it is necessary for public authority to intervene." *Rerum Novarum*, par. 52. Pope John XXIII synthesized the Church's understanding of the function of governmental intervention this way: "The State, whose purpose is the realization of the common good in the temporal order, can by no means disregard the economic activity of its citizens. Indeed it should be present to promote in suitable manner the production of a sufficient supply of material goods, . . . contribute actively to the betterment of the living conditions of workers, . . . see to it that labor agreements are entered into according to the norms of justice and equity, and that in the environment of work the dignity of the human being is not violated either in body or spirit." *Mater et Magistra*, paras. 20-21.

58 *Quadragesimo Anno*, par. 79.

III

SPHERE SOVEREIGNTY,
CREATION ORDER, AND
PUBLIC JUSTICE

THIRTEEN

✕✕✕✕✕✕✕✕✕✕✕

PROGRESSIVE CALVINISM: AN INTRODUCTION
TO THE READINGS

R alph Hancock, in his reassessment of Calvin's political thought, suggests that Calvin may have been both more modern and more biblical than has been estimated by either medievalists or secular humanists.[1] Calvin emphasized both the transcendence of God above his creation and the immanent responsibility of human beings to God within the creation. Calvin sparked a renewed expression of inner worldly activity motivated by Christian service to the God whom he considered to be far beyond the access of human reason—at least in the way that Aristotle and Aquinas conceived of reason. Calvin, according to Hancock, undermined the Aristotelian vision of a natural-rational order of being ranging from the lowest potentiality up to God himself. Calvin began to break away from the great Thomist synthesis, but not in the direction of either an other-worldly retreat or a primitive communalism. Rather, he sought to clarify the antithesis between Christian and non-Christian views of life in order to renew progressive, differentiated Christian action in this world.

According to the modern Calvinists whom we consider in Part III, Calvin promoted one kind of secularization process and rejected another. He promoted the ongoing differentiation of society which meant, to some degree, undermining the legitimacy of a hierarchical social order under church domination. At the same time, he stood opposed to the spirit of secularizing humanism that rejected God's sovereignty and sought complete autonomy of human action in this world. Calvin wanted to heighten the sense of human responsibility before God in all of life by stressing God's direct sovereignty over every sphere of human endeavor—a sovereignty not mediated hierarchically by means of church authorities.

This is the basis on which Calvinism began to flourish again in the nineteenth-century Netherlands. Abraham Kuyper, following Groen van Prinsterer's lead, sought to revive Christian cultural engagement in order to promote the ongoing differentiation of society and culture. He tried to do this by radicalizing the Christian meaning of life in this world. The social philosophy and political action that emerged from this movement take history seriously, stress the antithesis between fundamental religious motives, and look to God's creation order for the structural (ontological) norms of multiple social spheres. Kuyper and his followers are critical, therefore, of historical reductionism, particularly when it accommodates liberal and revolutionary claims of human autonomy. They are also critical of all Christian attempts at synthesis with pagan motives and philosophical visions—including attempts such as Thomism which is perhaps the most significant and powerful synthesis in Western civilization.

The philosophy of social pluralism that has developed out of the modern Dutch Calvinist tradition starts with Calvin's recognition of the sovereignty of God the Creator who fully transcends his creation. Human beings are created in God's own image and endowed with responsibility before God on earth as his stewards who should live in accord with creation-order norms or creation ordinances. Part of the meaning of this human stewardship is found in the exercise of multiple, subordinate responsibilities that God has given to a variety of human institutions and organizations, each in its own sphere and in accord with its own typical structural principles. Family, school, business corporation, state, and countless other organizations and voluntary associations each has an identity and responsibility as part of God's historically unfolding creation, bound by his ordinances. Human creativity and historical power may give shape to thousands of forms of these societal structures, just as human beings have developed thousands of different languages. But humans are no more free to live without institutions and organizations or to create them arbitrarily (free from creation norms) than they are to live without language or to create languages without regard to the creation's linguistic norms.

God's norms or ordinances for creation (which Calvinists understand not as natural rational laws of a universal order of being) drive human beings to the development of the creation in a plurality of fields of endeavor, in a multiplicity of interconnected modes of response. The differentiated social expressions and institutions are more like cogs of a wheel than like lower and higher steps in a hierarchy. In this framework, the constitutionally differentiated state finds its normative identity and purpose as a territorial community of public justice—providing for the public-legal integration of all individuals and institutions under a government that lawfully monopolizes the use of force. The term "public justice" is thus a more specific and differentiated norm than that of the common good.

We have already uncovered some of the historical roots of the Dutch Calvinist tradition in the selections from Groen van Prinsterer, Otto Von Gierke, and J.N. Figgis in Part I above. While the Dutch Calvinists share much in common with Catholics and other Protestants, especially in northern Europe, they have also made a unique contribution in the social, economic, and political realms. During the twentieth century, the influence of their thought and action spread beyond Europe to North America and other parts of the world.

As we saw in Part II, a revival of natural-law philosophy emerged in late nineteenth-century Catholic circles as Pope Leo XIII led an effort to relate the philosophy of Thomas Aquinas to rapidly changing social, economic, and political circumstances. Among the Dutch Protestants (and those whom they influenced) a comparable effort was made to shape culture and society with a spirit of Christian reform. The emphasis here, as we shall see, has been on creation more than natural law, and on revelation more than reason. But these Calvinists are neither reactionaries nor romantic irrationalists.

Until the time of the French Revolution, most Protestant and Roman Catholic Christians had an outlook on life rooted in centuries of tradition. They saw themselves as moving through history on their way toward a supernatural destiny. The various social structures and cultural patterns that defined their lives were accepted, for the most part, as the natural and God-given "furniture" of this world. The church was the primary institutional vehicle that carried them toward their ultimate destiny in the Kingdom of God. As Christopher Dawson explains:

> it hardly entered into men's minds that the existing order could be radically transformed. The European social order was an organic development—the result of centuries upon centuries of unconscious growth. The family and the state, kingship and authority, the different orders and classes with their functions and privileges, were not artificial creations. They had always been there and had gradually changed their form under the influence of new circumstances and different environments. And thus they were regarded as part of the natural

order, ordained by God, and were accepted as men accepted the changes of the seasons and the other laws of nature.[2]

This is not to say that creative social changes did not take place in Europe before the French Revolution, or that all thinking was uncritically supportive of the status quo. The Protestant Reformation was momentous in shaping the culture of seventeenth- and eighteenth-century Europe. Dutch Protestants in those centuries were deeply indebted to John Calvin, Johannes Althusius, and others in their line.[3]

Nevertheless, the French Revolution seemed to burst upon the European scene at the end of the eighteenth century as a sudden shock, certifying for nearly everyone that human beings do not simply ride through history; they actually *make* history. The revolutionaries believed so strongly in their own autonomous power and freedom to make history that they thought they could start from scratch, ignoring or discounting any natural law or creation order.

In Part I we noted the reaction of some who appealed to history (either by way of tradition or by looking to the future) in order to base society's structure on something deeper than revolutionary willfullness. Those who develop historical arguments for a plural society want a rationale that can transcend the desires of the moment and the conflicts among autonomous individual wills. They think they can find that normative order in the power and validity of history itself, either past or future.

One of the figures introduced in Part I was the Dutch aristocrat Groen van Prinsterer, who participated in the renewal of Protestant political thought in the Netherlands in the middle of the nineteenth century. His Christian faith had been revived through contacts with those who recalled the glorious days of the Protestant Reformation in the Low Countries. Yet Groen was not willing to fight the revolutionary movement simply by means of conservative reaction. He called for opposition to the spirit of the Revolution through a Christian revival and by means of cultural engagement that would take God's ordinances seriously. Groen remained far too dependent, however, on the "historical school" of thought to allow the idea of God's ordinances for society to become "a creational principle of universal scope."[4]

In the readings that follow, we see the full-scale development of the idea of creation principles as the basis for social pluralism. Groen van Prinsterer's younger colleague Abraham Kuyper first develops the idea in the course of a life dedicated to social, political, educational, and ecclesiastical reform. Kuyper's influence then spreads to the academic world of political and legal philosophy as well as into the ongoing course of Dutch politics. Herman Dooyeweerd and Bob Goudzwaard represent the twentieth-century Dutch world in this regard, while H. Evan Runner and his student Bernard Zylstra show the impact of the Kuyper tradition in North America and beyond.

NOTES

1 Ralph C. Hancock, *Calvin and the Foundations of Modern Politics* (Ithaca, NY: Cornell University Press, 1989).

2 Christopher Dawson, *The Gods of Revolution* (New York: Minerva Press, 1972), 10-11.

3 See James W. Skillen, "The Development of Calvinistic Political Theory in the Netherlands" (Ph.D. Diss., Duke, 1974), 180-273, and James W. Skillen, "The Political Theory of Johannes Althusius," *Philosophia Reformata* (Amsterdam), 39 (1974): 170-190; Rockne M. McCarthy, et al., *Society, State, and Schools: A Case for Structural and Confessional Pluralism* (Grand Rapids: Eerdmans, 1981), 30-50; and Gordon Spykman, "Sphere Sovereignty in Calvin and the Calvinistic Tradition," in David E. Holwerda, ed., *Exploring the Heritage of John Calvin* (Grand Rapids, MI: Baker Book House, 1976).

4 Herman Dooyeweerd, *Roots of Western Culture: Pagan, Secular, and Christian Options*, trans. J. Kraay, eds. M. Vander Vennen and B. Zylstra (Toronto: Wedge Publishing Foundation, 1979), 53. For a more detailed discussion of Dooyeweerd's criticism, see his "Het historisch element in Groen's Staatsleer," in H. Smitskamp, et al., *Groen's "Ongeloof en Revolutie"* (Wageningen: N.V. Gebr. Zomer en Keuning, 1949), 118-137.

Fourteen

※※※※※※※※※※※

The Antirevolutionary Program[1]
by Abraham Kuyper

Abraham Kuyper

Inspired and nurtured by Groen van Prinsterer, Abraham Kuyper (1837-1920) went on to become the chief organizer of Dutch Calvinists in politics, education, journalism, and the church. His passion was to seek the reformation of life according to God's ordinances rather than according to either the revolutionary claim of human autonomy or the more conservative appeal to historical development. The key phrases that unveil Kuyper's outlook and motivation are "God's ordinances" and "sphere-sovereignty"—both rooted in a particular conception of the structure of the creation.

Abraham Kuyper grew up in a Reformed pastor's family and went on to complete his doctoral work in theology at the University of Leiden at the age of 26. He entered the pastorate and was touched by the revival movement in Holland in his early years of ministry. Within the first decade of his ministry, he came under the influence of Groen and began to work in journalism and politics.

In 1872 he took over as editor-in-chief of *De Standaard*, a daily paper that spoke for the nascent Anti-Revolutionary Party. Soon after that, he also assumed the editorship of *De Heraut*, a weekly Christian paper. For more than 45 years he filled both posts. In 1874 Kuyper was elected to a seat in the lower house of the Dutch Parliament, and from that position he helped to organize the Anti-Revolutionaries as a mass party by 1879. As if his pastoral, journalistic, and political labors were not enough, the young leader led the way in founding the Free University of Amsterdam in 1880.

Leading the Anti-Revolutionary Party for decades, Kuyper eventually became Prime Minister of the Netherlands (1901-1905) in a Calvinist-Catholic coalition government. He also continued his writing, lectures, and organizing efforts in other spheres of society up to the very end of his life in 1920. In 1898 he visited the United States, where he delivered the Stone Lectures at Princeton Theological Seminary and received an honorary doctorate.[2]

In the first selection below, drawn from a series of articles that he published in *De Standaard* soon after he became its editor, Kuyper contrasts his Calvinist outlook with that of both political liberals and other Christians (including the Catholics). Between 1849 and 1888 the public life of The Netherlands came to be dominated by liberal leaders in both church and state. The formation of the Anti-Revolutionary Party under Groen's and then Kuyper's leadership was an effort to give the vote to commoners so they could exert a Christian influence in public life.

By "anti-revolutionary" Kuyper, like Groen, does not mean a counter-revolutionary reaction that seeks a return to the prerevolutionary status quo. Rather he intends a progressive movement that will operate with principles opposed to the relativistic, atheistic autonomy claims of the revolutionaries and of many liberals. The liberal establishment resisted Kuyper's persistent attempts to foster a system of genuine political pluralism. It sought instead the liberalizing of public life while trying to confine religious influences to the private periphery of society—in churches and homes. Under Liberal Party leadership around the middle of the nineteenth century, especially under the great Dutch Prime Minister J.R. Thorbecke, only a few well-to-do men had the right to vote (about 100,000 out of a population of several million). This Liberal elite did not want to appear completely relativistic and anti-Christian in a formally Protestant society, but it articulated a basis for its political programs and goals that clearly revealed its liberal assumptions. As Kuyper explains, some of the liberals wanted to downplay the basic dogma of liberalism, namely, the social-contract doctrine that grounds all authority in individuals themselves. But they refused to break with the system of thought that is inconceivable without that doctrinaire foundation.[3] Kuyper's series of articles on "God's Ordinances" was a direct response to the political opponents of his day who were misinterpreting his call for a distinctively Christian contribution to political life.

The essence of Kuyper's argument is that human beings cannot escape the heteronomous character of God's ordinances. The true law of life, including political life, comes from outside the human will; it comes from another—from the sovereign, personal God. The original and "normal" condition of human beings is a creaturely existence into which the Creator has "woven these ordinances" for life.[4] Among other things this means that God's ordinances are more than church ordinances or church directives about morality. The church must indeed heed the will and word of God for itself, but it is not the church's calling to direct the rest of human life by its authority. No, says Kuyper, the state (and every other "sphere" of life) must also respond directly to God's ordinances for itself. "We absolutely deny the church the right to establish political principles that would bind the state."[5]

The key to understanding and responding to God's ordinances, then, is to recognize them as God's ever present requirements of all human beings in the totality of their lives. The ordinances are given in creation and reiterated in biblical revelation. If it were not for sin and its consequent darkening of the human heart and mind through disobedience to God, God's ordinances would "reveal their rule through man's progressive development. . . ."[6] But sin is a reality, and the hope of a progressive, uninterrupted, rational development of human society, as the liberals expect, "doesn't deliver as promised."[7]

> Faced with the painful fact that in case after case, in system after system, although the demands of human nature have been expressed in the political realm, with the attempts to satisfy those demands having yielded nothing but disappointment, aren't we prompted to think of a harp whose strings are sprung and which is out of tune?[8]

Recognizing or not recognizing the realities of sin and redemption—that is what divides the people of faith from the followers of the Revolution, according to Kuyper. For the reality of sin should lead one to accept God's redemption in Christ. Christians believe and revolutionaries reject the truth that the "distorted life can never reveal the law for normal life."[9]

Turning to God's revelation, however, does not mean turning away from a careful observation of life. To the contrary, Christian citizens and politicians must study the reality of political life in the light of biblical revelation in order to respond obediently in given circumstances to the will of God expressed through his creation ordinances. Christians should not aim to hold on forever to a supposedly unchanging pattern of social life; nor should they try to launch out into the future with a revolutionary faith in their own autonomy. The proper human response should always be one of reformation—an attempt to reform the deformed, abnormal world through a progressive unfolding of creation in tune with God's ordinances now illumined by redemption in Christ.

Kuyper's perspective differs from that of both liberals and Catholics. His understanding of the incarnation of Christ, for example, is illuminating:

> The relationship one posits between God's life and the human world governs one's undertakings. One can completely separate them, or one can relate them externally, or one can allow them to permeate one another inwardly. The revolutionary chooses the first way. His religion, so he pretends, has nothing to do with his politics. Roman Catholicism takes the second way. Relying solely on spiritual givens, the church decides what spiritual substratum will undergird the church, allowing the statesman henceforth to decide the material issues on purely profane grounds. Our intentions aspire to the third position. We claim a mutual inter-penetration of the givens of God's Word and the givens derived from a study of nations.
>
> Does not the Christian notion of the incarnation of the Son of God pose precisely this claim? The divine does not just hover above us, nor just position itself beside the human, but it enters into human life, just as sin did, in order to permeate it and ennoble it.[10]

Kuyper felt that, in contrast to liberal humanism, Calvinist Christianity had a deeper appreciation for, and could make a greater contribution to the free development of science, art, industry, representative government, business, trade, and education. Kuyper's stance against the "modernists" was one of opposition to their fundamental assumptions about the meaning of earthly life that all people hold in common. And he stood opposed precisely because he believed that this common life is governed by God. Kuyper also had some basic disagreements with Roman Catholics with whom he cooperated to a great extent throughout his life.[11] Even in the course of political cooperation Kuyper wanted nothing superficial. He always tried to confront principle with principle so that what is true and what is false in competing Christian views of life could be brought out into the open in all spheres of society.

Kuyper's attempt to deal with the question of what is common to all people is presented most thoroughly in his multi-volume work *De Gemeene Gratie* (Common Grace).[12] First of all, Kuyper believes that Christians are the only ones able to account adequately for the problem of evil—the sinfulness which is common to all persons.[13] Liberals, who believe in inevitable progress, have to ignore the ever present evidence that individuals are not inherently good. Liberals try to explain away disorder and injustice by blaming particular institutions or certain kinds of people. But this simply covers over the questions of who establishes institutions and why only some people are "bad." Socialists also ignore the common disorder among all people, blaming a particular class or institution for the evils of life. Christians, by contrast, do not identify evil only with the "others." In this respect Calvinists have taken an even more forthright approach than Catholics in their assertion that all people have become totally depraved through their disobedience to God.[14] This account goes to the root of the problem, recognizing that people build institutions in accord with their nature and that immanent reality is bound by ordinances that judge its evils and distortions.

But if all individuals are sinful at the root of their being, if the cause of life's disruption and agony is the denial of God by those who have been created to serve him in all of life, then how can we account for what is good and orderly and positive in life—even among those who refuse to repent of their sin and turn back to God? The answer, according to Kuyper, who follows Calvin and Augustine here, can be nothing other than the *common grace* of God which maintains the creation in spite of sin and restrains the full consequence of human sinfulness. This grace Kuyper calls "common" because it works for the benefit of all people, not only for those who confess Christ as the Lord and Redeemer of life. Common grace is both preserving and restraining. It preserves the creation and restrains sin.

With this confession Kuyper remains true to his faith in God's sovereignty as Creator and Lord. God and his creation remain the foundation for all human social life. Of course, not all people believe this, and that is why there are opposing camps within the same nation and within this one world. But Kuyper puts the burden of proof on those who would deny God's sovereignty and reject human accountability to God. If individuals can prove that they really are the authors and creators of their own world, free of sin and distortion; if they can indeed show that the Revolution, by casting out the so-called myths of religion and asserting the rational sovereignty of the individual, can uncover the meaning of human existence and provide the kingdom of peace which overcomes injustice, then and only then will Christians be put on the defensive with their "unrealistic" account of reality.

Kuyper's perspective, therefore, is both confident and cautious. He stands for the truth of Christianity against all who deny it. But he refuses to conclude that Christians alone possess all the truth in some gnostic mystery or that they are the only good people on earth. He especially emphasizes that in the earthly domain under common grace Christians must submit to the structures of this domain. The Christian aim can never be revolution. As S. U. Zuidema explains in his penetrating study of Kuyper's thought, the basic theme that Kuyper emphasizes over and over again is the seriousness with which Christians must regard the original creation order.

A Christian marriage is an ordinary marriage, a Christian society is an ordinary society, a Christian family is an ordinary family, a Christian state is an ordinary state, a Christian association is an ordinary association—according to the ordinances that obtain for marriage, family, society, state and associations. The Christian family is no miniature church; the Christian church is not also a state; the Christian state is not a Christian church; a Christian marriage is no supernatural cloister but simply a conventional marriage; and even a Christian political party is just that—an ordinary party! Christian action is the opposite of overturning the Divine structural principles that are normative for this temporal, visible life.[15]

As long as some degree of goodness and order remains on earth, it is essential that Christians should work together for the positive development of a common social and cultural life which God preserves by his grace. At the same time this means both involvement by confessing Christians in society as well as a full respect for the rights and freedoms of those who cannot agree with the Christian confession.

Somewhat in contrast to the Catholic Church's revival of Thomist philosophy, Kuyper does not want to revive Calvin's theology in detail as his authority for social and political life. Kuyper believes that Calvinism can make a major, systematic contribution to life in the modern world, but to do so Calvinism itself has to be continually reformed.[16] Calvinism has to be liberated from various unbiblical chains that still hold it in check. Not the least of these bondages in Kuyper's day was the old Roman and medieval view of politics that did not allow for the independent unfolding of political life in accord with God's ordinance of public justice. The unhealthy alliance of church and state which, in Calvin's day, had led to such things as the burning of Servetus was something from which Calvinism had to be set free. As Kuyper puts it in his Princeton lectures of 1898:

> The duty of the government to extirpate every form of false religion and idolatry was not a find of Calvinism, but dates from Constantine the Great, and was the reaction against the horrible persecutions which his pagan predecessors on the imperial throne had inflicted upon the sect of the Nazarene. Since that day this system had been defended by all Romish theologians and applied by all Christian princes. In the time of Luther and Calvin, it was a universal conviction that that system was the true one. . . .
>
> Notwithstanding all this, I not only deplore that one stake, but I unconditionally disapprove of it; yet not as if it were the expression of a special characteristic of Calvinism, but on the contrary as the fatal after-effect of a system, gray with age, which Calvinism found in existence, under which it had grown up, and from which it had not yet been able entirely to liberate itself.[17]

In this passage we see how, in Kuyper's view, the differentiation of social spheres goes hand in hand with the development of political pluralism. And this is closely connected with the question of "secularization." Implied in the readings from Kuyper, but not fully articulated there, is a peculiarly modern Calvinist interpretation of the secularization process as we noted above.[18] On the one hand, Kuyper, along with many Catholics and other Protestants, is a vigorous opponent of secularization, if by "secularization" is meant the out-working of the spirit of liberalism and revolution which claims that human beings have no master in history and no ordinances from God to bind them— the claim that human beings are autonomous in their freedom to shape politics, art, science, education, and all of culture. Yet, unlike most Catholics and many Protestants of his day, Kuyper is a strong promoter of the secularization process if by "secularization" is meant the liberation of different social "spheres" from ecclesiastical control.[19] Kuyper believes that politics, art, science, education, and other areas of life should be free to unfold in direct obedience to God's ordinances for them. Each sphere of life should be free of direct control by any other so that each can learn obedience to God's special ordinances for its own domain.

This is the main burden of Kuyper's famous speech on "sphere sovereignty" given at the opening of the Free University of Amsterdam in 1880, excerpts from which appear below. Artists must be free to obey God's norms for art; they must not be forced to heed what ecclesiastical or political officials believe is good art. Teachers and scholars must be free to respond obediently to God's ordinances for reasoning, exploration, argument, and learning; they must not be under orders to teach and publish only what ecclesiastical or political authorities approve as the truth. Each area of human societal life "comprises its own realm, each has its own sovereign within the bounds of that realm."[20]

Kuyper's argument is different from that of "subsidiarity" which stresses a natural, *vertical* hierarchy of responsibilities in social life along with the rightful autonomy of the various parts within the societal "whole" which the state governs. In the subsidiarity argument the state is charged with the protection and promotion of the common good of the whole society, whereas Kuyper is suggesting a more *horizontal* concept of social spheres, among which the state has a less encompassing responsibility.

Consider the term "sovereignty," for example. Jacques Maritain avoids the term sovereignty in connection with the state because "there is no sovereignty, that is, no natural and inalienable right to *transcendent* or *separate* supreme power in political society."[21] Kuyper, on the other hand, retains the term and clarifies its meaning in order to make almost the same point that Maritain makes:

> What is sovereignty? Do you not agree with me in defining it as the authority
> that possesses the right and duty, and wields the power to break and punish all

resistance to its will? And does not an ineradicable conscience also speak within you, telling you that original, absolute sovereignty cannot reside in any creature, but must coincide with the majesty of God? . . . But then—and I stress this—then at the same time we must acknowledge that this supreme Sovereign has delegated and still delegates his authority to human persons, so that on earth one actually never encounters God himself directly in visible form, but one always sees his sovereign authority administered in human offices. . . .

Is this all-encompassing sovereignty of God delegated to a single person undivided? Or does an earthly sovereign possess the power to compel obedience only in a limited sphere, a sphere limited by other spheres in which someone else is sovereign, and not he?[22]

To the first of these questions Kuyper's implied answer is "No," to the second "Yes." In contrast to individualism, "sphere sovereignty" presupposes that the open field of human action is not a field without boundaries—not an arbitrary openness without limits. Kuyper is not arguing for the autonomous freedom of persons or spheres. To the contrary, dynamic, creative human actions are always either obedient or disobedient to divine ordinances. The norms are not created by autonomous individuals, nor should they be enforced by some central, controlling authority on earth. God's ordinances for creation, not autonomous impulses, are what allow human beings to develop a plurality of fields of endeavor and function in a multiplicity of social spheres. These differentiated social expressions are, therefore, more like "cogs" of a wheel than like lower and higher "steps" in a hierarchy.

THE ORDINANCES OF GOD

I

The term "ordinances of God," often used by us, has frequently led to misunderstanding not only by opponents but also by supporters. It is, therefore, necessary to clarify how the term should be understood from an Anti-revolutionary standpoint within the Reformed perspective. We can distinguish a dual confession in the use of this concept: 1) that ordinances, indeed, divine ordinances, do exist, and 2) that there is a way that we can come to know these ordinances. The first confession touches on the principle of Anti-revolution itself. The second pertains to the distinction between ourselves and related movements.

That ordinances exist, we confess over against the adherents of the social contract theory; and that these ordinances are divine, over against positivism in all its varieties.

Do you obey because you must, or because it suits you? Is your submission to existing authority dependent upon your voluntary recognition of it, or because it rules over you independent of your approval? Do you conform to the law because you see that it serves the general well-being, or because, despite the fact that it appears contrary to the general well-being, it nevertheless demands your obedience and conformity. In the first instance, it is you who, more by your consent and submission, grant legitimacy to authority and its laws. In the second instance, authority remains authority and law remains law, even if no one submits to it or obeys it.

It is undeniable that the social contract doctrine stands on the shifting sands of an authority dependent upon its subjects, who themselves establish that authority. According to its imperative, we are bound to obey because we made a contract to do so, whether personally by our own judgment or through an act of our forefathers. We could also have chosen not to enter into such a contract. This would have perpetuated anarchy and hindered order. Suppose, however, that, despite our respect for order, we had concluded that the price we had to pay for it in personal liberty was too high. We would then have had the equal right to abort that authority, that is, to prevent the birth of authority.

We need not be reminded that the Liberals, especially those in the Netherlands, would just as soon forget this social contract doctrine. They certainly are not enthusiastic about it. In fact, in many ways they themselves make fun of it. However, this is wholly irrelevant as long as they don't break with a system that is inconceivable without this doctrinaire foundation. One may close his eyes to the all-determining question concerning the principle of authority. One may pretend he doesn't see the issue. One may carefully avoid answering the question and satisfy oneself with authority as it actually exists. One may, thereby, evince a high degree of skepticism. However, as a point of departure for governmental policy it is superficial and arbitrary, and the first popular tumult would either lead to militarism or would deliver a deathblow to the moral strength of the state.

As long as Liberalism (and, as we know, in every fundamental issue Conservatism and Liberalism tread the same path) either conceals the credentials of its authority or can present none other than the social contract theory conceived in England and born in the court of France, every day it imprints more deeply upon the convictions of the nations the false thesis, the monstrous notion, the seductive word of rebellion: "The authority that constricts

you is something you yourselves have originated. There are no ordinances—
only consequences of an agreement, products of an accord, the results of a
contract."

The Antirevolutionary party denies this. There *are* ordinances. Authority
is the foundation of life; your life is not the foundation upon which authority
rests. Law holds, even if you refuse to lend it your seal of approval. It demands subjection, if possible, with your willing consent, but if need be, without it. Your subjection is ennobled if you conform your will to the law, if you
recognize its fruits and accede to its rightness; but this neither adds to nor
subtracts from the reality of subjection. Even at times when you still find your
will at odds with the law, even when its fruits are delayed and its rightness in
doubt, the obligation to submit is just as firm and decisive as ever. . . .

[There follows a discussion of the Mayflower Compact. Kuyper anticipates the counterargument that this event serves as an instance of a social
contract and that, therefore, it supports the assertion that Calvinism has been
receptive to this principle. He points out, however, first, that this compact
was signed only by the heads of households, and, second, that it declares that
the signers were establishing their colony to the glory of the Lord and before
his face. Both of these considerations are inconsistent with the social contract
theory which reduces everyone to individuals, not family members, and
which founds itself on man's will, not God's.]

II

This brings us to our second assertion: not merely that there are ordinances, but that these are ordinances of God. The addition of this phrase is
not superfluous. For even among those who with us oppose the arbitrary nature of authority there are those who do not derive the certainty of authority
from the will of a personal, living God, but from the constitution of our human nature. Sidestepping the question of how human nature originated, they
simply acknowledge the fact that man's nature is unique. This nature, they
argue, obeys unchanging laws and must, therefore, develop according to
those laws. If from this development it appears that this nature demands that
we organize ourselves into states, then it must be possible to discover in that
nature guidelines that can provide standards for the governance of the state.
The important thing, then, is to observe man as closely as one does the world
around him, to include the results of various experiments and to take into account the needs that reveal themselves, in order thereby to discover the laws
to which the life of states is subject, in order by this practical route to arrive
at the fixed rules for state polity. One can hardly charge this viewpoint with

being based on arbitrariness, still less with being based on chance insights. The proponents of this system concede that there is a binding, obligating, compelling power, that is, that there are ordinances. However, they recognize no higher authority for these ordinances than the constitution of our human nature. There simply is human life, which brings with it fixed laws, and violation of these laws takes its vengeance in a reduced quality of life.

It is this that the Antirevolutionary opposes, and, to my mind, rightly so. Laws, he argues, presuppose a Lawgiver. Even in the material world a law does not originate from itself. And even if we were to concede that the laws according to which matter moves and works, the genuine so-called laws of nature, are products of a material cause, this would say little if anything regarding the polity of the state. For in the state we are dealing with people, thus, with spiritual beings. It follows that the laws which govern the political life of the nations are of a moral nature, and moral laws are inconceivable apart from a personal will as the source from which they issue. Only if, along with the crudest materialism, one were to explain the spiritual expressions of human life as the condensation of gasses, would this argument (of ours) lose its force. As long as our opponents join us in loathing such materialism which debases man, they cannot escape the force of the argument: either there are no spiritual laws that rule the life of the state, or these laws presuppose a personal will.

III

Over against an arbitrary authority, which is the product of human self-consent, we advance the thesis: Ordinances are real. And over against the assertion that these ordinances are merely the laws of our nature, the thesis: These are divine ordinances.

This brings us to a statement to which we urge our readers to pay very close attention: acknowledgement of divine ordinances brings with it a recognition that scientific discovery of the laws that rule the lives of nations would be completely adequate to establish an unsurpassable constitutional law if there were no sin. We regard as incontrovertible the assertion that the laws governing life reveal themselves spontaneously in life. In the very process of painting and sketching and performing and sculpting our artists discovered the laws for the artistic enterprise. And it enters no one's mind to consult the Bible or ecclesiastical authorities when it comes to learning what the purpose of art is. (We are not talking here about judging the moral character of art objects.) The same is true of the laws which govern our thinking, the laws which govern commerce, and the laws which govern industry. We learn to know the laws of thought by thinking. By doing business we discover the art of commerce. Industry blazes its own path. The same is true for political life. To deny this truth is to fall short of respect for the Creator.

Respect for the Creator debunks the notion that man was created, if I may use this cliche, at the mercy of good luck, as if only afterward the laws which regulate his political life were then revealed. This is how man messes things up. God's creation, to the contrary, since its very beginning is fully equipped and endowed with all the powers it needs, carrying within it the seeds of all the developments to which it will attain even in its highest perfection.

The recognition that man, and therefore also the human race, is a creation of God leads to the unavoidable conclusion that, therefore, all the givens that govern the political life of the nations were present in human nature at its creation. If one assumes that man has developed normally, then we could raise no objection whatsoever to the argument of our opponents. Then the gradual development of mankind would have brought God's ordinances to light quite naturally.

We agree, moreover, that this development would have unfolded in two stages: first man thinks; afterward he discovers the laws of thought. Similarly, on this view, man would first have developed political life, and only thereafter would he have discovered the laws that govern it. This distinction cannot be denied. Life comes first; afterward reflection on that life. In the same way, by separating into states, mankind would first have brought his political life to completion more instinctively, more out of an immediate vital impulse. Only thereafter, entering into a higher stage, would man reflect that life in his consciousness, put those laws that rule it into words, and give an account of his actions. In the first stage there would simply be political life. Only in the second stage would, strictly speaking, political theory arise.

It should, therefore, strike no one as strange that our contemporary politicians recommend this method with such self-assurance or that their words are so well-received. Their construct is indeed completely right—as long as we neglect to ask whether human nature still exists in its normal condition. No objections can be raised against the view that the ordinances have proceeded from the Creator, or that he has woven these ordinances into human nature itself, or that these ordinances, first concealed within man's nature, necessarily reveal their rule through man's progressive development, or that, as a perceiving and thinking being, man learns the rules of political life from the facts, and after learning them consciously puts them into practice.

In applying this construct, the Revolution, perhaps more than it realized, approximated the original truth that is from God. Only by prominently displaying this truth was the Revolution able to draw the spirits and peoples in its wake. And it is mistaken if it thinks that Anti-revolutionaries oppose this position in principle. The moment we examine the application of this construct, however, we stumble over this one main point: It doesn't deliver as promised. . . .

IV

. . . A political theory that pays no attention to the reality of sin accordingly remains stillborn; it is a rarefied abstraction that fails to take real life into account. Anti-revolutionary political theory, therefore, seeks to steer clear of this reef. It emphasizes strongly this awful reality, not merely in its application, as Liberalism does, but, as is proper, in its principles as well as in its methods.

This leads to the question: Given the reality of sin, is the thesis still valid that the human mind by itself can come to know the rules and laws, or, if you prefer, the ordinances of God, for political life from the very life of states? This question divides the men of faith from the sons of the Revolution. To this question Liberals, Radicals and Conservatives all answer with a loud "Yes." Those who live by faith, on the other hand, whether they be orthodox protestants or orthodox Catholics or orthodox Jews, without hesitation answer, "No."

This response is based on two grounds. First, that distorted life can never reveal the law for normal life. Pathology alone can never lead to knowledge of healthy life. One cannot compose a harmony of tones from voices that are out of tune. One does not study logic in a madhouse. If it is an incontrovertible reality that nowhere on earth has there ever appeared any political life that was completely normal and not subject to the distortions of sin, then we declare that the actual life of nations has never revealed the laws of political life; sadly, such an object of observation just doesn't exist anywhere.

Secondly, even if such a set of states did exist, it would yet be questionable whether man still possesses in untainted form the power to observe such life rightly and truly. Doesn't psychology teach us that sensing the phenomena of the human spirit depends not so much on thinking as on the undisturbed harmony of man's inner life? From this the man of faith draws the discouraging conclusion that not only are the strings of the harp sprung, but also our ear for music has been distorted. These two factors by themselves make a true evaluation of tone completely impossible.

Summarizing our findings, we come to the following four conclusions:

1. Political theory, too, must first of all take into account the reality of sin.

2. If sin did not exist, observation of life would then be completely adequate to learn the laws of political life.

3. Since, however, sin does exist, there is no normal life to observe.

4. Since the reality of sin manifests itself as issuing from the heart of man, it has tainted his powers of observation.

Since it appears certain that a state polity which, nevertheless, clings to this method must inevitably end in frustration, it is worth asking, in rejecting this method, which route we must travel in order to arrive at a knowledge of the ordinances of God for the state.

V

Sin makes futile every effort to found political theory solely on the observation of life and causes it to fail. We were led to this conclusion not by an abstract concept of sin, but by a glance at the political history of European peoples. After all, again and again predictions of happiness were disappointed. That construct failed the test.

Does it follow, therefore, that the sooner we stop our observation of life the better, so that we can seek the rules of state polity outside life in Holy Scripture? This is how some mistakenly think that we reason; this is what some ascribe to us; this is what some keep writing about us in order, when it comes down to it, to inculcate in the people a distaste for our efforts. However, the opposite is true.

Calvinism has never supported this untenable position but has always opposed it with might and main. A state polity that dismisses and scorns the observation of life and simply wishes to duplicate the situation of Israel, taking Holy Scripture as a complete code of Christian law for the state, would, according to the spiritual fathers of Calvinism, be the epitome of absurdity. Accordingly, in their opposition to Anabaptism as well as the Quakers, they expressed unreservedly their repugnance for this extremely dangerous and impractical theory.

This is obvious, in the first place, from their attitude toward the state. While the Anabaptists and many other sects taught that the political organization of the nations was a necessary evil which found its reason for existence only in sin, Calvinism ceaselessly refuted this argument and roundly condemned every position that was bound to lead to a devaluation of government and contempt for authority. Only a poor knowledge of history can ascribe an opposite view to the Calvinists. The accusations constantly hurled at us: "wicked," "satanic," "demonic," and whatever else, rest quite simply upon misunderstanding.

If these accusers would just reflect for a moment, this would become plain to even the most hardened. One has but to look into the writings of our great leaders for the answers to three questions: 1) What must we think of the political life of antiquity? 2) What meaning does the organization of the Jewish state have for us? 3) What is the relationship between natural and special revelation? Unless stubbornness or deliberate misrepresentation enter in, the old charges will never again be repeated.

If we considered the political life of the nations as something unholy, unclean and wrong in itself, it would lie outside of human nature. Then the state would have to be seen as a purely external means of compulsion, and every attempt to discover even a trace of God's ordinances in our own nature would be absurd. Only special revelation would then be capable of imparting to us the standards for that external means of discipline. Wherever, thus, this special revelation is absent, as in the heathen world, nothing but sin and distortion would prevail, which would therefore not even be worth the trouble of our observation. This was also the judgment people came to wherever sectarian fanatics erased the boundary between ecclesiastical and political life. And this is the judgment that many fanatics still come to in their narrowness. However, if we open the works of Calvin, Bullinger, Beza and Marnix van St. Aldegonde, it becomes obvious that Calvinism consciously chooses sides against this viewpoint. The experience of the states of antiquity, the practical wisdom of their laws, and the deep insight of their statesmen and philosophers is held in esteem by these men, and these are cited in support of their own affirmations and consciously related to the ordinances of God. The earnest intent of the political life of many nations can be explained in terms of the principles of justice and morality that spoke in their consciences. They cannot be explained simply as blindness brought on by the Evil One; on the contrary, in the excellence of their political efforts we encounter a divine ray of light.

This is borne out by Calvinism's judgment regarding the meaning of Israel for our national life. If one rejects the efforts of the heathen world also in the area of politics as unclean and contaminated, then it is understandable that one should turn to the political order of Israel as a model by which the nations ought to be guided in all times and latitudes. As we all know, this opinion has always had its defenders; especially the Independents held fast to this position, and among us too we still read utterances that are explicable only on the basis of this peculiar position. What does Calvin say about this?

In the conclusion of his *Institutes* he writes: "For there are some who deny that a commonwealth is rightly organized, unless, making the common laws of the land inoperative, it introduces the Mosaic political system. I leave it to others to point out the danger of tumult among the peoples which lurks in this position; I will simply prove how false and foolish such talk is." (Bk. IV, XX, 14) He held that, like the ceremonial law, so also the judicial law of Moses for Israel was meant for Israel, not for us, and that it only served, by means of these shadows, to make Christ known to us. To his mind, we must distinguish between the form of these laws and the principle of love and mercy concealed in them in such a way that "every nation is left free to make its own laws, provided they are founded on that principle of love and mercy." (Bk. IV, XX, 15)

Coming now to the final point concerning the relationship between natural and special revelation, with proper rights we contradict the argument that Holy Scripture should be seen as the source from which a knowledge of the best civil laws flows. The supporters of this position talk as though after the Fall nature, human life, and history have ceased being a revelation of God and as though, with the closing of this book, another book, called Holy Scriptures, was opened for us. Calvinism has never defended this untenable position and will never acknowledge it as its own. Calvin already states in so many words that the revelation of Holy Scripture is like a pair of glasses that enables him to read once again with his weakened eyes the partially obscured revelation of nature. It reveals to us the ground rules, the primary relationships, the principles that govern man's life together and his relationship to the most holy God, not information concerning the individual parts of the state as a whole. What life itself, distorted and derailed by sin, could no longer reveal, God in his love made known in his Word, also for our political life. What the application of these principles to contemporary issues should be, however, how they ought to be adapted to the nature of various times and peoples, what kind of expression they should find in the laws and decisions of government, must be regulated so exclusively by the phenomena of life that Holy Scripture does not even opt for any single form of government, and allows Christian constitutional law to consider a monarchy as well as a commonwealth, an aristocratic republic as well as a democratic federation.

The press, which confronts us with the question of what these ordinances of God were for water and sewer and for telegraph lines, has therefore not even come close to touching our principle and only reveals an enormous gap in their own knowledge of history.

VI

We have refuted the notion that we entertain the foolish effort to patch together civil laws from Bible texts, and we have declared unconditionally that psychology, ethnology, history and statistics are also for us givens which, by the light of God's Word, must determine the standards for state polity. The question now arises, What then is the relationship between these givens and the Word of God?

Three kinds of answers have been given to this question.

There are those who think that God's Word has done its duty for the statesman when he has gleaned from it the demand for righteousness and love.

Others maintain that in state policy it is possible to distinguish between rules that can be established on the strength of God's revelation and rules that are left to human discretion. The first are then established by the church, and the state must act according to the pronouncements of the church.

Finally, a third group replies that it is the same God who reveals himself in the lives of the nations as well as in his Word, and that for every statesman knowledge of God's ordinances must be the result of a thorough knowledge of the nations and a fundamental knowledge of God's Word. These must not be conceived of as standing dualistically alongside one another, but, under the control of his conscience and under the influence of his faith, must be fused in his mind into a higher unity of insight.

The first view, as though a plea for righteousness and love itself already stamps a statesman as Christian, does not really belong to the faith-movement. I mention it only because in our parliament top men often speak as though such a plea implies the difference between Belief and Revolution. The simple observation that by this standard Solon and Cato, too, would be Christian statesmen is enough to refute this view. Those who speak in these terms misunderstand the character of Scripture, which distinguishes itself from the products of secular literature not by these general imperatives, but precisely by pointing the way to their fulfillment.

More can be said for the second view, which finds its support especially in Roman Catholicism. If there is a divine revelation, then of course one must look to that revelation for light on the principles and universal rules of state polity. However, if one doesn't recognize the organic character of revelation and ascribes to it a mechanical and therefore legalistic nature, then the expectation inevitably arises that one can find in it unambiguous statements and ready-made prescriptions for the life of nations. If the content and quality of

Holy Scripture fail to meet this expectation, and differences in exegesis threaten to undermine the certainty of its prescriptions, then as a matter of course the need is born for a church that can restore this sure foundation. This dilemma becomes even more pressing when we consider the fact that today there is more than one urgently important political issue that did not exist in antiquity and about which Scripture, therefore, says nothing. This then gives rise to the longing for a revelation that is not closed off with the last book of Scripture, but, living on with changing times, benefits us with its oracles for the problems of our time. For this reason people demand a church which, clothed with infallible authority, is the expositor of revelation given in the past and an organ of continually progressive revelation of God's will. Once people imagine that such a church actually exists, then every attempt to escape the implications of this construct naturally becomes futile. Then the state must, of course, adapt itself without reservation to the pronouncements of the church. Then every political theory that leads to a divergent result is sinful and inadmissible. Yes, then to rule according to laws that are in conflict with the oracles of the church is a political weakness, which may be tolerated tactically as a transitional measure but which in principle deserves to be unconditionally condemned.

Writers, such as a recent columnist, who view our efforts solely from the outside, imagine with good intent that we too adhere to this system. They think at least that they have a right to divide all thinkers into two categories: those who wish to derive the laws of life solely from life itself and those who wish to derive them from revelation under the supervision of the church. Only they concede that among the latter there are both proponents of a fallible and defenders of an infallible church, with the latter naturally having the advantage of consistency. We now protest this schema. We absolutely deny the church the right to establish political principles that would bind the state. The church is, of course, free to influence its members in the direction it deems desirable, but it may not establish rules that would bind the state. The reason it may not do so is obvious. To establish these rules, what is necessary is not just knowledge of Revelation but also knowledge of the temperament of the people, of history, and of politics, and these the church does not as church possess. Just as the state may not establish rules that bind the church and may exert influence on the members of the church only in their role as citizens, that is, indirectly, similarly the church may not arrogate to itself spiritual domination over the state. Church and state each have their own domain and should come into mutually mediated contact only through the persons who stand in relationship to both. Our resistance to the name "clerics," which some would force upon us, is therefore right and just. For, from our perspective, this term does indeed have an unfavorable connotation, because the concept that it embodies is an error which we oppose with all our might and which to the best of our knowledge smothers all healthy political development.

With the Roman Catholic statesmen we recognize that scientific study by itself is insufficient to discover the laws for the political life of the nations, and with them we also claim the light of revelation for the nation. However, in the application of this principle, we stand diametrically opposed to them. The dualism that lies at the basis of their view of revelation as well as of Christianity we reject as untenable and as repudiated by experience. We reject their construct of a unity of state and church, most aptly termed a church-state, in which the church by its spiritual authority decides in many respects what the rules of life for the state shall be. Such a construct is impractical for the state and harmful for the life of the church. Decisions about political issues ought to be made not by the clergy, that is, not by the ecclesiastical authorities as such, but by the citizens of the state and among them especially by statesmen and men of science. The church may influence these decisions, in my opinion, only through the spiritual training that it rightly and reasonably provides to these citizens and statesmen insofar as they are members of its fellowship. If it is able to persuade its members that God's Word should bind them also in their actions as citizens of the state and men of science, then these men, called by God to this task, will point out the right course for the state to follow. If it thereby exerts a spiritual power that enables its members to obtain positions of influence in the areas of politics and science, then by this fruit of its spiritual activity the church will actually be able to lead state polity along that course. However, it can command this immediate influence only as long as it binds its members to God's Word, trains its members to be persons of strength, and through them, assuming they are actually called to serve in the government, it enhances the well-being of the nation. To call this "clericalism" is a gross misrepresentation of the facts. To paint this viewpoint with the same brush as ultramontanism cannot stand up before the bar of honesty and good-will.

VII

One question remains to be answered. If it is the Christian statesman and not the church that must show the direction along which political life ought to move, by what method can the statesman acquire knowledge of God's ordinances?

We begin by admitting that our answer to this question is far from simple. Roman Catholicism has a much more direct solution. The church decides, and the only concern to the ultramontanist is the application of the church's pronouncements, not their discovery. The revolutionary statesman has a harder task than his ultramontanist rival because he lacks this *Roma locuta* and must draw his knowledge of the principles of political order from ethnology and history. Nevertheless, we must frankly concede that the process becomes even more difficult for the Antirevolutionary, for he must conquer two fields of knowledge. He must not only take on the task that the revolutionary shoulders, but must also penetrate into the spirit of Scripture, in order then to fuse these two approaches into a unity within the crucible of his own thought.

Incidentally, that simplicity is by no means a mark of truth appears convincing to anyone acquainted with the nearly endless combination of factors that rules the political life of a nation. Particularly if one is aware that the axles, cogwheels, and pivots of this composite organism have become obscured by the awful power of sin, then sensitivity to what is the most beneficial polity for the state tends to be more against than for a simple answer.

To my way of thinking, the fundamental idea of Christianity militates both against simplicity and for our viewpoint. When a few months ago I said that the incarnation of God's Son ought to be the principle also for a study of the state, some claimed not to understand the meaning of my statement. Let me explain.

The relationship one posits between God's life and the human world governs one's undertakings. One can completely separate them, or one can relate them externally, or one can allow them to permeate one another inwardly. The revolutionary chooses the first option. His religion, so he pretends, has nothing to do with his politics. Roman Catholicism takes the second way. Relying solely on spiritual givens, the church decides what spiritual substratum will undergird the church, allowing the statesman henceforth to decide the material issues on purely profane grounds. Our intentions aspire to the third position. We claim a mutual inter-penetration of the givens of God's Word and the givens derived from a study of nations.

Does not the Christian notion of the incarnation of the Son of God pose precisely this claim? The divine does not just hover above us, nor just position itself beside the human, but it enters into human life, just as sin did, in order to permeate it and ennoble it.

The former would have been easy to accomplish, but the latter cost Christ suffering and death. Yet only the latter was successful. It was successful because it revealed the omnipotence of his gracious love. Our method, thus, comes well-recommended. It carries the genuine stamp of Christian character on its forehead. The fact that it takes both givens into account—faith and science—certainly does not offer occasion to suspect it.

One of the implications of this method, however, is that it is impossible to supply a handbook for Christian political theory that is valid for all nations and all times. The Revolution claimed it could do so, precisely because it did not take life into account and wished to offer the same system ready-made for all nations in all ages.

The Christian statesman cannot placidly accept such neglect of the differences among nations and the changing times. Each nation, he finds, has its own character, and in the course of time he finds a perpetual fluctuation of circumstance. These facts demand attention. He wishes not to be speculative or doctrinaire, but historical, because reality constrains him to be so. Only the principles for which he stands up are eternal, valid for all nations and in force for all times.

Insofar as the content of Scripture forms part of history, that history teaches him that a nation is not an aggregate of individuals, but an organic whole. He knows that the purpose of national existence does not lie in the state, but in Him who created both state and nation—the King of kings, the Lord of lords. It is his conviction that mutual relationships among nations must be sought not in the fortuitous success of violence, but in justice. He cannot tolerate imperialism since the political unity of the nations lies not in Caesar but in Christ's future. He is convinced that justice is not made by the statesman, but that it exists before the very notion of justice crosses his mind, and he can only approximate it in this formulation of laws.

Authority, he firmly believes, does not originate by a human deed, but issues from God, and demands obedience not on the basis of a voluntary contract but on the basis of God's will. This authority may be entrusted to the father over his family, the rich man over his employees, the government over its citizens; and whether it be concentrated in the crown or spread among the people, it remains God's authority, and in themselves all those who bear authority are nothing but ordinary creatures and sinners like ourselves.

That (divine) authority recognizes no limitation other than itself. It exists primarily in Him who gave it. No earthly authority can ever assert itself contrary to the obedience we owe God. Similarly, this (earthly) authority can never nullify the authority with which others are clothed in their own spheres. The state cannot legitimately assert its authority over against the father, nor a prince over against the rights of other governing bodies and the people within their spheres of competence. Apart from these two limitations, however, authority is absolute.

Equally sacred to the Christian statesman, however, is the struggle for freedom and progress. For freedom, because God's Word desires a moral, not a violent triumph of the good, and because faith in the victory of truth gives him the courage and charges him with the duty to subdue every unspiritual bondage. But also for progress, because God's Word shows him a forward movement in the life of the nations toward a fixed goal—a movement which reactionism would retard and which stagnation would delay until it was too late.

Accordingly, the Christian statesman is motivated by the very opposite of a predilection for phony legitimacy and worship of royalty. Scripture teaches him to view Christian people as a free people, who may not be used as an instrument but who themselves act as a living member of the body politic. Recognizing the sinful seduction of ambition, self-exultation, and pride, he knows on the basis of God's Word that absolutistic rule, monarchy in an untempered sense, constantly threatens to turn into tyranny and must therefore be turned as swiftly as possible into a less dualistic form of state.

Besides these general principles, God's Word presents him with the history and political organization of a very gifted people that lived by these principles and found happiness or destruction in its faithfulness or unfaithfulness to these principles.

Standing thus on firm ground in his contemplation of basic principles, knowing what man is, knowing what a nation is and the purpose of the nations, knowing the source of justice and authority, knowing too where the claim to freedom and progress derives its impulse, he possesses the compass that points the way across the tossing seas even when there is no land in sight. The formulation of these principles must be the fruit of his own inner life. He himself must assimilate these principles into his own person and life so that he may find the thoughts, the expressions, the words, in which these principles can be embodied, not as from a code-book to which some would demote Scripture, but from that faith which takes up the Word of God into itself.

Once he has found this formulation, a formulation that must be purified and sharpened by each future generation, the task then awaits him to offer a critique of whatever there is in the polity of the state, in the dominant notions of his people, and in the tone-setting political opinions that undermine these principles; to present historical proof that the principles he professes have been found durable and able to stand the test; to seek that point-of-contact in the conscience of both the citizen and the statesman by which respect for these principles can be revived; and to sever every form of cooperation which would remove the question of principles from the order of the day. Finally, in

the application of his principles he is called to let himself be governed exclusively by the disposition of the national character, by the moral calling that
speaks in its history, by the demands of the time, and by the impulse toward
progress—all sanctified by critique in the light of these principles. . . .

SPHERE SOVEREIGNTY

How does the school I am introducing [The Free University of
Amsterdam] fit into the garden of Dutch society? Why does it brandish on the
point of its lance the cap of liberty? And why does it study the book of the
Reformed faith so intently? I can answer all three questions by pointing you
to the notion of sphere sovereignty as that which characterizes our institution
1) in its national significance, 2) in its academic aims, and 3) in its Reformed
character. . . .

[Only Kuyper's discussion of the first point follows.]

Its National Significance

The first part of my discourse aims to present the national significance of
our institution. In this awesome century our nation, too, is struggling its way
through a crisis, a crisis which it shares with all kindred nations, a crisis that
pervades the whole world of thinking humanity.

Every crisis centers on a threatened way of life, whose deterioration
prompts either prophecies of rejuvenation or predictions of decline unto
death. What is that way of life presently under assault? What is at stake in
this crisis also for our nation? And who would dare to repeat the customary
answers: that the battle is between progress and tradition, or between the
simple and the complex, or between the ideal and the real, or between the
poor and the rich? The inadequacy, unreasonableness, and shallowness of
each of these diagnoses has been exposed to the clear light of day. Some made
the slogans "clericalism" and "liberalism" the watchword, as though what
mattered was the abuse or purification of ecclesiastical influence. At last,
however, this pretense, too, was contemptuously torn away, until finally the
awareness grew that the present crisis of the nations does not center on inequality, self-interest, or justice, but on a living person, on Him who once
swore to being King, on Him who once sacrificed His life on the cross of
Golgotha for the sake of his claim to royal sovereignty—this awareness, first
grasped by the leading visionaries of our time, gradually spread from this nucleus to ever widening circles.

"The Nazarene: our holy inspiration, our animating ideal, our paragon of piety!" For a long time this is what people cried enthusiastically. But history passed judgment upon such praise as contradictory to the Nazarene's own claims. In His calm, divinely human consciousness, as lucid as glass, He claimed to be nothing less than the Messiah, the Anointed, and thus the King of kings, possessing "all authority in heaven and on earth." The scandalous sign tacked to the cross announcing the criminal arrogance for which He was sentenced to die was not that He was a hero of the faith or a "martyr to honor," but that He was the King of the Jews, that is, the Bearer of Sovereignty. It is this sovereignty, the existence or non-existence of the power of the One born of the virgin Mary, around which the thinking minds, the ruling powers, and the kindred nations are as greatly agitated today as in the first three centuries. This precisely is the question of sovereignty: the King of the Jews is either the saving truth to which all nations must say Amen or the principal lie which all nations must oppose. This issue, once encountered in the blood of the Nazarene, has now once again torn a rift through the entire world of our spiritual, human, and national existence.

What is sovereignty? Do you not agree with me in defining it as the authority that possesses the right and duty, and wields the power to break and punish all resistance to its will? And does not an ineradicable conscience also speak within you, telling you that original, absolute sovereignty cannot reside in any creature, but must coincide with the majesty of God? If you believe in Him as the Conceiver and Creator, the Founder and Director of all things, your soul must also proclaim the triune God as the only absolute Sovereign. But then—and I stress this—then at the same time we must acknowledge that this supreme Sovereign has delegated and still delegates His authority to human persons, so that on earth one actually never encounters God Himself directly in visible form, but one always sees His sovereign authority administered in human offices.

This embodiment of God's sovereignty in human office raises the very important question: how does this delegation occur? Is this all-encompassing sovereignty of God delegated to a single person undivided? Or does an earthly sovereign possess the power to compel obedience only in a limited sphere, a sphere limited by other spheres in which someone else is sovereign, and not he?

The answer to this question differs depending on whether one stands within the orbit of Revelation or outside it. The traditional answer given by those who excluded special revelation from their minds was, "As far as practical it must be undivided, but it must also permeate all spheres." They stipulated, "as far as is practical," because God's sovereignty over what is above falls beyond man's reach, and over nature beyond man's power, and over fate beyond man's control. But for the rest, they argue, we can do without sphere sovereignty. The state has unlimited power to command, disposing over persons, over their lives, over their rights, over their conscience, even over their faith. In ancient times there were many gods; as a result, in the slogan "united power makes for greater strength," the single, unlimited state was regarded as even more imposing and more majestic than the divided power of the gods. Eventually, therefore, the state itself, embodied in Caesar, became God—the divine state which could tolerate no other states beside itself. Thus the passion for world domination was born—*Divus Augustus!*—with Caesar worship as its religion. What a profoundly sinful notion, which eighteen centuries later for the first time was self-consciously elaborated into a theory of the state in Hegel's idea of "the immanent God".

In contrast, Jehovah causes the mouthpieces of Messianic prophecy to cry out in Israel, "This sovereignty must be delegated not 'as far as is practical' but wholly undivided and unbroken." And this human Messiah did appear, having power in heaven, power over nature, claiming power over all nations, and in all nations over conscience and faith. Even the bond between mother and child had to yield in the face of his call to obedience. This, then, is total sovereignty, extending over all things visible and invisible, over both the spiritual and the material, placed in the hands of a Man. This is not one kingdom among others, but the absolute kingdom. "To this end I was born, and for this cause I came into the world—to be king." "All power is mine in heaven and on the whole earth." "One day all enemies will be subdued and every knee will bow before me." This is the Messianic sovereignty once foretold by the prophet, to which the Nazarene laid claim, and whose beginnings He demonstrated in His miracles. It was, moreover, described by the apostles, and, on their authority, confessed by the church of Christ to be undivided, and yet delegated, or rather, assumed by Christ in order to be returned. For only if this sovereignty is returned from the Messiah to God himself, who will then be "all and in all," will that total harmony one day break through.

However—and here we encounter the glorious principle of liberty—this total sovereignty of the sinless Messiah implies at the same time the forthright denial and contradiction of all absolute sovereignty among sinful men on earth. It does so by dividing life into unique spheres, each with its own sovereignty.

Human life, with its material foreground which is visible and its spiritual background which is invisible, turns out to be neither simple nor uniform but constitutes an infinitely composite organism. Its composition is such that the individual exists only in terms of a group, and only in such groups can wholeness become manifest. Call the parts of this one gigantic machine cog-wheels, each revolving on its own axle under its own power, or spheres, each infused with its own animating spirit. The imagery is indifferent. As long as we recognize that there exist in life as many spheres as there are constellations in the sky, and that the scope of each sphere has been unerringly delineated by a unique principle, as its focal-point, namely, the apostolic injunction, "each in its own order" [I. Cor. 15:23]. Just as we speak of a moral world, a world of science, a business world, a world of art, so we can more properly speak of a sphere of morality, a family sphere, a sphere of social life, each with its own realm; and because each comprises its own realm, each has its own sovereign within the bounds of that realm.

There is accordingly a realm of nature in which its sovereign works formatively on matter according to fixed laws. Similarly, there is also a realm of the personal, of the family, of science, of social and ecclesiastical life—each of which obeys is own laws, and each of which stands under its own supreme authority. There is a realm of thought where only the laws of logic may rule. There is a realm of conscience where no one may issue commands sovereignly but the Holy One Himself. And finally there is a realm of faith where only the person himself is sovereign who through faith dedicates himself in the depth of his being.

All these spheres interlock like cogwheels, and precisely in acting upon one another and in meshing with one another, they produce the rich, multi-faceted variety of human society. But this also brings with it the danger that one sphere in life may break in upon another like a jerky cogwheel that shears off one cog after another until the operation of the entire machine is disrupted. This danger constitutes the rationale for still another sphere of authority, that of the state. The state must make it possible for the various spheres, insofar as they manifest themselves externally, to interact appropriately, and to keep each sphere within its proper limits. And since personal life may be suppressed by the group in which one lives, the state must protect the individual from the tyranny of his own group. Such a state is a sovereign power which, as Scripture succinctly puts it, "gives stability to the land by justice" [Prov. 29:4], since without justice it destroys itself and collapses. As the power that protects the individual and defines the mutual relationships among the visible spheres, the sovereignty of the state, therefore, rises high above all the other spheres by enjoining justice and utilizing force justly. It has no authority, however, within each of these spheres. Internally each sphere is ruled by another authority that descends directly from God, apart from the state. This authority is not conferred, but merely recognized by the state. And even in defining laws for the mutual relationships among these spheres the state may not adopt its own will or choice as the standard, but is bound by the decision of a higher will, as expressed in the nature and purpose of these spheres. The state must see to it that the cogwheels operate as they are meant to. Is it not so, that the ideal which beckons every nobler head of state is not to suppress life nor to shackle freedom, but to make possible the free movement of life in and for each of these spheres?

These two credos, thus, stand in sharp contrast. He who lives from the reality of revelation (and who lives consistently within that perspective) confesses that all sovereignty rests in God and that it can therefore only issue from Him; that this divine sovereignty has been bestowed totally and undividedly upon the man-Messiah; and that therefore human freedom is safe under this Son of Man as Sovereign. For the state as well as every other sphere of life is marked by an authority derived from Him, that is, it possesses sovereignty in its own sphere.

Those, on the contrary, who do not sense the reality of such a special revelation, and therefore deny it, insist on an absolute separation between the question of sovereignty and the question of faith. They assert, accordingly, that there is no other authority conceivable than that of the state, and therefore busy themselves to embody this high idea of sovereignty ever more perfectly in the all-powerful state. Hence, they can grant to the other spheres a freedom no more generous than the measure of rights the state allows them out of its weakness or confers upon them out of its absolute power.

I call these two positions "sovereignty credos," for they are fundamental convictions, not systems of thought. This is so because the gulf that separates them lies not in a different arrangement of ideas, but in a recognition or denial of the facts of life. For us who live by revelation, the Messiah lives, the Christ works, and He more certainly sits on the throne of God's power than you are sitting here in your seats. On the other hand, those who do not join in this confession must oppose it as a harmful illusion that poses an obstacle to the nation's development, a pernicious dogma, a meaningless phantasm.

These therefore stand as diametrically opposing confessions, which in cowardly fashion have been pushed aside repeatedly behind a long row of hybrid theories, mixed from more of one and less of the other, or from an equal portion of each. During critical periods, however, the principal credos from which these pale entities derive their basic hue repeatedly break through this unprincipled charade with a vengeance. Then in open array they once again challenge one another to combat, as the only two really great antagonists, which split life asunder at the roots. It is therefore worth risking one's life for this cause, even if it means disturbing the lives of other people.

Defending sphere sovereignty against state sovereignty—see, in summary form this is the history of the world, going back to even before the Messianic sovereignty was proclaimed. For the royal child of Bethlehem does indeed protect this principle of sphere sovereignty with His shield; but He did not create it. It existed from antiquity. It was embedded in the creation order, in the structure of human life. It existed before state sovereignty arose. But once state sovereignty arose, it recognized sphere sovereignty as its enduring enemy. Moreover, the power of the spheres to resist was weakened from within by the transgression of their own laws of being, that is, by sin. Thus the ancient history of all people confronts us with the ignominious drama of how, despite stubborn and sometimes heroic resistance, freedom within the various spheres dies out and the power of the state triumphs, turning eventually into Caesarism. Socrates drinking the cup of hemlock, Brutus driving his dagger into Caesar's heart, the Galileans whose blood Pilate mingles with their sacrifices—these are all wildly heroic convulsions of a free, organic way of life that finally collapses under the iron hand of this Caesarism. As antiquity draws to a close, freedom is lost. There are no longer nations. There are no longer free spheres. Everything had become one sphere, a single world empire under a single sovereign state-will. Only by intoxicating itself in dehumanizing luxury could a humanity, thus plunged into self-contempt, drown out the pain of that ignominy.

The one man who through supernatural power, through the power of faith, once again created a free sphere within the uniformity of an iron-clad state, and within this sphere a free sovereignty, was Jesus the Nazarene. With God in His heart, one with God, Himself God, He withstood Caesar, broke down the iron gates, and posited the sovereignty of faith as the deepest axis upon which the sovereignty of all spheres rests. Neither Pharisee nor disciple understood that, beyond the salvation of the elect, His cry "It is finished!" also embraces the idea of a "salvation of the cosmos," a liberation of the world, a world of liberties. Jesus, however, did see this, as the sign "King" on His cross testifies. He appeared as Sovereign. As Sovereign, He did battle with the usurping "Prince of the World" for authority over the world. No sooner did His followers form their own circle then they also came into conflict with the sovereignty of the state. They succumbed and their blood was shed. But the shedding of their blood could not wipe out Jesus' sovereign principle of faith. "Christ as God" or "Augustus the divine" became the shibboleths that would decide the destiny of the world. Christ won and Caesar was toppled. Every liberated nation came forth again with its own king, and within the realm of these kings with its own spheres, and in these spheres with its own liberties. Then at last, with honor, and crowning itself with nobility, life began to manifest all the energy and all the glory that sphere sovereignty implies in the increasingly richer organic unity of guilds and orders and free societies.

NOTES

[1] Selections from: (1) Kuyper's articles in *De Standaard*, October 16 – November 7, 1873, reprinted in Abraham Kuyper, *Ons Program* (Amsterdam: 1879), translated and edited by Harry der Nederlander, with Gordon Spykman; and (2) Kuyper's inaugural address at the opening of the Free University of Amsterdam, October 20, 1880—*Souvereiniteit in Eigen Kring* (Kampen: J. H. Kok, 1930 [1880]), translated and edited by Harry der Nederlander, with Gordon Spykman.

[2] For more on Kuyper's life and in critique of his work, see Frank VandenBerg, *Abraham Kuyper: A Biography* (St. Catharines, Ontario: Paideia Press, 1978); S.U. Zuidema, "Common Grace and Christian Action in Abraham Kuyper," in S. U. Zuidema, *Communication and Confrontation* (Toronto: Wedge Publishing Foundation, 1972), 52-106; Justus M. VanderKroef, "Abraham Kuyper and the Rise of Neo-Calvinism in the Netherlands," *Church History*, 17 (1948): 316-334; and McKendree Langley, *The Practice of Political Spirituality*, (St. Catharines, Ontario: Paideia Press, 1984).

[3] Kuyper, *Ons Program*, 117. See Dirk Jellema, "Abraham Kuyper's Attack on Liberalism," *Review of Politics*, 19 (1957): 472-485.

[4] Kuyper, "De Ordinantien Gods," 120.

[5] *Ibid.*, 126.

[6] *Ibid.*, 120.

[7] *Ibid.*

[8] *Ibid.*, 121.

[9] *Ibid.*, 122.

[10] *Ibid.*, 127-128.

[11] In 1891 Kuyper opened the First Christian Social Congress in the Netherlands with an address on "The Christian Religion and the Social Question." In the same year, but before Kuyper delivered his speech, Pope Leo XIII published *Rerum Novarum*. See Abraham Kuyper, *Christianity and the Class Struggle*, trans. D. Jellema (Grand Rapids: Piet Hein Publishers, 1950).

[12] *De Gemeene Gratie* (Amsterdam: Hoveker and Wormser, 1902-04), 3 vols.

[13] *Ibid.*, 1: 179-217, 439-446.

[14] *Ibid.*, 2: 49ff.

[15] Zuidema, "Common Grace," 73.

[16] See Abraham Kuyper, *Lectures on Calvinism* (Grand Rapids: Eerdmans, 1931). These were Kuyper's Stone Lectures at Princeton University in 1898.

[17] *Ibid.*, 100.

[18] Note especially Kuyper's argument below in "Sphere Sovereignty." See also Herman Dooyeweerd *The Secularization of Science*, trans. R. Knudsen (Memphis, TN: Christian Studies Center, 1954), first published in French, "La sécularisation de la science," *La Revue Réformée*, 5 (1954): 138-157.

[19] On the differentiation of life spheres see Kuyper, *Lectures on Calvinism*, and Herman Dooyeweerd, *Roots of Western Culture: Pagan, Secular, and Christian Options*, trans. J.

Kraay, eds. M. Vander Vennen and B. Zylstra (Toronto: Wedge Publishing Foundation, 1979), 62-87.

[20] Kuyper, *Souvereiniteit in Eigen Kring* (Kampen: J.H. Kok, 1930 [1880]), 11. Page citations here and below are from the original Dutch; the translation is by Harry de Nederlander and Gordon Spykman from the excerpt included below.

[21] Jacques Maritain, *Man and the State* (Chicago: University of Chicago Press, 1951), 24.

[22] Kuyper, *Souvereiniteit in Eigen Kring*, 8-9.

FIFTEEN

✕✕✕✕✕✕✕✕✕✕

ROOTS OF WESTERN CULTURE[1]

by Herman Dooyeweerd

Herman Dooyeweerd

One of the most influential of Kuyper's followers was the legal philosopher Herman Dooyeweerd (1894-1977), who played a role in Dutch
Protestantism similar to that played by Jacques Maritain in Catholic circles of
Europe and Latin America. Following his study at the Free University where
he received his doctor of laws degree, he became, in 1922, assistant director
of the Anti-Revolutionary Party's research center in The Hague. In 1926 he
returned as professor of law to the Free University where he worked until his
retirement in the 1960s.[2]

During his years at the Free University, Dooyeweerd helped to develop a
wide-ranging systematic philosophy based on a Christian *Weltanschauung*
(world-and-life view) that views the creation as a unity governed by God's
ordinances. Central to his philosophy is a recognition of the antithesis or opposition between different "ground motives" (basic, controlling, religious
drives or forces) that direct life and thought.

The first selection below shows how far Dooyeweerd takes this insight
which he received from Groen van Prinsterer and Abraham Kuyper. It also
helps to show why he thinks a Calvinist philosophy of the creation order differs from a Catholic natural-law philosophy. Dooyeweerd distinguishes four
major ground motives in Western culture, reaching back to the early Greek

and biblical traditions. First he discusses the Greek ground motive of "form and matter," rooted in the conflict between early nature religions and the later culture religion of the Olympian gods. The second ground motive is the Roman Catholic "nature and grace" motive which is a synthesis of Greek and Christian basic motives that establishes itself as a new force in Western civilization. Not included in this selection is Dooyeweerd's discussion of the biblical ground motive of "creation, fall, and redemption" and the modern humanist motive of "nature and freedom."[3]

Working with the same reforming zeal that inspired Groen and Kuyper, Dooyeweerd wants to free Christian philosophy and social theory from its synthetic accommodation of Greek religion and philosophy in order that its integral power can bear fruit in the contemporary world. Grounded in a motive of uncompromising commitment to biblical revelation about the order of creation, the radical character of sin, and the transforming power of God's redemption in Christ, a Christian social philosophy can contribute powerful insights to the complex and differentiated societies in which we live today. With this orientation and purpose, Dooyeweerd not only goes beyond Kuyper in articulating a philosophy of sphere sovereignty, he also seeks to give an empirical, phenomenological account of the multiplicity of "aspects" or "modes" of creaturely life that undergird and structure all the entities and institutions of life.[4]

The modes or aspects of creation, according to Dooyeweerd, are the universal dimensions of its structure. We know about the meaning of the aspects of life primarily because of the work done by special sciences through abstraction and analysis. Biologists analyze the biotic aspect of creation, psychologists analyze the psychical mode or dimension, and so forth. Just as one sphere of social life should not be reduced to another, but should be recognized as having independence in its own realm, so also scientists should not seek to reduce one mode or aspect of existence to another in their analytic interpretation of the created order. Each modality or aspect is sovereign in its own sphere, and each (together with all the others) governs or structures the entire creation. Dooyeweerd uses the language of "modal sphere sovereignty" to describe the irreducible but interrelated character of these aspects. His mature philosophy constitutes an intricate interpretation of the interconnection of "modal" and "societal" sphere sovereignty.

The second selection from Dooyeweerd provides an introduction to his philosophy of sphere sovereignty, rooted as it is in an effort to clarify the implication of the Christian basic motive of creation, fall, and redemption. In the second selection, Dooyeweerd carefully distinguishes between the "whole-part" relationship and sphere sovereignty.[5] This distinction helps to clarify the difference between the "subsidiarity" principle and the interrelationship of spheres as conceived by Calvinist thinkers.

Perhaps Dooyeweerd's greatest contribution is his interpretation of the fundamental importance of ontology in every social and political philosophy. He argues that "every theory concerning the structure of human society is based upon a specific conception of the basic structure of reality."[6] He believes that "the ontological question really lies at the foundation of every analysis of empirical societal facts. Human society belongs to reality."[7]

When Dooyeweerd analyzes social reality and discusses actual institutions and communities such as the family, state, and church, he is concerned with what he calls the normative structural principles of these distinct entities. In reality, he says, we confront particular "individuality structures" or "identity structures" of concrete reality. Each thing, person, and institution functions in all aspects or modes of reality and is to be distinguished from the multiple functions that it exhibits in all the modal aspects.

Dooyeweerd's general theory of society is neither individualistic nor collectivistic. He recognizes a variety of types of social structures in creation. Communities and institutions (such as families, schools, or businesses) exist according to their own internal structural principles. Social life and its institutions are not arbitrary, contractual creations by autonomous, atomized individuals.[8] Dooyeweerd also insists that there is no such thing in creation as a monistic social whole (whether the state or something else) that embraces all lesser communities and individuals as its parts.[9] He rejects the idea of a "total bond of all temporal society" on earth. Instead of individualism or collectivism, Dooyeweerd argues for social pluralism as the expression of the creation's complex unity under God.

This is not to say that Dooyeweerd sees no interconnection among the diverse social entities and relationships. To the contrary, he believes that all of life is intimately interrelated as a creational unity. Sphere sovereignty does not mean mutual isolation but rather real distinctions on the basis of which the interrelationships or "interlacements" exist. Dooyeweerd calls the interconnection or interlacement of social reality "enkapsis."[10]

Enkapsis is the corollary of sphere sovereignty because no single structure of individuality can be realized apart from "inter-structural intertwinements with other individuality structures."[11] In other words, enkapsis refers to the intimate, structural integration of different irreducible societal spheres. Especially important is Dooyeweerd's emphasis that enkaptic interlacement cannot be explained in terms of the whole-part relationship. Bernard Zylstra explains Dooyeweerd's point by using an example of a civil marriage ceremony.

This ceremony establishes a link between the marriage community and the state. Here we have an example of an intertwinement between two intrinsically different social relationships which leaves their respective inner nature intact. . . . [Dooyeweerd] insists that the relation of enkapsis between two heterogeneous social spheres must be sharply distinguished from the relation of a whole to its parts. The latter is present for instance in the relation between a state and its provinces. But a part-whole relation does not obtain between social spheres of different inner nature. That is, if a social bond exhibiting a distinct structure of individuality is bound "enkaptically" within another social bond of a different nature, the former will attain an enkaptic function within the latter which does not belong to its inner sphere. But within its own *inner* sphere— determined as it is by its particular structural principle—the social bond has "sphere sovereignty" and maintains its intrinsic typical character. In short, a civil ceremony enkaptically links marriage to the state without making it a state institution. And similar conclusions can be arrived at with respect to other interlacements. A university, a political party, an industry or a trade-union may all be more or less closely connected with the state. But if they are genuinely expressive of their normative internal structural principle they will maintain an authentic existence which is not derived from the state and which is not characterized by typically political processes.[12]

All of this is important for Dooyeweerd's understanding of the state. For he believes that marriage, family, education, industry, and others, have important enkaptic functions within the state apart from which the modern differentiated state could not exist. But these are not "parts" of the state community; they are not even lower, autonomous, subsidiary parts. The church, he says, is defined by a binding confession of Christian faith for its members, whereas the state should not have such a binding confession.[13] The state may not assume to itself attributes of the church nor may the church assume attributes of the state.

The public justice of the state finds its boundaries in the internal private communities of law of the other societal relationships. Thus also, the Christian state as such can reveal itself in the area of faith only within the boundaries of its own inner structural principle, and may not assume the structure of a church-institute. For the state is not, like the temporal church-community, qualified as a community of believers in Christ. This is to say, neither the state, nor any other non-ecclesiastical societal relationship has as its typical goal the area of faith and confession.[14]

In other words, Dooyeweerd's argument is that even in a state where most citizens acknowledge Christ as the supreme Lord, the government of that state should not use its monopolized sword power to establish a church or to enforce a public confession of Christ upon its citizens under penalty of

state punishment. The state, in accordance with its task of juridically governing the public good, should give equal and fair distribution of its rights and
services to all ecclesiastical and religious communities within the realm, including those that are non-Christian in confession. This is what it means for a
state to do public justice to the human faith of all its citizens. Furthermore,
the state's concern for doing justice to religion cannot be limited to a concern
for ecclesiastical and cultic institutions alone. It must recognize the *religious*
character of all of life and seek to do justice to all the diverse communities of
belief within its realm as they express themselves in and through education,
industry, science, and the arts.

Here is one point of great difference between sphere-sovereignty, as it
concerns church and state, and the liberal idea of the separation of church
and state which still largely controls American thinking on the subject.
Insofar as liberalism wanted to safeguard the freedom of church life over
against the state, according to Dooyeweerd,

> it could not do otherwise than (1) effect a watertight division between state and
> church, and (2) introduce the "religionless state," where faith is completely
> excluded. The freedom of the church was then derived from the absolute consti-
> tutional rights of the "religious individual." The church became a private asso-
> ciation, and in it the "general will" of the members was declared sovereign.
>
> Scriptural Christianity, on the other hand, can never take over this liberalistic
> slogan of separation of church and state without spiritual suicide. Sphere-
> sovereignty does not yield a watertight compartment or mechanical division
> among the areas of life. It is, as we have seen, an organically most deeply coher-
> ing principle, for it begins with the religious root unity of the life-spheres. The
> various social structures by which sphere-sovereignty is internally guaranteed
> do not stand alongside each other in isolation. In temporal life they are inter-
> twined and interwoven. All other societal relationships also have a function
> within the state, just as conversely the state functions in all other societal rela-
> tionships. But all these structural interplays remain in the final analysis of an
> external character with respect to sphere-sovereignty.[15]

The guarantee of true religion and just government, in Dooyeweerd's
view, is God's Word of creation and redemption in Christ by whom and
through whom all things are being set right and revealed in truth. Present
human responsibility is to seek out the proper principles, norms, tasks, limits,
and interrelationships of each human community and social relationship. By
God's grace, Christians should seek to understand and to actualize ecclesiastical and state institutions, each according to its divinely given structural principle. These two independent institutions cannot be kept isolated from one
another, but neither should they be collapsed into one another. They must be

properly interrelated, each performing its own functions in the religious life of persons according to its own internal structural principle.

The distinctive identity of the state (by virtue of divine ordinance) is to be found in its character as a public legal community. In the classical and Thomistic arguments, says Dooyeweerd, "it is impossible to see 'common good' as a truly *jural* principle."[16] Only by clarifying the foundation function of the state in its monopolization of political force within a territory, and by recognizing its guiding (or qualifying) function of public justice within that realm, is it possible to understand the kind of positive exercise of authority the state may employ within society. External limits are not enough—limits such as the procedural rule of due process, or the principle that non-state groups should be free to do whatever they are able to do for themselves. The actual internal purpose and task of the state must be specified so that its own sphere of sovereignty can be distinguished from that of other spheres. The norm of public justice is much more definite and specific than the norm of the common good, since the latter is applicable to all societal spheres.

THE GREAT SYNTHESIS OF PAGAN AND CHRISTIAN RELIGIONS

Early Setting

When the Christian ground motive entered the Hellenistic, late-Greek world of thought, its indivisible unity was threatened on every side. Already in the first centuries of its history, the Christian church fought a battle of life and death in order to keep its ground motive free from the influences of the Greek ground motive and the ones that later intermingled with Greek religion in its contact with the different near-eastern religions, notably Persian Zoroastrianism.

All of these nonbiblical ground motives were of a dualistic nature, divided against themselves. Torn by inner contradictions, they knew neither God the creator, the absolute origin of all things, nor man in the root of his being. In other words, they were apostate in their direction.

The Greek form-matter motive originated in an unreconciled conflict within Greek religious consciousness between the older nature religion and the newer culture religion of the Olympian gods. The spiritual momentum of this internally divided ground motive led mature Greek thought to accept a twofold origin of the world. Even when Greek thinkers acknowledged the existence of a cosmic order originating through a divine design and plan, they still categorically denied a divine *creation*. Greeks believed that whatever came into existence arose merely through a divine activity of giving form to an already present and formless matter. They conceived of divine formation only in terms of human cultural activity. The "rational deity" was merely a "heavenly architect" who formed a given material according to a free design. He was not able to forestall the blind, autonomous activity of the matter principle.

Just as the rational deity found the autonomy of the matter principle over against himself, so also the "rational soul" of human nature confronted an earthly, material body. The actual center of the rational soul was theoretical thought, which was divine in character. The soul was the invisible "form" of human existence, and as the faculty of theoretical thought it was immortal. By contrast, the material body, the "matter" of man's being was subject to the stream of life and blind fate.

In the Hellenistic period it was not difficult to combine the Greek ground motive with the dualistic ground motives of the near-eastern religions with which the Greeks had already made acquaintance. The ground motive of the Persian Zoroastrian religion consisted of a battle between a divine principle of light and an evil principle of darkness. Thus one could easily identify the Greek form motive with the Zoroastrian motive of light and the Greek matter motive with the evil principle of darkness.

The Temptation of Dualism

The Christian church realized the enormous danger the Greek-Zoroastrian ground motive posed for the pure ground motive of divine revelation. In its life-and-death struggle against this motive the church formulated the doctrine of the divine unity of the Father and the Son (the Word or *Logos*) and soon afterwards the doctrine of the trinity of Father, Son, and Holy Spirit. This determination of the basic doctrinal position of the Christian church was not intended as a scientific-theological theory but as a necessarily imperfect formulation of the living confession of the Body of Christ, in which the pure ground motive sought expression.

The orthodox direction of Christian thought reached a high point in Augustine. Augustine placed his stamp on Christian reflection through the thirteenth century, and even afterwards he maintained a considerable influence. The ground motive of his thought was undoubtedly scriptural. After his conversion his powerful, talented intellect increasingly drew from this source. However, the Christian theology of his day was confronted with philosophical problems whose solutions could not be avoided. Insofar as the church fathers had been philosophically educated—Augustine very much so—they had come to absorb the Greek way of thought. They had appropriated its views of cosmic order, human nature, and human society. The church fathers attempted to rid these conceptions of their pagan elements and to adapt them to the Christian religion. However, they failed to see that these elements were rooted in a pagan ground motive. They failed to understand that this ground motive controlled not merely a few components but its entire foundation and elaboration. In other words, they failed to see that because of its radical character the ground motive of the Christian religion demands an *inner reformation* of one's scientific view of the world order and of temporal life. Instead of *reformation* they sought *accommodation*; they sought to adapt pagan thought to divine revelation of the Word.

This adaptation laid the basis for *scholasticism*, which up to the present impedes the development of a truly reformational direction in Christian life and thought. Scholasticism seeks a *synthesis* between Greek thought and the Christian religion. It was thought that such a synthesis can be successfully achieved if philosophy, with its Greek basis, is to be made subservient to Christian theology. . . .

The Roman Catholic Ground Motive

The effort to bridge the foundations of the Christian religion and Greek thought necessarily entailed the further attempt to find a deeper reconciliation between their respective religious ground motives. During the Middle Ages, when the Church of Rome gradually gained control over all of temporal society, this attempted religious synthesis produced a new dialectical ground motive in the development of Western culture: the well-known motive of "nature and grace" (nature and supernature). Its inherent ambiguity and disharmony dominated even the thought of the Reformation to a great extent, although in principle the Reformation had overcome its dialectical tension by returning to the scriptural teaching of the radical significance of the fall for human nature and to the confession of justification by faith alone. . . .

Like the Greek form-matter motive, the ground motive of nature and grace contained a *religious dialectic* which drove life and thought from the natural pole to the supranatural pole. The naturalistic attitude summoned the ecclesiastical truths of grace before the court of natural reason, and a supernatural mysticism attempted to escape "nature" in the mystical experience of "grace." Ultimately this dialectic led to a consistent proclamation of the unbridgeable rift between nature and grace; nature became independent, losing every point of contact with grace. Only the official authority of the Roman

Catholic Church was sufficiently powerful to uphold the religious pseudosynthesis by formally denouncing the heresies that sought a following on the basis of this motive. Its defense drew heavily on the philosophy of Thomas Aquinas (1225-1274), the prince of scholasticism.

Thomas Aquinas

For Thomas "nature" was the independent "stepping-stone to grace," the substructure of a Christian superstructure. He construed the mutual relation between these antithetical motives in Greek fashion, understanding it as a relation between "matter" and "form." He believed that nature is matter for a higher form of perfection bestowed upon it by grace. In other words, the Redeemer works in the manner of a sculptor who shapes his material into a new form. . . .

Thomas maintained that the principle of matter was the principle of imperfection, arguing that what "comes into being" is still imperfect. Conversely, he continually called the "thinking soul," the "rational form" of human nature, "divine." He never referred to matter as divine. Clearly, the Greek form-matter motive led to a dualism in Thomas's conception of the creation, a dualism reinforced by the contrast between nature and supernature. How, for example, could a principle of imperfection originate in God? Unintentionally, Thomas allowed the Greek form-matter motive to overpower the creation motive of the Christian religion. Although he did acknowledge God as the "first cause" and the "ultimate goal" of nature, he divided the creation order into a natural and supranatural realm. And his view of the "natural order" stemmed from Aristotle. . . .

The Roman Catholic View of Natural Society

The philosophical system of Thomas Aquinas stands behind the official Roman Catholic view of the state and of the other societal spheres. It is undoubtedly true that in Roman Catholic circles some adhere to conceptions other than those of Aquinas. Augustinian trends are certainly not unimportant. But Thomistic philosophy, supported by official recommendation in a series of papal encyclicals, has a special status among Roman Catholics. The two famous social and socioeconomic encyclicals *Rerum novarum* (1891, from Leo XIII) and *Quadragesimo anno* (1931, from Pius XI) are based on a Thomistic foundation. They present guidelines for a solution to social questions and to the problems of economic order from a Roman Catholic vantage point.

Thomas's view of human society was completely dominated by the religious ground motive of nature and grace in its Roman Catholic sense. The main lines of his view of *natural* society were derived from Aristotle. We have already noted that in conformity with Aristotle he conceived of human nature as a composition of form and matter. This conception of human nature is the basis for Thomas's view of society. Man's "form" was the rational soul, and his "matter" was the material body, which owed its real being to the soul. Every creature composed of form and matter arose and came into being, and the principle of form gave this becoming the direction toward a goal. By nature, every creature strove to reach its perfection through a process whereby its "essential form" realized itself in the matter of its body. Thus a plant naturally strove to develop its seed into the mature form of a plant, and an animal developed itself toward its mature form. The natural perfection of man consisted in the complete development of his rational nature which distinguished him from plants and animals. His rational nature was equipped with an innate, rational, natural law that urged him to do good and to refrain from evil. Thus, according to Thomas, man *naturally* strove toward the *good*. This conception radically conflicts with the scriptural confession of the total depravity of "human nature."

Thomas also believed that man could not attain his natural perfection as an isolated individual. He came into the world naked and helpless, and therefore he depended on society, which had to aid him by providing for his material and moral needs. Thus for Thomas a social inclination or a predisposition toward society is also innate in rational human nature. This social propensity develops in stages, through the formation of smaller and larger communities that are mutually related in terms of *lower* to *higher*, *means* to *end*, *part* to *whole*.

The lowest community is the family, which provides the opportunity for satisfying man's lower needs, such as food and sex. The highest community is the state, which brings man's social tendency to perfection. All the lower communities relate to the state as their completion; for, unlike the other natural societal forms, the state is the overarching and perfect community. It possesses autarchy and self-sufficiency, since in the natural realm it is the highest and most embracive community. The state is based on the rational disposition of human nature. Its essence is *characterized* by its *goal*, the common good. This natural goal is also the immediate basis of governmental authority, without which the body politic cannot exist. Thus, if the state is grounded in "nature," so is the authority of government. Thomas certainly recognized that *ultimately* the government's authority is rooted in the sovereignty of the creator but, in typically Roman Catholic fashion, *he inserted the motive of rational nature between man and the creator. . . .*

The Principle of Subsidiarity

The Greek nature motive with its dualism between the form principle and the matter principle permeated Thomas Aquinas's view of human society. In his opinion the state, based on the rational nature of man, was necessary so that the rational form of human nature could arrive at perfect development and so that the matter principle—expressed in sensuous desires—could be held in check. In conformity with Greek thought, Thomas held that the state was the total, all-inclusive community in the realm of nature. All the other life spheres were merely its subservient parts. Thomas therefore conceived of the relationship between the state and the other natural spheres of life in terms of the whole-part relation. Certainly he would not defend a state absolutism that would govern all of life from "above." The modern totalitarian regimes of national socialism and fascism would have met an unwavering opponent in Thomas, as they did among the modern Thomists. Thomas immediately added a restriction after declaring that individuals and "lower" communities were parts of the state; he maintained that they were parts only insofar as they were of the *same order*. To begin with, this limitation excluded the supranatural order from the jurisdiction of the state. Both the individual and marriage (in its sacramental superstructure) participated in the supranatural order, and the jurisdiction of the state did not extend beyond the natural. Secondly, this limitation signified that Thomas's view of the state was anticentralist in principle. Thomas argued that the state is constructed *from below* in a hierarchy of lower and higher communities. Whatever could be adequately taken care of by a lower community should not be subsumed by a higher community.

The famous principle of *subsidiarity* is rooted in this train of thought. The encyclical *Quadragesimo anno* (1931, from Pius XI) defended "subsidiarity" as a guide for delimiting the state's task in the organization of labor and industry. The principle of subsidiarity holds that the state should contribute to the common good only those elements which the individual person cannot provide, either by himself or by means of the lower communities. At first glance this principle seems to be another name for "sphere sovereignty." Those who agree with Groen van Prinsterer's views concerning the structure of the state will be congenial to the idea that the state should be organized not from above but from below. Yet a decisive difference exists between the principles of subsidiarity and sphere sovereignty.

Roman Catholic social theory developed the principle of subsidiarity on the basis of the Thomistic view of man's "rational nature," which itself was derived from the Greek concept of nature. Man's natural perfection, which consisted in realizing the "rational essential form" of this nature, could not be attained in isolation. He came into the world naked and helpless, with the result that he depended upon the community for providing him with his "material" and "rational-moral" needs. Hence a social propensity lay implanted in his rational nature, a propensity that developed step by step in the societal forms which began with the lowest (the family) and ended with the state, the perfect and highest community in natural society.

Meanwhile, the human being as an *individual* always remained the Thomistic point of departure, for he alone was truly a *substance*. In the context of Greek thought this meant that the individual possessed an *independent* existence while the community was regarded as merely a *unity of order* borne by the individual. In this pattern of thought a community like the state does not possess *the same reality* as the individual, just as one cannot ascribe the same reality to the *color* red as to a red *rose*. The color red is only a property of the rose and presupposes the rose as its bearer.

For analogous reasons the official Roman Catholic view maintains that the state and the lower societal communities cannot exhaust the reality of the individual as a "natural being." The rational law of nature holds that man depends on the community only for those needs which he himself cannot fill as an individual. The same natural law also holds that a lower community like the family or the school depends on the higher communities (ultimately on the state) only for those interests that it itself cannot handle. Basically, this hierarchical structure describes the content of the principle of subsidiarity.

But Thomism still conceived of both the individual and the lower societal communities in the natural realm as parts of the whole, as parts of the state. It is against this (essentially Greek) view of human society that the scriptural principle of sphere sovereignty directs itself. Rooted in the creation motive of revelation, sphere sovereignty compels us to give a precise account of the intrinsic nature of the life spheres. God created everything according to its own nature. Two parts that completely differ in kind can never become parts of the same whole.

This insight into the inner structure and nature of the differentiated spheres was alien to Thomistic social theory. Thomism distinguished communities only in terms of the immediate *purpose* they served in their cooperation toward the natural perfection of man. For example, marriage (apart from its ecclesiastical, sacramental dimension) was understood as a juridical institution grounded in human nature for the sake of the procreation of the human race. Does this definition focus at all on the intrinsic nature and structure of the community of marriage? If so, what should we say of a marriage in which children are no longer expected? What is the inner norm of the marriage bond in its internal character? Does one really identify the *inner* nature of married life by describing it as a *juridical* institution? Would not marriage be sheer hell if the juridical point of view would guide all of its affairs?

Following Aristotle, Thomas looked upon the family as a natural community serving the lower economic and sexual needs of life. The family consisted of three relations: husband and wife, parents and children, and master and servants. Does this in any way approach the internal character of the family? Does the family really include the servants? Is it true that the family serves only the "lower needs?"

Lastly, Thomistic social theory considered the state to be the perfect human community. Its goal was the "common good" of its members. I ask: *how can this teleological goal orientation help us define the internal nature and structure of the state?* The concept of "common good" in Thomistic political theory was so vague that it applied also to the "lower" societal structures. For example, the modern Thomist does not hesitate to speak of the "public interest" of an industrial corporation in distinction from the "specific interest" of the persons who work within it. For the Thomist the "common good" in the body politic can only refer to the interest of the "whole" that embraces all the "lower" communities and the individuals as "parts." From this perspective, however, it is impossible to indicate an inner criterion for the "common good," since a Thomist does not see the state according to its own intrinsic nature and structure. We know how even the most revolting state absolutism seeks to justify itself with appeals to the common good. As we mentioned earlier, Thomism certainly does not desire an absolute state, but it has no defense against state absolutism other than the principle of subsidiarity, a principle derived not from the intrinsic nature of the life spheres but from the Aristotelian conception of the "social nature" of man and of the "natural purposes" of the various societal communities.

SPHERE SOVEREIGNTY

The scriptural ground motive of the Christian religion—creation, fall, and redemption through Christ Jesus—operates through God's Spirit as a driving force in the religious root of temporal life. As soon as it grips a person completely, it brings about a radical conversion of his life's stance and of his whole view of temporal life. The depth of this conversion can be denied only by those who fail to do justice to the integrality and radicality of the Christian ground motive. Those who weaken the absolute antithesis in a fruitless effort to link this ground motive with the ground motives of apostate religions endorse such a denial.

But the person who by grace comes to true knowledge of God and of himself inevitably experiences spiritual liberation from the yoke of sin and from sin's burden upon his view of reality, even though he knows that sin will not cease in his life. He observes that created reality offers no foundation, foothold, or solid ground for his existence. He perceives how temporal reality and its multifaceted aspects and structures are concentrated as a whole in the religious root community of the human spirit. He sees that temporal reality searches restlessly in the human heart for its divine origin, and he understands that the creation cannot rest until it rests in God.

Creation and Sphere Sovereignty

Created reality displays a great variety of aspects or modes of being in the temporal order. These aspects break up the spiritual and religious root unity of creation into a wealth of colors, just as light refracts into the hues of the rainbow when it passes through a prism. Number, space, motion, organic life, emotional feeling, logical distinction, historical development of culture, symbolic signification, social interaction, economic value, aesthetic harmony, law, moral valuation, and certainty of faith comprise the aspects of reality. They are basically the fields investigated by the various modern special sciences: mathematics, the natural sciences (physics and chemistry), biology (the science of organic life), psychology, logic, history, linguistics, sociology, economics, aesthetics, legal theory, ethics or moral science, and theology which studies divine revelation in Christian and nonchristian faith. Each special science considers reality in only one of its aspects.

Imagine now a science that begins to investigate these distinct aspects of reality without the light of the true knowledge of God and self. The predicament of this science is similar to that of a person who sees the colors of the rainbow but knows nothing of the unbroken light from which they arise. If one were to ask him where the different colors came from, would he not be inclined to consider one color the origin of the others? Or would he be able to discover correctly the mutual relation and coherence between them? If not, then how would he know each color according to its own intrinsic nature? If he were not color-blind he would certainly make distinctions, but he would likely begin with the color that strikes him the most and argue that the others were merely shades of the absolutized color.

The position of a man who thinks he can find his basis and starting point for a view of temporal reality in *science* is no different. Time and again he will be inclined to present one aspect of reality (organic life, feeling, historical development of culture, or any of the others) as reality in its completeness. He will then reduce all the others to the point where they become different manifestations of the absolutized aspect. Think for instance of Goethe's *Faust*, where Faust says: "Feeling is all". . . [*Goethe's Faust*, Walter Kaufmann, line 3456]. Or think of modern materialism, which reduces all of temporal reality to particles of matter in motion. Consider the modern naturalistic philosophy of life, which sees everything one-sidedly in terms of the development of organic life.

Actually, what drives us to absolutize is not science as such but an idolatrous ground motive that takes hold of our thinking. Science can only yield knowledge of reality through the theoretical analysis of its many aspects. It teaches us nothing concerning the deeper unity or origin of these aspects. Only religion is sufficient for this task, since in calling us to know God and ourselves it drives us to focus whatever is relative toward the absolute ground and origin of all things. Once an apostate ground motive takes hold of us, it compels our thinking to absolutize the relative and to deify the creature. In this way false religious prejudices darken our conception of the structure of reality.

Whoever absolutizes one aspect of created reality cannot comprehend any aspect on the basis of its own inner character. He has a false view of reality. Although it is certainly possible that he may discover important *moments* of truth, he integrates these moments into a false view of the *totality* of reality. They are therefore the most dangerous and poisonous weapons of the spirit of the lie.

Historicism

Today we live under the dominion of an idolatrous view of reality that absolutizes the historical aspect of creation. It calls itself dynamic, believing that all of reality moves and unfolds historically. It directs its polemic against static views that adhere to fixed truths. It considers reality one-sidedly in the light of historical becoming and development, arguing that everything is purely historical in character. This "historicism," as it is called, knows of no eternal values. All of life is caught up in the stream of historical development. From this viewpoint the truths of the Christian faith are just as relative and transient as the ideals of the French Revolution. There are many moments of truth in the historicistic view of reality. All temporal things do indeed have a historical aspect. Historical development occurs in scientific endeavor, in society, in art, in human "ideals," and even in the revelation of God's Word. Still, the historical remains merely one aspect of the full reality given to us in time. The other aspects cannot be reduced to it. It does not reach the root unity and absolute origin of reality. Because historicism absolutizes the historical aspect, its individual truths are dangerous weapons of the spirit of deception. Like the tempting words the serpent spoke to Eve in paradise, "You will be like God, knowing good and evil" [Genesis 3:5], historicism contains a half-truth.

The scriptural ground motive of the Christian religion liberates our view of reality from the false prejudices imposed upon us by idolatrous ground motives. The motive of creation continually drives us to examine the inner nature, mutual relation, and coherence of all the aspects in God's created reality. When we become conscious of this motive, we begin to see the richness of God's creation in the great pluriformity and colorfulness of its temporal aspects. Since we know the true origin and the religious root unity of these aspects through God's revelation, we do not absolutize one aspect and reduce the others, but we respect each on the basis of its intrinsic nature and its own law. *For God created everything after its kind.*

The various aspects of reality, therefore, cannot be reduced to each other in their mutual relation. Each possesses a sovereign sphere with regard to the others. Abraham Kuyper called this *sphere sovereignty.*

The creation motive of the Christian religion is engaged in an irreconcilable conflict with the apostate tendency of the human heart to eradicate, level, and erase the boundaries between the peculiar and intrinsic natures that God established in each of the many aspects of reality. For this reason the principle of sphere sovereignty is of powerful, universal significance for one's view of the relation of temporal life to the Christian religion. This principle does not tolerate a dichotomy (division) of temporal reality into two mutually opposing and mutually separable areas, such as "matter and spirit" which we observed in the orphic Greek view. A dualistic view of reality is always the result of the operation of a dualistic ground motive, which knows neither the true religious root unity nor the true absolute origin of temporal reality.

The principle of sphere sovereignty is a creational principle which is unbreakably connected with the scriptural ground motive of the Christian religion. It tells us of the *mutual irreducibility, inner connection,* and *inseparable coherence* of all the aspects of reality in the order of time. If we consider logical thinking, for example, we find that it is embedded within the logical aspect of temporal reality. While this aspect is irreducible to the others, sovereign in its own sphere, and subject to its own sphere of divine laws (the laws for logical thought), it nevertheless reveals its internal nature and its conformity to law only in an unbreakable coherence with all the other aspects of reality. If one attempts to conceive of the logical function as absolute, that is, as independent of and apart from the functions of feeling, organic life, historical development of culture, and so on, then it dissolves into nothingness. It does not exist by itself. It reveals its proper nature only in an inseparable coherence with all the functions which created reality displays within time. We therefore acknowledge readily that one can think logically only insofar as one has a perishable body which functions organically and physicochemically. Our hope of immortality is not rooted in logical thinking but in Christ Jesus. By the light of God's Word we know that our temporal life in all its aspects has a spiritual, religious root unity that will not decay with our temporal existence. This unity, which transcends our bodily life, is the imperishable soul.

Two Types of Structure

The principle of sphere sovereignty has a concrete meaning for our view of reality. As we saw earlier, the scriptural ground motive radically transforms one's entire view of temporal reality as soon as this motive begins to penetrate one's life. It then causes one to know again the true *structure* of reality.

There are two types of structure within temporal reality. The first is the structure of the various aspects or modes of being we listed earlier. One is familiar with these aspects only indirectly in everyday life, where we experience them by way of the individual totalities of concrete things, events, societal relationships, etc. In the ordinary experience of our daily life our attention is focused entirely on concrete things, events, and societal relationships; and we are not interested in focusing on the *distinct aspects as such* within which these concrete things, etc. *function*. The latter focus occurs first in the *scientific* attitude of thought.

A child, for example, learns to count by moving the red and white beads of an abacus. He begins to learn numerical relationships by means of these beads, but soon he sets the abacus aside in order to focus on the relationships themselves. This process requires a theoretical abstraction foreign to ordinary experience. For the child the numerical aspect and its numerical relations become a problem of logical conceptualization. At first this raises difficulties. The child must learn to set reality aside in his thinking, so to speak, in order to focus on the numerical aspect alone. To carry out such a theoretical analysis, he must subtract something from the full, given reality. The logical function, with which one forms concepts, thus assumes a position over against the nonlogical aspect of number, which resists the attempt to conceptualize it.

In everyday experience reality does not present itself in the aspects that thought abstracts from it, but in the structure of different individual totalities, such as things, events, acts, and societal relationships (involving the family, the state, the church, the school, industry, etc.). This is the second, the *concrete* structure of reality as it reveals itself to us in time and in which it shows itself in the experience of daily life. This structure is inseparably related to the first. If one views the latter wrongly, it is impossible to gain correct theoretical insight into the former, as we will see later.

Sphere Universality

If one desires to understand the significance of the creational principle of sphere sovereignty for human society in its full scope, then the meaning of sphere sovereignty for the intrinsic nature, mutual relation, and coherence of the *aspects* of reality (including the aspects of society) must first be understood. Earlier we observed that the various aspects arise from a single religious root, just as the colors of the rainbow originate in a single unbroken light. Despite their distinctiveness, the aspects cohere and interconnect in the all-embracive order of time. None exists except together with all the others. This universal coherence and inter-connection expresses itself in the structure of each aspect.

Consider, for example, the psychical aspect of reality. In its core or nucleus it is irreducible to any other aspect. Nevertheless, in emotional life one discovers the expression of an internal coherence with all the aspects displayed by reality. Certainly, feeling has a life of its own: psychical life. But psychical life is possible only on the basis of a series of connections with the other aspects of reality. For example, psychical life requires organic life, even though it is itself not organic life. In its "life moment" the psychical aspect is intrinsically interwoven with the organic aspect of reality. Likewise, feeling has an emotional moment that binds psychical life to the physicochemical process of bodily motion. Even though emotion, which is nothing but the movement of feeling, cannot be reduced to the mere motion of particles of matter in the body, the movement of feeling cannot occur without chemical movement. Thus there is an intrinsic coherence between the psychical aspect and the aspect of motion. Similarly, the feeling of spaciousness points to the connection between psychical life and the spatial aspect. This moment corresponds to the sensory space of awareness in which one observes colors, sounds, hardness or softness, and other sensorily perceivable properties. Sensory space is certainly quite different from mathematical space. Finally, the aspect of feeling also manifests an internal plurality of emotional impressions; this plurality expresses the connection between feeling and the numerical aspect.

Human psychical life is not limited to a coherence with the aspects that precede feeling. It also unfolds itself in logical feeling, historical and cultural feeling, lingual feeling, feeling for social convention, feeling of economic value, aesthetic feeling, moral feeling, and the feeling of faith certainty. In other words, the structure of the psychical aspect reflects a coherence with all the other aspects.

The universal scope of psychical life cannot be limited. In its own sphere psychical life is the integral and complete expression of God's creational work. Together with all the other aspects of one's temporal being, it finds its root unity in the religious focus of existence: the heart, soul, or spirit, where it is impossible to flee from God. From the religious creation motive of Holy Scripture one discovers the expression of creation's integral and radical nature in each of the aspects of God's work of creation. In other words, sphere sovereignty, which guarantees the irreducibility and protects the distinct laws of the different spheres, finds a correlate in *sphere universality*, through which each aspect expresses the universal coherence of all the aspects in its own particular structure.

Sphere universality provides the context for absolutizing an aspect of God's immeasurably rich creation. Let us take an example. Misguided by an apostate ground motive, a person may be searching for the basic certainty for his life in feeling. When he sees that all the aspects are reflected in psychical life, what will prevent him from declaring that feeling is the origin of number, space, motion, logical thinking, historical development, and so forth? Why not ultimately identify *faith* with the *feeling* of trust and certainty? Our own faith can easily be undermined and impoverished by this false emotional mysticism. In Goethe's *Faust* the simple Margaret asks Dr. Faust whether or not he believes in God; he, the thinker who has fallen into Satan's power, replies by pointing to the feeling of happiness that flows through us when we contemplate heaven and earth and when we experience love in courtship. He continues with these words:

> ... Then let it fill your heart entirely,
> And when your rapture in this feeling is complete,
> Call it then as you will,
> Call it bliss! heart! love! God!
> I do not have a name
> For this. *Feeling is all*;
> Names are but sound and smoke
> Befogging heaven's blazes.

[*Goethe's Faust*, Walter Kaufmann, lines 3451-3458. The emphasis is Dooyeweerd's.]

Idolatry of the other aspects of reality stands beside idolatry of the psychical aspect. Vitalism, which deifies an eternally flowing stream of life, is no less idolatrously directed than the religion of feeling. Modern historicism, which sets its hope for humanity on unending cultural development, is no less idolatrous than modern materialism, which declares that the aspect of motion investigated by the natural sciences is the beginning and end of reality.

Have we now begun to see how the religious ground motive of our life governs and determines our whole view of reality? Is it not obvious that an irreconcilable antithesis is at work between the Christian religion and the service of an idol? In the light of the conflict between the different ground motives, can we still maintain that the Christian religion is meaningful only for our life of faith and not for our view of reality? Certainly not! At this point we cannot escape from ourselves. The Christian religion cannot be bartered. It is not a treasure that we can lock away among the relics in an inner chamber. Either it is a leaven that permeates all our life and thought or it is nothing more than a theory, which fails to touch us inwardly.

But what does the Christian ground motive have to do with the concrete needs of political and social action? This is the key issue today, especially for those who witnessed the liquidation of the various Christian political parties and organizations during the war. After all, one might argue, the Christian *confessions* offer no answers to the political and social questions of the present time. Certainly it is true that the church confessions do not address these problems. Their ecclesiastical character prevents them from venturing into social issues. But if the *ground motive* of the Christian religion works in our lives, then it radically changes even our view of the inner nature of the state and its relation to the other societal spheres. With the Christian ground motive we discover the true principles for political life and for societal life as a whole. Hence, the antithesis between these principles and those of an apostate orientation must necessarily be expressed.

Society and Sphere Sovereignty

As a principle of the creation order, sphere sovereignty also pertains to the second structure of reality. It applies to the structure of societal forms, such as the family, the state, the church, the school, economic enterprise, and so on. As with the *aspects* of reality, our view of the inner nature, mutual relation, and coherence of the different *societal spheres* is governed by our religious point of departure. The Christian ground motive penetrates to the root unity of all the societal spheres that are distinct in the temporal order. From that root unity it gives us insight into the intrinsic nature, mutual relation, and coherence of these spheres.

In terms of the scriptural ground motive, what is the unity of the different spheres in society? It is the *religious root community of mankind* which fell in Adam but was restored to communion with God in Jesus Christ. This community is the foundation of all temporal, societal relationships, and on its basis the Christian religion stands in absolute antithesis to every view of society that absolutizes and deifies any temporal societal form. . . .

What then is the significance of sphere sovereignty for human society? Sphere sovereignty guarantees each societal sphere an intrinsic nature and law of life. And with this guarantee it provides the basis for an original sphere of authority and competence derived not from the authority of any other sphere but directly from the sovereign authority of God.

Since the time of Abraham Kuyper the term *sphere sovereignty* has become common property in the Netherlands. But the profundity of his insight with respect to the nature of the social order—an insight based on the ground motive of the Christian religion—was appreciated by only a small number of persons. The less men realized that this fundamental principle was rooted directly in the scriptural ground motive of the Christian religion, the more it dissolved into an ambiguous political slogan which each could interpret in his own way. At the same time, the increasingly historicistic way of thinking robbed the principle of its religious root, thereby contributing to its erosion. If one takes sphere sovereignty as no more than a historical given, somehow grown on Dutch soil as an expression of Holland's love of freedom, then one automatically detaches it from the constant, inner nature of the societal spheres.

In the light of this historicism, the principle of sphere sovereignty assumes a purely "dynamic" character whose contents can be filled according to the specific needs of a particular period. In this way, this very principle, in which the *antithesis* (opposition) between the scriptural and the antichristian starting points receives such a lucid elaboration in one's view of reality, is used as a building block in the most recent attempt to find a *synthesis* (reconciliation) between Christianity and humanism. For the new phase of history which we have entered, the principle of sphere sovereignty would have approximately the same meaning as the conception of *functional decentralization* propagated by modern socialism. In this conception the legislative and executive organs of the central government must be "relieved" of a sizable share of their task by a transfer of their authority to "new organs" derived from "society" itself. The different spheres of society must be incorporated into the state by means of public-legal organization. But at the same time these spheres must maintain a relative independence, a measure of *autonomy*, just like counties, municipalities, provinces and other parts of the state. These new organs would then take over an important part of the state's task by establishing regulative jurisdiction pertinent to their own affairs under final supervision of the central government. The regulations of these new organs would be maintained with public-legal sanctions. In this way "authority" and "freedom" are to be united in a harmonious manner. The principle of functional decentralization would thus provide a basis for cooperation for members of the socialist, Roman Catholic, and Antirevolutionary political parties. And the sphere sovereignty of the societal structures would receive a historical form and expression suitable to the new era.

How can one explain this basic misunderstanding of the principle of sphere sovereignty? This we will consider next.

History and Sphere Sovereignty

To find an answer we must recall that the nineteenth-century Historical School in Germany strongly influenced antirevolutionary political thought, particularly in its view of history. Although the founders of this school were devout Lutherans, their world view was completely dominated by the historicism that gained ground in humanist circles after the French Revolution.

By "historicism" I mean the philosophical conception that reduces the whole of reality to an absolutized historical aspect. Historicism sees all of reality as a product of ceaseless historical development of culture. It believes that everything is subject to continual change. In contrast to the rationalistic thinkers of the French Revolution, the historicists do not seek to construct a just social order from abstract, rational principles which have no relation to historical development and the individual traits of a specific national character. Rather, the fundamental thesis of the new historical way of thinking is that the entire political and social order is essentially a historical and developmental phenomenon. Its development originates in a nation's individual character, the "national spirit" (*Volksgeist*), which is the historical germ of an entire culture. The national spirit generates a culture's language, social conventions, art, economic system, and juridical order. Following the example of the mathematical and natural sciences, earlier humanistic theory had always sought after the universally valid laws that control reality. It constructed an "eternal order of natural law" out of the "rational nature of man." This order was totally independent of historical development, and was valid for every nation at all times and in all places. The earlier rationalistic humanism displayed little awareness of the individual traits of peoples and nations. All individual things were regarded as mere instances or examples of a universal rule and were reduced to a universal order. This reduction highlights the rationalistic tendency of this type of humanistic thought.

But as a result of the polarity of its religious ground motive, humanism veered to the other extreme after the French Revolution. Rationalistic humanism turned into irrationalistic humanism, which rejected all universally valid laws and order. It elevated individual potential to the status of law. Irrationalistic humanism was not inspired by the exact mathematical and natural sciences but by art and the science of history. Art revealed the "genius" and uniqueness of individuality. This "romanticism," which for a time dominated Western culture during the Restoration period after Napoleon's fall, was the source of the view of reality defended by the Historical School.

When the Historical School attempted to understand the whole of culture, language, art, jurisprudence, and the economic and social orders in terms of the historical development of an individual national spirit, it elevated the national character to the status of the origin of all order. It therefore denied the truth that *the individual creature always remains subject to law*. It argued that if the individual potential of a man or nation is the only law for development and action, then this potential cannot be evaluated in terms of a universally valid law. Accordingly, any nation was considered to act rightly and legitimately if it simply followed the historical fate or goal implicit in its individual potential or disposition.

This view of reality was historicistic in the sense explained above. Although the Historical School principally rejected the validity of general laws, it nevertheless replaced them with a substitute by a kind of compromise with the Christian belief in "divine providence." It viewed divine providence as a "hidden" law of history, arguing that God's providence rules the history of a nation. Where the Christian mask was laid aside, "providence" was replaced by *Schicksal*, the historical destiny or fate of a nation. *Schicksal* played the same role as divine providence; it operated as a norm for the development of a national character.

Careful readers will have noted how closely this view approaches the spiritual atmosphere of national socialism and its appeal to providence, to the "Destiny of the German People". . . . We will do well to keep the affinity between national socialism and the Historical School in mind, for later we will see that nazism must be considered primarily a degenerate fruit of the historicism propagated by the Historical School.

The Historical School strongly emphasized the bond between past and present. It held that culture, language, art, law, economics, and the social order arise and develop from the national character both unconsciously and apart from any formative influence of the human will. For the Historical School, tradition works as an unconscious power in history. It is the operation of God's providential guidance or, expressed less Christianly, of *Schicksal*, the destiny of a people. . . .

Guillaume Groen van Prinsterer

. . . [I]n the Netherlands Groen van Prinsterer fought for an idea of the state along *historical-national* lines which would suit the Dutch national character in its historical development. He was the first person to use the phrase "*souvereiniteit in eigen sfeer*" (sovereignty within its own sphere) with respect to the mutual relation of church and state. But he did not yet view this principle as a *creational principle of universal scope*. He only demanded *autonomy* for the societal "corporations," as [Friedrich Julius] Stahl had done. For him, trade and industry were only organic members of national life, just like municipalities and provinces. Their autonomy within the state was a merely historical principle rooted in the Dutch national character under God's guidance. At the same time, Stahl and Groen van Prinsterer saw very clearly the basic differences between the state, the church, and the family. Driven by the scriptural ground motive of the Christian religion, both held that the state should not interfere with the internal life of the other societal spheres. But their compromise with the world view of the Historical School prevented them from consistently applying this scriptural motive in their political thought.

Abraham Kuyper

Abraham Kuyper was the one who first understood sphere sovereignty again as a creational principle and thus fundamentally detached it from the historicistic outlook on human society. In his initial formulation of this idea, however, traces of a confusion of sphere sovereignty with municipal and provincial autonomy founded in Dutch history were still present. When he listed the various sovereign spheres he included the municipalities and provinces with the family, the school, science, art, economic enterprise, and so forth. Municipalities and provinces, however, are not sovereign spheres themselves but truly "autonomous" parts of the state, and the boundaries of their autonomy are dependent upon the requirements of the whole, the needs of the common good. Autonomy is authority delegated to a part by the whole.

What was the result of this confusion in political life? It became impossible to offer a principial criterion for the limits of autonomy. Increasingly, what originally fell under the autonomous jurisdiction of the municipalities and provinces needed regulation by a centralized government. Since this autonomous jurisdiction has been described as "sovereignty within its own sphere," Kuyper's followers began to be embarrassed with the principle itself, particularly because Dutch antirevolutionary political thought had never severed its links with the Historical School and had remained more or less infected with historicism.

Had Kuyper then erred when he founded sphere sovereignty in *creation*? Was his immutable principle actually no more than a historically alterable and variable given in the Dutch national character?

Confronted with questions of this sort, many antirevolutionaries, especially among the more educated, began to endorse an attitude of caution. They hesitated to honor certain slogans with the word *principle*. "Eternal principles" were considered safe if they were limited to directives "explicitly revealed" in Holy Scripture. The Bible, it was argued, contains no direct texts about sphere sovereignty. Thus the infection of the historicistic outlook surreptitiously influenced many in the ranks of the antirevolutionaries.

But the foundation laid by Kuyper was so firm that the principle of sphere sovereignty in its scriptural sense could not be completely erased from the religious consciousness of those who lived by the Word of God. Certainly, "purification" and further elaboration were still necessary. The important elements of truth in the teachings of the Historical School had to be freed from the framework of the historicistic world view if they were to become parts of a truly scriptural view of history.

It is high time that such purification and elaboration take place. The "new age" has no mercy for principles that are internally undermined. Our spiritually uprooted nation has never needed the explication and implementation of the creational principle of sphere sovereignty as urgently as today.

Autonomy and Sphere Sovereignty

Kuyper's great achievement was that he grasped the principle of sphere sovereignty as a creational principle. Earlier, however, we saw that the influence of the Historical School was evident in the way in which he sought to apply this principle to society. When in his general list of the life spheres he placed municipalities and provinces alongside of the family, the school, art, science, economic enterprise, and even the church as a temporal institution, he confused genuine sphere sovereignty with a historically founded autonomy of parts in the body politic.

Especially today, when the issue of the proper relationship between political, social, and economic structures demands immediate, principial solution, it is utterly crucial that we avoid this confusion. For we have already seen that the historicistic world view has an immense influence in our time. . . .

Historicism nourishes itself on the absolutization of the historical aspect of reality. Against it there is only one antidote: exposing the hidden religious ground motive which operates behind a seemingly neutral mask of supposedly profound scientific insight. All the false masks of apostate ground motives become transparent under the searching light of divine truth through which man discovers himself and his creator.

Autonomy of the parts of a whole and sphere sovereignty of radically distinct societal relationships are principially different matters. In a differentiated society the degree of autonomy depends upon the requirements of the whole of which the autonomous community remains a part. Sphere sovereignty, however, is rooted in the constant, inherent character of the life sphere itself. Because of their intrinsic natures, differentiated spheres like the family, the school, economic enterprise, science, and art can never be part of the state. . . . What does *historical individualization* mean? We must pursue this further, for it is here that the scriptural view of history immediately comes to the fore.

It cannot be said often enough that historicism, which today is much more influential than the scriptural view of history, arises out of the absolutization of the historical aspect of reality which is investigated by the science of history. But the integral, complete, and radical (penetrating to the root of created reality) character of the scriptural motive of creation makes us see this aspect in its irreducible nature and in its unbreakable coherence with all the other aspects of reality. In its core it is irreducible to the others, but at the same time in its inner structure it displays a complete expression of this aspect's universal coherence with the other aspects. This expression is the work of God's creation, which is integral and complete.

Earlier I discussed the universal coherence of the aspects in connection with the psychical aspect, calling this coherence the sphere universality of each aspect. It is the correlate of sphere sovereignty. In order to perceive God's ordinances for historical development, it is necessary that we search for them in the historical aspect and in its unbreakable coherence with the structures of the other aspects. If this search is not to go astray, then the scriptural ground motive of creation, fall, and redemption through Jesus Christ must be our only point of departure and our only religious motivation.

Biblicism

Some may object as follows: is such an intricate investigation really necessary to gain insight into God's ordinances for historical development? Is it not true that God revealed his whole law in the ten commandments? Is this revelation not enough for the simple Christian? I answer with a counterquestion: is it not true that God placed all the spheres of temporal life under his laws and ordinances—the laws that govern numerical and spatial relationships, physical and chemical phenomena, organic life, emotional feeling, logical thinking, language, economic life, and beauty? Are not all these laws grounded in God's creation order? Can we find explicit scriptural texts for all of them? If not, shall we not acknowledge that God gave man the task to discover them? And admitting this, can we still hold that it makes no difference whether we start from the ground motive of the Word of God or from the guidance of unscriptural ground motives?

Those who think they can derive truly scriptural *principles* for political policy strictly from explicit Bible texts have a very mistaken notion of scripture. They see only the letter, forgetting that the Word of God is spirit and power which must penetrate our whole attitude of life and thought. God's Word-revelation puts men to work. It claims the whole of our being; where death and spiritual complacency once held sway in us, it wants to conceive new life. Spiritually lethargic persons would rather have the ripe fruits of God's revelation fall into their laps, but Jesus Christ tells us that wherever the seed of God's Word falls on good soil, we ourselves must bear fruit.

Today Christians face a fundamental question posed by the "new age": what historical yardstick do we possess for distinguishing reactionary and progressive directions in history? We cannot derive this criterion from the ten cannot derive this criterion from the ten commandments, for they were not meant to save us from investigating God's creational ordinances. To answer this basic question, one needs insight into the specific ordinances that God established for historical development. There is no easy path to such insight. It requires investigation. Our search will be protected against derailment if the creation motive of God's Word claims our life and thought integrally.

Barthianism

But another objection arises, this time from the followers of Karl Barth. The objection is this: what do we know of the original ordinances of creation? How can we speak so confidently of creation ordinances, as if the fall had never happened? Did not sin change them in such a way that they are now ordinances for *sinful* life? My reply is as follows.

The ground motive of the divine Word-revelation is an indivisible unity. Creation, fall, and redemption cannot be separated. In effect, a Barthian carries through such a separation when he confesses that God created all things but refuses to let this creation motive completely permeate his thinking. Did God reveal himself as the creator so that we could brush this revelation aside? I venture to say that whoever ignores the revelation of creation understands neither the depth of the fall nor the scope of redemption. Relegating creation to the background is not scriptural. Just read the Psalms, where the devout poet rejoices in the ordinances that God decreed for creation. Read the book of Job, where God himself speaks to his intensely suffering servant of the richness and depth of the laws which he established for his creatures. Read the Gospels, where Christ appeals to the creational ordinance for marriage in order to counter those who aimed at trapping him. Finally, read Romans 1:19-20, where the creational ordinances are explicitly included in the general revelation to the human race. Whoever holds that the original creational ordinances are unknowable for fallen man because of the effects of sin, does basic injustice to the true significance of God's *common grace* which maintains these ordinances. Sin changed not the creational decrees but the direction of the human heart. Man's heart turned away from the creator.

Undoubtedly, this radical fall expresses itself in the way in which man discloses the power that God enclosed in creation. The fall affects natural phenomena, which man can no longer control. It expresses itself in theoretical thought led by an idolatrous ground motive. It appears in the subjective way in which man gives form to the principles established by God in his creation as norms for human action. The fall made special institutions necessary, such as the state and the church in its institutional form. But even these special institutions of general and special grace are based upon the ordinances that God established in his creation order. Neither the structures of the various aspects of reality, nor the structures that determine the nature of concrete creatures, nor the principles which serve as norms for human action, were altered by the fall. A denial of this leads to the unscriptural conclusion that the fall is as broad as creation; i.e., that the fall destroyed the very nature of creation. This would mean that sin plays a self-determining, autonomous role over against God, the creator of all. Whoever maintains such a position robs God of his sovereignty and grants Satan a power equal to that of the origin of all things.

Certainly, then, this objection from the Barthian camp may not keep us from searching for the divine order for historical development as revealed in the light of the creation motive. . . .

Ideal Types and Creational Structures

Ultimately, all the fundamental problems of sociology seem to converge in the question of how it is possible to bring together in a comprehensive theoretical perspective the great diversity of modal aspects revealed by society. The various special sciences concerned with social relationships, such as social biology, social psychology, history, linguistics, economics, legal theory, etc., may restrict themselves to study these relationships under a specific modal aspect, such as the aspect of organic life, the aspect of feeling, the historical aspect, the aspect of language, the economic, or the jural aspect. However, sociology cannot adopt this restricted perspective of a special science. Rather, it is the essential task of sociology to bring together all these aspects in a typical comprehensive theoretical perspective. This presupposes that one has an idea of the mutual *interrelation and coherence* of the aspects, the respective *place* which each of them occupies in the entire order of the aspects, and, finally, the *manner* in which the aspects are arranged within the typical totality structures of reality to form individual wholes.

In other words, our whole theoretical understanding of the underlying structures of reality is at stake here. The fundamental problems we have raised are indubitably of an intrinsically *philosophical* nature. But sociology gains nothing if it tries to brush these questions aside with a sweeping gesture, proclaiming that it is content to conduct research into *empirical* phenomena, while the philosophical root problems can be left to a social philosophy. After all, is it not exactly the question of the *empirical* character of the reality of social relationships which is at issue here? The typical structures within which empirical social relationships are ordered—such as the structure of marriage, nuclear family, lineal family, state, church, business, school, labour organization, social intercourse, relations of war, etc.—are not sensorily perceptible entities presented to us in an objective space of sense perception. In principle, these typical structures embrace all modal aspects of reality without exception; they arrange or group these aspects in a typical manner to form individual totalities; and they make possible our experience of the concrete and temporally variable social phenomena. The question regarding the *inner nature* of these social structures simply cannot be evaded if one wishes to investigate empirical phenomena in a truly *scientific* manner.

Let us take an example from a sociohistorical inquiry into the factual development of the life of the state. Is it not imperative first to reflect on what one understands by a "state"? Were the primitive kinship communities, clans, sibs, and tribal communities really "states"? Is it correct to apply the term *state* to the medieval fiefdom of the bishopric of Utrecht? Did the state have its origins in the family or in conquest? Is the state merely the instrument of power wielded by the ruling class in order to keep the oppressed class in subjection? How are the physical, biotic, psychical, historical, economic, jural, ethical, and other aspects interrelated within the structure of the state? Does law play the same role in the state as in other social structures; or, in its empirical reality, is the state nothing but an organization of historical power, while the enforcement of the legal order represents only one of the numerous *purposes* of the state and as such is extraneous to a sociological understanding of the state? Can all these questions be answered objectively on the basis of sense perception? Surely, anyone who has retained a measure of critical awareness will not assert that this is the case!

Is there an alternative solution? Are we to operate in sociology with so-called "ideal-type" concepts which we have extracted in arbitrary fashion from the variable social phenomena as these are presented to us under the historical aspect of reality? Such "ideal types" ultimately are nothing but subjective constructions which cannot contribute anything to our insight into the typical totality structures of *reality*. Max Weber, the well-known German scholar who introduced these so-called "ideal types" into the conceptual framework of sociology, expressly acknowledged their relatively arbitrary and derivative character and only wishes to utilize them as aids toward a better understanding of the historical individuality of phenomena, especially of the subjective sociohistorical meaning of human action. He explained that "ideal types" are achieved by consciously exaggerating certain traits within "historical reality" and abstracting these from all other traits. He readily admitted that one will never simply come across such an ideal type within reality itself. As example one can point to the ideal type of *homo economicus*, the fantasy image of a person who is driven only and exclusively by his own economic self-interest and who chooses, in a strictly rational fashion, the means whereby he will be able to realize his goals. In a similar manner, one might construct an ideal type of the modern bureaucratic state, of church and sect, of the medieval city, of medieval crafts, etc.

However, the real structural problem we have brought to light has not even been raised here; that is, the question of how the various aspects which manifest themselves in society are arranged within the distinctly typical totality structures to form wholly unique individual entities. Yet this is the basic question of all sociology. One reads a great deal in various writings and daily newspapers about the "structures" of society and about structural changes. But it is far from clear what exactly is understood by this. Quite often these terms conceal a scientifically defended notion that economic factors are really decisive and determine the entire coherence of a "society." It is also quite common that the expression "social structure" conceals a pseudoscientific conception of society as an "equilibrium of forces" whose disruption will necessarily effect structural changes.

Anyone who has seen the urgent necessity for the development of a sociology based on a scriptural-Christian foundation must inevitably assume a skeptical attitude toward this pseudoscientific methodology which eliminates the real structures of reality, for he understands that these structures are grounded in the creation order. We have seen, of course, that modern sociology did not receive its spiritual dynamic from the ground motive of Christianity—creation, fall into sin, and salvation through Jesus Christ—but from the humanistic ideal of science, either in its classical natural-scientific form, or in its modern historicistic form. And this ideal of science depended throughout upon man's faith in his own autonomy as understood in characteristic humanistic fashion. This faith could not tolerate the acceptance of a creation order to which man, quite independently of his own subjective thinking and volition, is subject. Thus sociology, inspired by this ideal of science, began immediately with eliminating the modal structures of the aspects and thought it could grasp the empirical reality of society apart from its underlying structural matrix.

The elimination of a normative perspective from social reality led, of necessity, to the elimination of all those aspects of reality which, in accordance with their modal structure, bear a normative character. As we have emphasized, after such elimination one is not left with an empirical social reality, but with an arbitrary, abstract, and scientifically unsound construction of that reality. The elimination of the modal structures of the aspects directly implied the elimination of the typical totality structures or individuality structures of

social reality, since the latter depend on the former. Therefore, since our first
objective must be to acquire insight into the typical totality structures of society and into the different ways these structures are mutually intertwined, we
must begin our own inquiry with an analysis of the modal structures of the
various distinct aspects of society. We will see how such analysis will, in a
surprising manner, provide us with insight into the entire sequence of these
aspects and thus into the place each aspect occupies in this sequence.

NOTES

[1] Selections from Chapters Two, Five, and Eight of Herman Dooyeweerd, *Roots of Western Culture: Pagan, Secular, and Christian Options*, trans. J. Kraay, eds. Mark Vander Vennen and Bernard Zylstra (Toronto: Wedge Publishing Foundation, 1979). This work first appeared as a series of articles in the weekly *Nieuw Nederland* from August, 1945 to May, 1948. The articles were then published in book form, edited by J. A. Oosterhoff, *Vernieuwing en Bezinning om het Reformatorisch Grondmotief* (Zutphen: J. S. Vanden Brink, 1959). Capitalization of certain words has been changed from the 1979 edition to standard usage.

[2] On Dooyeweerd see Bernard Zylstra's "Introduction" to L. Kalsbeek, *Contours of a Christian Philosophy*, eds. B. Zylstra and J. Zylstra (Toronto: Wedge Publishing Foundation, 1975), 14-33; G. Puchinger, et al., "Dr. Herman Dooyeweerd," in *Perspectief*, ed. W. Van Dijk (Kampen: J. H. Kok, 1961), 43-86; and James W. Skillen, "The Development of Calvinistic Political Theory," (Ph.D. Diss., Duke, 1974), 14-18.

[3] For a detailed discussion of ground motives, see Herman Dooyeweerd, *In the Twilight of Western Thought* (Philadelphia: Presbyterian and Reformed Publishing Co., 1960), 35-52; and Skillen, "The Development of Calvinistic Political Theory," 332-377.

[4] Dooyeweerd's philosophy of modal aspects is developed in detail in vol. II of his *A New Critique of Theoretical Thought*, trans. D. Freeman, H. de Jongste, and W. Young (Philadelphia: Presbyterian and Reformed Publishing Co., 1953-1958), 4 vols. A critical study evaluating the difference between Dooyeweerd's view of "cosmic law order" and that of "natural law" is O. J. L. Albers, *Het Natuurrecht volgens de Wijsbegeerte der Wetsidee* (Nijmegen: Janssen, 1955).

[5] Dooyeweerd, *Roots of Western Culture*, 55-58.

[6] Dooyeweerd, *A New Critique*, 3: 222.

[7] *Ibid.*

[8] *Ibid.*, 222-237.

[9] *Ibid.*, 194-221; 236-61.

[10] Dooyeweerd explains that he got the word "enkapsis" from Theodor L. Haering in his work *Über Individualität in Natur- und Geisteswelt* (Leipzig and Berlin: B. J. Teubner, 1926) and that Haering borrowed it from the anatomist Heidenhain. *A New Critique*, 3: 634-5.

[11] *Ibid.*

[12] Bernard J. Zylstra, *From Pluralism to Collectivism: The Development of Harold Laski's Political Thought* (Assen, The Netherlands: Van Gorcum, 1968), 216-17.

[13] Dooyeweerd, *A New Critique*, 3: 505-506.

[14] Herman Dooyeweerd, *The Christian Idea of the State*, trans. J. Kraay (Nutley, NJ: The Craig Press, 1968), 45-46.

[15] *Ibid.*, 49.

[16] *Ibid.*, 43. See Skillen, "The Development of Calvinistic Political Theory," 400-426.

SIXTEEN

✕✕✕✕✕✕✕✕✕✕✕

SCRIPTURAL RELIGION AND POLITICAL TASK[1]
by H. Evan Runner

H. Evan Runner

Evan Runner (b. 1916) is one of the important links between the contemporary English-speaking world and the Calvinist tradition of Groen van Prinsterer, Abraham Kuyper, and Herman Dooyeweerd. Born near Philadelphia into a family with Scotch-Irish-Welsh roots, Runner grew up in the circles of Presbyterian evangelical piety that had become adjusted quite comfortably to the American way of life. As a youngster he knew little of the complex historical roots of the Presbyterian-Calvinist tradition and nothing of the Dutch Calvinist movements of the nineteenth century.[2]

Inspired by the desire to become a missionary in some foreign setting, the young Runner set out in 1932 for Wheaton College in Illinois—the foremost evangelical college of the day where Billy Graham, Carl F. H. Henry, and other future evangelical leaders would also be trained. He graduated from Wheaton in 1936 and then went to study at the newly formed Westminster Theological Seminary in Philadelphia. Westminster was established as a consequence of the liberal-fundamentalist conflict in the northern Presbyterian Church which led several prominent Princeton seminary professors to leave Princeton to start a more orthodox school. J. Gresham Machen and Cornelius Van Til were among Westminster's founders.[3]

By the time Runner left Wheaton and entered Westminster, he had become immersed in theological and philosophical questions concerning the place of Christianity in modern society. At first he thought of this as chiefly a theological challenge, so from Westminster he traveled to The Netherlands in 1939 to study at the theological school of Kampen to which he had been introduced by Van Til. In that Dutch academic setting he became more and more aware of the broad range of intellectual and spiritual conflicts in the West since the time of the Renaissance and Reformation, and especially since the French Revolution. Taking up classical studies, he then went in search of the foundations of Western civilization.

In 1940, Runner returned to the United States to enter Harvard University where he studied classics with Werner Jaeger and ancient church history with George LaPiana and was a member of the distinguished Society of Fellows. In 1946, he returned to Holland to study the history of philosophy with D.H.T. Vollenhoven, a close associate of Herman Dooyeweerd, at the Free University of Amsterdam. By this time, Runner had become thoroughly acquainted not only with the writings of Groen, Kuyper, and Dooyeweerd, but also with the political and cultural movements in Holland that had been inspired by the modern revival of Calvinism.

On the completion of his studies, Runner accepted a position at Calvin College in Grand Rapids, Michigan in 1951 to teach philosophy. For the next 30 years, until his retirement, he remained at Calvin. While not a prolific writer, he lectured widely in the U.S. and Canada as well as in Europe, encouraging cultural initiatives ranging from new magazines to the formation of the Christian Labor Association of Canada. In all of this, he appealed for integral Christian thinking and action of a kind that would break with "synthesis thinking" that robs Christianity of its full power.[4]

A significant number of Runner's students went on to pursue graduate study at the Free University of Amsterdam in a variety of fields. Many of them came from families that had emigrated from Holland to Canada and the U.S. Others came from Australia, England, and even from the Orient. By the late 1960s a movement was afoot to organize an educational enterprise that would concentrate on developing the philosophical and scientific work of Dooyeweerd and Vollenhoven in North America. Runner had more than a little to do with this venture. In the early 1970s, several of Runner's former students, now with doctorates from the Free University, took up residence in Toronto where their work led to what is now the graduate Institute for Christian Studies (ICS).[5] In many respects, the founding of the ICS was sparked by Runner's conference lectures in the three summers of 1959, 1960, and 1961 in Toronto. His lectures were later published in two books—*The*

Relation of the Bible to Learning and *Scriptural Religion and Political Task*.[6] The selection below is from the second of these books, and it is important for two reasons. First, Runner shows the impact of Groen and Dooyeweerd in particular on his own understanding of the French Revolution and of the ongoing conflict between different basic religious motives in the modern era. The problems raised by historicism, liberalism, and collectivism are not simply intellectual or political difficulties that can be solved pragmatically or technically. They are deeply rooted in conflicting views of life. To understand the shaping influences in our day, says Runner, one must grasp the conflict between competing religious motives—between revolutionaries and Christian reformers, between Christianity and anti-Christian humanism. Groen's insights, which had such a lasting affect on Kuyper and Dooyeweerd, are not something peculiarly Dutch, according to Runner, but have universal significance for Western and now global history.

In the second place, Runner's critical assessment of the modern understanding of "reason" is especially important for our purposes. The Dutch Calvinist tradition is not anti-rational or irrational in its appeal to divine revelation, but neither does it incorporate human rationality into its social philosophy in the same way that the historicist and recent Catholic traditions do. Just as "sphere sovereignty" represents something different than "subsidiarity," so also the place and function of human reason is interpreted differently by the progressive Calvinists than by other pluralists.

Runner's explanation of the connection between modern rationalism and the conflict of religious motives helps both to account for the uniqueness of the progressive Calvinist vision and to relate the insights of that tradition to the North American political context. Neither conservatism nor liberalism as we know it today in the United States, is adequate to bring about the social and political reforms needed to restore health to society. A deeper renovation is necessary, Runner says, and that can only arise from the power of the Christian gospel—a power that is oriented toward the judgment and renewal of all creation, not simply toward the future salvation of souls.

Scriptural Religion and Political Task

The French Revolution and Rationalism

What, then, was the French Revolution? In all the writing of the last century and a half the constellation of events that goes by this name stands out above everything else. From the first, men everywhere were somehow fascinated by it. Almost without exception English men of letters greeted the revolutionary movement in France as the dawn of a new day of hope for all mankind. You recall how Wordsworth, reflecting later upon those first days of the Revolution, penned the oft quoted lines:

> Bliss was it in that dawn to be alive,
> But to be young was very Heaven.

Burke, on the other hand, abhorred what he saw. But all men, however they viewed it, had a kind of presentiment that what was taking place there in France had to do with them. Ever since, men have unceasingly been attempting to determine their positions with respect to that awesome event. . . .

Discussions of the underlying meaning of the Revolution often relate it to the movement of the human spirit in the eighteenth century that we speak of as the Enlightenment, or as the Age of Reason. To this I have no objection, provided that we also see this eighteenth-century Enlightenment as a second stage in the continuing development of the new spirit of rationalism, the revolutionary movement of thought that arose in the seventeenth century and dominated both it and the following two centuries. This rationalistic spirit signified modern man's radical break with the Christian religion.

"There is in the thought of the Enlightenment," Charles Frankel once wrote, "an identifiable pattern, a unity of objective and assumptions which has had a decisive effect on subsequent history."[7]

The special effort of the Enlightenment, therefore, was to find a foundation in every field, "from the profane sciences to revelation," "from music to morals," and "theology to commerce," such that thinking and action could be made independent of speculative metaphysics and supernatural revelation. Religion was treated mainly as an appendage to morals and discussed as though it were a part of physics. History was written to place European life in balanced perspective among other ways of life, none of which enjoyed the special sanction of God. In politics, the conceptions of divine right and supernatural providence were replaced by "the social contract," so that governments could be evaluated as instruments of human desire. In moral philosophy the effort was to base moral codes on Natural Law or on the "well-established facts" of human psychology.[8]

It is important to notice what is said here about politics. Although the statement is oriented more to eighteenth-century Enlightenment, the fact is that the eighteenth century did not really develop a new political theory; it called for political action on the basis of the rationalistic theory of the seventeenth century. Rousseau is the key figure here. For he is regarded as the one who gave to the French Revolution its definitive character—its tendency toward abstract organization. He is the exponent par excellence of liberalism. Yet the ideas of his *Contrat Social* and other political writings are largely to be found in Locke and Grotius and Pufendorf. These ideas belong to the modern rationalist movement generally and can be found as early as Grotius' *The Law of War and Peace* (1625). Their revolutionary character is to be seen in the hope Grotius cherishes of an international amity based on a law of nature. According to French historian Paul Hazard,

> War, violence, disorder, which the law of God does not repress but suffers rather, and even justifies, as being part of an inscrutable design, all the ills which man is heir to—perhaps the day will come when some human law will bring about their mitigation, their abolition. Thus it is that we are invited, with manifold excuses for such boldness, to pass from the Order of Providence to the Order of Humanity.[9]

Instead of an Order of God an order of man. Instead of the Law of God the social contract. Instead of the sovereignty of God the sovereignty of the people.

The Spirit of the Age

Since Christians in America often argue that the French Revolution was related primarily to continental thought, more radical than our Anglo-Saxon background, and that therefore such analyses as we are here engaged in are really irrelevant to an understanding of North American cultural life, it may be well to call attention to the name of John Locke in the above account. Locke and the English deists had a great influence upon Voltaire, who revivified these ideas upon his return to France. One cannot really distinguish English and continental here. The ideas are common to the modern rationalist movement. We have to do here with the spirit of an age. The ideas are everywhere. Let me quote Ernst Cassirer on the subject.

The political rationalism of the seventeenth century was a rejuvenation of Stoic ideas. This process began in Italy, but after a short time it spread over the whole of European culture. In rapid progress New-Stoicism passed from Italy to France; from France to the Netherlands; to England, to the American colonies. . . .

When Thomas Jefferson, in 1776, was asked by his friends to prepare a draft of the American Declaration of Independence he began it by the famous words: "We hold these truths to be self-evident, that all men are created equal; that they are endowed by their Creator with certain unalienable rights; that among these are life, liberty, and the pursuit of happiness. That, to secure these rights, governments are instituted among men, deriving their just powers from the consent of the governed." When Jefferson wrote these words he was scarely aware that he was speaking the language of Stoic philosophy. This language could be taken for granted; for since the times of Lipsius and Grotius it had a common place with all the great political thinkers. The ideas were regarded as fundamental axioms that were not capable of further analysis and in no need of demonstration. For they expressed the essence of man and the very character of human reason. The American Declaration of Independence had been preceded and prepared by an even greater event: by the intellectual Declaration of Independence that we find in the theoreticians of the seventeenth century. It was here that reason had first declared its power and its claim to rule the social life of man. It had emancipated itself from the guardianship of theological thought; it could stand its own ground.[10]

Concept of "Ratio"

We must take a closer look at this concept of Reason if we wish to understand the revolutionary character of the modern movement of rationalism. René Descartes can best be used to illustrate its meaning. This man, often called the father of the "modern" way of philosophizing, found that after having enjoyed the best secondary education available in Europe his mind was a curious mixture of truth and falsehood. His (religious!) need for certainty led him after a while to consider the system of geometrical thought of his day as a model of the perfect clarity he desired in all his experience. In the proofs of geometry every step carries its clarity and necessity with it. A particular step in the proof of a theorem follows with the necessity of logical demonstration from the previous step, and each previous step out of the foregoing, until at last we get back to the first axioms and postulates from which the entire system is generated.

And what about the foundations of geometrical thought? They, too, are clear and necessary. Not in the way of logical (deductive) demonstration, but because they shine by their own rational light. They are self-evidencing. They are absolute Truth. Descartes now proceeds to use this pattern that he finds in geometry as the model—the very structure—of all human thought. All successive steps of reasoning can be proved by logical deduction; the starting-points are certain *innate ideas*, bearing in themselves the Light of Truth. This body of innate ideas—the ideas of Plato that were made *a priori* concepts in the philosophy of the Hellenistic Age and that can be found clearly in the reasoning of Aurelius Augustine—Descartes called the *ratio* or *lumen naturale* (natural light or light of nature, if by "nature" one understands human rational nature).

Here in this *ratio* or Reason we find the key to the religious and revolutionary character of the rationalist movement generally, more specifically now of the Enlightenment and the French Revolution. This *ratio* is not just our human power of understanding. It is the understanding, directed by supposed *a priori* or innate ideas that are considered to be the original Light and Truth that show us how to conduct our lives. The *ratio* or Reason of the rationalist is more than mere rational thinking; in this concept thought contains within itself the *Principium* (the first principle) of life which directs all our ways. This concept is the result of apostate religion; it is a repressing substitute for the Word of God which is the true *Principium* that leads us into ways of salvation. Reason is thus an idol—something that does not truly exist but can be conceived only because in the Truth of the divine Word there is a true *Principium* of life. In modern rationalism men have replaced God's sovereign and gracious Word of redemption with their own deepest, rational self as the Light, the Law-word, the directing Principle of our entire life. . . .

Political Rationalism as the Basis of Modern Democracy

These assumptions of Descartes and of the rationalist movement became the intellectual—actually, religious—basis for the social and political institutions of modern democracy. If the diversity of our opinions is the result merely of the fact that we do not all find an adequate way of applying our rational powers, then a system of universal, public education is all that is needed to raise all men to the level of enlightened and responsible citizenship. This was the conclusion a subsequent century drew. On the basis of universal, rational education, we would all then be able to put our confidence in the popular will and the popular vote, and acquiesce in the will of the majority. This rationalistic basis of our modern democracies is one form—a subjectivistic one—of the theory of natural law (where "natural" refers to our rational nature, which is the Law). Besides being, as was thought, self-evidencing, this theory could appeal to an unbroken history from the time of Hellenistic (to an important degree Stoic) philosophy, through the Roman jurists, the Church Fathers, the scholastic philosophers and the conciliarists of the late medieval church. This long and unbroken history, in turn, convinced men the more of the self-evidencing character of the rationalist theory. It is to this long history that Walter Lippmann refers when he speaks of the "public philosophy." In his book *The Public Philosophy* Lippmann, quoting Ernest Barker, says: "For over two thousand years . . . European thought has been acted upon by the idea that the rational faculties of men can produce a common conception of law and order which possesses a universal validity."[11] This natural law or law of human rational nature, Lippmann continues, is a rational order of human society "in the sense that all men, when they are sincerely and lucidly rational, will regard it as self-evident."[12]

The American and French revolutions at the end of the eighteenth century, and the political regimes they established, were among the best fruits of these assumptions of rationalism. In the nineteenth century the assumptions came to be questioned and even, in many quarters, rejected. One of the major problems of contemporary political theory is how to rehabilitate this old basis or to discover a satisfactory new one.

One of the supposedly self-evident "axioms" of this rationalistic political thought was the doctrine of the state-contract. This meant that the political order could be reduced to free individual acts—to a voluntary contractual submission of the governed in what they took to be their own interest. Here there is no idea of a corporate society to which God has given offices, but only a collection of equal individual rational men. Here there is no idea of a service of God and an administration, in his name, of the whole earth, but only a contractual agreement in the interest of the contracting individuals. (This is undoubtedly the deepest religious reason for the development of modern politics as interest-group politics.) In this theory of contract we see the individualism of rationalist political theory. It denies that the Law-word of God has laid down in the Order of Creation a typical state-structure with its own (delegated and limited) authority, and that we men were created for this and other law-structures. In the beginning, according to the theory, there are only individual men, who then contract together, in their own interest, to live together in a political community. The Law-word that constitutes the State lies in the *ratio* of each thinking individual.

At the same time, on the ground of the supposed (axiomatic) commonness of Reason, there was in this individualistic outlook the possibility of community. The very self-evidencing character of the innate concepts of common Reason should compel a common acknowledgment. This common acknowledgment of what each thinking man is sure to find as his own deepest Light and Truth, assures true community among all right-thinking men. . . .

The Modern Rationalistic Mind

It is now possible for us today to see how fundamental a thing this theory of rationalism is in the history of modern Western man. It is so fundamental an idea that it led to a reconstruction (revolution) of European society in its entirety. In the concept of Reason, man tries to assure himself with respect to the two basic (and related!) needs of certainty and community. Conceived as having his most essential roots in this *ratio*, man is the sovereign possessor of Truth; indeed, in his deepest self he is the Truth, and thus cannot be estranged from it. He is basically at home in a world that yields up its secrets to rational penetration. There is no need of salvation; man is right with the world; and, as to the future, he is wholly confident of his gradually increasing control of his environment by rational-technical means. It is just a question of working out the details. Rationalistic man is optimistic. Continual innovation and endless experimentation are the way to mastery. There is no revelatory Light of a Creation order. There is no Order for which he is created. Reason, as original Light, can ignore any question as to a Light of Creation. It generates its own Order out of itself as creative thought. It makes its world. Being always and everywhere the same, it will ultimately produce one world. The kingdom of blessed souls, the kingdom of good or right-thinking men is assured if only we act in accordance with reason. Proceeding by its light, men will progress onwards and upwards until they achieve a natural, earthly, and common City of Man. The universal community.

There is no place in this rationalism for a deep, fundamental antithesis of direction in human life. Christ and the Holy Spirit's work have been made superfluous. There is no thought here of Christ's returning to put down the enemy and set up His Kingdom. The possibility of community resides not in a conversion and common obedience to Christ, but in a working out of our commonly shared rationality. Here we have the background for the faith that so many of our contemporaries have in the salutary consequences of shared beliefs, democratic discussion, the Town Meeting. When Franklin Roosevelt went to Yalta to talk with Stalin, he felt assured that if only emotion and historical misunderstandings (prejudice) could be cleared up, rational analysis would reveal to all participants commonly the truth of the situation, all rational men would be governed by the light of that truth, and a world-community of nations might then be erected.

If all this is involved in the new "mind" of the seventeenth and eighteenth centuries, we can well understand the enthusiastic processions to the shrine of the goddess of Reason that characterized the hey-day of the French Revolution. And we can now see why I said earlier that this Revolution can serve, not only as a point of orientation, but as a kind of norm for fixing the meanings of the two poltical movements of the last two centuries. For then the French Revolution is indeed fundamentally the breaking out into the open of man's religious abandonment of God—the open expression in everyday life of his heart-deep rejection of the Law of God and his substitution of his own creative rational thought for that law. Then Burke and Groen van Prinsterer are right that the Revolution has crucially to do with the radical religious direction of man's life on earth. Only such an estimation of it can adequately account for the very peculiar fascination it has for so many men.

As an overturning of the divine Order it reveals itself as Revolution in the religious sense, a revolution against the Law and Order of God, against the Rule of Christ, against the witness of the Holy Spirit—in short, against the scriptural revelation of the Truth.

After the first stage of the Revolution had run its course, the direction of Western political life fell largely to the Liberals or Moderates, to whom the Radicals or confident believers appeared extremists. These Liberals have taught us to believe that the Revolution went wrong because of the excesses of the Radicals. Groen makes clear, however, that it was not the excess that was wrong, but the essential revolutionary direction of events. The *Principium* heralded by the revolutionaries is not the true *Principium* of life; it is an antithetical distortion. To follow its leading, in whatever tempo, can only lead to a sickening of society and its ultimate destruction. Apart from the intervention of God, who always maintains His creation order and restrains the destruction of the wicked, complete chaos would already be upon us.

Significance of Groen van Prinsterer

It was this that Groen van Prinsterer saw, and his prophetic insight and evangelical obedience elevate him above all the other conservatives of his time. Christian insight is, in fact, what led him to break with conservatism. His act of evangelical obedience has given The Netherlands another political history in the nineteenth and twentieth centuries than the Anglo-Saxon countries. The difference is not a matter of national or racial differences; it is a difference in religious insight. In his religious insight Groen got beyond conservatism. His fundamental analysis can be summed up in one or two sentences: To get rid of the evil it is not sufficient to combat its symptoms, but the germ has to be removed. The only antidote to systematic unbelief is belief.

Conservatism sensed better than liberalism that the principle operative in the new political movement and driving it on in its course was a wrong principle. But conservatism was not in a position to reassert the Word of God in its integral revelatory sense as the only possible antidote. From the beginning the conservative political movement belongs to the modern world. Edmund Burke came out of a Whig background and had imbibed many notions of the prevalent humanism and "enlightenment." There was no thought of bringing to political articulation the religious split between acceptance of the Word of God as integral directing Principle of life and acceptance of an antithetical pseudo-principle. In Christian circles theologism, mysticism, and pietism had already greatly weakened whatever insight Christians had into the scriptural sense of the Word of God and the Christian religion. But, beyond that, conservatism was not a specifically Christian movement. This explains its powerlessness to change the religious direction that political life had taken.

Conservatism appealed to a rational or intelligible order that was visible in history, an order that rational man could deal with and talk about. Because Christians since the time of the earliest church Fathers had accepted Greek views about a rational order of "nature," they were unable to see the dangers of assuming a common political witness with unbelievers, and generally they joined in a movement with conservatives against the revolutionary movements. Unfortunately for the whole modern world, conservatism could not be genuinely "anti-revolutionary." Groen, a confessor of the Gospel, was that, in principle.

Christians should have witnessed to the Order of Creation that is anchored in the Creator's Will (and republished in the Gospel). They should have been single minded in attempting to obey the central law of love in various divinely ordained (and revealed) offices in human life. They would then have been compelled to break with the static, intellectualist-reductionist natural law theories, and they would have been able to bring a very relevant and urgently needed word (from the revelation of God) into the modern cultural discussion. For we need a sure Law that yet allows for dynamic historical development by man.

Conservatism and the Historic Right School

But conservatism did nothing of the sort. Conservatism falls into an identification of the Order of God with what has developed in history. Over against the abstract rationalistic thought-constructions of Voltaire, Rousseau, and the famous Declaration of the Rights of Man, Burke put the organic growth of English constitutional law and institutions. The conservative movement became closely allied with the Historic Right School of jurisprudence. "The founders of the 'Historic Right School'," Cassirer tells us, "declared that history was the source, the very origin of right. There is no authority above history."[13]

For conservatives, the rights of man are not those abstractly conceived "natural rights" of the revolutionaries, sanctioned supposedly by the *a priori* law-ideas of a Reason that is looked upon as the ultimate ordering authority. The conservative sees the sanction for the rights of men and of institutions and organizations in the hoary antiquity of these rights. The Law of God, which declares everywhere what is good and right, is drawn down into history and identified with the "finger of God," the gradual working out of the right in the development of history. The religiously accountable nature of office is brought down and identified with what in the course of history has acquired authority.

Thus, the scriptural view of reality has here, in fact, been reduced to a form of historical relativism. Whatever has established itself and gained recognition in the slow growth of history is right. Here we see a fundamental kinship to the enlightened view of the positive rightness of all that is—the eighteenth-century optimism about universal cultural evolution. There is here no divine Law apart from and above historical development, no awareness of deviation or religious apostasy working itself out in the positivizing labors of man in all areas of life. Conservatives do not sense the need of religious reformation in all areas of life—reformation by men whose hearts have been renewed, illumined, and directed by the sovereign Word of God and who have been restored in Christ to offices of responsibility before God. Is all historical change merely organic growth? Are there in history no irreconcilable conflicts that express a fundamental antithesis of religious direction in human life? To raise these questions here is sufficient to point up the anti-scriptural background of conservative thought.

The Failure of Conservatism

Having once taken his position within historical development, the conservative is lost. For history presents us with a continuous flux. At first, the conservatives, true to their criterion of historically acquired rights, defended the traditional orders and classes of European society. Against the innovations of the new, purely rationally conceived society, they tried to maintain the old patriarchal conditions—society as an organism. But straightway their real problem began to press them. If rights are historically acquired, what about the "rights" of the new revolutionary movement? This movement was gaining wide support among the rising industrial classes (because they too were either ignorant of or alienated from a scriptural view of their life), and had become consolidated in the time of Napoleon. How far would this historical development have to go, and how long would it have to prevail before it too became integrated into the slow growth of history? In other words, how ancient is "hoary" ancient? How happy would the Christians who attached themselves to the conservative movement have been with their conservative ideology in an Asiatic or African country where the Christian church had no historically acquired rights, but cannibalism, say, did?

The conservative, unless he became more aware of the urgent need of a radically Christian answer to the problems involved, as Groen van Prinsterer did in principle, could follow one of two paths. He could fall back into a reactionary defense of the past, of already vested interests, and thus lose all genuine relevancy since he would have no significant understanding of the dynamic, the novel, in history. Or he could find himself in the most unhappy position of simply following along after the more progressive accomplishments of the liberals, serving chiefly as a brake upon the dynamic movement of innovation. Especially as the power of the Christian faith waned in a quickly secularizing Europe, the position of conservatism came to be more and more that of a middle-road, take-it-easy correction to the more vital course developed by the liberals.

You can see now why the charge has been leveled that conservatism as an ideology lacks what might be termed a substantial ideal, i.e. a norm or principle of its own by which it can develop a distinctive standpoint. The tag "conservatism" has been used to justify any existing order, at any stage of history; thus, one does not find in conservative circles any clear indication of the character of the political institutions and way of life that conservatism as an ideology would be interested in defending. . . .

The Failure of Liberalism

We have seen something of the way in which conservatism deteriorated and became empty of meaning in the course of the nineteenth century. But liberalism, a compromise of bourgeois capitalists from the beginning, also underwent further deterioration. The collapse of faith in metaphysical constructions, which characterized the middle decades of the century, cooled whatever convictions men still held as to the capacity of Reason to direct their lives. In the further course of the century an awareness was dawning that men do not reason alike in all ages and places. Anthropological and ethnological investigations taught Europeans the relativity of rational insight. The Enlightenment belief in a common reason began to fade. But, with it, the religious strength of the revolutionary movement also faded. It did not take long to draw the conclusion that if men's reasoning is different in different situations, it may not be an authoritative Director or Principle out in front (a priori) to guide us through life, but may only be an instrument of adaptation to a contingent physical environment. Where such a conclusion was drawn men were left without a guiding Principle in a swirling world of factual political circumstances.

Though they understood it differently, both liberals and conservatives inherited the apostate religious belief in the fundamental oneness of man's rational processes. Now, both find themselves immersed in a supposedly common factuality which either speaks commonly to men or can be mastered by the application of a common technology. Typically the liberal movement experiments more progressively towards a new and enlarged freedom. Conservatives serve more as a brake upon innovation, seeking to maintain the established order.

The argument is frequently heard today in North America that the two-party or two-movement system necessarily presupposes a fundamental commonness of commitment to ultimates, and that the two poles of our political life, instead of providing radical alternatives, should be thought of as complementary to each other. We need, it is then said, both bold experimentation and the maintenance of historical continuity, but on the background of a common fundamental belief. Walter Lippmann writes: "For the toleration of differences is possible only on the assumption that there is no vital threat to the community. Toleration is not, therefore, a sufficient principle for dealing with the diversity of opinions and beliefs. It is itself dependent upon the positive principle of accommodation. The principle calls for the effort to find agreement beneath the differences."[14]

Here Lippmann can be seen signing the death warrant of those who would live radically and integrally by the powerful Word of the living God. Christianity will be tolerated where and only where it allows itself to be integrated with the rest of humanity's life. The confession that human life is characterized by a fundamental split of religious commitment is *intolerable*. The irony of the situation is that Lippmann derives hope for his rationalistic scheming from the long history of accommodation that is typical of the synthesis mind. . . .

But the closer we get to the root of the political crisis of our times, the more we are made aware of the root-dividedness of our human race in its ultimate loyalty, its ultimate faith. There is an Antithesis in our life, and the belief that the human race is fundamentally one in its confession of the Truth is a false belief. No cultural articulation of such a false faith could ever be salutary for human beings; it is not based on realities. But, meanwhile, as long as Christians try to live within the area of belief and action that Western man decrees to be tolerable, our lives will be constantly drawn in the direction of the final Catastrophe, the Destruction that is justly meted out to the oldest Rebel and his Revolution of Nihilism.

NOTES

1 Selections from Lecture II of Runner's *Scriptural Religion and Political Task* (Toronto: Wedge Publishing Foundation, 1974, first published in 1961), edited by James W. Skillen, with the author's permission.

2 Bernard J. Zylstra, "Preface" to H. Evan Runner, *The Relation of the Bible to Learning,* 5th rev. ed. (Jordan Station, Ontario: Paideia Press, 1982 [1960]), 9-34. See also the interview with Runner by Harry Van Dyke and Albert M. Wolters in John Kraay and Anthony Tol, eds., *Hearing and Doing: Philosophical Essays Dedicated to H. Evan Runner* (Toronto: Wedge Publishing Co., 1979), 333-361.

3 Zylstra, "Preface," 10. On the background of the liberal-fundamentalist controversy, see George M. Marsden, *Fundamentalism and American Culture: The Shaping of Twentieth-Century Evangelicalism, 1870-1925* (New York: Oxford University Press, 1980).

4 See Bernard J. Zylstra, "H. Evan Runner: An Assessment of His Mission," in Henry Vander Goot, ed., *Life is Religion: Essays in Honor of H. Evan Runner* (Jordan Station, Ontario: Paideia Press, 1981), 1-14.

5 The Institute for Christian Studies in Toronto offers several masters degrees and a Ph.D. program in conjunction with the Free University of Amsterdam. Its nine graduate professors and numerous adjunct faculty teach primarily in the humanities and social sciences.

6 Runner's *The Relation of the Bible to Learning* is now in its fifth edition. His *Scriptural Religion and Political Task,* from which we have taken a selection, has been reprinted several times.

7 Charles Frankel, "The Philosophy of the Enlightment," in V. Ferm, ed., *A History of Philosophical Systems* (New York: Philosophical Library, 1950), 266.

8 *Ibid.,* 267.

9 Paul Hazard, *The European Mind (1680-1715),* trans. J. May, (New York: New American Library, 1963), 271-272.

10 Ernst Cassirer, *The Myth of the State* (New Haven: Yale University Press, 1946), 166-167.

11 Walter Lippmann, *The Public Philosophy* (New York: Mentor Books, 1955), 81.

12 *Ibid.,* 95.

13 Cassirer, *The Myth of the State,* 182.

14 Lippmann, *The Public Philosophy,* 132.

SEVENTEEN

✖✖✖✖✖✖✖✖✖✖✖

THE UNITED STATES CONSTITUTION AND THE RIGHTS OF RELIGION[1]

by Bernard J. Zylstra

Bernard J. Zylstra

Born in Friesland, The Netherlands, Bernard Zylstra (1934-1986) was still a youngster when his family emigrated to the United States. He grew up on a farm with eight siblings where he remembers being drawn into a wide world of learning. In his Calvinist home, reading included not only the Bible and American literature but also works from the Kuyperian tradition.

When he entered Calvin College, he took up the study of philosophy under the tutelage of Evan Runner. From that point his horizons kept enlarging to include theological, historical, and legal subjects. After college he went first to Calvin Theological Seminary and then to law school at the University of Michigan, completing degree programs at both institutions. Though Zylstra found many of the narrow technicalities at seminary and law school too confining, he was nevertheless well prepared after those years to take up the study of the philosophy of law and political theory which had become the central focus of his interest.

Zylstra returned to The Netherlands where he pursued graduate study primarily under Herman Dooyeweerd at the Free University of Amsterdam. In 1968 he published his doctoral thesis *From Pluralism to Collectivism: The Development of Harold Laski's Political Theory*.[2] Soon thereafter, he returned to

North America to become one of the first lecturers at a fledgling Christian study center in Toronto. By the time that study center had become the Institute for Christian Studies and established itself, in reputation as well as in law, as a graduate school, Zylstra was serving as its principal and would soon become its first president.

In addition to his doctoral thesis, which Paul Hirst describes as "the best book" on Laski's political theory,[3] Zylstra wrote articles on a wide range of subjects and guided graduate students into many diverse corners of political and legal thought.[4] Nevertheless, the time and energy spent in helping to develop and to administer the Institute for Christian Studies kept him from pursuing with full vigor the research and writing he wanted to do. Sadly, at the very time when he was choosing to relinquish his administrative responsibilities to return to scholarship, he was struck with cancer that led to his premature death in 1986.

The selection we have chosen from Zylstra's writings is an essay first presented as an address at a conference organized by the Christian Legal Society. The theme was the relation of law to religious liberty. While clearly focusing on that subject, he does much more than one might expect to find in an essay on the First Amendment. The writing is clear and forceful, requiring little introduction, and it will become apparent that Zylstra's evaluation of law and religion in the American context is deeply indebted to the insights gained from Kuyper, Dooyeweerd, and Runner.

When, for example, Zylstra says near the beginning that the different conceptions of justice held by Aristotle, Locke, and Marx illustrate their dependence "on different world views,"[5] he is already working to expose competing religious "ground motives." That insight deepens as the essay unfolds, leading him to argue that the American Constitution embodies the "eighteenth-century Enlightenment in its moderate form." The Enlightenment, he continues, "marked the unfolding of humanism, the religion which idolizes the self-realization of human personality."[6]

The essay also explains the importance of institutional and associational rights, not just the rights of individuals. His rejection of individualism and collectivism in favor of a genuine social pluralism is spelled out in a manner that goes beyond an appeal to religious freedom for churches and liberty of conscience for individuals. The insistence that different kinds of institutions and associations should be free to pursue their distinct "callings" and "offices" shows Zylstra's dependence on the Kuyperian insight into sphere sovereignty.

Finally, the essay stresses the idea that the state exists to establish the "*salus publica*, the public good"[7] qualified by the norm of justice for a public legal order. With this conception of the state—an institution called by God to establish justice in a society consisting of a multiplicity of institutions organized by people with different religious world views—Zylstra argues through to his conclusion that genuine religious freedom requires the disestablishment of secularism in the public arena and the protection of religious liberty for schools, hospitals, and other non-ecclesiastical institutions. The United States Constitution, properly interpreted, permits this and the United Nations Universal Declaration of Human Rights demands it, he argues. In the context of the full Bill of Rights, Zylstra concludes, future battles for religious freedom "should be fought much more in terms of *rights*, which the courts are called upon to defend, rather than in terms of *religion*, which the courts are not legally competent to define."[8]

THE UNITED STATES CONSTITUTION AND THE RIGHTS OF RELIGION

In order to address the question of the impact of law on religious expression and freedom, it is appropriate to begin with the meaning of *law*. Webster defines it as "the whole body of . . . customs, practices, or rules constituting the organic rule prescribing the nature and conditions of existence of a state or other organized community." This "organic rule" allocates the rights, duties, freedoms and privileges in the state or other organized community. The key word here is *right*, for we are concerned with the rightful expression of religion in society.

The civilization of the West is the heir of the Roman law definition of right, viz. *suum cuique tribuere*, to render to each his due. But what is one's due? To what does one have a right? What is a just claim which, by way of the public legal system, one can expect society to meet? Questions like these are asked each day by politicians and parliamentarians, by theorists and theologians, but particularly by the poor, the prisoners, the persecuted. Answers are not nearly as numerous as the questions. Nonetheless, answers are constantly given in the way societies distribute resources and in the philosophies of the world's great thinkers. Aristotle argued that persons have a natural right to an equal share of society's wealth—though he immediately made distinctions between proportionate and numerical equality.[9] John Locke asserted that one has a right to what he has worked for. Karl Marx stated that one has a right to what he needs.

All of these conceptions of justice contain an element of truth. We intuitively sense that equality, merit and need are basic components of justice. But the singling out of one component as the key factor in justice illustrates the dependence of these conceptions on different world views. How, then, should the Christian deal with conceptions of justice in the context of non-Christian patterns of life and thought? I believe that the partial insights of both pagan and secular thinkers can be meaningful in the development of a view of justice built on the biblical world view. The Bible pictures the world as God's good creation, fallen into sin, and now in the cosmic process of redemptive restoration because of Christ's substitutionary death and the Spirit's regenerative work in the hearts of men and women. A biblical conception of justice reflects this threefold picture of creation, fall, and redemption.[10] It begins by taking seriously the biblical teachings on creation. Here Emil Brunner is helpful.

> The Christian conception of justice . . . is determined by the conception of God's order of creation. What corresponds to the Creator's ordinance is just—to that ordinance which bestows on every creature, with its being, the law of its being and its relationships to other creatures. The "primal order" to which every one refers in using the words "just" or "unjust," the "due" which is rendered to each man, is the order of creation, which is the will of the Creator made manifest.[11]

In this light one can say that *human beings have a right to fulfill the calling God gives them.* All creatures are God's servants (Psalm 119:91). Every creature has a right to be servant of God, to fulfill its particular office for His glory. In the most fundamental link between creatures and Creator—which is the link of the covenant[12]—the Creator speaks His Word and the creature is called upon to do that Word.[13] Creatures have the right to do the words of God. Here the correlation between rights and duties is clear. Creatures differ, and thus their respective rights, because God made them "after their kind." He addresses differing words to them; their callings and offices are thus distinct. The entire creation story in the book of Genesis is filled with a description of callings, of divine assignments. God set the sun and the moon in the firmament of the heavens, the greater light to rule the day and the lesser light to rule the night. He created plants to yield seed and fruit trees to bear fruit upon the earth in order to feed mankind. And He created mankind, male and female, to till and keep the garden of Eden, to fill the earth and subdue it, to love God above all and neighbor as self. Indeed, the very meaning of creatureliness lies in service, in being subject to divine ordinances which are the pointers to blessing, shalom, the life that is good. Creatures have the *right* to perform these divine assignments. They have a right to the institutions and the resources needed to carry them out.

The legal framework in a society like ours consists fundamentally of three types of rights—the rights of persons, of institutions and associations, and of the state.

First, personal rights. The norm of justice requires a social order in which men and women can express themselves as God's imagers. To put it another way, justice requires social space for human personality. By personality I mean the human self whose calling lies in love of God and love of fellowman. It is at this point that one can again see clearly the correlation between rights and duties. The duty to love God is ineradicable from the covenantal bond between God and humans; sin does not eliminate that duty. At the same time, the right to love God is inalienable. We cannot surrender it because it defines our very existence, our humanness, our creatureliness as male and female.

In the revelation of Christ, the Word made flesh, we know what love is. But at this point we are also confronted with what is perhaps the most difficult problem in the history of human rights. Because of sin, the gods men love are many, and for centuries the lovers of God have denied the right of others to love their god. If *in Christ* we know what it means to love God, do persons who claim to love God as revealed by Buddha or Mohammed have a right to the fulfillment of their claim? And what about persons who claim that the god they are called upon to love is human personality itself? A just society may not discriminate between one religion and another. The wheat and the tares are allowed to coexist until *God's* final day of judgment. This does not mean that the social order is neutral with respect to religions. Societal orders ought to be so structured that a multiplicity of religions can flourish side by side. This will be of increasing import when we will see a rapid growth of interchange among the world's civilizations and cultures. Religion is the prime factor not only in the value systems of persons but also in the fabric of cultures and civilizations. If the society of the future will be one of peace and justice, it must be one where the right to freedom of religion is accorded preeminence, where there are no laws "respecting an establishment of religion, or prohibiting the free exercise thereof." (First Amendment, U.S. Constitution)

The rights of persons to fulfill their callings implies *the right to be*, the right to life itself, the right to be unharmed. Again we are reminded of our dependence on the Roman law.

Iuris praecepta sunt haec: honeste vivere, alterum non laedere, suum cuique tribuere.[14]

The precepts of law are these: to live honestly, not to harm another, to render to each his due.

This right to be is not merely that of the human species. It belongs to every individual human life, from the beginning of its existence at conception to its end at death. Human life on earth always exists in bodies of flesh and blood and bones. These individual bodies have a right to remain whole, not to be harmed, aborted, maimed, tortured, molested, placed in hostage, terrorized. The basic needs of individual bodies to food, nurture, shelter and care are implicit in the right to life. The biblical message pointedly indicates that the fulfillment of such needs is not a matter of charity but of justice, and is therefore a matter of the structure of the public order. Justice requires such an allocation of material and cultural goods that human life is made possible, is protected, enhanced, and enabled to carry on a multiplicity of tasks in history. The building of cultures and societies entails the use of "nature" and its resources. Again, this is not a right of the human species or the human community. The earth is the Lord's; and *persons* have the right to a stewardly possession and use of it. In this sense, the right to private property is as essential as the right to privacy in a developed, highly differentiated society like ours.[15]

2.   The second category of rights is that of institutions. I employ the word "institution" here in a specific sense to refer to communities and associations of which persons are members. Typical communities are marriages, families, churches and states. Associations are generally dependent upon the principle of voluntary joining and leaving on the part of their members.[16] These include schools, universities, industrial enterprises, philanthropic and artistic organizations, political parties, labor unions, social clubs, the media, and the hundreds of freely established associations characteristic of modern democratic societies.

Communities and associations have an identity that is directly dependent upon their office, the service they render society. Their rights are correlative with their office. The right of an institution is its authority to make legally binding decisions for its members pertinent to its office.[17] A society is genuinely free when both persons and institutions can exercise their rights in this sense, without interference by external powers. With reference to the question of the impact of law on religious expression and freedom, we have to address the issue of whether religious freedom is primarily a matter of personal rights and the right of churches or whether that freedom is also essential for non-church institutions.

3.   But first let's consider the third category of rights—those of the state. Since the state is also an institution, its rights do not in principle need sepa-

rate attention. However, since the impact of *its* "law" on religious freedom is our focus, practical considerations justify this in the present context. The state has rights peculiar to it because it has a unique office. That office is of divine origin: it is God's servant for our good. (Cf. Romans 13:4.) Its distinctive office is to establish and maintain a public realm in which the rights of persons and institutions are recognized, protected, and guaranteed. The state does not create these rights; instead, it must acknowledge divinely sanctioned and given rights, and establish spheres of freedom within which persons and institutions can exercise rights for the fulfillment of their respective offices, callings, and responsibilities.

The "good" which the state is called upon to establish is the *salus publica*, the public good. This has a variety of implications. In the first place, it means that the state's administration of justice must protect each person within its realm, irrespective of belief, race, class, or sex. Each person must be deemed equal before the law of the land. In the second place, the state is a public institution in that its membership—citizenship—must be open to everyone born within its borders. Under no circumstances is the state allowed to annul the citizenship of its members. In the third place, the state is public in that the legal order which it establishes ought to be one in which the spheres of freedom for the nonpolitical institutions and associations are guaranteed and protected from external interference. It must do that in such a way that no person or institution exploits, usurps, or abuses another. The state is called upon to guarantee peace for the commonwealth so that communities and associations domiciled within its territory can develop the "inner law of their being," the specific mandate for which the Creator called them into being through the historical deeds of men and women in time. In the fourth place, the state is a public institution because it has the calling—with other states— to establish an international framework of law which maintains peace and justice among nations and among multinational powers. Finally, states are public because they have the right to exercise "the power of the sword" within the entire territory over which their jurisdiction extends. Only states can have a monopoly of that power; as soon as they lose that monopoly they cease to be states. Though that power is immense, it is limited both in kind ("sword") and in use (public justice). Acquisition of different kinds of power results in tyranny at home and imperialism abroad.

Along with the biblical setting and the legal framework, we must also consider the constitutional structure. After all, when we speak of the impact of *law* on religious expression and freedom, we are in the final analysis speaking of *constitutional law* because legislative stipulations and administrative regulations affecting religion will, if challenged, have to pass the test of constitutionality.

A constitution is the body of fundamental rules which determines "the exercise of the sovereign power in the state"[18] and guarantees certain rights to the people. Two questions must be distinguished here. First, does the U.S. Constitution contain provisions which adequately protect the people's rights of religious expression and freedom? Second, has the U.S. Supreme Court properly interpreted these provisions? I will focus primarily on the first question because, in my view, the public debate concerning it leaves a great deal to be desired.

The Constitution has withstood the test of time. Though formulated by representatives from thirteen thinly populated former colonies of diverse cultural and religious leanings, it provided the base for 200 years of development of the United States into the most powerful nation on earth. It was one of the most formative powers that kept this body politic together and could, at times of crisis, be amended to meet new needs. A political document of such stature has an aura of invincible splendor that humbles the student of constitutional law.

Moreover, the clauses affecting religion in the First Amendment— "Congress shall make no law respecting an establishment of religion, or prohibiting the free exercise thereof"—have exercised a benignant impact on American society. The establishment clause prevented the legal primacy of any denomination so that the equality of each citizen before the law became a reality, at least from a formal point of view. The fact that membership in the traditional Anglo-Saxon denominations carried with it definite social, economic and even political advantages must be attributed more to the cultural moorings of American civilization than to its legal structure. And the free exercise clause eliminated potential legal obstacles in the way of the stunning diversity of ecclesiastical life in the United States—a diversity unique in the modern age. Nonetheless, these outstanding features of the Constitution should not blind us to its shortcomings that today not only contribute to confusion in the relation between religion and the public realm but also hinder the proper expression of religious freedom in American society. These shortcomings are related to the biblical underpinnings of human rights and the threefold societal diversity of rights.

The Constitution is an embodiment of the eighteenth-century Enlightenment in its moderate form.[19] The Enlightenment marked the unfolding of humanism, the religion which idolizes the self-realization of human personality. In its radicality, humanism views the autonomy of the human will as the final source of "values" for ethics. Since the eighteenth century, humanism considered technical rationality in science as the most fitting instrument in extracting nature's resources in industrial production. And humanism, in its late bourgeois phase, viewed the acquisition of material abundance for our bodily needs as the goal of progressive history.[20] Humanism is the post-Christian religion of the West. In its most radical forms it *negates* the relevance of God's existence, the light of biblical revelation, the created structure of natural and social entities, the spiritual essence of human nature, the openness of human beings toward God, and the rootedness of cultural traditions and social institutions in the Christian foundations of Western civilization. Humanism is a secularized version of the Christian religion: it places the transcendent spiritual realities of the Christian faith within the confines of an immanent historical process subject to the control of the autonomous human will.[21]

Immanentized spiritual movements as a rule express themselves historically in three dialectically interrelated ways: radicalism, moderation, conservatism. (The political movements that parallel these expressions are generally referred to as the left, the center, and the right.) In the modern age, France was the center of radicalism, England of moderation, and Germany of conservatism. Moderate humanism took into consideration the importance of continuity in cultural and social change, and it accommodated itself politically to the Christian religion by making the public realm secular and by confining religion to the private spheres of home and church. John Locke (1632-1704) was the political philosopher who most clearly articulated the political accommodation between the Christian religion and modern, individualist humanism. Because of Locke's influence on the Founding Fathers, it is essential that we understand his position on the relation between religion and society. One doesn't have to deny Locke's personal commitment as a Christian to be aware of his basic post-Christian stance in sociopolitical matters which he shared with Thomas Hobbes.

> Both men began with a common point of departure, the assumption that man is a product of his experience and that his nature is rooted in material reality rather than in divine ordination. The assumption was revolutionary; it swept away the belief in providence that underlay medieval society and instead pointed to man's potential for ordering society as he saw fit.[22]

In distinction from Hobbes, the radical, Locke searched for a moderate political accommodation with the Christian religion. He did this perhaps most clearly in *A Letter Concerning Toleration*, published in 1689. Here Locke first presents his view of the state. It is a radically secular, even materialist conception. It is best to quote his own words.

> The commonwealth seems to me to be a society of men constituted only for the procuring, preserving, and advancing of their own civil interests.
>
> Civil interests I call life, liberty, health and indolency of body; and the possession of outward things, such as money, lands, houses, furniture, and the like.
>
> It is the duty of the civil magistrate, by the impartial execution of equal laws, to secure unto all the people in general, and to every one of his subjects in particular, the just possession of these things belonging to this life.[23]

After thus reducing the scope of government to "secular interests"[24] which in effect amounts to the "preservation of property,"[25] Locke defines the church.

> A church, then, I take to be a voluntary society of men, joining themselves together of their own accord in order to the public worshiping of God in such manner as they judge acceptable to Him, and effectual to the salvation of their souls.[26]

After this speedy reduction of religion to the pursuit of soul salvation, Locke turns to the question of the relation between state and church. He makes two points. "The only business of the church is the salvation of souls, and it no ways concerns the commonwealth."[27] But he is aware that in certain circumstances the interests of the church may collide with the interests of the state. In that case the church must give in to the state. "But those things that are prejudicial to the commonweal of a people in their ordinary use, and are therefore forbidden by laws, those things ought not to be permitted to churches in their sacred rights."[28]

With this defense of toleration, Locke in effect provided the basis for secular society in its moderate, liberal form. This basis comprised several elements, two of which are indispensable: first, the state is secular, governed by the rational consent of the governed; and second, religion is a matter of the salvation of the soul, best achieved in the church of one's choice. The First Amendment of the Constitution embodies these principles. The establishment clause severs the link between the state and church, and, in an ever increasing manner, the link between the state and religion. Further, the free exercise clause guarantees the individual's religious freedom in whatever church he seeks to express it.

There is one additional complication. The conception of society, both in Locke and in the Founding Fathers, was individualistic. This meant that societal relationships were viewed in terms of the wills of the individual persons comprising these relationships. In the realm of law, it meant that the rights of individuals are protected in the Bill of Rights while the rights of communities and associations are not mentioned except indirectly in the Third

Amendment, where the privacy of the family is protected ("No Soldier shall, in time of peace be quartered in any house, without the consent of the Owner...")

With this background, it should come as no surprise that with reference to the expression of religious freedom we are in a constitutional bind. The two centuries of American history have witnessed an amazing proliferation of communities and associations in the form of churches, schools, colleges, universities, industries, labor unions, charitable organizations, and, especially in recent decades, caring institutions for the very young and the very old, for the disabled and the handicapped. The expression of religious freedom is guaranteed in the churches. But it is of the very nature of religion to express itself also in these "mediating structures"[29] that fill society between the individual and the state. Precisely because they are mediating structures, they inevitably have links with individuals, who are their members, and with the state, which must acknowledge, protect and guarantee the rights peculiar to their nature, identity, and office. These mediating structures are established by ordinary people for a great variety of reasons—profits of money, pleasures of the body, and praise of God. I suspect that the latter reason is still foremost. How then can we have a free society when the rights of the mediating structures organized for the praise of God are not constitutionally protected? From the schools parents expect for their children an education that is in tune with their basic world view. From the colleges and universities we expect the development of the mind. From the caring institutions we expect legal adoption arrangement for children, medical care for the sick, assistance for the physically and mentally disabled, protection for the elderly. These concerns overlap with those of the state. But does this overlap mean that the religious character of these mediating structures must be eradicated as soon as the state becomes involved, especially when public funds are used? If that is the meaning of the establishment clause, its effect is "the establishment of a religion of secularism," as Justice Potter Stewart hinted in his dissent in the *Schempp* case.[30] The U.S. Supreme Court has indeed interpreted the establishment clause in this way, especially since the *Everson* case.[31] In view of this, we are today faced with the compelling need for "Disestablishment a Second Time."[32]

The disestablishment we need today is not a severing of the link between the state and its established church, as in the eighteenth century, but rather a severing of the links between the state and the secularism established and imposed in mediating structures that are closely connected with the state, especially in the areas of health, education, and welfare. I am not advocating a universal severance of the links between the state and the mediating structures operating in these areas. I am not advocating a medical, educational, or social laissez-faire policy (although a cutting back of governmental bureau-cracy and an increase in personal and institutional responsibilities in these ar-eas ought to be welcomed). Nor am I advocating a states' rights solution to these problems (as if local and state governments are inherently less secular than the federal government). The solution I am advocating is *the disestab-lishment of secularism* in the mediating structures on the part of every level of government and *the equal protection of the free exercise of religion* in these structures. In the area of education, for example, governments are legitimately involved because without education citizens cannot assume political respon-sibilities in a democracy. But parents are equally interested in education. The interests of the government and the interests of the parents can be met in a system of governmentally certified and funded schools religiously differenti-ated according to the religious convictions of the parents whether they be secular, Jewish, or Christian. Similar solutions are possible in the areas of health and welfare.

I am aware that what I am advocating involves a fundamental restructur-ing of the American legal system. I dare to defend this proposition since I am convinced that the establishment of secularism is a tyranny that prohibits free exercise of both personal and institutional rights.

Does a restructuring of the legal system require constitutional reform? I would like to answer this question first by pointing out that there is a major example of juridical reflection that better covers this area than the U.S. Constitution, and secondly, by suggesting that the U.S. Constitution can serve as the legal basis for expanding the free exercise of both personal and institu-tional rights. The documents to which I refer are the Charter of the United Nations adopted on June 26, 1945, and the Universal Declaration of Human Rights, drafted by the United Nations Commission on Human Rights under the chairpersonship of Eleanor Roosevelt and adopted by the General Assembly on December 10, 1948. The Charter sets out the internal structure of the United Nations; the Declaration is in effect a universal Bill of Rights. This Declaration is a document born within the civilization of the West, re-vealing the impact of both humanism and Christianity. It displays many weaknesses, but it is the most adequate statement of rights the civilized world has formulated, even if it has not managed to live up to its demands. It is im-portant because it has gone beyond the individualism of the Enlightenment world view reflected in the U.S. Bill of Rights. The personal rights recognized in the U.S. Bill of Rights are incorporated in the Declaration, but in addition there is a surprising list of institutional rights which has not received the attention it deserves. Here are the relevant articles.

Article 16. 1. Men and women of full age, without any limitation due to race, nationality or religion, have the right to marry and to found a family . . . .
3. The family is the natural and fundamental group unit of society and is entitled to protection by society and the State.

Article 18. Everyone has the right to freedom of thought, conscience and religion; this right includes freedom to change his religion or belief, and freedom, either alone or in community with others and in public or private, to manifest his religion in teaching, practice, worship and observance.

Article 20. 1. Everyone has the right to freedom of peaceful assembly and association.
2. No one may be compelled to belong to an association.

Article 26. 1. Everyone has the right to education. Education shall be free, at least in the elementary and fundamental stages. Elementary education shall be compulsory. . . .
3. Parents have a prior right to choose the kind of education that shall be given to their children.

Article 29. 1. Everyone has duties to the community in which alone the free and full development of his personality is possible.
2. In the exercise of his rights and freedoms, everyone shall be subject only to such limitations as are determined by law solely for the purpose of securing due recognition and respect for the rights and freedoms of others and of meeting the just requirements of morality, public order and the general welfare in a democratic society.

As its Preamble states, the Universal Declaration of Human Rights was proclaimed by the General Assembly of the United Nations "as a common standard of achievement for all people and nations." It is not binding law in any state, but serves as an excellent model for constitutional reform because it recognizes the rights of such institutions as marriage and family, the freedom of association (including the indispensable corollary—the freedom *not* to belong to an association), and the freedom without distinction of any kind to manifest one's belief, either alone or in community.

The United States is not going through a period of constitutional reform, and amendments do not readily receive the required support, as the history of both the proposed Equal Rights Amendment and the Anti-Abortion Amendment shows. How then can the disestablishment of secularism be legally achieved? How can the free exercise of religion without discrimination in the health, education, and welfare institutions be guaranteed? I believe that within the present constitutional framework there are three available avenues. First, there is ample historical evidence that the establishment clause was included in the First Amendment to disestablish churches.[33] The question of religious freedom *in schools* is not properly a matter of the establishment clause (except when the state uses schools to establish the religion it prefers.) Constitutional lawyers should argue this strict interpretation of the clause.

In the second place, the nature, content and scope of religion is not defined in the First Amendment.[34] The rights pertinent to the free exercise thereof can only be defined by its adherents, and the exercise of these rights should not be prohibited unless such exercise conflicts with the legitimate demands of the public realm itself. (For example, the refusal of parents, on religious grounds, to permit the administration of blood transfusion to save the life of their child would—in my view—constitute an offense against the public realm.) In recent decades the Supreme Court has begun to acknowledge that the free exercise of religion cannot possibly be confined to personal belief and ecclesiastical practice. It has protected the free exercise of religion even when this collided with the interests of the state, as in the conscientious objectors cases.[35] Constitutional lawyers will have to pursue this argument further, to extend to the expression of religious freedoms in the various spheres outside of the church. The Constitution itself does not prohibit such an extension.

In the third place, there are three amendments to the Constitution whose provisions can be properly used to defend a relation between religion and the state radically different from the "absolute separation" imposed on American society by the Supreme Court on the basis of a misinterpretation of the establishment clause. The Fourteenth Amendment, in part, reads as follows: "No State shall make or enforce any law which shall abridge the privileges or immunities of citizens of the United States; nor shall any State deprive any person of life, liberty, or property, without due process of law; nor deny to any person within its jurisdiction the equal protection of the laws." In my view, any state which funds secular public schools while refusing to fund independent private schools abridges the privileges of the citizens who support the private schools, deprives them of property without due process, and denies them the equal protection of the laws. The same argument holds for similar discrimination in the areas of health and welfare.

And then there is the Tenth Amendment: "The powers not delegated to the United States by the Constitution, nor prohibited by it to the States, are reserved to the States respectively, or to the people." The Founding Fathers established a nontotalitarian state. This means that the state does not have a monopoly of power in society. Other sectors have powers of their own. We acknowledge a plurality of power when we defend free enterprise in the economic sector. There is no constitutional prohibition of a defense of a plurality of power in the cultural sectors, whose powers today are increasingly absorbed into the political system.

Finally, the Ninth Amendment reads: "The enumeration in the Constitution of certain rights, shall not be construed to deny or disparage others retained by the people." The rights of the people to the free exercise of religion in the nonchurch spheres of society are today both denied and disparaged. As a rule, rights have to be fought for; they don't come on a golden platter. The Ninth Amendment provides a constitutional base for this battle.

By suggesting that religious rights should be dealt with in the light of these three amendments I am really saying that the future battle should be fought much more in terms of *rights*, which the courts are called upon to defend, rather than in terms of *religion*, which the courts are not legally competent to define. The disestablishment of the religion of secularism must be achieved by getting the combatants out of the prison of the Supreme Court's interpretation of the First Amendment's establishment clause, which is largely irrelevant to the issues at stake. The establishment clause cut America off from the Constantinian entanglement of church and state, and did so properly. The Bill of Rights *as a whole* laid the basis for a free society, including the expression of the rights of religion. Let's then bring the entire Bill of Rights into the picture!

At the beginning of the modern era the societies of western Europe were torn by the wars of religion. The colonies along the eastern seaboard and later the independent United States were havens for those driven from their homelands because of religious persecution. The Constitution established channels for a society of toleration. Today we realize that these channels are partly blocked because secularism has become the religion of the public realm. The establishment of this religion brings with it both injustice and discrimination, and thus the danger for new wars of religion, undoubtedly fought with different weapons. This danger can be averted. Let us openly and honestly recognize that the American citizenry is religiously divided. And then let us avail ourselves of the constitutional weapons so that the legitimate rights of each religious segment in the citizenry are properly acknowledged, not only in the private spheres of life but also in the public realm.

NOTES

[1] Selection from Bernard J. Zylstra, "Using the Constitution to Defend Religious Rights," in Lynn R. Buzzard, ed., *Freedom and Faith: The Impact of Law on Religious Liberty* (Westchester, IL: Crossway Books, 1981), with minor editorial revisions.

[2] Bernard J. Zylstra, *From Pluralism to Collectivism: The Development of Harold Laski's Political Theory* (Assen, The Netherlands: Van Gorcum and Co., 1968).

[3] Paul Q. Hirst, ed., *The Pluralist Theory of the State* (New York: Routledge, 1989), 46.

4 Zylstra was instrumental in bringing the English translation of several Dutch works to publication, including Herman Dooyeweerd *Roots of Western Culture* (Toronto: Wedge Publishing Foundation, 1979), from which we have excerpted above, and L. Kalsbeek, *Contours of a Christian Philosophy: An Introduction to Herman Dooyeweerd's Thought*, eds. B. Zylstra and J. Zylstra. (Toronto: Wedge Publishing Foundation, 1975) to which Zylstra contributed a substantial introduction. Among Zylstra's many other essays are: "The Bible, Justice, and the State," in James W. Skillen, ed., *Confessing Christ and Doing Politics* (Washington, D.C.: Center for Public Justice, 1982), 39-53; "Philosophy, Revelation and Modernity: Crossroads in the Thought of George Grant," in Larry Schmidt, ed., *George Grant in Process: Essays and Conversations* (Toronto: House of Anansi Press, 1978), 148-156; "Voegelin on Unbelief and Revolution," in C. Bremmer and M.N.G. Kool, eds., *Een Staatsman ter Navolging: Groen van Prinsterer Herdacht (1876-1976)* (The Hague: CDA, 1976), 191-200; "Modernity and the American Empire," *International Reformed Bulletin*, No. 68/69 (1977): 3-19; and the "Preface" to H. Evan Runner's *The Relation of the Bible to Learning*, 5th rev. ed. (Jordan Station, Ontario: Paideia Press, 1982), 9-34.

5 Zylstra, "Using the Constitution," 94.

6 *Ibid.*, 101.

7 *Ibid.*, 99.

8 *Ibid.*, 111.

9 Aristotle, *The Politics of Aristotle*, trans. Ernest Barker (London: Oxford University Press, 1946), 65n.

10 Here it should be kept in mind the Bible presents a fundamental antithesis between the sin of mankind and the work of God in creation and redemption. It does not present an antithesis between creation and redemption. Redemption is the restoration of creation by divine grace. Christian world views which proceed from the (relative) autonomy of creation lead to a natural law conception of justice, dominant in classical Roman Catholic thought. See John Courtney Murray, *We Hold These Truths: Catholic Reflections on the American Proposition* (New York: Sheed & Ward, 1960); and its Protestant parallel, Carl F.H. Henry, *Aspects of Christian Social Ethics* (Grand Rapids: Eerdmans, 1964). Christian world views which (tend to) isolate redemption from creation lead to a Christomonistic conception of justice. Because of the eclipse of the doctrine of creation in modern Christian thought, such Christomonistic conceptions are dominant. See Karl Barth, *Community, State and Church* (New York: Doubleday, 1960); Jacques Ellul, *Le fondement théologique du droit* (1946); and John Howard Yoder, *The Christian Witness to the State* (Newton, KS: Faith and Life Press, 1964). Finally, Christian world views that take as their point of departure the fall into sin tend to reject the inherent goodness of creation and perceive redemption as entirely innovative, often implying the elimination of the existing (sinful) order. In certain types of dispensationalism—made popular by the writings of Hal Lindsey—this annihilation of the existing order will occur when Christ returns in the eschaton. In certain types of liberation theology, Christians are called upon to engage in the destruction of the sinful, existing capitalist order. See José Miranda, *Marx and the Bible: A Critique of the Philosophy of Oppression* (Maryknoll: Orbis Books, 1974). These various Christian world views have their counterparts in post-Christian secular thought, such as modern natural law, Marxism, and the radical wing of the counterculture from Rousseau to Roszak.

11 Emil Brunner, *Justice and the Social Order*, trans. M. Hottinger (New York: Harper and Row, 1945), 89.

12 For a treatment of the history of biblical revelation in the light of the covenant, see S.G. de Graaf, *Promise and Deliverance*, 4 vols. (St. Catharines, Ontario: Paideia Press, 1977-1981) and H.E. Runner's "Translator's Introduction" to *ibid.*, 3: 11-21.

13 Cf. Bernard J. Zylstra, "Thy Word Our Life," in James H. Olthuis, et al., *Will All The King's Men?* (Toronto: Wedge Publishing Foundation, 1972), 153-221.

14 Justinian, *Institutiones* I.1.3.

15 Cf. Hannah Arendt, *Crises of the Republic* (New York: Harcourt Brace Jovanovich, 1972), 211ff.

16 Herman Dooyeweerd's sociological distinctions of the various kinds of human relations in a differentiated society are helpful. For a quick survey, see Kalsbeek, *Contours*, 196-268.

17 This matter of the authority and rights of institutions outside of the state is being given increasing attention in sociology of law. F.W. Maitland's Introduction to Otto von Gierke's *Political Theories of the Middle Age* (Cambridge: Cambridge University Press, 1900), vii-xiv is a classic statement of the issue by a legal historian. Herman Dooyeweerd's doctrine of sphere sovereignty deals with this question; cf. his *Roots of Western Culture*, 40-60. For an introduction to the relevant literature, especially European, see Zylstra, *From Pluralism to Collectivism*, 206-220; and James W. Skillen, "The Development of Calvinistic Political Theory in The Netherlands, with Special Reference to the Thought of Herman Dooyeweerd," (Ph.D. Diss., Duke, 1974.) See also H. Evan Runner, "Sphere Sovereignty," in H. Evan Runner, *The Relation of the Bible to Learning*, 2d ed. (Toronto: Wedge Publishing Foundation, 1981), Lecture V.

18 Cf. A.V. Dicey, *The Law of the Constitution* (London: MacMillan, 1959), 23.

19 Cf. Henry F. May, *The Enlightenment in America* (New York: Oxford University Press, 1976), 96ff.; Carl Becker, *The Heavenly City of the Eighteenth-Century Philosophers* (New Haven: Yale University Press, 1932); Hannah Arendt, *On Revolution* (New York: Viking Press, 1963).

20 Cf. Bob Goudzwaard, *Capitalism and Progress* (Toronto: Wedge Publishing Foundation; Grand Rapids: Eerdmans Publishing Co., 1979), especially Part One.

21 For a more extensive discussion of the development of secular humanism, see Bernard J. Zylstra, "Modernity and the American Empire," *International Reformed Bulletin*, 68/69 (1977): 3-19, and the literature cited there.

22 James Laxer and Robert Laxer, *The Liberal Idea of Canada: Pierre Trudeau and the Question of Canada's Survival* (Toronto: James Lorimer, 1977), 80.

23 John Locke, *A Letter Concerning Toleration* (Indianapolis: Bobbs-Merrill, 1950), 17.

24 *Ibid.*, 19.

25 John Locke, *The Second Treatise of Government* (1690), par. 94.

26 Locke, *A Letter Concerning Toleration*, 20.

27 *Ibid.*, 36.

28 *Ibid.*, 40.

29 This term is from Peter Berger. Cf. his essay, "In Praise of Particularity: The Concept of Mediating Structures," in Peter Berger, *Facing up to Modernity: Excursions in Society, Politics, and Religion* (New York: Basic Books, 1977), 130-141.

30 *Abington School District v. Schempp*, 374 U.S. 203 (1963) at 226.

31 *Everson v. Board of Education*, 310 U.S. 1 (1947).

32 See Rockne McCarthy, James W. Skillen, and William A. Harper, *Disestablishment a Second Time: Genuine Pluralism for American Schools* (Grand Rapids: Eerdmans and Christian University Press, 1982). See also Rockne McCarthy, *et al.*, *Society, State, and Schools: A Case for Structural and Confessional Pluralism* (Grand Rapids: Eerdmans, 1981).

33 See Anson Phelps Stokes, *Church and State in the United States* (New York: Harper, 1950) 3 vols., vol. 1, [552-61].

[34] See Sharon L. Worthing, "'Religion' and 'Religious Institutions' under the First Amendment," *Pepperdine Law Review*, 7 (1980): 313-354.

[35] See, for instance, *United States v. Seeger*, 380 U.S. 163 (1965).

EIGHTEEN

CHRISTIAN POLITICS IN A GLOBAL CONTEXT[1]
by Bob Goudzwaard

Bob Goudzwaard

The final excerpts in Part III are from Bob Goudzwaard (b. 1934), a contemporary Dutch economist who served for a number of years in Parliament and in leadership positions in the Anti-Revolutionary Party. The historical continuity with Kuyper and Dooyeweerd appears in the fact that Goudzwaard is now a professor at the Free University of Amsterdam. The continuity with the work of Evan Runner is evident from the many visiting lectures that Goudzwaard has given at the Institute for Christian Studies, Calvin College, and other related institutions in North America, Latin America, and other parts of the world.[2]

The occasion for much of Goudzwaard's writing in the 1970s was similar to that for Dooyeweerd's in the 1940s. In the immediate postwar period all segments of Dutch political life were seeking common ground for cooperating to rebuild the country.[3] In the mid-1940s Dooyeweerd argued that the Christian principles of the Anti-Revolutionary Party should not be quickly relinquished in the interest of a wide but temporary consensus with liberals, socialists, and Catholics. The important issues that had been debated for more than a century in Europe regarding the normative structure of society and the task of the state are still important, Dooyeweerd argued, precisely at a time when people long to work together for Dutch recovery.

Goudzwaard rose to political influence at the height of debates 30 years later regarding the basis for Christian politics—particularly the debates about whether Protestant and Catholic Christians should try to build a new inter-party unity.[4] Just as Kuyper felt compelled to criticize Calvin, and Dooyeweerd felt compelled to criticize Groen and Kuyper, so Goudzwaard feels compelled to criticize his Party's use and misuse of the term "sphere sovereignty" in the ongoing course of Dutch politics. Though he is more willing than Kuyper or Dooyeweerd to encourage the unification of Christian political parties, Goudzwaard is not willing to give way to a merely pragmatic politics that dismisses the principled insights and commitments of the Anti-Revolutionary tradition. In fact, his refusal to stay in the union of Christian parties in Holland in the early 1980s was due, in part, to his conviction that the new "Christian Democratic Appeal" (CDA) would likely become a merely pragmatic party. The CDA was formed in 1980 from the merger of the Anti-Revolutionary Party, the Christian-Historical Union (also Protestant), and the Catholic Peoples Party.

The first excerpt from Goudzwaard below is a simple and brief articula-tion of the principle of sphere sovereignty coupled with his criticism of some misuses of that principle in his circles.[5] One of Goudzwaard's special con-cerns is with the way sphere-sovereignty was being used to justify a rather liberal conception of economic life in its relation to the state. With the over-whelming impact of economic growth and development ideas in the post-war period, Goudzwaard expresses the need for a renewed and progressive rearticulation of "sphere sovereignty" so that Christians do not end up simply defending the unjust structures of life that have been established. As both se-lections from Goudzwaard show, the issues of economic life are not merely domestic but are also international in scope. In Goudzwaard more than in Kuyper or Dooyeweerd we see a struggle with issues of economic life with which José Míguez Bonino, Pope Leo XIII, Pope Pius XI, Jacques Maritain, and the American Catholic Bishops have also struggled.

Against the backdrop of Goudzwaard's clarification of what he means by sphere sovereignty, the second excerpt on international economic life should be quite understandable.[6] The norms of stewardship, justice, and social well-being have meaning as dynamic words from God showing his creatures how to deal with one another and with the earth's resources so that justice can unfold throughout the globe. Goudzwaard's exposition of these norms is closely parallel to Dooyeweerd's articulation of the meaning of economic, le-gal, and social aspects or modes of life. Spheres of responsibility (sovereignty) must be differentiated and protected, Goudzwaard writes; public justice must be implemented. The framework of societal life in which these norms should be implemented, however, goes far beyond the confines of the various domestic economic orders of today's states. The norms are global in their application.

> In regards to the role of the national state in relation to the international economic order, it is best to speak of a duty to act in accordance with the norm of public justice—a norm which may induce the national state to participate in international agreements and lead to the establishment of international or supranational institutions. This responsibility includes the duty to (help) create the juridical and institutional framework within which also non-government persons and agencies are bound to abide by public norms of cooperation, participation, and stewardship.

> It is clear that precisely in the area of international economic relations there are large gaps in the formation and administration of justice. While it is true that within the Western national states the expansion urge of big corporations has in the course of years been curtailed and limited and given a place within a balanced whole of social legislation (environmental legislation, the right of competition, and the like), outside the national territory the right of the strongest is still often determinative.[7]

Sphere sovereignty, as a principle expressing God's direct rule over all of life, should be recognized as a phrase that points to the normative demands of God upon our diverse, ongoing responsibilities in a changing world. As Goudzwaard argues, to the extent that Christians get caught up in the false ideologies and drives of the contemporary world their attempts to use the phrase "sphere sovereignty" will prove destructive to themselves and unjust for society. But to the extent that they yield to divine norms as truly dynamic standards of judgment, they may be able to contribute much to the reformation and ongoing development of society and politics in our rapidly differentiating and integrating globe.

CHRISTIAN POLITICS AND THE PRINCIPLE OF SPHERE SOVEREIGNTY

The gospel will continue to have political significance as long as it is preached and people are willing to receive it as a message of salvation. To illustrate the truth of this assertion. Professor Van Niftrik once pointed out that on the day of Christ's resurrection the disciples were gathered behind closed doors and windows because they were afraid of the Jewish authorities. Although they had no intention of engaging in politics, this gathering of that small group of fearful disciples was seen as a political act by their enemies. Accepting the message of the gospel is a religious and a personal fact, but it is also a social and political fact. It brings us into a new relationship with God, but also with our fellow men in every aspect of our lives.

The meaning of the gospel of Christ is not just an inner question, but also a matter of outward renewal. Its meaning is not limited to the salvation of the soul, but also extends to the body. It is related not only to a new heaven, but also to a new earth. In his pamphlet, "Christ and Social Problems," published in 1895, the same conviction led Abraham Kuyper to complain bitterly about the prevailing sermons in the church of his day. He said, "They constantly remain caught up in the spiritual, continually plodding around in the same circle of ideas, and in doing so they neglect to preach the full Christ, whose gospel so clearly shows that he also wished to influence the life of society, that he condemned society as it was, and wished to sanctify it to be something better." The gospel of Christ does indeed prompt us to a renewal of our thinking about social and political matters.

As we all know, the history of attempts by Christians to arrive at this renewal of political thought spans several centuries. In that history we encounter, among other things, the principle of sphere sovereignty. This principle was, as it were, an echo within political thought of a deep biblical truth, namely, that we ought to obey God rather than man. Therefore, so this principle argues, no human institution has the right to lay a total claim on human life. Human institutions are authorized to lay their claim upon us and exercise authority over us only within their own sphere.

We find the kernel of this concept of sphere sovereignty already present in the time of the Reformation, namely, in Calvin's discussions of the civil state. However, only with the Christian statesman Ernst Ludwig von Gerlach and the Dutch political leader Groen van Prinsterer does it receive a more structured delineation and elaboration. In the January 5, 1871 issue of *Dutch Reflections* [*Nederlandse Gedachten*], Groen cites von Gerlach approvingly when the latter says that "God's law does not stand alongside of or under the spheres of diplomacy, politics, and war but embraces these spheres with its sovereign authority as it does that of private life. God's law, therefore, is their supreme guideline." Von Gerlach also says, "National needs and wants . . . must submit themselves humbly to the holy majesty of God's commandments, which every child learns at school but whose depth and height no human mind can fathom." As is clear from his famous inaugural address, "Sphere Sovereignty," given at the Free University in 1880, Kuyper embraced this common heritage of Calvin, von Gerlach, Althusius, and Groen van Prinsterer.

We, however, are living now in the late twentieth century. The realm of political activity has reached a level of complexity in our time that Groen and Kuyper in their day could hardly have imagined. Not only has the complexity of political life increased; so also has the interlacement of political life with all other domains. Especially in social-economic affairs the spheres of government and business have influenced one another strongly. The state has taken upon itself considerable direct economic responsibility, and government is deeply involved in numerous social and economic matters. This automatically raises the question: Has not the concept of sphere sovereignty been rendered wholly obsolete by the developments of our time? To even broach the topic at this time seems clearly out-of-date. Is it still meaningful to speak of distinct authorities that must be respected in their own spheres, whatever those spheres may be? Nowadays the principle of sphere sovereignty is either not mentioned at all or it is used, it seems, only by the committed proponents of almost total state non-intervention. The principle of sphere sovereignty seems to have developed into a sort of holy haven for those Christians who cannot keep up with the pell-mell pace of our civilization. It seems to be a concept fit only for people who, for example, want to interpret every effort by workers for a share in management as a violation of the employer's God-given authority. Because of all this, we are tempted in our time to proclaim the complete bankruptcy of this principle, a principle that once was one of the most important expressions of a uniquely Christian politics. This does, however raise a question. If it is true that the principle of sphere sovereignty was once a product of genuine biblical thought, can such a principle then become completely outworn and outmoded by historical developments? In my opinion a good principle is valid not simply as long as circumstances permit but forever. But if this affirmation is true, only one possibility remains: namely, that this principle has gradually become outdated through a series of distorted interpretations. Perhaps our own ideas and interpretations have spoiled its original meaning and thus deprived us of an insight that would serve us extremely well in approaching the complex reality of our day.

I will, therefore, now attempt quite deliberately to remove the dead husk surrounding this almost forgotten concept of Christian politics and seek anew the living kernel beneath all the scholastic layers of dirt and paint which in the course of time have obscured it.

A Threefold Misinterpretation

To this end, I draw your attention to a possible threefold misinterpretation of the principle of sphere sovereignty, viewed in terms of its origin. In the first place, there is the misinterpretation that would turn a norm-oriented principle into one oriented to authority. Secondly, there is a misinterpretation that would turn an appeal to a dynamic calling into a static barrier. Thirdly, there is a misinterpretation that would apply this principle one-sidedly, namely, only to the government's authority over society.

In other words, I wish to present the principle of sphere sovereignty as a principle that is by its very nature norm-oriented, one in which the dynamic calling of government and society in their mutual interrelation comes to expression. In so doing, I wish to distance myself from every viewpoint that sees this principle as a static rule that demands from all existing authority relationships in society a one-sided respect for government.

1. Norm versus authority

The contemporary interpretation of the principle of sphere sovereignty is especially slanted toward respect for external authority. When this principle is under discussion, for example, it is customary to point out the necessity of fully respecting all expressions of the employer's authority and of the authority of business in economic life in general. This authority—these powers or offices—must always be respected in what they do.

Respect for authority is indeed something good. In its proper context it can even be a biblical demand. It is also true that the principle of sphere sovereignty has everything to do with differences in human office. But is respect for every given authority indeed the historical core or root of this principle? I doubt this very much, and I do so on what I consider good grounds.

The word "sphere" is certainly important in this connection. A characteristic of every sphere or circle is that it cannot exist without a center. What is this center according to Kuyper and Groen, for example? Is this center some human—though God-given—authority? Then this authority would be the thing to which every sphere of human life owes its peculiar character and from which it derives its peculiar inner coherence. This sounds too fantastic to be true, although I will admit that sometimes Kuyper sounds as though this is what he means.

The center of every sphere of life, the source of its own unique coherence, is naturally not the existence of human authority, but the existence of divine norms characteristic for that sphere. Groen van Prinsterer expressed this when he spoke of the validity of God's law for every sphere of life. With strong approval he quotes von Gerlach's statement that God's will encompasses all human spheres with a sovereign authority that acts as their supreme guideline. This divine—"sovereign"—authority is the center of every sphere of life. Only when this divine sovereignty is no longer acknowledged do the various spheres lose their inner coherence and unity.

This may seem to be quibbling, especially in view of the numerous problems of contemporary social and economic policy. But it isn't. For example, in discussing the participation of workers in the management of an enterprise, if we follow the authoritarian interpretation of the principle of sphere sovereignty, then all such claims must be seen as a challenge to God-given authority and must, therefore, be repudiated as an attack on the sovereignty of that enterprise. If it is true, however, that God's norms for economic life form the basis of its sovereignty, one implication of this principle may well be that we should strenuously promote the co-responsibility of workers in business. For if stewardship is God's norm for all of economic life—and it is—then it is the calling of every enterprise to become a genuine institution of stewardship. This is a calling in which all working people must share, in keeping with their occupations.

Professor P.S. Gerbrandy, prime minister of the Netherlands during World War II, and a committed advocate of worker participation, once put it this way: "In the life of the nation the principle of sphere sovereignty, originally Christian, is being perverted into a sort of employer sovereignty which excludes the participation of all others. The characteristic thrust of this principle, however, is right—namely, the sovereignty of divine ordinances in a given sphere, before which both employer and worker, both government and people must bow." From a Christian viewpoint it is indeed unthinkable that authority should ever be allowed to exist in a normative vacuum, and that it should be viewed as something that ought to be revered as an end in itself, without taking into account the way this authority is exercised. Such modes of thinking seem rather to derive from humanist notions of autonomy. In interpreting the principle of sphere sovereignty we must proceed from divine norms which enable us to understand the limits of human authority, rather than proceeding from human authority which would make the latter into an unlimited norm.

2. Dynamic versus static

This conclusion, however, brings us to a second misunderstanding of the principle of sphere sovereignty, namely, that which interprets it as a static barrier instead of a dynamic calling. A static barrier, a line of defense against all government interference—this is the primary political conclusion which follows when the principle of sphere sovereignty is transposed into a principle of unlimited respect for authority. Then indeed every government measure relating to the market mechanism and free enterprise stands as an attack on the sphere sovereignty of free enterprise. But can we draw the same conclusion if we proceed from the normative interpretation of the principle of sphere sovereignty?

The question is almost rhetorical. For if it is true that the primary norm for every government is to do justice in all matters of public concern, and if it is also true that no industry may set aside the command to act as a genuine steward, it is then clear that if the employer does not act as a good steward, it may be a matter of just governmental action to bring it back to its original calling. Radical intervention by government in social and economic life may then be necessary. Preventing industry from severely polluting our environment, for example, is a matter of public justice. Legislation to prevent such pollution is, therefore, not a violation of the principle of sphere sovereignty; on the contrary, the latter demands such legislation. In this way the government restores public justice to the economy and it does so on the grounds of a deep respect for the unique norm of economic life, namely, the norm of stewardship. For stewardship presupposes that every enterprise should demonstrate direct concern for its natural environment. When the government drives irresponsible enterprises back to their calling, it expresses not a desire to destroy the sphere sovereignty of free enterprise but a desire fully to honor it.

It should be obvious that in this way the principle of sphere sovereignty does not work as a static barrier but as a spur to a dynamic interpretation of the calling of government and business.

In our time we see that through the continual influence of a one-dimensional, materialistic lifestyle, industries often lack completely the dimension of human values in the work environment and display shortcomings with respect to normative economic behavior toward their consumers, their employees, and toward the well-being of their natural surroundings. Instead, they are often nothing more than institutions which pour out the greatest possible stream of consumer goods—industrial sites for combining the factors of production. Is this a salutary existence in accordance with God's norms for economic life, norms that speak of service to one's neighbor, of work fit for people created in the image of God, and of the mandate of stewardship? Of course not. As long as, or as soon as free enterprises are unable or unwilling to open themselves up to these norms for their own sphere, and in doing so cause harm to citizens' legitimate interests, government must intervene to correct the public derailment of these private enterprises. The government will even have to create the public conditions to prod and stimulate every enterprise to open itself up to genuine obedience to these norms of stewardship. Contemporary government has a preeminently dynamic calling to promote in its own way—that is, in a just way—the sphere sovereignty of free enterprise and to do so by directing it to economically responsible behavior toward nature, out of consideration for our fellowmen, with an eye to scarce natural resources, and in service of society as a whole. The closed tunnel of employer behavior must be opened up. Trampled grass must be given a chance to recover. For God's norms—not our own cheap, one-dimensional desires—must be sovereign in economic life.

3. Two-sided versus one-sided

I wish to close my essay by pointing to a third misunderstanding of the principle of sphere sovereignty, namely, that this principle can and must function in only one direction, that is, as a means by which to protect private offices in society from acts of public agencies.

Perhaps this statement flabbergasts some. Is it possible in this matter also to turn the question around? Is it possible to speak of the necessity of asserting the sphere sovereignty of the state over against the actions of private enterprise? This idea would seem to be applicable only in times of bitter revolution, and, therefore, very remote from our wealthy, civilized western world.

At this point, too, I wish to stress how important it is to understand sphere sovereignty as a norm-oriented principle if it is to speak effectively. The state is not an end in itself. The government has the divinely imposed duty to obey the norm of justice in all matters of public interest. This means, however, that it must also have the real possibility to act and react in accordance with that norm. For if citizens impede government in carrying out its task justly toward society, this in fact constitutes a direct assault upon the unique sovereignty of the state. Yet this is precisely what happens in many cases in our modern society. Think of the way that pressure groups try to turn the power of the government into an extension of their own private interests. Or of the techniques used to turn a president into a commercial product that can be sold to the people. And, not least of all, I remind you of the rise in our time of a type of government which is no longer grounded in striving for justice but in seeking endless compromises, which means attempting to divide the booty among the economically powerful and leaving the weak and small to toddle along in the rear. Here, if anywhere, we see a blatant challenge to the sovereignty of biblical norms for the public actions of government. For the central obligation of every government is precisely to protect the weak and to defend the powerless.

A totalitarian state is a demonic thing. It openly ignores the fact that God has given unique norms for family life, for economic life, and for social life, and that in all these spheres people live *coram Deo*, directly before the face of the living God. He is the only One who has the right to lay a total claim on our lives; therefore, a state that tries to do so is demonic. It thereby tries to take the place reserved for God alone. This, however, should not lead us to the conclusion that the only real danger of totalitarianism comes always and solely from the state. This danger can also come from so-called free enterprise when it systematically attempts to make the government an extension of its private, commercial interests and when it continuously tries to transform the family into a platform upon which it can dump an endless stream of consumer goods, even when the cost of it is nothing less than a perpetual steamrolling of current consumer tastes in conformity to the model of its latest advertising campaigns. For what do you think the future is for the unique spheres of government and family in a society whose only hope of happiness is the increase of material welfare and power? I tell you that in the end all these institutions will then be transformed into growth-machines, into institutions that are forced to serve that central goal of our life. They will then lose almost entirely their full diversity of character. For wherever norms lose their authority within the distinct spheres of life, the unique character of each of these spheres will then also disintegrate. We can be crushed by a totalitarian society, but we can also create one ourselves.

Conclusion

Two conclusions may be readily drawn from this entire argument. The first is that the manner in which we are inclined to interpret the principles from which we profess to proceed is more important than those principles themselves. In current interpretations of the principle of sphere sovereignty, also in contemporary American literature, the deepest motives are often more humanistic than Christian, often oriented more to human autonomy than to a consciousness of norms, often directed more to our economic advantages than to the duties of stewardship.

My second conclusion is that, resting upon its biblical foundation, the principle of sphere sovereignty has not only retained a certain validity right up to the present day; but, although nearly forgotten, it has now perhaps reached its point of highest urgency: for we live in a Western culture that in its reductionistic materialism, with its whittling away of all differences, is close to becoming totalitarian.

NORMS FOR THE INTERNATIONAL
ECONOMIC ORDER

Introduction and Statement of the Problem

The purpose of this essay is to ask what norms ought to be applied today and in the future to create a more just international economic order. With a topic like this we immediately face the danger of sliding into daydreaming. In the first place, even back in antiquity compassion was hardly a prominent characteristic of the economic process. "I saw something else under the sun: In the place of judgment—wickedness was there. . . . I saw the tears of the oppressed—and they have no comforter," wrote the Preacher many centuries ago. He added in the same breath, "Power was on the side of their oppressors—and they have no comforter" (Eccl. 3:16; 4:1, *NIV*),

Injustice is a misuse of power. The fight against injustice, which is rooted in the commandment to do justice and love the neighbor, always demands, therefore, a confrontation with what is powerful. Anyone who recognizes this is not about to be overconfident.

Secondly, the development of the world economy points to an aggravation rather than a melioration of injustices. The "trends" which prognosticators detect in what is happening indicate that injustice will increase rather than decrease. A striking example of this is the brief sketch by Rajni Kothari in which he ascribes a partly evil effect to the West's persistent striving for modernization.[8]

> The widely accepted model of modernization along a preconceived course of change has already released forces that will accentuate ethnic and class cleavages, internal violence and armed conflicts between neighbors. The economic gap will continue to widen, minimum conditions will become increasingly hard to achieve except in a few fortunate or favored nations, and patterns of dominance will continue, with at least some of the big powers trying to exploit the existing misery with ready aid, distorting economic policies and mortgaging all future generations to mounting burdens of debt repayment. Poorer countries will continue to be told to engage in family planning to restrain their populations, to integrate their ethnic minorities and "motivate" their illiterate farmers, if necessary through coercive methods, and to leave the real problems of world power and its distribution to be tackled by the big powers through appropriate balances and spheres of influence.[9]

Kothari's sketch is likely one-sided, but his bitterness—he speaks from the context of his experiences in India—is rooted in trends that are very apparent. He summarizes his prediction of the future this way:

> The upshot of all this is a growing dualism in the world, in large part expressed along a North-South hiatus. As this hiatus cannot be resolved militarily—thanks to the oligopolistic control of the balance of terror—and as the institutional structure of international economic relationships will militate against a viable domestic economic solution, the poorer and dependent countries will continue to engage in militant anti-colonial postures, exploited by local power-seekers and demagogues without any regard for the welfare of their people.[10]

Domination, modernization prompted by self-interest, exploitation by the already affluent West which has become hooked on its goals of continuous economic and technological expansion, these factors are threatening to tear the world apart and to arouse counterforces that are themselves not capable of promoting greater justice.

In 1970 the poorest 40 percent of the world's population received 2.9 percent of the gross world product. In 1980 their percentage had fallen to only 2.1 percent. This decline is an indication that even in times of prosperity the economic systems of East and West tend to aggravate injustice rather than to lead to a more just distribution of goods in the world economy. No wonder that since the early 1970s the poor countries of the world have formed power blocs as a counterbalance. They know that the struggle for a more just world economic order will be illusory so long as its creation is dependent only on the good will of the rich countries.

The achievement of justice in international economic relationships is a matter of rowing against the stream, a stream moreover which keeps dragging us back, sometimes beyond the point where the struggle began. . . .

A Short Excursus on the Science of Economics

At first glance it might seem very unnatural to connect the problem of justice in international economic relations with the methodology of economics as a science. The connection between both subjects becomes clearer, however, when we realize that economics as a science is inclined to start with human needs as ends which should be satisfied through the free choice of available means. Consequently, the economist as a student of science expresses himself only with regard to the application of appropriate means to achieve or fulfill those ends.

Economics calls itself an "aspect-science" (concerned only with the economic aspect or dimension of life). Economists acknowledge that in human activity ethical considerations can also play a role. But as a consequence of this "means-ends" construction they tend to regard ethics as connected only with the goals and not with the means of any activity. When considering the means, only one norm is considered valid, namely, that of economic efficiency—the best possible way to accomplish the given goals. Once goals are identified, the economist pretends he knows for sure how the economic subjects will use their means.

This conception of science is striking because of its ideologizing effect. Human needs are, as it were, put first, and are treated as the source for determining the correctness or incorrectness of human economic behavior. Whatever is efficient or useful, whatever optimally satisfies the existing needs, is assumed to be the correct or right means. This is a typically Western conception of science which, instead of being neutral or objective as it pretends, supports a society which proclaims the goals of an ever expanding income and the satisfaction of needs as its central purpose. This is a society, moreover, which tries to use or allocate the means (the necessary labor and capital) in such a way that the obvious needs of the consumer and government are satisfied in the most efficient manner, even when that efficiency brings about, for instance, the alarming loneliness of the laboring man. There is no room, in other words, for any extra-economic normativity in the use of the means; extra-economic norms are recognized only in determining the goals.

This short exposition teaches us anew that when economic *goals* are made central, however responsibly chosen and however ethically responsible, they cannot and may not be a substitute for the immediate validity of *norms* in human society. For the validity of norms concerns not only our chosen goals but also the means we choose and the mode of their application.

The modern student of science (and the politician) is deluded if he thinks that he can contemplate and change the world without starting from a deep respect for given norms. The "values" one chooses on the basis of one's goals will either conform to what is normative or will begin to function as pseudo-norms. Pseudo-norms will, by their very nature, subject society to a process of ideologization which distorts culture and deprives it of freedom.

The scholar who acknowledges *heteronomous norms*—that is, norms that come from the outside—is usually assumed to be at a disadvantage. But, to the contrary, he is more open in his choice of goals and has more of an eye for relativity, while in the application of instruments and means he always asks the question of whether he is doing the right thing. For this very reason such a person is able to make the deepest possible appeal to nations and to their

political and social leaders. For the question concerning what is good and just
is the question which addresses people and societies on the level of their
deepest responsibilities toward God and fellow man. This is the question that
calls people back to the divine norms which have held for human life from
the very beginning. The question of what is good and just is more important
than the questions about what people may be able to accomplish in the future. With the latter question there is only an opening toward results which
we must bring about. With the first question there is an opening toward the
blessing evoked by listening to norms—the law as *Thora*. For blessing is, by
definition, a result which cannot be guaranteed ahead of time.

Basic Norms for the Ordering of Society

Speaking about fixed, given, valid norms for international economic relations, we do not mean thereby fixed and concrete behavioral guidelines.
Rather we are speaking of basic norms which have the character of a
"*Weisung*" (*Thora* for Martin Buber) which open up a path toward the future
on which one can safely walk. Justice is one such basic norm which again and
again must be recognized, developed and followed by men.

Speaking about and searching for norms for international economic relations entails no idealism, only realism. Idealism is characteristic of those
modern designers of the future who by means of planning want to create an
entirely renovated world. In contrast, it is realistic to acknowledge that no society can be permanent if there is not a certain respect for basic norms.

From the perspective of Christian conviction, it can be posited that the
core of human responsibility in this created world is to listen to divine norms.
Only in and through the response of justice, of love for the neighbor, of caring for nature entrusted to us, does this created world reach its destination.
When these norms are negated—which means that power, technology, prosperity do not "open up" to the service of God and fellow men but are given an
independent and autonomous existence—then this created world is bound to
react adversely. The pollution of the environment, malnutrition, loneliness,
and long-term unemployment ought not to be interpreted as a fate but rather
as a failure of human responsibility. They are signs on the walls of this creation that we ourselves have been weighed in the balances and found wanting.

This implies at the same time the possibility of an appeal to ourselves
and others. There are divine norms, and they are valid for everyone—for all
people and for all cultures and societies. "Culture is response" (*Onvlee*). The
awareness of evil in the world might be misshapen and distorted, but where it

exists it points to the validity of norms for people and their societies which cannot and may not be transgressed with impunity.

Where it concerns giving form to an international economic order and correcting the evils that occur on this level, those norms are especially important which apply directly to the economic aspect, the judicial aspect, and the social aspect of the world society. How can we give a more specific designation of these norms without ourselves falling into some ideology, choosing the interpretation which is colored by what we secretly want to safeguard or achieve?

With a "Western" awareness of norms marked by ideals of modernization, desires for power, and dreams of prosperity, there is no possibility of a genuine solution. For it will be clear that in this regard we cannot trust ourselves. To every interpretation of a norm we add our own distortions. But as Christians, it is precisely at this point that we must acknowledge the great importance of a biblical mode of thinking which we must constantly search out anew. For the Bible contains revelation to every man and every society for what is really "good," "true," and of service to our neighbor.

1. The Economic Norm

Economics has become a colorless term, a more or less neutral designation of all human activity that has to do with scarcity. To the degree that in the West it still has a normative significance (economic versus non-economic), it contains no more than a reference to waste and/or a lack of efficiency.

As we noted, that designation of the economic norm contains an ideological restriction which is stamped by the Western mentality that has elevated the expansion of material prosperity to a goal in itself. It is striking that Aristotle contrasted two conceptions of economics: *Chrematistike*, the pursuit of more monetary possessions as good in itself (gain for gain's sake), and *Oikonomia*, the net profitable management of the *Patrimonium*, the goods inherited from the fathers for the benefit of all who are dependent on them for their livelihood. Naturally there is in Aristotle, in his perspective, a certain distortion of the norm. In his thinking the idea of *Oikonomia* serves at least partially to conserve an existing, patriarchal order of society. Moreover, in his thinking moderation is recognizable as an independent human virtue. Aristotle's designation reveals, nonetheless, an important element of truth, which in Western economic expansion has been suppressed for a long time, namely, the mandate calling for the careful management of whatever has been entrusted to humanity for the sake of the welfare of many. The Bible also speaks of the human economic challenge in terms of stewardship, a term which makes clear immediately that human beings are supposed to govern the world by regarding it as belonging to someone else.

In the economic norm of stewardship the following elements can be detected:

a. *Conservation*—the care for this creation and its fruitbearing potential for this and for future generations. To "rob" the world, to exploit it totally for one's own good, clashes with the norm of stewardship.

b. *Avoidance of waste*—the avoidance of the senseless loss of possibilities for use. This normative concept is misused by making it independent and reducing it to (mere) monetary "efficiency," but at its core it remains a legitimate element in our economic mandate. Whatever is of value or has been obtained by labor should not be lost by spendthrift recklessness or lack of insight.

c. *Urgency*—giving preference to those forms of use which are the most urgent in the totality of the fulfillment of our human challenge. Here ideology has also had its influence. Western individualism speaks of the order of priority, of human needs as a purely individual concern, in which everyone autonomously or sovereignly may go to work for himself. But this is a dangerous bypassing of the recognition that the fruits of the world, God's creation, are intended for all people (Calvin). There is the constant danger that "man as steward" will be replaced by "man as owner."

The criterion of urgency involves the distinction between quasi or unnecessary needs and real needs. It is uneconomic (in the sense of violating a divine norm of stewardship) when in a world economy the fulfillment of artificial, advertising-induced needs makes the fulfillment of basic needs impossible or very difficult. That is not only unjust, it is likewise uneconomic. It is an unjust way of managing scarce means in a world economy.

What the basic needs are (that is, needs which deserve priority in the satisfaction of human needs) cannot be determined equally for all times and cultures. They are, however, always connected with what is of vital significance for human existence and for the fulfillment of every human calling. Necessary nutrition, clothing, and shelter belong to it, and likewise the possibility of meaningful labor. It also involves a minimum of common needs, such as the need for education and medical care.

2. The Norm of Justice

Emil Brunner has said that the wealth of the rich is unjust because it makes the poverty of others necessary. This formulation expresses an authentic element of the norm of justice in its validity for economic relations, namely, that no one may be pushed aside or cheated out of what he is entitled to. This holds for persons, but likewise for races, classes, and national groups.

Here too it must be noted that ideologies have done a thorough job. The ideology of the "class struggle" has bent the norm of justice in its own direction by positing that the totality of what has been produced belongs either to the governing class or to the laboring class (in Marx every form of profit and interest is *by definition* exploitation). The ideology of "statism" maintains that to the state belong both the ownership of the land and the means for production as well as the fruits of all human labor—whereby the state from its side obligates itself to support its subjects. The "prosperity" ideology of the West has by and large reduced the norm of justice to a common sharing in the prosperity, for which reason there must constantly be growth (here justice stops with the giving of a financial payment—so-called "social justice"). In contrast the "equality" ideologies hold that everyone should receive an equal share of the total goods and/or products of society (apparently through some governing body, which thus is bound to have a very unequal share in the total exercise of power in society). Finally, we may also mention here the "national" ideologies which bend the demands of justice in the direction of a servility fixed in advance which aims at the preservation of the identity of one's own nation or national existence, even when this creates permanent economic disadvantage or discrimination for those who are not members of the nation but only live in that area. Considering all this, it seems nearly impossible to speak properly about the norm of justice as it pertains to the international order. Nevertheless what follows are some carefully formulated annotations derived from the biblical idea of justice (*tzedeka*).

a. In biblical revelation, justice is never without a double address. It is first of all a call addressed to those who have the right to give orders: to the prince because he has received authority from God, to the judge because he has to pronounce justice, to the property owner because his property gives him the obligation of enabling his neighbor to make a living. Justice always has a specific address, and it *presupposes* existing responsibility.

In the second place there is always a personal address to those who should be the beneficiaries of justice. The widows, the orphans, the Levites without land, the debtors, the laborers—they are always mentioned by name. Though the demand of justice is not limited to those who are mentioned here, it is nevertheless undeniable that to be subject to injustice is particularly the lot of the weaker ones in society. Important to note, also, is that this addressing of specific groups of people again and again exceeds the boundaries of race, nation, social level, and class: the foreigners and sojourners in Israel share in the nation's social and civil legislation. Justice, including its orientation to personal situations, is always specifically oriented; it does not just hang in the air.

b. Justice always includes an emancipation motif. It is never a question of simply giving money or sharing power. It is a motif of liberation, of the comprehensive restoration of life to those who are suppressed and have lost the perspective of a fruitful and happy life. In Biblical revelation, justice and reconciliation belong together. The Bible speaks, therefore, of a justice which must exceed the righteousness of the Pharisees. Justice involves the relief of the oppressed and help to build a new life; prisoners are not only to receive their freedom but they are also to be received again as members of society. The demands of justice must be differentiated from paternalism and humiliation. Justice implies that the other (human being, nation) is restored to *his* rightful place in order to resume and fulfill his own calling.

c. Justice in the biblical sense is not in the first place a choice for or against certain forms of possessions, but it concerns whether the available property is open or closed to people. Justice in ancient Israel demanded of every farmer that he not harvest his entire land, but leave something for all who would pass by, and also that he deposit in the gate one-tenth of his yield for those who might need it. In the legal order of Israel property is not the exclusive title to something.

This rule holds for financial property as well. The poor are entitled to what the rich can give or lend them, without interest payments entering into the picture. In this legal order goods and money connect people, instead of dividing them into classes and groups. Property is subject to every rightful claim of the neighbor.

These elements of biblical thinking on justice will have to be included as criteria for evaluating every international order. At this point it can be said that with respect to each of the three above-mentioned elements in the norm of justice our international order is woefully deficient. In the relationship between the poor and the rich countries one notices that the rich countries consistently seek their own advantage. With respect to the application of the norm of justice, they look first of all within their own borders. It is, moreover, a meager and condescending justice which is "practiced"—there is no attempt to help other countries to achieve their *own* development in accordance with their *own* calling. Another observation is that the social systems of East and West can be called typically closed systems. The possessions of the rich nations are not open to the rightful claims of the poor nations. Rather, exclusive claims are made on raw materials outside the rich countries' own borders in the very heart of countries who may later badly need these same raw materials for their own development.

3. The Social Norm

The economic norm—stewardship—and the norm of justice contain several social aspects. Yet, having said that, it seems that the normativity which is to be characteristic of the social contact between people and nations has not yet been described sufficiently. Social life is also characterized by a normativity of its own. As regards the relation of one person to the other and of one nation to the other, there must also be a direct relation in a bond of "actual" solidarity and respect. For precisely in international *economic* relations there is the danger that mutual relations will be limited to the context of money, goods, and power, dominated by what Martin Buber once called the "I-It" relationship, which can threaten the vital "I-Thou" relationship and also supersede it. Respect for cultures other than one's own deserves an obvious place in all international contacts. If we understand "culture" to be the total mode of association of people with one another and their relationship to nature, then two additional terms can be used to explain what social norms imply— "participation" and "cooperation."

Participation does not require total equality in the power to decide. It does imply that people and nations are directly involved in decisions that have a bearing on their own destination. This norm stems from the creation of each person in the image of God. One may not deal with fellow human beings and fellow nations as if they are will-less objects without their own judgment, their own conscience, their own input. Participation involves, therefore, a direct co-responsibility.

Cooperation includes more than the preparedness to reckon with each other; it expresses the necessity of working together. Without cooperation every form of living together will eventually collapse. Cooperation, too, has its foundation in biblical revelation. People have not been created with differences in order to be unequal, but precisely in order that, as equals, they may depend on each other all the more (Calvin). Cooperation emphasizes the necessity of human societal formation to fulfill responsibilities which can only be born jointly; it is, therefore, the complement of human responsibility. For example, without cooperation, even an idea which in itself is correct, such as that of *self-reliance*—the formation according to one's own insights of one's own society, culturally, socially, and economically—will founder in a limited attempt to achieve autonomy or autarchy. The development of one's own culture ought to be respected, yet at the same time it ought to remain open for service to others.

International Society as the Junction of Norm Realization

. . . The economic systems of East and West have arisen as incarnations of the individualistic or collectivistic technical-material striving of human beings toward progress. This is how an international economic order is distorted—a distortion characterized in the past by Western colonialism and today by economic neocolonialism and an unquestioning quest for modernization.

We must, therefore, not be afraid to plead for concrete reforms and perhaps make or support daring proposals, relative to the international societal order. The point of contact, however, is always the question of where in the existing societal order there are *concrete evils* which involve fundamental deviations from such divine norms as justice and stewardship. With this approach we not only throw up a counterweight to excessive goal-oriented thinking, but we can also gain a clearer understanding of which responsibility is not being fulfilled. We can then appeal to the proper persons or institutions for change in the direction of international economic justice.

To raise the question of responsibility for the failure to establish a reformed international order is important. The preservation and upbuilding of a societal order is always a matter of competencies, of a variety of responsibilities. Insofar as an international economic order is shaped by the action of cooperating national states it is necessary to deal directly with the responsibility of government. Governments have received power in order that they may righteously serve society, without, however, having to regulate everything in it. There exists a personal area of life which ought to be respected. The responsibility of government is always a *public* responsibility. In other words, not every form of injustice, not every evidence of uneconomic or unsocial behavior is a matter of government concern (or, on the international level, of concern to cooperating governments). Such issues only become a government matter when the interests of the entire nation or society of nations are involved.

In regards to the role of the national state in relation to the international economic order, it is best to speak of a duty to act in accordance with the norm of *public justice*—a norm which may induce the national state to participate in international agreements and lead to the establishment of international or supranational institutions. This responsibility includes the duty to (help) create the juridical and institutional framework within which non-government persons and agencies are bound to abide by public norms of cooperation, participation, and stewardship.

It is clear that precisely in the area of international economic relations there are large gaps in the formation and administration of justice. While it is true that within the Western national states the expansion urge of big corporations has in the course of years been curtailed and limited and given a place within a balanced whole of social legislation (environmental legislation, the right of competition, and the like), outside the national territory the right of the strongest is still often determinative. Trade organizations do exist on the international level, but they are often not very effective. In important respects, the market economy of the 19th century is still dominant in the world economy of the 20th century.

This situation is most harmful for the countries of the Third World. The voluntary adoption of rules undertaken by multinational corporations (under the auspices of the United Nations, for example) is a nice gesture, yet it is also an illustration of the lack of public formation of law in this area. The argument that the countries of the Third World should establish their own laws—including national policy for protection of the environment and prevention of the exhaustion of raw materials—is hardly an option. Third World countries cannot do this for the simple reason that most of them remain too much dependent on Western corporations established in their countries and on the need to continually attract Western capital.

Clearly we cannot expect Third World countries to compete against economic and political superpowers and, at the same time, bridle and tame them. Furthermore, we should not lose sight of the fact that outside the territory of Third World countries, and also outside of the territories of the First and Second Worlds, there are the world oceans where the hunt for raw materials is still very much a free-for-all. Wherever the economic power goes, there justice must go along to correct that power and, where necessary, to limit and restrain it. But that implies the necessity of an international order of justice which is able to issue regulative and binding directives on the basis of public norms for justice in international economic relations. The establishment of such an international order would provide the peoples of all countries the opportunity to work through their governments to achieve global cooperation. This would also be a way in which those who are involved with the global duty of being good stewards could better exercise their calling in the world.

NOTES

[1] Selections from (1) Bob Goudzwaard's "Christelijke Politiek en het Principe van de 'Souvereiniteit in Eigen Kring'," *Anti-Revolutionaire Staatkunde* (March, 1977), translated and edited by Harry der Nederlander with the assistance of Gordon Spykman; and (2) "Norms for the International Economic order," edited from a paper by Bob Goudzwaard with the assistance of John van Baars, first presented at the Second International Conference of Reformed Institutions for Christian Higher Education at Calvin College, August, 1978. The papers of that conference were published under the title *Justice in the International Economic Order*, Proceedings of the Second International Conference of Reformed Institutions for Christian Higher Educaiton (Grand Rapids, Michigan: Trustees of Calvin College, 1980).

[2] Goudzwaard's translated books include *Idols of Our Time* (Downers Grove, IL: Inter-Varsity Press, 1984); *Capitalism and Progress: A Diagnosis of Western Society*, trans. J. Zylstra (Toronto: Wedge Publishing Foundation, and Grand Rapids: Eerdmans, 1979); *Aid for the Overdeveloped West* (Toronto: Wedge Publishing Foundation, 1975); and *A Christian Political Option* (Toronto: Wedge Publishing Foundation, 1972).

[3] See Herman Dooyeweerd, *Roots of Western Culture: Pagan, Secular, and Christian Options*, trans. J. Kraay; eds. M. Vander Vennen and B. Zylstra (Toronto: Wedge Publishing Foundation, 1979), vii-xii, 1-6.

[4] Some of Goudzwaard's articles as well as those of others in these debates, can be found in the quarterly *Anti-Revolutionary Staatkunde*, and in the bi-weekly *Nederlandse Gedachten* from the early 1970s until the early 1980s.

[5] Goudzwaard, "Christelijke Politiek," 63-77.

[6] Goudzwaard, "Norms for the International Economic Order," 223-253.

[7] *Ibid.*

[8] Rajni Kothari, "World Politics and World Order: The Issue of Autonomy," in Saul H. Mendlovitz, ed., *On the Creation of a Just World Order: Preferred Worlds for the 1990's* (New York: The Free Press, 1975), 39-69.

[9] *Ibid.*, 40.

[10] *Ibid.*

IV

THREE VIEWS OF
SOCIAL PLURALISM: A CRITICAL
EVALUATION

NINETEEN

✠✠✠✠✠✠✠✠✠✠

HISTORY, THE UNFOLDING OF SOCIETY, AND HUMAN FULFILLMENT: AN EVALUATION

E arly in the book's Introduction, when we explored the context of the contemporary American debate over the plural structure of society, we considered, among others, the work of Robert Nisbet, Theodore Lowi, and Michael Walzer. Criticizing American individualism, interest-group liberalism, and political egalitarianism, these authors appeal to history. We raised questions at that point that bear directly on our critical evaluation of the writings of Edmund Burke, Groen van Prinsterer, Otto von Gierke, J.N. Figgis, and José Míguez Bonino. We asked, for example: What is the source of the norms or standards that the American thinkers use for recognizing the proper boundaries of different social spheres? If the boundaries are not natural or heteronomous but only artificial, then how can one make a normative argument about how those spheres *ought* and *ought not* to be shaped? Do the multiple spheres of a differentiated society have any grounding in a natural or divine order which is less historically relativistic than the American authors assume?

We now return to these questions as we evaluate the arguments from history, because each of the readings in Part I seems to confront the same problems and limits. While arguments from history seek to hold on to, or point toward, a certain kind of society, their philosophical or ontological basis for recognizing the proper and legitimate identities, tasks, and rights of diverse institutions remains unclear. This is as evident in the thought of "backward lookers" Burke, Gierke, Figgis, and Groen as it is in the thinking of "forward looker" Míguez Bonino.

Burke and Figgis

There are some striking similarities in the writings of Burke and Figgis. For example, they react negatively to the destructive leveling forces unleashed by the French Revolution. As a bulwark against the atomization of society they both appeal to history and to the variety of associations and institutions that have become differentiated over time. And similarly, much of the ambiguity in their thinking about the basis of a differentiated social order can be traced to the same three factors: (1) they fail to distinguish adequately between society and the state; (2) they often use social-contract terminology (based on what Burke refers to as "analogical precedent, authority and example") in defense of a diversified social order; and (3) they continue, to some extent, to rely on traditional Christian and natural-law arguments without sufficient critical and systematic reflection on what is old and new in their thinking. As a result Burke and Figgis do not develop the philosophic basis for an account of the identity, tasks, and rights of differentiated institutions in society.

In reference to the first factor, neither Burke nor Figgis adequately distinguishes between society and state. For Burke, these two are virtually the same, as illustrated by the following statement:

> Society is indeed a contract. Subordinate contracts for objects of mere occasional interest may be dissolved at pleasure—but the state ought not to be considered as nothing better than a partnership agreement in a trade of pepper and coffee, calico, or tobacco, or some other such low concern, to be taken up for a little temporary interest, and to be dissolved by the fancy of the parties.[1]

This ambiguity means that sometimes when Burke refers to society or the state he has in mind an organic union of all spheres of a social order which has evolved and matured in the course of history. At other times he uses the word "state" to refer specifically to government in contrast to the other spheres of society. The failure to account adequately for the difference between society and state means a lack of clarity regarding the basis for, and the structure of, a differentiated social order. In fact, the lack of clarity leaves an opening for collectivist assumptions to creep in as they did around the time the English pluralists found themselves reacting to state absolutist claims in Great Britain.

Figgis' argument from history is plagued by the same ambiguity. Instead of clearly distinguishing state from society, Figgis views the state as a *communitas communitatum* (society of societies).[2] The state is a composition of social entities, "a synthesis of living wills."[3] The state is not itself an institution which possesses a separate identity from society. Indeed, a person is a member of the state only through membership in other institutions of society, as Figgis sees it. And thus, because the state is a "society of societies" Figgis writes about churches *in* the modern state rather than churches *and* the modern state.[4] Though his intent is obviously to affirm the multiplicity of "societies" in the state, his reasoning leaves him open to universalist claims by the state over all of society. Thus, when he says at one point that the state is to "control and limit within the bounds of justice, the activities of all minor associations whatsoever,"[5] he is unable to give a strong philosophical or legal argument for what he means by "the bounds of justice."

Fearful of the growing power of a centralized state, Figgis looks for a way to deny the state any substantive authority within other spheres of society. But in the process he does not articulate the state's specific, limited responsibility to govern "within the bounds of justice." He tries to replace state sovereignty with the sovereignty of nonpolitical institutions without ever clarifying how "the bounds of justice" are to be established if the state has only a limited role to perform in society. And if the state is restricted in its responsibility for society, how is a just social order to be preserved? Figgis' view of the state is essentially a negative one, and provides no answer to these important questions.

Figgis' understanding of pluralism, which rests on an appeal to the variety of institutions that have appeared in the course of history, does not provide him with an adequate basis for identifying each societal structure. This is particularly evident in the case of the state. He is unable to define a norm or standard by which to judge between a just and an unjust state, other than to point to Dutch and English examples which he approves. But pointing approvingly to certain examples of limited states is not sufficient as a normative argument for the proper distinction between state and society. Arguments from history can as easily give authoritative sanction to non-pluralist societies which have gained a historical foothold.

A second reason for the ambiguity in Burke's and Figgis' understanding of a differentiated social order can be traced to the fact that they often use social contract terminology to support their views. In this case, the impact is in the direction of individualism rather than collectivism. Burke speaks of civil

society as the "offspring of convention" and of the presence of "artificial institutions" in society.[6] Further, when he refers to "the great primeval contract of
eternal society," and contends that societal entities are linked in a fixed compact, "each [entity] in their appointed place," the basis for such a diversified
order, apart from the historical accumulation of individual contracts, is never
made clear.[7] At times his language sounds very much like the radicals whom
he criticizes so vigorously. If social institutions grow from "conventions" ar-
tificially, why can't people create new institutions at will, in any shape they
desire, as history unfolds? What is so sacred or rational about what existed
prior to the French Revolution or what now exists? Why should we side with
Burke rather than with the revolutionaries in history?

There is a danger in concluding too much from Burke's use of social-
contract terminology. For example, John MacCunn points out that Burke's
words are often those of the eighteenth century even though his thinking is
closely related to nineteenth-century organic views of society.[8] Crane Brinton
agrees that it would be a mistake to believe that just because Burke used social-contract language his social philosophy is rooted in Lockean individualism. Brinton concludes that Burke's thought is clearly tied to concepts of the
medieval Christian tradition.[9] But whether Burke's perspective is to be identified more with a medieval Christian view or with a nineteenth-century organic view of society, the point is that we may find it easier to understand
what Burke opposes than to grasp the principled basis he has for defending a
diversified social order. This problem, we believe, is intrinsic to every
"argument from history." History rather than the "individual" or "society" is
absolutized, and yet "history" cannot itself provide the norms or standards for
the structure of society. At best, the weight of history bears testimony to the
success or failure, the progress or regress of human social development, depending on the norms to which one appeals in making judgments.

The lack of a clear, ontological basis for the independent identity, tasks,
and rights of social entities becomes even more evident when Burke employs,
by analogy, an essentially individualist argument to enlist respect for the civil
institutions of society. Burke argues: "We procure reverence to our civil institutions on the principle upon which nature teaches us to revere individual
men: on account of their age and on account of those from whom they are descended."[10] This analogical argument rests on nothing more than the hope
that an appreciation for the age and ancestry of persons can be transferred to
a reverence for the age and ancestry of the many institutions that have become differentiated in the course of history.

To Burke's credit, even though he relies heavily on the argument from
analogy, he is conscious of its abuse. He says that we should not speculate in

using an argument from analogy. To affirm that states go through stages of infancy, adulthood, and old age is only a loose analogy.

> Parallels of this sort rather furnish similitudes to illustrate or to adorn, than supply analogies from whence to reason. The objects which are attempted to be forced into an analogy are not found in the same classes of existence. Individuals are physical beings subject to laws universal and invariable. The immediate cause acting in these laws may be obscure; the general results are subjects of certain calculation. But commonwealths are not physical but moral essences. They are artificial combinations, and, in their proximate efficient cause, the arbitrary productions of the human mind. We are not yet acquainted with the laws which necessarily influence the stability of that kind of work made by that kind of agent.[11]

This statement manifests Burke's caution in view of the potential abuse of an argument from analogy. But it also shows how he uses individualist and historicist language ("artificial combinations," "arbitrary productions of the human mind") to make his case.

Burke's argument based on "analogical precedent, authority and example" is repeated by Figgis. Figgis follows the lead of Gierke in contending that groups in society— institutions such as the family, church, school, and trade union—possess real personalities. Groups, according to Figgis, should be considered living and organic entities, having a mind and will of their own.[12] Just as freedom demands that room be given to individuals for their self-development, so, too, the development of the real personality of associations— that is, of their freedom—is necessary for true liberty to exist. Figgis' argument from analogy is clearly stated in his critique of state absolutism which he believes was "the child of the Renaissance and [Reformation] and the grandchild of the Pagan State." He continues:

> Now the State did not create the family, nor did it create the Churches; nor even in any real sense can it be said to have created the club or the trades union; nor in the Middle Ages the guild or the religious order, hardly even the universities: *they have all arisen out of the natural associative instincts of mankind, and should all be treated by the supreme authority as having a life original and guaranteed, to be controlled and directed like persons.* . . .[13]

Figgis' appreciation of Dutch history and particularly the work of Johannes Althusius comes from his conviction that the post-Reformation experience of the Netherlands set the stage for the best forms of the modern constitutional recognition of free and differentiated societies.

But why should we agree with Figgis that Althusius and the early Netherlands came closer than others to the norm for a plural society? History also took shape in other directions, and Figgis believes that some regress also occurred in The Netherlands. So, clearly, his standards of judgment do not simply arise *from* history. Whence do they come, and do they amount to anything more than his self-assertive preferences? In the perspective of Burke and Figgis the ontological and normative basis for a differentiated order is missing. Their historical (frequently historicist) arguments do not provide a framework for judging between legitimate and illegitimate, healthy and unhealthy institutions that come into historical existence. If we agree with their view of life, then we too will appreciate Althusius and Gierke, but what has history actually proved?

Otto von Gierke

Gierke's historical reasoning is more complex, organic, and dialectical than that of Burke and Figgis. Gierke's interpretation of the five periods of European history shows, for example, the manner in which he recognizes the differentiation of the state from society in the contemporary (fifth) period. In fact, Gierke's insight into the peculiar nature of modern social differentiation is, from our point of view, perhaps his most important contribution.

Unlike medieval fellowships, which tended, as Gierke explains, "to extend each group of fellows over the whole person and simply make it into a community [*Gemeinschaft*],"[14] modern fellowships take a far more differentiated shape. The *"purposes of each individual association are precisely defined, and its organisation adapted and its significance limited accordingly. . . . It is, in short, the general rule today that freely formed associations are confined to single specialised purposes."*[15] Hand in hand with this differentiation process, the state itself —"the highest association"—takes on a more limited scope and more precisely defined purposes.[16]

Yet Gierke, in our view, offers only a rudimentary normative account of the distinct identities and characteristics of these groups. To say that modern associations form around specialized purposes does not say enough about the distinguishing identities and characters of different groups. Might any group organize for any purpose and define its membership in any fashion? Do the chosen "purposes" define a group, or does the special nature of a group circumscribe and give birth to its purposes? Why cannot, or should not, a family set as its purpose to be a business enterprise, or a church to be a political lobby group, a counseling center, a worship community, and a relief agency all at the same time? Is there anything that would be inappropriate about a modern, differentiated association trying to become an undifferentiated *Gemeinschaft*, seeking to extend itself over the whole life of its members?

Though Gierke describes a wide variety of groups and even shows how they have expressed themselves in law, the actual differentiation appears to be grounded in nothing more than the historical unfolding of an organic, human sociability. In other words, all social structurations arise from human freedom and take on group personalities. But how does Gierke escape the conclusion that each fellowship at any given point in history exhibits its identity as a matter of simple arbitrariness, as a relative accident? Gierke may believe, as Walzer and Jeffrey Stout believe, that the boundaries and the virtues of diverse social structures do not arise from thin air and that distributive justice requires that public law respect diverse associations. But if all the norms and boundaries are relative to historical change, then the moral argument for what *ought* to exist seems to erode.

Furthermore, if the organic, historical unfolding of national communities has an inevitable character to it, how does Gierke escape the problem of determinism which leaves no room for human freedom or for human actions based on normative judgments? In other words, how can history take any course other than the one it is taking?

Antony Black argues that Gierke's method of interpreting history is not strictly speaking idealist.

> He insists that the relation between ideas and actual "forms of life" is one of "two-sided causality" or "reciprocal action" . . . . He speaks of institutions as embodying ideas. The nearest he comes to a general historical *explanans* is the German people, in whose national life and consciousness (*Volksbewusstsein*) fellowship and lordship ebb and flow. But even here he does not, I think, imply that people develop institutions because they have a mind to: that would be a necessary but not a sufficient condition, for he clearly thinks that circumstances have to be appropriate.[17]

When Gierke turns his attention to the modern state, recognizing as he does its historical differentiation from other associations, he still does not go beyond "the people" in offering a ground for the formation of every other association. The modern association movement, says Gierke, "draws the whole nation into its circle,"[18] and is thereby beginning "to relocate the state itself within the people."[19]

> For, through a representative constitution, public control of the administration, the participation of the people in law-making and the restoration of traditional [*volksthümlich*] criminal adjudication, it [the modern association movement] has given expression to the idea that the state is nothing other than the organised people. It has built up the state under sovereign leadership but on the basis of a fellowship of citizens.[20]

But, we may ask, what should keep the people from trying to do anything and everything with and through the state, thereby obliterating many if not all of the rights of their other associations? What is the necessary, normative character of the state that ought to limit it with respect to other fellowships of citizens? Apart from emphasizing that politically free human beings have, in the modern period, been forming many associations and therefore would not countenance state absolutism, Gierke does not adequately answer these questions.

In fact, Gierke's somewhat Hegelian interpretation of historical development in Germany raises most of the same questions about the source of the norms for his judgments that we raised about Burke's and Figgis' arguments from history. The fact that for Gierke Germany plays such a crucial and distinct role in the historical emergence of groups only accentuates the question about universal normativity. In what respect may we assume that the German experience is, as Gierke seems to assume, normative for other nations and peoples? Even if Gierke is accurate in his historical account of social change in Germany, what allows his description to become a normative judgment about universal history?

It seems clear that Gierke's careful study of law and historical change in German lands is strongly guided by romantic, nationalist prejudgments and presuppositions. He is convinced that history is moving forward, however dialectically, toward the realization of a synthesis of human freedom and ordered unity which will become fully manifest in pluralistically differentiated nations bound together in the highest fellowship of representative, constitutional states. This *ought* to be the direction of history for all peoples, Gierke implies, and Germany simply represents the vanguard of history. According to Black, "Gierke's reading of history clearly had a millenarist aspect, similar to what we find in Hegel and Marx: today is witnessing the consummation of historical development, and all the promise of the past ages is going to be fulfilled in the not too distant future."[21]

If Gierke's presuppositions and view of the direction of history are accurate, then his moral argument transcends German history. But if Gierke's judgment is truly the fruit of the German experience and is reflective of a distinctly German contribution to world history, then his normative argument about the direction of history is surely relative in its entirety to Germany's and his own historical moment. Rather than bearing the burden of universal truth, his argument drowns in a sea of relativism. If romantic nationalism is the "truth" of history, then Gierke's argument cannot transcend his own history. If, on the other hand, the truth about history's direction and aim is universal, then the basis of that truth must be deeper than the historical experience of the German people.

According to Black, Gierke moved away later in his life from the emphasis on social diversity to an increasing preoccupation with the supreme fellowship of the German nation state. Much like Laski's shift "from pluralism to collectivism,"[22] Gierke shifted from complex pluralism to an almost "mystical nationalism."[23] After 1868, says Black, Gierke "made hardly any noteworthy contribution to the question of how the state and association are related."[24] Whatever the causes for such a shift, we believe that the lack of a non-historicist, ontological basis for social pluralism allowed Gierke to make the shift more easily than might otherwise have been the case.

Groen van Prinsterer

Like Burke and Figgis, Groen van Prinsterer opposes the abstract reasoning of the Revolutionaries, the leveling tendency of their ideas, and their radical repudiation of the past. He also shares with Gierke a degree of organic, romantic nationalism. Groen's opposition to the French Revolution and liberalism, however, is inspired by a more explicitly articulated desire for Christian social reform. Groen discerns the religious roots of the revolutionary events; he recognizes the conflict of *religious motives* at work in the different conceptions of society. He describes the deeper meaning of the Revolution as an attempt to overturn the divine order. He recognizes that history can be misshaped and therefore that its weight can be negative as well as positive.

Groen's primary concern, is not to defend the political, economic, or social order of the *ancien régime* or even of the contemporary social order of the mid-nineteenth-century Netherlands. It is, rather, to point out that the revolutionaries rejected faith in the revelatory light of God's Word and placed their faith in human reason. Groen demonstrates how this new faith manifested itself in the social order designed by the French revolutionaries. Groen, more than Burke, Figgis, or Gierke, concentrates on the religious root of the Revolution—on the conflict of religious motives in the shaping of history. He believes that the Revolution represented human abandonment of the "law and ordinances of God." He concludes that Enlightenment unbelief was the basis upon which the revolutionaries attempted an "artificial reconstruction of society"—the rebuilding of society in an abstract and unhistorical way.[25]

At the same time, however, Groen shares some characteristic habits of thought with Burke, Figgis, and Gierke. While he does not fully subscribe to the position that the meaning of events emerges entirely from within the stream of historical development, nonetheless, his argument "from revelation" is closely bound up with his argument "from history."[26] At times Groen argues that God's revelation is "the foundation of justice and morality, of freedom and authority for private persons as well as for nations and governments."[27] But at other times he argues that "In essence my whole argument will be *historical*. . . . History alone will be our instructor."[28] This historicist tendency leads Groen to refer to the antirevolutionary movement in The Netherlands as the "Christian-historical position."[29]

Early in his career, Groen was influenced not only by Burke, but by other conservatives like Karl Von Haller and Friedrich Julius Stahl.[30] Dutch philosopher J. D. Dengerink contends that there were two main periods in Groen's intellectual development:[31] (1) in the first period, he was influenced by von Haller's private-law conception of governmental authority, a period, which culminated in the publication of *Unbelief and Revolution*; (2) in the second period after 1847, Groen came increasingly under the influence of Stahl and started to place greater stress on the public-law character of the state.

Von Haller denied the existence of an original state of nature, devoid of social relationships. Human beings have always existed in society through a hierarchy of communities, with the highest ones having no further power above them. These superior communities are merely the most highly developed forms of private associations. Their distinctive character lies only in their ultimate independence—their sovereignty.

Groen, following von Haller, says that the state is the most highly developed form of a private association. It is characterized by private law, the reflection and influence of which can be found in all other social relations. The state distinguishes itself only by its independence, and recognizes only God above itself.[32] In this view there is no awareness of the state as a distinguishable *res publica*—an institution established for the sake of public justice. Also missing is the recognition of civil law which recognizes persons as being endowed with public legal rights distinguishable from their rights, identities, and memberships in different private communities. The state, for the early Groen, then, is the central organ around which all other associations (including municipalities and regions) are grouped. The relative autonomy of each association is acquired historically (by organic analogy) only within this hierarchy; it does not derive from a distinguishable inner character of each association in its own right.

In the earlier period, Groen does not seek to provide an account of the distinct internal identity, tasks, and rights of different social institutions and relationships. He perceives no essential difference between the authority exercised by the head of a family or a trade union president and that exercised by a king or prince. The state is different only in having supremacy or independence, i.e., sovereign authority. While he defends the external freedom of the lower communities or spheres of society against steady trends toward political centralization, this seems to have been little more than a conservative stance in face of the French centralizing influence in The Netherlands following the Napoleonic era.[33]

Later, under the influence of Stahl, Groen comes to a broader conception of government as a *res publica* under the sovereignty of God. He conceives of the state as a public institution that cannot be classed according to private property rights. But, under Stahl's influence, Groen also imbibes a form of historicism by which he attributes the structure of society to the historical unfolding process. While he insists that all earthly authority is obliged to comply with God's revealed will, he does not conceive of the different associations or spheres of society as owing their normative identities to God's creation order. The various societal spheres are for Groen merely the historical off-shoots of particular national communities. In this sense, Groen is very much like Gierke.

A national community such as The Netherlands, according to Groen, should not be thought of as a mass of individuals, but as an organic whole, composed of the multitude of social relations and acquired rights. These historically-acquired rights demand respect. The government should recognize the independence of established associations or institutions. A relative individuality or independence of the subordinated parts must be upheld if the whole national community is to live in peace. But why should we follow Groen in accepting as normative the character of society in the Netherlands at any particular stage in its history? Groen cannot answer this question to our satisfaction.

As in the case of Burke, Figgis, and Gierke, Groen fails, even later in his career, to differentiate adequately between society and state. The problem is rooted in his understanding of the historical unfolding of the national community. For him the state represents the "whole," while other spheres, except for the church, are organic parts of it. Only when considering the relation of church and state does Groen come close to transcending this type of organic historicism. Here he tries to articulate the principled differences between two institutions without falling back on organic analogies and arguments. With respect to church and state Groen offers something different from the idea of a national community identified as the "whole" of which all social relationships are "parts." The spiritual and temporal areas should be separated, he says,

> in order to submit Church and State, each in its own sphere, to the immediate power
> of Him to Whom has been given all power in heaven and on earth, in order to
> establish not an atheistic but a lay (secular) state; not an absolute state, but a
> state subordinated to the divine will, a Christian state.[34]

Groen suggests that church and state are two independent spheres, each having its own authority in direct responsibility to God. The state, then, should not be Christianized by bringing it under church control but by recognizing the unique character and position of its authority under God. At the same time the purity of the church's confession ought not to be determined by state intervention, and it is not simply an organic natural part of the national community. The state should not have authority to establish doctrine. That power and authority belong to the church itself. Groen is not entirely consistent, however, even in this conception. He wants to allow the church to lean on state support, for example, when it is struggling against those who oppose the church's doctrine from within.

Groen is the first to use the phrase "sovereignty in its own sphere" (*souvereiniteit in eigen sfeer*) when trying to articulate the principled basis for distinguishing different social structures and identities. But he applies the phrase only to the relation of church and state. He does not work it out as a creational principle of universal societal scope.

In summary, Groen's reaction to Enlightenment individualism is influenced by historicism. He assumes that institutions acquire their identity, tasks, and rights in the course of historical development. Concerning this point, H. Evan Runner makes two important observations that also apply to some degree to Burke, Figgis, and Gierke. First, he notes that Groen's argument provides at best only a relative guarantee for the independence of the various associations and spheres of society. Runner asks, "For what—except the will to be a conservative . . . gives the right to call a halt to historical change at any particular stage of it?"[35] "If rights are historically acquired," Runner asks, "what about the 'rights' of the new revolutionary movement?"[36] How far would the revolutionary movement "have to go, and how long would it have to prevail, before it too became integrated in the slow 'growth' of history?"[37] Second, Runner observes that by taking historically-acquired rights as the criterion of independence there is "no satisfactory way of judging what are really independent spheres."[38] Groen leaves himself with no adequate basis for accounting directly for the identity, tasks, and rights of the many institutions in society.

José Míguez Bonino

Míguez Bonino takes history as seriously as did Burke, Figgis, and Groen. But, unlike the "backward lookers," he looks to the future unfolding of history for the transformation of social structures and for the liberation of the poor and dispossessed in Latin America and elsewhere. A true liberation movement, however, will require "a coherent and all-embracing method of sociopolitical analysis."[39] His "quest for a new society" leads him to look for such a method in a synthesis of Christian and Marxist assumptions regarding the nature of social reality. If Burke, Figgis, and other English pluralists sometimes come close to ontological individualism in their mode of historical argument, Míguez Bonino certainly comes close to Marxist collectivism in his.

In order to appreciate Míguez Bonino's social philosophy, we must understand his hermeneutical method because for him, as for Groen, the truth of biblical revelation transcends all social theory, ideologies, and actual social structures. He also firmly believes that correct theology and social theory must be developed in close relationship to the concrete events of history. In the midst of historical practice people should look to the Bible and the Christian theological tradition in order to find answers to their questions about what *ought* to exist.[40] But this cannot be done by individuals alone. Míguez Bonino argues that "a Christian hermeneutics is unthinkable as a purely individual undertaking. It necessarily presupposes a 'hermeneutical community'."[41] For him the hermeneutical community is the Christian church engaged in the struggle for liberation.

Míguez Bonino does contend that contemporary social life in Latin America can best be described by using traditional Marxist terms such as "class struggle." The experiences of history are proof that the poor and the dispossessed are an oppressed class, he argues. This fact is an analytical judgment that emerges objectively out of the historical conditions of modern societies.

> Class struggle is a fact. . . . When a fact is introduced in Christian reflection, one cannot be satisfied with merely recording it; it demands to be understood both in its operation and significance and to be theologically evaluated. At this point the Marxist analysis is, I think, indispensable. It must be corrected and refined in the context of action and theory, but it is, so far, the best instrument we have to understand the fact.[42]

Classes and their conflict function as a major category in Míguez Bonino's understanding of history.

Although he does not hesitate to use Marxist categories when he believes they accurately reflect the way things are, he also contends that it is possible to separate Marxist "facts" from Marxist revolutionary theory or ideology. This must be done because a revolutionary theory moves beyond scientific observation to offer (1) an account of the causes, dynamics, and direction of the process of social reality; and (2) a strategy for overcoming what is judged to be unjust and antihuman in the present structure of society.[43] Míguez Bonino is thus willing to accept a Marxist "fact" at the same time that he wants to correct Marxist revolutionary theory on Christian ethical grounds. Moreover, he believes that while the non-Christian revolutionary and the Christian often find themselves bound together in a common struggle as they seek to create a new society, they actually relate their immediate revolutionary goals to their conceptions of final destiny in different ways. Míguez Bonino thus attempts to separate "fact" from "value." He assumes it is possible to divorce a Marxist fact (class struggle) from Marxist theory (goals and tactics).

Curiously, while Míguez Bonino is highly critical of dualist tendencies in the thought of others, he accepts without qualm this kind of fact/value distinction which disguises the real conflict between deep religious motives— between Christian and Marxist visions in history. More like Burke and Figgis than like Groen, Míguez Bonino fights against what he believes is an unjust social order without being able to sort out the conflicting religious motives behind Marxist and Christian views of humanity and society. But whereas Burke and Figgis appeal to the past against a degenerating present, Míguez Bonino appeals to the future against an unjust past and present.

Although Míguez Bonino uses Marxist "facts" in his evaluation of injustices, he reaches for Christian categories to find an alternative social vision, though a biblical social ideal is never developed in any detail. For example, he suggests that an appreciation of the relation between creation and salvation in the Bible might provide the basis for an alternative theological framework and vision for society.[44] The creational and soteriological themes are expressed in the biblical language of "covenant of creation" and "covenant of redemption."[45] By the "covenant of creation" Míguez Bonino is referring not to "the rational order of things," to which conservatives often appeal in order to support the status quo—a static and stratified society. Rather, his reference is to the dynamic unfolding of humanity's God-given possibilities within history. "Creation," he says, "is the installation of a movement; it is an invitation and a command to man to create his own history and culture, creatively to transform the world and make it into his own house and to explore the configurations of human relationships available to him."[46]

However commendable this statement may appear to be, it does not illumine normative criteria by which people should shape and judge the quality and legitimacy of a diversified society. It does not provide the criteria for judging the errors made in history by people creatively transforming the world. It appeals to a future constructive expression of human freedom against past experiences of oppression. But without articulating biblical covenant boundaries, this sentiment is hardly distinguishable from liberal and Marxist appeals for freedom, neither of which depends on biblical covenant categories. His statement remains confined, at best, to what reformed theologians call the "cultural mandate" in creation (Genesis 1:28). The cultural mandate is God's command to develop and subdue the earth (in the biblical sense)—a dynamic call to be fruitful and to draw out all the possibilities of creation to the glory of God. Even though sin prevents human activity from bringing creation to its proper fulfillment, God has upheld the cultural mandate by his common grace. Human cultural activity remains a response to God's command to discover, develop, disclose, open up, and actualize the creation. This divine command accounts for the forward-looking meaning of history.

But one should not, as Míguez Bonino seems to do, confuse the cultural mandate with the *order* of creation itself. Biblically speaking, the normative structure of creation is not antithetical to human historical responsibility. The creation order is, therefore, not historically rigid or static. But there is more to the creation than an open-ended cultural mandate. The creation, with humanity as its crown, is an expression of the holy will of the Creator. It represents the totality of created things, plants, animals, and humans, as well as the ordering principles of all social relationships and institutions. The cultural mandate should, therefore, be conceived as the dynamic call to humanity to heed the order of creation in obedience to the Creator.

What is lacking in Míguez Bonino's perspective, as in Groen's, Burke's, Figgis', and Gierke's is a developed philosophy of creation. While he looks ahead to the unfolding of a just and differentiated social order—an order which should come to expression in "the corporeality of history"—he is no more able to provide an ontological basis for a differentiated society than was Burke, Figgis or Groen. If history has brought us only injustice and oppression to date, why should we have confidence that the future will be different? If God will release captives and overcome the oppressive structures of contemporary society, what structure will the future society have? By what creational principles should we evaluate the future shape and interrelationships of state, church, family, school, business enterprise, and individuals? If people follow Marx, what is to keep them from falling into collectivist oppression as they escape from capitalist oppression?

Míguez Bonino regards the "covenant of redemption" as the soteriological work of Jesus Christ in history. The church is commissioned to proclaim God's salvation in Jesus Christ. This means "the forgiveness of sins, namely man's freedom in God's grace to take up again, in whatever circumstances and after whatever failure and destruction, the work committed to him in creation. It means, also in traditional terms, the call to the sanctification of man, namely, the invitation to effective love and the freedom to love."[47] This soteriological work of Christ—this "covenant of redemption"—is the basis of all human liberation, according to Míguez Bonino. In order to comprehend the truth of this gospel message we must consider the covenant of redemption in relationship to the covenant of creation. To emphasize the soteriological role of Christ in isolation, as so many Christians do, can lead to an individualistic and other-worldly understanding of the gospel. Instead, we should recognize "the significance of the soteriological without swallowing up the creational."[48] But Míguez Bonino does not develop this comment. His future-oriented hope for a new society never really goes beyond the expression of a freedom ideal. He does not look for society's ontological foundation in the order of creation. A normative, creationally grounded framework for a pluralist society that is neither individualist nor collectivist does not emerge from the writings of this theologian of liberation.

Gary J. Dorrien is especially critical of Míguez Bonino's Marxist-Christian synthesis. Dorrien admits that Míguez Bonino does not actually advocate a centralized collectivist "solution" for Third World oppression. Liberation theology calls for freedom, not for new forms of oppression. But, says Dorrien, the problem with Míguez Bonino's socialist project "is that it *isn't* very concrete. It largely avoids, for example, the questions about centralization of authority, market freedom, and political rights."[49] Consequently, Míguez Bonino is unable to be as critical as he should be of "economic inefficiency and bureaucratic authoritarianism that have characterized the various command economies of the past century."[50] In the hope of seeing a more just society in the future, Míguez Bonino calls for the further unfolding of history toward a full range of diversified human achievements and fulfillment. But his use of Marxist "facts" in conjunction with a biblical prophetic appeal is insufficient to chart a normative course for social and political reform that will ring true to the Bible's revelation about creation order, human sin, and divine redemption in history.

The "argument from history" then, whether orientated to the past or the future, raises many questions for those who are looking for a solid foundation on which to develop a theory of social pluralism. Many of those questions have not been (and we think, cannot be) answered from the "facts" and the "course" of history alone. For example, how does one avoid arbitrariness, historicism, traditionalism, or revolutionary negation in judging the legitimacy or illegitimacy of particular institutions and groups that have arisen in the past or that will be created in the future? What criteria does one use to decide when particular forms of social life are enslaving? What constitutes positive, liberated social life? What kind of state, in particular, is legitimate for a pluralistic society? Once individualism or collectivism has gained a foothold in history, on what basis is it to be opposed? Burke, Figgis, Groen, Gierke, and Míguez Bonino seem to be more certain of what they reject as unhealthy forms of society than of what they accept as the principles or standards for diversifying social structures. Is there a genuine social pluralism implicit in their arguments, or are they simply rejecting individualist and collectivist options? Moreover, while there is a concern for social diversity in their perspectives, the fact that the nature and task of the state remain ambiguous (or are by Míguez Bonino perhaps rejected altogether) means that it is not clear how societal coherence and integration are to be achieved and preserved.

Just as our earlier discussion of Nisbet, Lowi, and Walzer led us to a consideration of the arguments being offered today by Alasdair MacIntyre, Jeffrey Stout, and Michael Novak, so too, this evaluation of the selections from Burke, Groen, Gierke, Figgis, and Míguez Bonino drives us forward to the selections representing recent Roman Catholic social thought. If arguments from history are to avoid the pitfalls of relativism, arbitrariness, and pragmatism, can they find redemption in an appeal to nature, or to a more traditional understanding of reason guided by revelation? Is there some idea of the common good of society that can provide a clearer basis for differentiating the role of the state in a complex society? Does modern Catholic social thought offer something more and better at this point than do the historical arguments of the figures we have just considered?

NOTES

1 Edmund Burke, *Reflections on the Revolution in France*, ed. with intro. T. Mahoney (New York: Liberal Arts Press, 1955), 110 (emphasis added).

2 John Neville Figgis, *Churches in the Modern State* (New York: Russell & Russell, 1973), 8, 48-49.

3 *Ibid.*, 92.

4 See David Nicholls, *The Pluralist State* (New York: St. Martin's Press, 1975), 79.

5 Figgis, *Churches*, 251.

6 Burke, *Reflections*, 67, 39.

[7] *Ibid.*, 110.

[8] John MacCunn, *The Political Philosophy of Burke* (New York: Russell & Russell, 1965), 58-59.

[9] Crane Brinton, *The Shaping of Modern Thought* (Englewood Cliffs, N.J.: Prentice-Hall, Inc., 1950), 178-179.

[10] Burke, *Reflections*, 39.

[11] Edmund Burke, *Regicide Peace*, Letter 1, in *The Works of The Right Honourable Edmund Burke* (London: George Bell and Sons, 1877), 5: 153.

[12] Figgis, *Churches*, 33, 41-42.

[13] *Ibid.*, 47 (emphasis added). Compare Figgis' similar judgments in his appreciative discussion of Althusius in the selection above taken from his *Political Thought From Gerson to Grotius: 1414-1625* (New York: Harper Torchbook 1960), 234-235. See also Paul Q. Hirst, ed., *The Pluralist Theory of the State* (New York: Routledge, 1989), 10-11, 16-41.

[14] Otto von Gierke, *Community in Historical Perspective*, trans. M. Fischer, ed. A. Black (Cambridge: Cambridge University Press, 1990), 120.

[15] *Ibid.*

[16] *Ibid.*

[17] *Ibid.*, xxvi.

[18] *Ibid.*, 122.

[19] *Ibid.*

[20] *Ibid.*

[21] *Ibid.*, xxv.

[22] This is a reference to the title of Bernard J. Zylstra, *From Pluralism to Collectivism: The Development of Harold Laski's Political Thought* (Assen, The Netherlands: Van Gorcum & Co., 1968).

[23] Gierke, *Community*, xxii.

[24] *Ibid.*

[25] Groen van Prinsterer, *Unbelief and Revolution*, in Harry Van Dyke, *Groen van Prinsterer's Lectures on Unbelief and Revolution* (Jordan Station, Ontario: Wedge Publishing Foundation, 1989), Lectures VIII and IX, 180-223 of Groen's text. All references to Groen below, unless otherwise noted, are to this text.

[26] Much of nineteenth-century conservatism was identified with what Ernst Cassirer refers to as the "Historic Right School." Against the abstract rationalist order of the revolutionaries, Savigny, Schelling, Schlegel, and others argued that history was the source of the origin of right. On the basis of historically acquired rights the conservatives defended the traditional orders, classes, and institutions of European society. See Ernst Cassirer, *The Myth of the State* (New Haven: Yale University Press, 1946), 182-183.

[27] Groen, *Unbelief and Revolution*, 22.

[28] *Ibid.*, 16-17.

[29] *Ibid.*, 22.

[30] Much of the following evaluation of Groen's perspective is taken from James W. Skillen, "The Development of Calvinistic Political Theory in the Netherlands" (Duke, Ph.D. Diss., 1974), 217-225. For a thorough background, see Van Dyke, *Groen van Prinsterer's Lectures on Unbelief and Revolution*, 1-150. For a criticism of the "historicism" and "organicism" in Groen, see Herman Dooyeweerd, "Het historisch element in Groen's staatsleer," in L.C. Suttorp, et al. eds., *Groen's "Ongeloof en Revolutie"* (Wageningen: Zomer en Keuning, 1949), 118-137. For the influence of Burke on Groen, see J.C.H. de Pater, "Edmund Burke," *Antirevolutionaire Staatkunde*, 2 (1926): 449-64. Von Haller was a Swiss nobleman and member of the supreme council of Berne whose most important work was

Restauration der Staatswissenschaft, which appeared in six parts between 1816 and 1834. Stahl was a German jurist from the center of Lutheran conservatism in Erlangen. He championed the divine right of kings and led a clerical party in the Prussian upper house. For a discussion of Stahl's political views, see Herbert Marcuse, *Reason and Revolution* (Boston: Beacon Press, 1960), 360-374. See F.J. Stahl, *The Present-Day Parties in the State and the Church* (State College, PA: Blenheim Publishing House, 1976).

31 J. D. Dengerink, *Critisch-Historisch Onderzoek naar de Sociologische Ontwikkeling van het Beginsel der "Souvereiniteit in Eigen Kring" in de 19e en 20e Eeuw* (Kampen: J.H. Kok, 1948), 71-74.

32 Groen, *Ongeloof en Revolutie*, 37-41, 51-56.

33 Groen's perspective is summarized in the following comments regarding the traditional structure of society in The Netherlands before the advent of radical thought:

> In their day, every family head, every corporation, every estate was entitled, within the sphere of its competence, to dispose of person and property, to make rules for its subordinates, to regulate its affairs as it pleased; in short, to exercise a form of government that differs from sovereign authority only in this respect that it lacks independence, which is the distinguishing mark of sovereignty. They believed that general prosperity was inseparable from the free development of the orders, of the estates composing the state, whose rights were held to be sacred until the Revolution came, when they were called scandalous.

> Behind the rebuke you recognize the bias for *centralization*. We shall have to come back to that many times. Centralization always begins by destroying the rights of provinces and municipalities and, if forced to be consistent, ends by tolerating in fact no right or activity or existence except under its supervision and control, as a benign favour. It has no place for autonomy, for independence within one's own sphere.

Ibid., 48.

34 Groen van Prinsterer, *Le Parti anti-revolutionaire et confessionnel dans l'Église réformée des Pays-Bas* (Amsterdam, 1860), 89.

35 H. Evan Runner, *The Relation of the Bible to Learning*, 5th rev. ed. (Jordan Station, Ontario: Paideia Press, 1982), 183.

36 H. Evan Runner, *Scriptural Religion and Political Task* (Toronto: Wedge Publishing Foundation, 1974), 93.

37 *Ibid.*

38 Runner, *The Relation of the Bible to Learning*, 183.

39 José Míguez Bonino, *Doing Theology in a Revolutionary Situation* (Philadelphia: Fortress Press, 1975), 147.

40 *Ibid.*, 165.

41 *Ibid.*, 154.

42 *Ibid.*, 119. Míguez Bonino continues: "It [Marxist analysis] teaches us to see class struggle, not as a general consequence of sin, nor as a deplorable accident, but—as Calvin himself saw—as a war prompted by greed and power. More specifically, in our Western capitalist society, it is an effort of the dominating class to protect and maintain the present economic system beyond the time of its ability to provide for the basic needs of all mankind and to organize the productive forces of man and his technological discoveries in such a way that all men may realize their creative potentialities. Class struggle is, finally, the effort of the oppressed to break into a new form of economic and social organization in which work will be related to need and creation and not to profit. It is a struggle for the power to reshape society. It is not a mere outlet for resentment, or an instrument of

revenge—although these things are by no means absent—but a means for attaining a new and more just situation. When the fact of class struggle—in itself a brute fact unleashed by the capitalist organization of work and production—is consciously assumed by the working class and deliberately used for its liberation, it becomes a political act. It is as such that it must be theologically evaluated." *Ibid.*

43 *Ibid.*, 113.

44 *Ibid.*, 165. The only Reformed theologian to whom Míguez Bonino specifically refers is the Dutch theologian serving in Argentina, Lambert Schuurman. Compare also José Míguez Bonino, *Toward A Christian Political Ethics* (Philadelphia: Fortress Press, 1983), 84-86.

45 Míguez Bonino, *Doing Theology*, 165.

46 *Ibid.*, 166.

47 *Ibid.*, 167.

48 *Ibid.*, 165-166.

49 Gary J. Dorrien, *Reconstructing the Common Good: Theology and the Social Order* (Maryknoll, NY: Orbis Books, 1990), 158. There is a "missing element in Miguez Bonino's assessment of the historical legacy of Communism," says Dorrien. "In his sincere desire to avoid self-righteousness he refuses on principle to examine the implications of Communist terror, totalitarian rule, and economic bankruptcy. What is missing is any acknowledgment of the meaning of . . . the mass graves of Cambodia or the hatred for Communism shared by all of the otherwise differing countries of Eastern Europe." *Ibid.*, 155.

50 *Ibid.*, 158. An even more recent evaluation of Míguez Bonino in the context of the moderating shift of liberation theology is Paul E. Sigmund, *Liberation Theology at the Crossroads: Democracy or Revolution?* (New York: Oxford University Press, 1990). Cf. also Michael Novak, *Will it Liberate? Questions About Liberation Theology* (New York: Paulist Press, 1986), and Gordon Spykman, et al., *Let My People Live: Faith and Struggle in Central America* (Grand Rapids: Eerdmans, 1988).

TWENTY

SUBSIDIARITY, NATURAL LAW, AND
THE COMMON GOOD: AN EVALUATION

Historical arguments for the plural structure of society appear to take us only so far. There can be no doubt that historical development occurs, that human beings do make history and shape society with a degree of creative liberty, and that we live today in highly complex and differentiated societies that could not have been anticipated a few centuries ago. A single, fixed form of human social order has not persisted through time. But when we ask, What does history teach us about what *ought* to exist? and Why is a pluralist philosophy of society *better* than an individualist or collectivist view?, we enter a domain requiring moral arguments and normative considerations that transcend the so-called "facts" and the multiple interpretations of history. We need more than historical arguments to judge between Edmund Burke and Jacques Maritain, between Pope Leo XIII and Herman Dooyeweerd, between José Míguez Bonino and Bob Goudzwaard.

One enduring tradition of argument for a plural social order, which appeals to more than history for its norms, is Thomism—a philosophy given special prominence and moral approval by the Roman Catholic Church. Key ingredients of this philosophy, as we saw in the selected readings above, are (1) natural law and natural reason; (2) subsidiarity and autonomy; and (3) the common good.[1] In the social thought of Pope Leo XIII, Pope Pius XI,

Jacques Maritain, the Bishops of the Second Vatican Council, and the American Catholic Bishops, there is clear evidence of the desire to reject both universalism and individualism. However, from our viewpoint, it is not clear that this philosophy offers an adequate normative argument for the kind of social diversity and coherence necessary to safeguard the identities, tasks, and rights of society's many institutions. We evaluate each of the key ingredients of this philosophy in turn.

In Critique of Natural Law and Natural Reason

At the heart of recent Catholic social thought, rooted in the philosophy of Thomas Aquinas, is the assumption that human reason, unaided by faith, is capable of grasping the governing principles of nature and the normative structure of a plural society. This is possible, the argument goes, because natural law which is the norm or standard for social life is open to anyone who possesses rational faculties. In the words of Pope Leo XIII, all persons may "through the natural light of reason alone" and "without any admixture of error" comprehend certain basic truths about God's design for human social life.[2] The structure of social life may be known by all, irrespective of a person's religious convictions or lack of them, for "God did not instill the light of reason into the human mind in vain."[3] Human beings may, therefore, be able to reach a common understanding of generally accepted principles for the structuring of society.[4]

The Catholic argument that natural moral norms for a diversified social order are open to all people through natural reason is not without its problems. The "reason alone" argument of Pope Leo XIII has not, for example, proved to be a very effective instrument for convincing most people of the validity of pluralism and the invalidity of individualism and collectivism. At issue, therefore, is Thomism's claim of universal rational validity. Even if one accepts Thomism, it would appear to be necessary, as Alasdair MacIntyre argues, both to accept the full tradition in which its meaning has emerged as well as to contend with others who reject it on the bases of other rationalities. Moreover, it seems clear to us that Catholic social philosophy must give greater attention to the issue of conflicting basic religious motives in view of the high degree of diversity even in the West regarding the nature of human rationality.

If, as a matter of fact, non-Thomist views of reality dominate in the shaping of contemporary societies, what does this say about the natural rationality that all people are supposed to share? At the very least, it suggests that history is made and society shaped by irrational or anti-normative motives and desires. In that case, the appeal to natural law through natural reason should try to give an account of how and why history can be misshaped. It ought to be able to make a convincing moral case for why people should act rationally (naturally) rather than irrationally (unnaturally). Is the Thomist synthesis of Aristotle and Christianity adequately equipped to answer these questions and to meet these challenges? Have Catholics since the time of Pope Leo XIII found Thomism sufficient for these purposes?

Werner Wiesner, for one, is not so sanguine about the health and strength of Thomism as a modern social philosophy, given its own inner tensions.

> The idea of a law of nature does not arise out of Scripture, but is pre-Christian. And even in the new form which Christianity gave it the doctrine has never quite been able to repudiate this heathen and pre-Christian origin. So that in the conception of a law of nature we are not dealing with an idea of reason, but with a very complex historical entity; it has roots in the past which must be known if one is to understand and judge it.[5]

Wiesner seeks to uncover the Greek-Christian tensions in Thomism by showing that its view of natural law cannot be separated from an essentially pagan idea of nature.[6] The Greek view of the cosmos gave birth to a philosophical doctrine of "Being" which, according to Wiesner, "abides eternal amid the change of phenomena."[7] For Greek philosophy "this Being, which is independent of all change and at rest within itself, is nature, and the eternal order of nature is the law of nature."[8] The very conception of natural reason and natural law, in other words, is not religiously neutral and universal but arises from the world of the Greek *polis*.

There appears to be a basic incompatibility between the all-encompassing classical idea of Being and the biblical revelation that God the Creator is independent of, and sovereign over, his creation. Biblically speaking, God is not the supreme pinnacle of the great chain of Being; he is not Aristotle's pure thinking about thinking, or pure actuality at one end of the potentiality-actuality continuum. The biblical God is the independent and self-sufficient Creator of everything that exists—he is the historically engaged, covenant-making God. Natural law, reason, and cosmic order are not elements that unite the biblical God with his creation. Rather, they are the essential ingredients of a philosophy that cannot adequately distinguish the Creator from his creatures. Thus, Thomism seeks to synthesize incompatible worldviews arising from conflicting religious motives.

The Thomist view of natural law and social order is, to a great extent, built on Aristotle's understanding of the cosmos. According to Aristotle, the cosmos, is ordered teleologically for the natural actualization of various inner potentialities.[9] All things that exist in the cosmos are structured to attain their goal (purpose, *telos*) by an internal "entelechy"—an almost biological unfolding of all parts toward fulfillment of the whole, as ordered by the laws implanted within them. In adapting this philosophy to Christianity, Thomism seeks to make an integral connection between the Greek idea of natural law and the biblical idea of God's eternal law.

Thomists have, of course, always insisted that in order for humanity to reach its highest destiny it must achieve a supernatural *telos*—something possible only by means of God's grace.[10] In other words, Aquinas and the Catholic Church have brought distinctively Christian elements into synthesis with Aristotelian concepts. The question is whether the synthesis can be achieved and maintained. For Aristotle, human reason stands in no need of divine grace in order for the individual to reach maturity and fulfillment. For Aristotle, there is no such thing as sin or the need for the forgiveness of sin through a Church which transcends the *polis*. He anticipates no supernatural destiny whatever.

In the Thomist perspective, however, divine law comes as part of God's supernatural revelation, as grace added to nature. Nature, including human nature, is part of the rationally ordered natural realm, but human beings have a higher, supernatural destiny as well. The realm of nature possesses an autonomy—a relative independence and self-determination—in distinction from the supernatural realm of grace. But grace completes and perfects nature. This formulation became scholastic dogma and has been referred to as the grace-nature synthesis.[11]

The grace-nature synthesis thus represents an accommodation of Christianity to Greek thought. The cosmic order is then divided into natural and supernatural realms. In Thomism, Wiesner explains,

> two heterogeneous elements are bound up together: the biblical conception of creation, at once limited and completed by eschatology, and the idea of the cosmos in late Greek philosophy. But these are mutually exclusive: the thought, pantheistic in its origin, of eternal law immanent in the world cannot be united with the biblical doctrine of creation. . . . This means that the Christian faith in God as Creator negates at the outset the theological and cosmological bases of the Thomist conception of the law of nature.[12]

Wiesner's judgment is not shared by Jacques Maritain and Alasdair MacIntyre, however. While Maritain and MacIntyre readily acknowledge that the concept of natural law is a legacy of a Greek-Christian synthesis, they do not agree that this is something illegitimate or problematic. Maritain believes that Greek philosophers and biblical writers held a similar idea of natural law. To support this position he argues that a "genuine idea of natural law" goes back farther than Aquinas or Augustine to the Church Fathers and St. Paul as well as to Cicero, the Stoics, and Sophocles.[13]

MacIntyre agrees that Aquinas confronted "the claims of two distinct and in important ways incompatible philosophical traditions" rooted in the work of Augustine and Aristotle. But the synthesis he achieved was genuine because Aquinas did not merely "supplement Aristotle"; he "shows Aristotle's account of teleology of human life to be radically defective."[14] So the Thomist synthesis now stands on its own feet as a new and integral achievement.

With respect to the biblical idea of natural law, Maritain appeals to Paul's statement in Romans 2:14 ("When the Gentiles who have not the Law, do by nature the things contained in the Law, these, having not the Law, are a law unto themselves . . . "[15]) to demonstrate that a person can gain a true understanding of social reality by means of the natural light of reason. Thomist scholars often use Paul's statement in Romans 1:18-20 to make this point:

> The wrath of God is being revealed from heaven against all the godlessness and wickedness of men who suppress the truth by their wickedness, since what may be known about God is plain to them, because God has made it plain to them. For since the creation of the world God's invisible qualities—his eternal power and divine nature—have been clearly seen, being understood from what has been made, so that men are without excuse.[16]

But is it not clear from this passage that *God* has revealed himself ("God has made it plain to them") through His creation, and that natural persons have *suppressed* the truth by their wickedness? In other words, doesn't Paul teach something quite different than the idea that human beings are able, regardless of sin and special revelation, to know the truth about the creation? Doesn't Paul's teaching point to a religious antithesis at a very basic level between the use of reason to suppress the truth and the use of reason to follow the truth revealed by God in creation?

If this reading of Romans 1:18-20 is correct, then God's revelation is heard, understood, and obeyed only in faithful obedience to God. Sin has affected human reason to the extent that it is impossible for people, except through God's renewal of human life in Christ, to comprehend the truth about God and his creation. The sinner suppresses the truth in unrighteousness. For this reason Paul attacked the sinful actions of a people who, claiming to be wise, became fools "and exchanged the glory of the immortal God for images made to look like mortal man and birds and animals and reptiles."[17] Paul did not advocate the self-sufficiency of natural reason, but rather uncovered the root cause of differences among human beings who reason from different starting points to different conclusions because of opposing basic religious commitments. This has significant implications for any judgment regarding the validity of a Thomist view of society in general and of society's plural structure in particular. If Thomism offers the correct view of reality, then its truth is not demonstrable by virtue of any universal contemporary assent to its terms.

An appeal to natural law by means of natural reason will have to demonstrate its power by the way it exposes the errors of individualist and collectivist ideologies in their impact on history. And if a genuine antithesis exists between Catholic social thought and other philosophies, then the character of that antithesis will have to be explained in contrast to the supposedly common rational basis that permits all human beings to grasp the truth of natural law.

In Critique of Subsidiarity and Autonomy

By calling into question the health and strength of Aquinas' synthesis of Greek philosophy and Christianity, we are led logically to question the adequacy of the principle of "subsidiarity" as the normative principle that undergirds social pluralism. Thomism and traditional Catholicism have defined the state as the ruling authority in a hierarchical social order that directs everything to the common good. According to the subsidiarity principle as outlined by Pope Pius XI, the state, though superior and prior, should only interfere in, or supplement the efforts of smaller communities when those communities are unable to fulfill their own tasks in society. Prudential diligence is required so that a "graduated order is preserved among the various associations" that make up the social order.[18]

The principle of subsidiarity rests on the Thomist conception of the "social nature of man" and the "natural purposes" of the various societal groups that comprise a differentiated, hierarchically structured order. The subsidiarity principle is supposed to guarantee genuine pluralism even though all differentiated groups are *parts* of a more encompassing whole. But given Aquinas' heavy dependence on Greek thought, especially Aristotle, the conception of parts within the whole pushes in the direction of a universalist conception of the social *whole*.

To be sure, one of the corollary concepts of subsidiarity is that the parts should enjoy relative autonomy within the whole. Although in a logical sense "the whole is of necessity prior to the part," in a historical sense the simpler or less universal parts of the body politic are the first to emerge from nature to fulfill human needs. The universal body politic is constructed of more limited social orders, not the other way around. Thus, while the state possesses the highest authority within the body politic it is not the most basic institution of society. The latter honor is held by the family, which like other groups in the body politic, possesses its own autonomy within the whole. Furthermore, according to the principle of subsidiarity, the intervention of a higher group (ultimately, the state) in a lower one is justified only when needed to coordinate, supplement, or encourage the efforts of a smaller community. Respect for the autonomy of parts within the whole is thus the key to protecting against the development of a totalitarian society.

The grace-nature duality is another constitutive element that is supposed to keep the part-whole relationship from being reduced to collectivism. The subsidiarity principle is tied directly to a hierarchical view of reality in which the distinction is made between the order of nature and the order of grace. Aquinas taught that individuals and groups are parts of a greater whole only insofar as they are of the same order. This means that a limitation is placed on temporal authorities by the very fact that, while the state is the leading authority within the body politic, that body is limited to the natural realm. There is a distinction between the higher order of grace and the lower order of nature. Because the ultimate "end" of the person and of redeemed society transcends temporal reality, temporal authority is limited to the natural order of life. For Aquinas this meant that

> as long as man's mortal life endures there is an extrinsic good for him, namely, final beatitude which is looked for after death in the enjoyment of God. . . . Now the same judgment is to be formed about the end of society as a whole as about the end of one man. . . . Consequently, since society must have the same end as the individual man, it is not the ultimate end of an assembled multitude to live virtuously but through virtuous living to attain to possession of God.[19]

The temporal order, in other words, is fit rather than unfit for a supernatural destiny. This shows up both in the moral conscience of individuals as well as in the sacramental dimensions of institutions such as marriage and the family. The task of guiding persons and institutions to their final destiny, then, belongs not to a temporal but to a sacred authority. The supra-temporal dimension of society (the sphere of grace) is thus removed from the jurisdiction of temporal authority. The Church has the primary responsibility to instruct and give direction on moral matters, whether those matters are social, economic, or political, because they all pertain to the Church's authority as the moral and spiritual leader of society.

The teachings of the encyclicals *Rerum Novarum, Quadragesimo Anno,* and the Church's other social teachings rest on this doctrine of subsidiarity. Pius XI was quite explicit on the authority of the Church in social and economic matters:

> That principle which Leo XIII so clearly established must be laid down at the outset here, namely, that there resides in Us the right and duty to pronounce with supreme authority upon social and economic matters. Certainly the Church was not given the commission to guide men to an only fleeting and perishable happiness but to that which is eternal. Indeed "the Church holds that it is unlawful for her to mix without cause in these temporal concerns," however, she can in no wise renounce the duty God entrusted to her to interpose her authority, not of course in matters of technique for which she is neither suitably equipped nor endowed by office, but in all things that are connected with the moral law. For as to these, the deposit of truth that God committed to Us and the grave duty of urging it in season and out of season, bring under and subject to Our supreme jurisdiction not only social order but economic activities themselves.[20]

The American Catholic Bishops speak from the same point of view:

> In our letter, we write as pastors, not public officials. We speak as moral teachers, not economic technicians. We seek not to make some political or ideological point but to lift up the human and ethical dimensions of economic life, aspects too often neglected in public discussion.[21]

From the perspective of the superior authority of divine grace and moral law, popes and bishops have criticized the injustices of fascist, Marxist, and liberal/capitalist states of their day. And through their criticisms they have raised the banner of a "third way"—a non-fascist, non-Marxist, non-liberal/capitalist view of the nature and task of the state in a pluralist society. Nevertheless, even with Aristotle's whole-part distinction and with the hierarchical sacred-secular distinction, the "parts" of temporal reality remain subject in one way or another to the social "whole" of the body politic. Is this framework sufficient to guarantee a genuine pluralism of temporal social institutions?

In our judgment, influenced as it is by Herman Dooyeweerd's contrast between "sphere sovereignty" and the "whole-part" relation, the principle of autonomy in a subsidiarity framework does *not* adequately define or safeguard the identities, tasks, and rights of multiple societal institutions. Autonomy can provide for the relative independence of parts within a whole, such as different government units within a state, or different academic units within a university, or different ecclesiastical offices within a church. It does not, however, provide an adequate basis for distinguishing the identities and responsibilities of different spheres of human life. A family, a school, a church, a business enterprise, a state, each has a different identity, requiring uniquely different human roles and responsibilities within it. These different social entities should not be viewed as parts of one another as autonomous subunits in a larger whole.

While it may be legitimate to define cities and counties as constitutional parts within a state, it does not seem legitimate to speak similarly of the family as a part of the state. The very nature of a political subunit is determined by the identity of the larger political whole of which it is a part. Cities and counties are lesser governmental administrative bodies which possess some autonomy (relative independence) within a single *political* whole. But the same thing should not be said of the many *non-state* institutions in society. They are not political subunits at all. A truly pluralist social order seems to require recognition of the fundamental and not merely the relative independence of different spheres and institutions in a differentiated society. To achieve this recognition, the ontological status of institutions must be grasped and upheld. In our opinion, the subsidiarity-autonomy framework does not do this.

In the teaching of the papal encyclicals and in the thought of Maritain, for example, the independence of persons is recognized, but the ontological status of institutions is not. Maritain does point to the importance of "an ontological perspective" for the development of "true philosophy."[22] In his discussion of human rights he argues that a person possesses an "ontologic structure" ("essential constitution") which defines the character of human life. Human rights, therefore, are possessed by every person and are intelligible to all through human reason.[23] The ontological issue is at the heart of Maritain's understanding of individual rights.

Maritain does not, however, extend this argument to social institutions and associations. While he is very concerned about the "essential rights and freedoms" of the multiplicity of particular societies that make up the body politic, he does not believe that institutions possess an ontic structure of their own.[24] Although "particular societies" should be as "autonomous as possible," they do not have an essence separate from that of individuals. Institutions, according to Maritain, "proceed from the free initiative of citizens," and, therefore, do not possess their own essential constitution.[25]

Institutions are the creation of individuals who alone possess a character that can be accounted for ontologically. On this basis Maritain develops his view that the social order is a pyramid in which "authority comes from below, through the people," and then rises in tiers one above another through many "particular and partial authorities" until reaching the topmost authority which is the state."[26] Particular and partial authorities merely possess a derived authority that comes from the people. Institutions, for example, do not possess authority based upon their own identity, tasks, and rights because they do not have such an identity. While he is clear that individuals are cultural agents who give form and shape to specific institutions, he seems to reduce institutional life to the expression of the will of individuals, albeit with the understanding that individuals are social, rational creatures and not isolated, willful automatons. Though Maritain rejects the Lockean belief in human sovereignty, his argument that "authority comes from below, through the people" is ontologically similar to that of the individualists.

How is it possible to account for this similarity? One explanation is that Catholic social philosophy remains too much in debt to the assumptions of Greek philosophy—some of which point in an individualist direction. For example, Aquinas, following Aristotle, takes the individual as the ontological point of departure because the person alone has *substance*. For Aristotle, according to Dooyeweerd, only the person possesses an independent existence and the community is merely "a *unity of order* born by the individual." The state "does not possess *the same reality* as the individual, just as one cannot ascribe the same reality to the *color* red as to a red *rose*. The color red is only a property of the rose and presupposes the rose as its bearer."[27]

The question of the ontological status of social institutions illumines the linkage of classical thought to both Catholic social philosophy and modern individualism. The similarity between Catholic and individualist social philosophies becomes particularly evident when attention is turned to an examination of human rights and the state.

Typically a consistent individualist speaks of the "rights" of individuals and the "duties" of the state. This distinction between rights and duties comes from the assumption that only individuals are real—only individuals have ontic status. Thus no social institution can claim to possess rights because institutions are merely the artificial creations of individuals. The state simply has duties to perform toward individuals who alone possess rights in society. For adherents of social individualism this view is supposed to ensure the freedom of individuals.

The emergence of modern individualism was in part a reaction to government absolutism experienced as despotism in the sixteenth and seventeenth centuries. By introducing the concept of the sovereignty of the people, Locke and others fundamentally rejected the idea that the state possesses rights. They revived the contractual theory of the state which goes back to the Epicureans and the Stoics. We may ask, however, whether the legitimate reaction against absolutism (through a constitutionally established bill of rights for individuals, etc.) requires the denial of all rights to the state and to multiple nonpolitical institutions in society?

The Catholic view of societal pluralism which aims to break with both individualism and collectivism seems, at this point, to make a basic accommodation in the direction of individualism even as it reaffirms the social identity of human beings. This shows up not only in Maritain's justification of constitutional democracy, religious freedom, and human rights but also in the post-Vatican II attempts to accommodate Catholic teaching to the modern doctrine of human rights.

The ontological accommodation to individualism can be seen in Maritain's view of the state. He believes that the state represents the highest authority within the body politic. But since he wants to guard against the dangers of absolutism and collectivism, he appeals to the principle of autonomy and subsidiarity as a way to uphold the "particular societies" within the body politic. Thus, while granting that the state possesses the leading authority within the body politic, he also says that it is "neither a whole nor a subject of right, or a person."[28]

> The State has a primary duty concerning justice, which should be exercised only in the manner of an ultimate supervision in a body politic basically just in its inner structures. . . . But this supreme authority is received by the State from the body politic, that is, from the people; it is not a natural right to supreme power which the State possesses of itself.[29]

In Maritain's attempt to champion a pluralist social model against the claims of collectivism, he denies an ontic status to the state because, he believes, it is "not a subject of right." He thus accepts a basic assumption regarding the state and other institutions that is characteristic of individualism. Consequently, both the state and the body politic remain mysterious and ambiguous entities without a clear delineation of their identity and boundaries.

Generally speaking, this idea of the body politic as a "unity of order" sustained by real individuals seems to be characteristic of recent Catholic thought. The American Catholic Bishops, for example, building on the American constitutional tradition of individual political rights, try to develop a framework for economic rights. The "new experiment" they advocate is a "partnership for the public good" that appeals for cooperation among all kinds of groups and institutions—particularly to help the poor. Their goal is to enhance community and the common good, but the "rights" tradition which they happily accommodate is heavily dependent on liberal individualism. Thus, at times they sound almost collectivist, at other times individualist, as they look for ways to enhance the justice of the body politic. In the absence of a principled ontology that defines the identities and responsibilities of various social institutions, including the state, their use of the subsidiarity principle tends toward pure pragmatism. As the following quote reveals, the ideal of creative cooperation can easily degenerate into the conflict between unrestricted government mandates and appeals for individual rights protection:

> The principle of subsidiarity calls for government intervention when small or intermediate groups in society are unable or unwilling to take the steps needed to promote basic justice. Pope John XXIII observed that the growth of more complex relations of interdependence among citizens has led to an increased role for government in modern societies. This role is to work *in partnership with* the many other groups in society, helping them fulfill their tasks and responsibilities more effectively, not replacing or destroying them. The challenge of today is to move beyond abstract disputes about whether more or less government intervention is needed, to consideration of creative ways of enabling government and private groups to work together effectively.[30]

Thomas Aquinas assumed that a society is "a union of men acting for a common purpose." But if a society is merely a union of persons, what is the status of entities such as the state? In an effort to answer this question Thomists distinguish between a "unity of substance" and a "unity of order."[31] It is assumed that a "unity of substance" corresponds to a substantial being. Wherever there is substantial being, there is also substantial unity, and where there is only a relationship between substantial beings, there is only a unity of relation—a "unity of order." From this perspective, the individual is a substantial being possessing a "unity of substance." By contrast, an institution such as the state represents a relationship of individuals. In comparison with the individual who is a "unity of substance," an institution represents a "unity of order" and is thus viewed as a less perfect unity—a quasi-unity.

Since individuals alone possess a unity of substance, only individuals have an ontic character. Institutions within the body politic such as the state lack substantial unity or independent existence, and, therefore, they do not possess an ontic status. Though institutions such as the state are essential expressions of human nature, they possess no more than a quasi-unity derived from individuals by an act of human intellect. Both Catholic and individualist viewpoints grant to institutions an axiological status (a place of value), but they deny them an ontic status. There is thus a basic ontological similarity between a Catholic and an individualist view of social reality at this level.

The subsidiarity principle, which assumes the autonomy of the parts within the whole, does not, therefore, seem to safeguard society from moving in either a collectivist or an individualist direction. It does not appear strong enough to resist purely pragmatic tendencies whether coming from above or from below.

In Critique of the Grace-Nature Schema

If the autonomy argument connected with the subsidiarity principle is insufficient to protect a diversified societal order from the dangers of state collectivism, on the one hand, and from individualist reductionism, on the other, can such dangers be avoided by appealing to a hierarchical arrangement where natural society is ordered under the guardianship of grace?

While a distinction between the temporal order of nature and the transcendent order of grace has been used by the Catholic Church to set limits to temporal authorities, the distinction also led at one time to an ecclesiastical dominance over European society from about the twelfth to the fifteenth centuries. Indeed, it has been argued that the institutional Church, standing above all temporal authority, actually impeded the development of a fully differentiated social order. Insofar as the Church *was* the state, according to Figgis, there existed a form of social cohesion that inhibited the historical development of social pluralism. Long before there was the phenomenon of modern state collectivism, there was the reality of what many would describe as an ecclesiastically managed social collectivism built on a grace-nature hierarchy.

One of the abiding questions associated with the grace-nature argument is how to determine the boundary line between the two spheres. Aquinas argued that making this determination is the sole responsibility of the Church:

> Thus, in order that spiritual things might be distinguished from earthly things, the ministry of this kingdom has been entrusted not to earthly kings but to priests, and most of all to the chief priest, the successor of St. Peter, the Vicar of Christ, the Roman Pontiff. To him all the kings of the Christian People are to be subject as to our Lord Christ Himself. For those to whom pertains the care of intermediate ends should be subject to him to whom pertains the care of the ultimate end, and be directed by his rule.[32]

The implications of his argument are clear: "Consequently, in the law of Christ, kings must be subject to priests."[33] In the final analysis, the Church on its own authority reserves the right to determine the boundary line between the spheres of grace and nature.

In 1302, Pope Boniface VIII in the bull *Unam Sanctam* affirmed the judgment that it is appropriate to speak of the two swords of spiritual and temporal authority, but "both swords are in the power of the church, the one by the hand of the priest, the other by the hand of kings and knights, but at the will and sufferance of the priest."[34] *Unam Sanctam* decreed in its closing sentence that "We therefore declare, say, define, and pronounce that it is altogether a necessity of salvation for every human creature to be subject to the Roman Pontiff."[35]

While subsequent papal encyclicals, and especially the declarations from Vatican II, acknowledged the legitimacy of religious freedom in secular states and softened the extreme assertion of papal authority in *Unam Sanctam*, the Church's argument that grace transcends nature and represents the highest and most authoritative realm of moral standards for society still stands. What does that claim to moral and spiritual authority mean today, however, in our highly differentiated societies? The contemporary circumstances of both the social order and official Catholic teaching do not seem to lend themselves to a strong hierarchicalism.

From the standpoint of classic Thomism, the notion of subsidiarity suggests a hierarchically ordered collectivity. Church and state are two universal authorities, each in a sphere where the boundaries are ultimately defined by the Church. According to the analogy of being, both the Church and the state have under them a series of subordinate orders over which they exercise ultimate jurisdiction. This view of society, we suggest, cannot escape the implications of collectivism. And these implications are softened only to a degree by the hierarchically motivated desire to affirm the relative autonomy of lower levels of social reality *within* the larger wholes of state and Church.

With the most recent tendencies in Catholic social thought showing movement toward a defense of human rights and freedoms in secular states, the more immediate question is whether Catholic thinking can avoid the pitfalls of liberal individualism. The hierarchical schema of a natural society aided by supernatural grace may continue to exist as a model in the minds of Catholic leaders, but it may have less and less relevance for actual practice in liberal societies. We return, then, to MacIntyre's question of whether Thomist thinking can function meaningfully in a liberal society, and particularly whether its philosophy of a hierarchically pluralistic society can still have meaning in our day.

In Critique of The Common Good

The primacy of the common good is the third element intrinsic to a Catholic view of social pluralism. The common good represents the moral standard of a society bound together as a just and coherent whole in the realization of the temporal welfare of humanity. Our question is this: Is an embracing concept of the common good adequate to circumscribe the contours of the unified good of a diversified society? We think not. This largely undifferentiated concept derived from the experience of a Church-unified, hierarchical social order does not appear to be sufficient to distinguish the sphere of public-legal justice in a highly complex and differentiated society.

In his short essay entitled "On Kingship," Aquinas argues that society would disintegrate unless it sustains a proper recognition of the welfare of all the institutions in society. And this can be accomplished only through an acknowledgment of the claims of the common good. Aquinas says that "what is proper and what is common are not identical."

> Things differ by what is proper to each: they are united by what they have in common. But diversity of effects is due to diversity of causes. Consequently, there must exist something which impels toward the common good of the many, over and above that which impels toward the particular good of each individual.[36]

It is not clear, however, upon what basis the distinction is to be made between what is "proper to each" and what is "common to all." With respect to the current diversity of social institutions, it is precisely an understanding of what is "proper to each" that must be developed in order to avoid having what is "common to all" become defined by either individualists or collectivists. Though Aquinas affirmed the importance of a differentiated social order, the overriding emphasis in his thought is upon that which is *common* to the whole. The result is that the concern for unity takes control of his thought before the basis of diversity is adequately established. This problem is compounded by the fact that the common good is supposed to define both the good of the whole as well as what is proper to each part within the whole. Once again the whole-part relationship defines all of temporal social reality. In the final analysis "every law is ordained to the common good."[37]

Aquinas' teaching about the common good in connection with the whole-part relationship has left Catholic social thought with a variety of unresolved problems. When Maritain, for example, discusses the essential rights and freedoms of the multiplicity of particular societies that comprise the superior unity of the body politic, he emphasizes that "the public welfare and the general order of law are essential parts of the common good of the body politic."[38] What this means is that the common good applies to all of life; it defines not only the superior unity of the body politic but also the particular unities of all the entities that make up the body politic. Maritain thus faithfully follows Aquinas when he declares that the common good is applicable to "both the whole and the parts."[39]

The common good is not only the collection of public commodities and services which the organization of common life presupposes: a sound fiscal condition, a strong military force; the body of just laws, good customs, and wise institutions which provides the political society with its structures; the heritage of its great historical remembrances, its symbols and its glories, its living traditions and cultural treasures. The common good also includes the sociological integration of all the civic conscience, political virtues and sense of law and freedom, of all the activity, material prosperity and spiritual riches, of unconsciously operating hereditary wisdom, of moral rectitude, justice, friendship, happiness, virtue and heroism in the individual lives of the members of the body politic.[40]

The common good apparently stands for the complete moral good of social life, but the concept does not clarify who is responsible in what respect for securing the common good. The concept is not narrowly a political concept, and yet it lends itself to recognizing political authority as chiefly responsible for ensuring the common good. In and of itself, however, the concept does not distinguish clearly the realm of governmental responsibility within the larger moral order of the common good. Just as the whole-part relationship constitutes the structure of societal reality, the common good is the norm which defines the goal of the whole together with its many parts.

What are the implications of allowing this teleological goal of the common good to define the good of both the whole and of its many parts? We believe that, without an inner *political* criterion delimiting the common *public* good, in distinction from various nonpolitical and private social goods, Thomism will remain highly ambiguous and problematic as a pluralist philosophy. Precisely because Thomists insist that the common good defines the whole-part relationship which structures all of social reality, there is an insufficient barrier against the universalizing or collectivizing impulses. This danger is what leads Michael Novak to react in the direction of liberalism for his political and economic philosophy while elevating the idea of the common good to an eschatological level.

Since we know from history that the most extravagant claims for state absolutism have come from those seeking to justify their actions with appeals to the common good, it seems clear that an undifferentiated concept of the common good will not be sufficient to protect the relative autonomy of all the social parts within the body politic. There is no doubt that Catholic social thought wants to offer a pluralist alternative to individualism and collectivism. Oswald von Nell-Breuning, who was commissioned to write the original draft of *Quadragesimo Anno*, argues that social pluralism stands at the heart of Thomist thought.

St. Thomas defines the nature of order as "unity in well-arranged multiplicity." This distinguishes order from mere uniformity. We cannot speak of order, order that really deserves this name, where everything is uniform. Millions of grains of sand can be poured on the ground; it is irrelevant where the individual grains come to rest, because they are alike; no one can bring order into them. They are neither capable of order nor subject to disorder. Monotony cannot approach the concept of order. But "unity arising from an apt arrangement of a multiplicity of parts" does not merely mean a multiplicity of different things; aside from diversity and multiplicity it includes arrangement whereby equal things are united and unequal things combined to a higher unity.[41]

Though we recognize and appreciate the sincere attempt of Catholic social philosophers and Church officials to offer an alternative to individualism and collectivism, we conclude that the combined weight of the idea of the common good and the concepts of subsidiarity and autonomy within a natural law framework do not supply an adequate, normative view of both the *diversity* and the *complex unity* of society. The very pattern of synthesizing ancient and modern philosophical perspectives under the guiding moral eye of the Church seems to open Catholic social thought to the conflicts among incompatible ingredients and the deeper antithesis between opposing religious basic motives at work in history. If there really is some kind of natural or divine order of heteronomous social norms, then it seems to us that an appeal to it ought to shed light on why society has frequently been shaped in disregard of that order. At the same time, that order must be shown to be the reason why misdirected attempts to shape society according to individualist and collectivist visions have failed or are illegitimate.

Is it possible, then, to conceive of an appeal to "natural law" or to "creation order" that does not bear the burden of ambiguity and inner tension which the Thomist synthesis bears? This question leads us back to the discussion of Ralph Hancock's thesis about Calvin and to Jeffrey Stout's sympathetic but critical evaluation of Alasdair MacIntyre's critique of liberalism. It also leads us to an evaluation of progressive Calvinism as developed by Abraham Kuyper, Herman Dooyeweerd, H. Evan Runner, Bernard Zylstra, and Bob Goudzwaard.

NOTES

[1] A number of Anglican and other Protestant theologians and philosophers such as William Temple, T. S. Eliot, V. A. Demant, William G. Peck, and Maurice B. Reckitt share with Catholic theorists some basic Thomist assumptions regarding social reality. For a discussion of the similarities between Catholic and Anglican perspectives see Dante L. Germino, "Two Types of Recent Political Thought," *The Journal of Politics*, 21 (1959): 455-

486. This insightful essay contrasts the political thought of Christian Rationalists (Catholic and Anglican) with that of so-called neo-orthodox figures including Karl Barth, Reinhold Niebuhr, and Emil Brunner).

2 Leo XIII, *Aeterni Patris* (1879), in J. Husslein, ed., *Social Wellsprings* (Milwaukee: The Bruce Pub. Co., 1942-43), 1: 258. The Encyclical *Aeterni Patris* ordered that the doctrines of Thomas Aquinas, "the pre-eminent guardian and glory of the Catholic Church," were to be taught in all its schools and academies. Leo XIII would later decree that if other writers and theologians disagree with Aquinas, the "former must be sacrificed to the latter." Quoted in William Ebenstein, *Great Political Thinkers: Plato to the Present* (New York: Holt, Rinehart and Winston, 1969), 224.

3 Leo XIII, *Aeterni Patris*, 249.

4 In his *Summa Theologiae* Aquinas answered the question, whether the natural law is the same in all men: "I answer that to the natural law belong those things to which a man is inclined naturally: and among these it is proper to man to be inclined to act according to reason. . . . Accordingly then in speculative matters truth is the same in all men, both as to principles and as to conclusions: although the truth is not known to all as regards the conclusions, but only as regards the principles which are called common notions." Quoted by Ebenstein, *Great Political Thinkers*, 236-237.

5 Werner Wiesner, "The Law of Nature and Social Institutions," in Nils Ehrenström, M. F. Dibelius, William Temple, et al., *Christian Faith and the Common Life* (Chicago: Willett, Clark & Company, 1938), 103.

6 *Ibid.*, 104.

7 *Ibid.*

8 *Ibid.* Compare Herman Dooyeweerd, *Roots of Western Culture: Pagan, Secular and Christian Options* trans. J. Kraay, eds. M. Vander Vennan and B. Zylstra (Toronto: Wedge Publishing Foundation, 1979), 15-22.

9 Wiesner, "The Law of Nature," 106.

10 *Ibid.*

11 See Dooyeweerd, *Roots*, 111-147.

12 Wiesner, "The Law of Nature," 106-107. In Dooyeweerd's view, Aquinas accommodated the Greek view of nature to the biblical view that all of creation emerged *ex nihilo* from the creative act of a sovereign God. The Greeks conceived neither the invisible order of the form of nature nor the cyclical stream of the matter of nature, as created. For Aquinas, according to Dooyeweerd, form and matter (nature) continued to be the "two metaphysical principles of all perishable existence" and "with respect to their origin Thomas was silent." While Aquinas acknowledged God as the "first cause" and the "ultimate goal" of nature, "he never referred to matter as divine." Nature, Dooyeweerd concludes, became for Thomas an independent (autonomous) stepping-stone to grace. Dooyeweerd, *Roots*, 118. The most thorough recent discussion of the incompatiblility of Greek and Christian bases of thought and of the religious roots of all theorizing is Roy A. Clouser, *The Myth of Religious Neutrality* (Notre Dame: University of Notre Dame Press, [forthcoming, 1991]).

13 Jacques Maritain, *Man and the State* (Chicago: University of Chicago Press, 1951), 84-85. For representative selections of writings on natural law from Aristotle through Maritain, see Paul E. Sigmund, *Natural Law in Political Thought* (Cambridge, MA: Winthrop Publishers, 1971).

14 Alasdair MacIntyre, *Whose Justice? Which Rationality?* (Notre Dame: University of Notre Dame Press, 1988), 168, 205.

15 Maritain, *Man and the State*, 85.

16 Romans 1:18-20 (NIV).

17 Romans 1:23 (NIV).

18 Pius XI, *Quadragesimo Anno*, in Terence P. McLaughlin, ed., *The Church and the Reconstruction of the Modern World: The Social Encyclicals of Pope Pius XI* (New York: Doubleday & Company, 1957), 247.

19 Aquinas, "On Kingship," in Ebenstein, *Great Political Thinkers*, 231.

20 Pius XI, *Quadragesimo Anno*, 232.

21 The National Conference of Catholic Bishops, *Economic Justice for All: Pastoral Letter on Catholic Social Teaching and the U.S. Economy* (Washington, D.C.: U.S. Catholic Conference, 1986), par. 7, vii.

22 Maritain, *Man and the State,* 84.

23 *Ibid.*, 85-86.

24 *Ibid.*, 11.

25 *Ibid.*

26 *Ibid.*

27 Dooyeweerd, *Roots*, 125.

28 Maritain, *Man and the State*, 24.

29 *Ibid.*

30 National Conference of Catholic Bishops, *Economic Justice for All*, par. 314, 155. Compare par. 28, 15; pars. 79-84, 40-44; and pars. 99-124, 50-62. Some worthy assessments of the American Catholic Bishops with respect to some of these questions can be found in R. Bruce Douglass, ed., *The Deeper Meaning of Economic Life: Critical Essays on the U.S. Catholic Bishops' Pastoral Letter on the Economy* (Washington, D.C.: Georgetown University Press, 1986), and Charles R. Strain, ed., *Prophetic Visions and Economic Realities: Protestants, Jews and Catholics Confront the Bishops' Letter on the Economy* (Grand Rapids: Eerdmans Publishing Co., 1989).

31 See the exposition of this distinction in John F. Cox, *A Thomistic Analysis of the Social Order* (Washington, D.C.: The Catholic University of America Press, 1943), Chapter V.

32 Aquinas, "On Kingship," 232.

33 *Ibid.*

34 Quoted by *ibid*, 262.

35 *Ibid.*

36 *Ibid.*, 226.

37 Aquinas, *Summa Theologiae*, quoted by Ebenstein, *Great Political Thinkers*, 235.

38 Maritain, *Man and the State*, 11.

39 *Ibid.*

40 *Ibid.*

41 Oswald von Nell-Breuning, *Reorganization of Social Economy: The Social Encyclical Developed and Explained* (New York: Bruce Publishing Co., 1936), 224-225.

TWENTY ONE

SPHERE SOVEREIGNTY, CREATION ORDER, AND PUBLIC JUSTICE: AN EVALUATION

T hose standing in the progressive Calvinist tradition, provide both criticisms of other traditions and elaboration and criticism of their own tradition. Common threads clearly exist in the Calvinist tradition, as each author builds on earlier insights into sphere sovereignty, creation order, and public justice. But both the distinct contributions and the limitations of this tradition will best come to light if we follow the development of thought of each author in turn.

Abraham Kuyper

At the basis of Kuyper's entire social philosophy is his faith in the trinitarian God who establishes or casts down, blesses or curses, all human formative efforts in culture and society. Kuyper believes in the living and enduring lordship of Jesus Christ revealed in history—the reign of the transcendent King who will one day bring the entire creation to its promised fulfillment under his rule.

> Christ's Kingship, which concerns the life of states and nations, must be explained precisely in connection with the process of history. Christ establishes all ages in terms of the Kingdom of heaven, not in terms of the kingdom of this

world. From the hour of His ascension, He has been busy bringing to fulfillment this Kingdom of heaven which is *His* Kingdom and in which He rules as the King. His reign embraces all that has already gone on in this life and which now awaits the glory on the other side of the grave. And it embraces all of this world here below with all that belongs to this life by virtue of creation and common grace.[1]

There is both similarity and dissimilarity between Kuyper's and recent Roman Catholic social thought. On the one hand, Kuyper distinguishes between common grace and special (or particular) grace in a manner that very nearly fits the Catholic distinction of nature and grace. The essential basis for special grace, he says, is the supernatural, while common grace is restricted to the natural realm.[2] Only Christians share in the supernatural grace which carries them toward the new heavens and new earth, while all people share in common grace which pertains only to the preservation of life in this world.

Kuyper has no doubt that the original creation is restored in the new creation and that common grace has no purpose outside of particular grace.[3] Nevertheless, the dualistic motif is strong, for example, in his description of church and state.

> The church has its starting-point in the Word of God and in re-birth. Both of these are miracles. A miracle is precisely a phenomenon which reveals powers in nature which are not in nature but above it and which are joined to it. The miracle does not arise from the creation but from the re-creation. The state, by contrast, has its point of origin in nature.[4]

While Kuyper is explicit in his reference to God's creation order as the basis for sphere sovereignty, he does not make sufficiently clear the difference between the motive of creation-fall-redemption and that of nature-grace.

Nonetheless, several dissimilarities between Kuyper and Catholic Thomism become apparent in the way he develops the idea of sphere sovereignty. Despite his political cooperation with Catholics in opposition to the anti-Christian programs of the liberals and revolutionaries, he is not fully at home with the Catholic idea of the state. For Kuyper, the state takes its place not *above* all other spheres, but rather next to them. Its high and overarching position is due not to a natural hierarchy but to the state's peculiar character as *public* authority. At this point Kuyper, like Calvin, stands at a considerable distance from Aristotle and Thomas. The state is in no way self-sufficient; it is not the natural *telos* of other associations or spheres of social life; it is not the whole of which the latter are parts.

Moreover, Kuyper does not agree with the Catholic interpretation of how Christians should function in society and culture outside the institutional church. According to the Catholic, cultural life needs direct contact with, if not direct supervision by, the institutional Church in order for it to be fully Christian. In all areas of life, Catholic Church members remained *lay* people, needing moral oversight by the *clergy*. Calvinism, says Kuyper, brings about an entire change in viewpoint—a change described above in terms of its acceptance of one view of secularization and its rejection of another. The meaning of God's common grace for the creation, says Kuyper, is that it

> relaxes the curse which rests upon it, arrests its process of corruption, and thus allows untrammelled development of our life in which to glorify Himself as Creator. Thus the Church receded in order to be neither more nor less than the congregation of believers, and in every department the life of the world was not emancipated from God, but from the dominion of the Church. Thus domestic life regained its independence, trade and commerce realized their strength in liberty, art and science were set free from every ecclesiastical bond and restored to their own inspirations, and man began to understand the subjection of all nature with its hidden forces and treasures to himself as a holy duty, imposed upon him by the original ordinances of Paradise: "Have dominion over them." Henceforth the curse should no longer rest upon the *world* itself, but upon that which is *sinful* in it, and instead of monastic flight *from* the world the duty is now emphasized of serving God *in* the world, in every position in life.[5]

The basis for Kuyper's political thinking and action, therefore, is neither the Aristotelian philosophy of nature and society nor Enlightenment rationalism. Even though there is a strong thread of nature-grace duality in Kuyper, his philosophy of culture and society is rooted in a somewhat more unified view of God's sovereignty through Christ over the integral creation order—a sovereignty that upholds the creation, including all human creatures, through common grace and that demands a response to God in every sphere of life without hierarchical mediation by state or church. Despite his dualistic inclination, therefore, S.U. Zuidema writes,

> A full picture of Kuyper is not given unless it is also shown that he did not halt before his self-imposed problem, but broke through to the confession that truly Christian action is possible also in the domain of common grace. The fear of the Lord, not distinguishable from the confession and the experiencing of Jesus Christ as our Lord and King, is totalitarian in that it embraces not only the mystic life of the inner soul and not only the life of the hereafter but embraces no less our life "in all areas of life" in the present dispensation.[6]

Kuyper insists that cultural and political activities must themselves be conducted with a view to Christian reform. Jesus prayed for his disciples not that they be taken out of the world but that they be preserved in the world.

The apostle Paul wrote that Christians were to live differently from others in the world. This, says Kuyper, means

> that the calling of the Christian can in no way be fulfilled only within the church. The Christian also has a calling in the midst of the life of this world. And to the question, "How is this possible," "How is it thinkable that a child of God can still have business with a sinful world?" comes the loud, clear answer: "This is possible and necessary because God Himself still has business with this world!" Moreover, God's business with the world is precisely that which is declared to us in His *common grace*.[7]

Another point of contrast between Kuyper and the Catholics is the stress that he places on the religious antithesis between the Kingdom of God and the kingdom of darkness, between the religious motive of biblical Christianity and that of human claims of rational self-sufficiency. The basic antithesis or opposition on earth is not between church and society, or between past and present, or between liberals and conservatives, but between the spirit of Christian reformation and the spirit of anti-Christian deformation in all areas of life.[8] Deformation can occur even in the institutional church, while definite Christian reformation (according to God's ordinances) can also take place in politics. This view of creation under God's judgment and renewal is what gives unity to Kuyper's Christian social theory. It calls forth his program of organized, non-ecclesiastical activity by Christians in all spheres of life. On this foundation he stands apart from the humanists who do not recognize the normative ordering of human life by the transcendent Creator God. On this foundation he also takes some distance from Catholics who see the church institution as the primary sacramental and supervising force for anything that is specifically Christian on earth.

Kuyper stands radically opposed to the individualist conception of human nature that underlies liberal contract theories of society and government. Human beings are social creatures.[9] Kuyper thinks about human social nature and politics differently from Aquinas, however. The state is not "natural" in an inherent teleological way as it is for Thomists. Civil government comes as a gift of God's common grace for the preservation and advancement of human society *after*, not before, the fall into sin.

Features of Kuyper's view of the state should be emphasized. First, although the state was established due to sin the state itself is not evil or inherently sinful. On the contrary, it is a good and great blessing in view of human sinfulness.[10] Second, since earthly governments are a gift of God's common grace, they do not derive from the original unity of creation.[11] According to Kuyper, the entire human race was, by virtue of creation, one tremendous or-

ganism. By contrast, state life is not an organic unity but a mechanical association which holds together the parts and broken pieces of our sinful human
race which otherwise would disintegrate in anarchy. There would have been
no need for the state had humanity not turned away from obedience to God.

Whereas the state is, for Catholic thinkers, the inherent, natural development of a higher unity in human society, it appears to Kuyper to be more
like a dike against the flood of chaos produced by the brokenness of sinful
human beings. After all, Kuyper reasons, we have only ever seen states, never
the state. In sin the human race has become divided; by God's common grace
partial unity is recovered here and there through civil governments. Thus, we
see that God's common grace is directly and intentionally embodied in the
civil state.

Kuyper's ambiguous conception of nature and grace reappears in this line
of argument. Even if we grant that God's grace restrains sin and that human
states can only have a limited task in recovering human community, it is still
difficult to grasp what God's grace "creates" that is not implicit in the original
order of creation. If humans had not sinned, would there not have been a
public, civil order which would be visibly actualized under God's
sovereignty? Is this not the normative order that underlies the public legal
authority of earthly states? Kuyper suggests that this would be the case, and
that the state rises from nature not from grace, but he does not elaborate.[12]

Kuyper says that in the state nothing exists which has not been taken
from nature.[13] There is a territory; there is someone who comes to exercise
the governmental authority; laws are made; rules are established; and so forth.
None of this, he says, is the result of a supernatural miracle. It is all wholly
natural, developing through the course of history. Apparently, then, Kuyper is
not talking about something ontically new brought in from outside the original creation order. Common grace expressed in the formation of states is
simply a preserving, restraining act of God for the sake of his creation.
Nevertheless, at points Kuyper does seem to imply that God has, by means of
common grace, injected something new into the world which human beings
in their sinfulness could not and would not possess or develop.[14] Not only is
it difficult to get a clear idea of how the pre-fall order of creation is related to
the post-fall order, but it is also difficult to understand the relationship of
common grace to special grace. On the one hand, Kuyper tries to distinguish
them sharply, but, on the other hand, he wants to show their close connection.

> The kingdoms of the world live their own lives. The powers which work in our
> states do not come from Christian ordinances but from common grace. The
> earthly powers form together as it were the great body of visible things. But also

in this body there is a spiritual power at work which is the power of Christ. Through this spiritual power, which Christ exercises in the body of the king- doms of this world, He makes these kingdoms serviceable to His high and holy purpose, that is, to the revelation of the Kingdom of heaven.[15]

Finally, we must say that Kuyper's political philosophy does not grow and deepen to the point where he is able to elaborate on the notion of public justice as the norm of state life. Undoubtedly part of the reason for this is his immersion in practical political, ecclesiastical, educational, and journalistic affairs of his day. He had little time for extended philosophic reflection. Another part of the reason is that his concept of the state itself is quite ambiguous. He knows that the state has a different identity and purpose than the church or family or school. He is convinced that the state should not try to be a church or some other kind of institution. He affirms in countless ways that government's task is to protect confessional and societal pluralism. And yet the meaning of public justice as a creational norm for political life retains some of the same looseness and ambiguity that the phrase "common good" holds for Catholic thinkers.

Herman Dooyeweerd

Dooyeweerd grew up in, and continued Kuyper's line of thought and ac- tion—a line that goes back through Groen van Prinsterer to Johannes Althusius and John Calvin. The spirit of reformation meant for these Christians the necessity of continually reforming life and thought in the light of biblical revelation. For this reason, Dooyeweerd does not hesitate to criti- cize the tradition in which he stands. He confronts the ambiguities of Kuyper directly.

Dooyeweerd finds in Kuyper two different lines or directions of thought. One derives from the biblical religious motive which Dooyeweerd summa- rizes by using the phrase "creation, fall into sin, and redemption of the cre- ation through Christ." The other line of thought is more traditionally Thomistic or scholastic, displaying the synthesis of classical Greek and Stoic convictions with biblical themes.[16] The scholastic conception of human na- ture, for example, is that of a rational soul and a material body.[17] Kuyper ac- cepts this, though at various points in his writing he insists that human na- ture is an integral whole as expressed by the biblical word "heart."[18] Dooyeweerd argues that these two approaches in Kuyper cannot be recon- ciled, and therefore Dooyeweerd chooses to develop more consistently the biblical, non-synthetic line of Kuyper's thought.[19] Dooyeweerd expects his own efforts to be criticized in turn. He believes that the critical refinement of

Calvinism in the modern Dutch tradition up through Kuyper led to a more and more self-consciously biblical approach to social and political thought. He wants to continue the process of criticism and reform.

The first thing to stress is that Dooyeweerd begins with creation order as the full meaning of ontic (or ontological) reality. In other words, everything that exists, including all of human reality, needs to be understood as depending on and referring to God the Creator. Life in this world does not have a natural meaning (whether as substance, or matter, or something else) that can be grasped rationally apart from its divinely created meaning and dependency. The identity of everything is to be found in its dependent character as the revelatory creation of God. God's sovereignty, then, as Dooyeweerd understands it, is not simply an overwhelming or superior power above the "natural" world that brings it to judgment and redemption. Rather, God's sovereignty is expressed first of all in the creation order that he made and still upholds. Nothing, no meaning, exists outside the relation of creatures to the Creator.

This is the key to understanding Dooyeweerd's development of the concept of "sphere sovereignty." The concept of sphere sovereignty is valuable not, first of all, because it helps to justify our presently existing differentiated society or because it can be used to block movements toward a totalitarian society. Rather, sphere sovereignty points us to God as the author of all diversity and unity and meaning in life.[20] God's ordinances hold us accountable in this vast and complicated creation of which we are a part. Social diversity is always connected with creational unity from a Christian point of view. Our creaturely obligation is to ask, How may we serve God obediently? How should we serve our neighbors and develop all aspects of creaturely life in allegiance to God? The answer is that we should direct all of life, our whole heart, to God by seeking to obey all his ordinances in thankfulness for his creative and redeeming love. This means looking carefully to see how the full diversity of social life should be developed properly, each according to its own created nature—science, art, education, economic enterprise, politics, and so forth. Sphere sovereignty is simply a shorthand phrase to express the idea that a diversity of creational arenas call for human obedience to God as part of humanity's unified service to the Creator.

What Dooyeweerd does that Kuyper did not do, is to take this basic insight into the creation's unity and diversity and develop the implications of sphere sovereignty in more consistent philosophic detail. As we saw in the excerpts from his writings, Dooyeweerd distinguishes two different horizons or dimensions of the creation's ontic structure, both of which can be referred to with the concept of sphere sovereignty.

The first and most immediate horizon of our experience, he argues, is the concrete experience of multiple institutions and associations of which we are a part. Kuyper appropriated the phrase "sphere sovereignty" from Groen to refer to that diversity of social life. Dooyeweerd continues that usage while going on in more detail to describe and analyze the complex nature of the typical "identity structures" (or individuality structures) of social reality.

The second "horizon" of our experience to which Dooyeweerd points is the "modal" structure of reality. These ontic modes or functional dimensions of life are not experienced directly as things and institutions; rather, they are the universal qualifying boundaries of our experience which tell us "how" things exist, not "what" exists. Kuyper had done little if anything to describe or explain this horizon of the creation's structure, whereas Dooyeweerd makes his most creative contribution at this point.

Dooyeweerd argues that each existing thing, including every social entity, reveals a distinct qualifying aspect while functioning in all the modal dimensions of the creation. For example, a family is "qualified" differently than a state or a business enterprise. A family exists normatively as a community of kinship love. A state, on the other hand, is qualified by a guiding juridical norm. And a business enterprise can be identified by its qualifying obligation of economic stewardship. Each of these institutions functions in all modalities of creation; each functions juridically, economically, ethically, linguistically, etc., but each is qualified by a different modal "leading function" which is constitutive of its peculiar identity and purpose. Thus, when the "whole" institution or organization is analyzed with regard to its sphere of responsibility (or sphere of sovereignty), it displays a typical character (a distinguishable "identity structure").[21]

In Dooyeweerd's hands sphere sovereignty is deepened as a concept for interpreting the ontic identity of diverse social structures. He takes history seriously since he recognizes a historical modal function structuring all of reality; but he does not reduce the complex structure of society to its historical modality. He takes rationality seriously since he recognizes a modal function of logical thought in everything human; but he does not absolutize reason as the means of access to a universal order of nature or being. Logical reasoning is part of the creation and does not transcend it; rationality is only one among many important human functions. Sphere sovereignty refers to both the complex modal character and the diversified social character of creational meaning whereby God upholds the boundaries and identities of creaturely life.

With respect to this philosophy of creation order, Dooyeweerd is closer to the natural law thinkers than to historicists because he acknowledges heteronomous principles that hold for human beings in this world. Nevertheless,

Dooyeweerd rejects the rationalism and the naturalism of the natural law tradition.[22] God's obligating norms or ordinances are not rational principles of universal, natural being. God's laws hold for the creation, including human thought and all modes and societal spheres, in ways that are not reducible to rational principles. Dooyeweerd rejects, on biblical grounds, the relatively independent naturalism and rationalism of the Greek and Roman traditions as they became synthesized in Thomism. Just as he wants to distance himself from the scholasticism latent in Kuyper's thought, so he wants to find a more consistently and integrally biblical understanding of creation order than he finds in the mainstream of Thomist natural law doctrine.

The principle of subsidiarity, for Dooyeweerd, relies too much on the general idea of a natural, rational hierarchy of being without a sufficiently differentiated interpretation of the identity and meaning of each social unit, each in its own sphere. The idea of the common good also remains too general and undifferentiated to provide an adequate qualifying norm for the state or political community.

With his twofold account of sphere sovereignty as both social and modal, Dooyeweerd offers a creative approach to an understanding of the ontic status of social institutions and associations. He neither reduces all social entities to the individuals who compose them, nor does he look for static forms or ideal models of institutions in a transcendent world. For Dooyeweerd the entire creation is what it is by virtue of divine creativity. God created different creatures, all of which have their identity in relation to his ordinances. The creation is not substantial matter to which God has given different rational forms. There is only God and his creation, and his creation is the diversity of things he has created, each bound by his laws and ordinances. The fact that a family or a school or a business enterprise is not an individual person does not mean that it has no ontological identity; it simply means that it does not have the same identity that an individual person has. A family, or school, or state is each a different type of human community or social structure. There is more to the reality of human life than individual persons. Human beings have their distinct and unique identities in and through communities and associations. These social entities are differentiated expressions of human community. They express human life in different kinds of organized activities and sustained relationships—all on the basis of creation ordinances, both modal and associational.

The ontic identity of any particular institution or association, therefore, is to be found in the way that it expresses a particular type of social life in all the modal dimensions of the creation. That is to say, the ontic foundation of social life is neither a substance in general nor "substantial" individual persons. Rather, it is the creation order which exists by design of the Creator and shows itself in the various creatures God has made. Human creatures exist in a variety of institutions and relationships each of which, with its own structural identity, is bound by all the norms of physical, rational, historical, linguistic, social, aesthetic, juridical, ethical, and other modes of life.

Dooyeweerd's analysis certainly does not guarantee that one can always interpret the meaning of human existence correctly, much less that human beings can thereby be assured of success in shaping human institutions. What his philosophy does is to direct our attention to the creationally normative meaning of that diverse reality. Or, to put it another way, Dooyeweerd points the way towards avoiding reductionism in all its varieties. Instead of explaining away all social entities by reference to their individual members, or historical origins, or rational character, Dooyeweerd takes seriously the differentiated character of society. Instead of dissolving social diversity into one political or social whole, he acknowledges both the diversity of society and the enkaptic, public-legal integrating functions of the state. He recognizes social structures for what they are, namely, essential diversified expressions of human community. Instead of looking for "substance" underneath or behind reality, he accepts the reality of individual and social life as the actual world in which human beings serve either the true God or false gods in all that they do. Instead of making too much or too little of social institutions and associations, particularly the state, he accepts all these realities as part of what constitutes the creation.

If Dooyeweerd's strength is to be found in the philosophical framework he has developed for a more detailed interpretation of the ontic basis of diverse societal structures, his weakness is evident in having not sufficiently articulated the implications of this perspective for an understanding of the state as a concrete institution in our everyday experience.[23]

Dooyeweerd's criticism of "liberalism" helps to overcome the reduction of politics to mere contractualism. His criticism of historicism shows how to appreciate the historical foundation of the state while still recognizing that the state is not simply a historical thing. His criticism of Thomism points to the need for a more specific understanding of the state as a differentiated community of public justice rather than as a community of the common good. Dooyeweerd's development of the idea of social sphere sovereignty opens the way to an ontological differentiation of institutions and relationships in a way that the subsidiarity principle is incapable of doing.

Nevertheless, Dooyeweerd's interpretation is dominated by *modal* rather than *institutional* analysis. Modal analysis is crucial because, as Dooyeweerd shows, the modal horizon of our experience is fundamental for all of life. If we examine political life carefully from a modal point of view, then we can understand more clearly the state's unique function in all modalities—ethical, aesthetic, juridical, linguistic, etc.—because of its particular identity structure. But modal analysis focuses on a horizon of our experience that is secondary in immediacy. Modal or functional analysis of the state is a theoretical analysis that abstracts from the state the multiple aspects of its existence. Modal analysis does not focus on the state in its concrete actuality and fullness as an integral and functioning entity of our everyday experience.

Dooyeweerd himself shows that the horizon of everyday experience (what he calls "naive" or immediate experience) is prior to theoretical reflection and abstraction. In other words, theoretical analysis of the modalities of experience presupposes everyday, naive experience. Our direct experience of political life is prior to the possibility of analyzing the modal dimensions of that experience. But the state as an integral community of public justice receives only very slight development in Dooyeweerd's hands.

One of the most valuable insights that he provides, however, is his distinction between the "whole/part" relationship and "sphere sovereignty." This allows for a better understanding of how the state can, through public law, integrate into a community of public justice all other institutions and societal relationships without thereby reducing them to "parts" of a single whole. Such reductionism is the danger of the subsidiarity principle with its idea of the broader common good. Subsidiarity and common good do not account for the particular identity of each societal institution.

Dooyeweerd's analysis also shows up the weakness of the liberals' attempt to define a limited state purely by means of external boundaries, constitutional restraints, and a stress on the priority of the individual as the only ontological reality. The state is a true community, a real social institution which requires an appreciation of its actual, internal identity and boundaries. The state is not a boundless, function of human will or reason; it is a limited, identifiable institution of citizens and government qualified by its own normative principles, called to fulfill its own ends, purposes, and means. If the state moves in a totalitarian direction, this calls for more than external restraint; it demands a normative recall of the state to its own proper purpose of maintaining a community of public justice which is, by definition, distinguishable from all other institutions and communities which the state may not dominate or take over as parts of itself.

H. Evan Runner

The selection from Runner above displays clearly the many lines of thought drawn together from Groen, Kuyper, and Dooyeweerd. His criticism of the French Revolution, showing both its religious character as well as its deep historical roots, carries forward Groen's thesis. His profound insight into the meaning of *ratio* (reason)—both in its classical and modern senses—carries forward Dooyeweerd's work on the religious roots of all theorizing and sheds further light on both Kuyper's and Dooyeweerd's struggle with synthesis thinking in Christian circles. His critique of liberalism and conservatism depends on Kuyper's and Dooyeweerd's work along the same line.

Though his published writings do not take it far enough, Runner's critical assessment of North American political thinking and practice is especially valuable for our purposes in this volume. If one compares the selections from Runner with those from the American Catholic Bishops' pastoral letter and from Míguez Bonino, for example, one will notice significant contrasts. All three call for the renewal of a biblical, covenantal vision and for a Christian-inspired reform of society. All three criticize liberalism and conservatism. All three sense deep injustice in contemporary societies. But whereas the American Catholic Bishops are quick to appeal to the common reason of all citizens, and whereas Míguez Bonino is quick to synthesize Marxism and biblical revelation, Runner challenges all synthesizing efforts and argues that an uncritical appeal to a common rationality is actually antithetical to an appeal for reform based on distinctly Christian principles.

Runner also displays some interesting contrasts with Edmund Burke and J.N. Figgis. Runner's criticism of historicism goes to the heart of the weakness in Burke's and Figgis' approaches. While the latter two wish to find a basis for pluralism, they can do little more than establish the weight of the past against the present. But once the past becomes a world that has been shaped by several generations of liberals or radicals, it is no longer a past that earlier conservatives would have wanted to hold onto. On what grounds of historical argument, therefore, may newer conservatives now distinguish between the historical factors they approve and those which they disapprove? Historicism collapses into relativism or arbitrariness at this point.[24] Simply by noting the contrast between Runner's treatment of Hugo Grotius as one of the first modernists and Figgis' treatment of Grotius as one of the fathers of healthy constitutionalism, one will see how different are the glasses through which Runner and Figgis are looking. Compared to Runner, Burke and Figgis are hardly conscious of the deep religious roots of the conflicting social and political philosophies of their times.[25]

What Runner most helps us to do is to make connections between many of the selections in this volume and the work of the North American authors whom we dealt with in our Introduction. Ralph Hancock, for example, notes that a large part of the controversy over Calvin concerns the question of whether he had a medieval or a modern view of reason. Hancock only indirectly stumbles over the question of contrasting religious motives that shape the diverse answers to this question. Runner helps to show why a Calvinist attempt to think through the consequences of the creation's complete and utter dependency on God must lead to a critical rejection of both classical reason (Aristotelianism, Stoicism) and modern rationalism (Descartes, Grotius, Locke). A biblically motivated theory and political practice (à la Calvin) simply does not fit into either medieval or modern humanist camps. Calvinism of the sort that Runner applauds must be understood in terms of a different basic religious motive.

Alasdair MacIntyre who appears to accept the Thomist synthesis and Jeffrey Stout who does not, both wish to find grounds for supporting a society of multiple institutions in which many different and sound virtues can flourish. Both reject the leveling influences of liberalism and capitalism. Runner's explanation of the conflict between a Reason which serves as law-giver and a Creator who establishes the creation's laws for rationality (as well as for everything else) helps to show why neither Stout's pragmatism nor MacIntyre's rational/natural traditionalism will be able to fulfill all the demands of normativity for human thought and moral action. Runner's insight into the incompatibility between a humanistic "community ideal" and the actual conflicts among people rooted in different religious motives also helps to explain the reason for the incompatibility among different "rational" traditions that MacIntyre struggles so carefully to expose.[26]

What Runner does not offer is any particular advance in the interpretation of sphere sovereignty and public justice for North American politics. Given the multiple questions of normativity regarding the task and limits of the state in a complex society shaped by liberalism, conservatism, Christianity, and the classical traditions, we must ask today, What are some of the implications for our constitutional order to be drawn from the work of Dooyeweerd in particular?

Bernard Zylstra

In the selection from Zylstra we find an attempt to work out some of the implications for American constitutionalism of the Kuyperian tradition.

First, if the state is a community under public law in which its citizens should receive their due, then we must ask what is due to them? What are their civil rights? The question of public justice, Zylstra shows, is specifically a question of public legal rights and duties, not a question of an undifferentiated common good or of mere historical precedent.

Second, individual persons are not alone in requiring the protection of their rights. If government's task is to give to each its rightful due, then institutional and associational rights must not be ignored or reduced to individual rights.

Third, if human beings are by their very nature religious creatures serving different gods (whether transcendent or earth-bound), then religious rights of citizens ought to be protected by the Constitution in ways that permit them genuinely to practice their religions. In other words, we must cut through the dominant public secularism of American society that allows public law to predefine religion as a private matter, which may legitimately be confined to individual conscience and to churches. The religious practice of citizens, Zylstra argues, also extends to the way they educate their children, heal the sick, and otherwise shape their culture.

In this light, the American Constitution should be reinterpreted and American law should be reformed to recognize the freedom of diverse religious practices both by individuals as well as by institutions and associations beyond the churches. Only by granting citizens these rights can each person and social entity be given its due in public law. "How can we have a free society," Zylstra asks, "when the rights of the mediating structures organized for the praise of God are not constitutionally protected?"[27]

In order to advance public justice in the American republic, the sphere sovereignty of different institutions and associations must be protected. This requires disestablishment of secularism but not the disconnection of the state from other institutions. "I am not advocating a medical, educational, or social laissez-faire policy," writes Zylstra. "Nor am I advocating a states' rights solution to these problems (as if local and state governments are inherently less secular than the federal government)."[28] Rather, he argues, the state should give each person and institution its due, its rights, including equal protection of the free exercise of religion in all spheres of life.

By appealing to the First, Ninth, Tenth, and Fourteenth Amendments of the Constitution of the United States as well as to the United Nations Universal Declaration of Human Rights, Zylstra points the way to a recognition of institutional rights and to going "beyond the individualism of the Enlightenment world view reflected in the U. S. Bill of Rights."[29] The result will be a genuine social pluralism—both religious and structural—that can clarify the state's unique task and limits to establish public justice and to protect the creationally grounded sphere sovereignty of other institutions and associations.

"Let us openly and honestly recognize," Zylstra concludes, "that the American citizenry is religiously divided. And then let us avail ourselves of the constitutional weapons so that the legitimate rights of each religious segment in the citizenry are properly acknowledged, not only in the private spheres of life but also in the public realm."[30]

Although Zylstra's insights here and elsewhere remained underdeveloped at the time of his death, they have had a catalytic effect in the work of scholars as well as organizations such as the Association for Public Justice in the United States and Citizens for Public Justice in Canada.

Bob Goudzwaard

Goudzwaard's essay on sphere sovereignty advances the development of that concept primarily by confronting some of the conservative distortions and misuses of it in The Netherlands from the time of Kuyper to the present. Perhaps Goudzwaard's most important point is that sphere sovereignty should be understood as an attempt to articulate the normative character of God's will for creation. It may not be used as a rationalization of the historical status quo—as a simple justification of the rights of people who hold authority in various institutions as presently structured. Both those in authority and those under authority must bow before divine law—the creation norms. Goudzwaard emphasizes in a somewhat different way Dooyeweerd's argument that sphere sovereignty points us first of all to God's sovereignty over human life.

Goudzwaard's emphasis on the dynamic meaning of normativity is also important in this regard. The idea of sphere sovereignty has frequently been misunderstood as a justification for a particular arrangement of social institutions. Kuyper was even used by some Afrikaner philosophers to justify apartheid, though Kuyper's idea of sphere sovereignty does not identify nations or races as social spheres. Sphere sovereignty does not make reference to racial groups or to race-based national sovereignties. Nor does it stand for a static form of differentiated institutions or cultural groups. Rather, it points to divine mandates that call human beings to creative shaping and reshaping of society. The differentiation of social institutions and relationships which conform to such transcendent norms as justice, stewardship, and love should be welcomed and appreciated, but they never exist without some sinful distortions and can never be frozen as if time and history can be stopped. Divine norms for society's structure always call to account unjust, unstewardly, unloving institutions, and thus, call human beings to reformation and renewal.

Also important in this regard is Goudzwaard's development of the contrast between "norms" and "goals" in his essay on the international economic order. Just as it is necessary to contrast "norm" with "form" in order to see the principle of sphere sovereignty, so we must recognize that a norm is not a subjectively projected goal. Human beings do set goals for themselves, and their institutions will inevitably set goals to guide their actions into the future. But goal-setting is part of the subjective *response* to divine normativity as humans seek to shape social life. Projected goals should never be allowed to stand in the place of divine norms. Rather they must be held accountable by the norms which determine whether the institutions and their goals are just or unjust, stewardly or unstewardly, economical or uneconomical, and so forth. Goudzwaard's development of this contrast is an important extension and clarification of Kuyper's and Dooyeweerd's understanding of the meaning of sphere sovereignty.

Despite Goudzwaard's extensive discussion of "norms," we are not satisfied, however, that he has adequately articulated and developed the meaning of social sphere sovereignty, especially with respect to the nature of the state and its character as a differentiated community of public justice. In this regard, while Goudzwaard benefits greatly from Dooyeweerd's modal analysis of juridical, economic, and social norms, he also seems to remain limited by Dooyeweerd's underdeveloped discussion of the social sphere sovereignty of concrete institutions and relationships in our everyday experience. This comes through especially in the second selection on international economic norms.

When Goudzwaard says that a just government may have to "bring back" an unstewardly business enterprise "to its original calling,"[31] he seems to suggest something more in keeping with the *Catholic* idea of the "common good." Is public justice a norm that gives governments a universal scope of responsibility for society? On what basis does a government decide what is the proper calling of a business enterprise? If government may call back an unstewardly business to its original calling, may it also call back an unloving family, or a heretical church, or an unscholarly university to its original calling? Are there no boundaries beyond which government may not go in addressing these malformed, nonstate institutions?

Goudzwaard may, of course, be saying simply that government is responsible to redress *public* injustice which arises from the distortion of public law and order by unstewardly business enterprises. He may intend to say simply that public laws against pollution, for example, are necessary to keep industries from exceeding the proper bounds of their responsibility leading to the destruction of the public welfare. This is consistent with the idea that the specific sphere of responsibility belonging to government in a state entails respect for the specific sphere of responsibility of a business enterprise. The public trust is not the kind of universal domain that gives government an undifferentiated right of responsibility for all of society. As Goudzwaard says in his discussion of the international order, "Governments have received power in order that they may righteously serve society, without, however, having to regulate everything in it. . . . In other words, not every form of injustice, not every evidence of uneconomic or unsocial behavior is a matter of government concern (or, on the international level, of concern to cooperating governments)."[32]

Those with governmental authority indeed ought to appeal to business and labor leaders to change their internal operating procedures in view of public problems that arise from those private activities. Government may even need to take public legal action (through pollution laws, child labor and other laws) to protect civic rights and the public trust if businesses fail to act in ways that are conducive to public justice. But this is something different from suggesting that government may decide what the original and proper calling of a business enterprise is and then legislate the internal laws and purposes of any enterprise.

By analogy, governments may, indeed, have to begin warning parents and drawing up new public laws such as curfews to govern juveniles if crime, drug addiction, and other habits detrimental to the public continue to grow. But this is something quite different from the government attempting to "bring families back" to their original calling by deciding what a good family should be and then preempting parental responsibility by laying down the laws and rules for internal family behavior.

Even if Goudzwaard's statements are not more ambiguous than the statements of those Catholics who appeal to the common good, he, nonetheless, leaves himself open to the charge that the norm of "public justice" is too undifferentiated to serve as a guiding principle for government within its specific sphere of responsibility. Goudzwaard, like Dooyeweerd, does not fully develop the idea of the state (or political community) as a particular differentiated institution among others with its own unique responsibility, dictated by the norms of public justice. For those who wish to make the most of the Kuyperian tradition, this remains one of the greatest challenges.[33]

This problem is especially important when it comes to considerations of international public justice. Goudzwaard rightly calls for greater international justice by means of public institutions. Here the need is for transnational public authorities that can lay down and enforce laws for global, or at least regional, public justice. But, without greater clarity about the nature of a public legal order in contrast to nonpublic institutions and relationships, an appeal for greater international justice can sound like an opening in the direction of a dangerous global totalitarianism. The fact is, however, as Goudzwaard shows, that much of the world suffers from grave injustice and a lack of freedom precisely because of the present international arrangements. What is needed is greater justice. The economic dimension of international justice is only one part of public justice. Development of the idea of institutional responsibility and accountability is necessary if we are to be able to point properly to a transnational public sphere of responsibility for governmental authorities. Goudzwaard's discussion which is confined mostly to general modal analysis of economic, social, and juridical norms is not sufficient to clarify the nature of societal sphere sovereignty.

The final point that Goudzwaard makes in the first selection is especially important in face of all the contending pluralist and nonpluralist approaches to social and political theory. Sphere sovereignty is not a one-way street; it is not a principle designed simply to keep government out of economic or religious life. It must not be misused by ideological liberals in the individualist tradition to justify laissez-faire economic policies. It must not be allowed to serve as a tool for any ideological position that wants to use government as a means to other ends. The state has its own rights; government has its own obligation to foster a just political community. A constitution must articulate more than the obligations of government toward its citizens and nongovernmental institutions. Citizens and nonpublic institutions and associations must also respect and honor the rights of the state.

Here again, however, Goudzwaard makes too little of government's specific responsibility for public law and public governance. He is properly concerned about distortions in public life because of the way that business enterprises, for example, have influenced the shape of bad public laws. But he needs to show how this produces an unjust *public* community—a community that requires reformation of its own public laws. It is not enough to point to the mistaken (perhaps even selfish) intentions of business enterprises as if society could have greater public justice if it could only reform business and redirect the decisions of business leaders.

In conclusion, we should underline the importance of Goudzwaard's contribution to the discussion of economic justice. Clearly in our day the economic issues, both domestic and international, are among the most urgent and pressing issues we face. The issues recently raised by Míguez Bonino and the American Catholic Bishops are of urgent importance in our shrinking globe. A pluralist alternative to individualism and universalism must prove itself by the way it takes on and attempts to resolve the great problems of political economy—the relation of business to government and of business to labor, the terms of international trade and finance, freedom for economic activity which is not allowed to overwhelm a healthy public order, employment, ecological balance, care for the poor and elderly, and much more.

This is not to say that questions about the proper sphere of responsibility of families, schools, churches, and other institutions and organizations have all been answered and that only economic questions remain. But clearly the problems that confront every attempt to build a truly pluralistic and just society along with a just and differentiated global order are problems that call us again and again to urgent economic considerations. Goudzwaard has done much, from out of the Kuyperian tradition, to point the way toward dealing with economic matters so that structural pluralism can be strengthened and defended.

NOTES

1 Abraham Kuyper, *Pro Rege* (Kampen: J.H. Kok, 1911-12), 3: 268-269. Much of the critique of Kuyper's perspective in this section is taken from James W. Skillen, "The Development of Calvinistic Political Theory in the Netherlands" (Ph.D. Diss. Duke, 1974), 225-273.

2 Abraham Kuyper, *De Gemeene Gratie* (Amsterdam: Hoverker and Wormser, 1902-04), 3: 105.

3 See S.U. Zuidema, "Common Grace and Christian Action in Abraham Kuyper," in S. U. Zuidema, *Communication and Confrontation: A Philosophical Appraisal and Critique of Modern Society and Contemporary Thought* (Toronto: Wedge Publishing Foundation, 1972), 94-101.

4 J. D. Dengerink, *Critisch-Historisch Onderzoek naar de Sociologisch Ontwikkeling van het Beginsel der "Souvereiniteit in Eigen Kring" in de 19e en 20e Eeuw* (Kampen: J.H. Kok, 1948), 101.

5 Abraham Kuyper, *Lectures on Calvinism* (Grand Rapids: Eerdmans, 1961 [1898]), 30. For a further consideration of the debate over secularization as it relates to The Netherlands, see James W. Skillen and Stanley W. Carlson-Thies, "Religion and Political Development in Holland," *Publius (The Journal of Federalism)* 12 (Summer, 1982): 43-64.

6 Zuidema, "Common Grace," 96-97.

7 Kuyper, *De Gemeene Gratie*, 3: 14.

8 Kuyper, *Pro Rege*, 1: 498-509.

9 "In the beginning God did not create individuals, but men who together constituted one human race, who formed an organic unity, and who together with all that existed constituted the world." *Ibid.*, 3: 253.

10 Kuyper, *De Gemeene Gratie*, 3: 30-34.

[11] *Ibid.*, 99; Kuyper, *Pro Rege*, 3: 229.

[12] Kuyper, *Lectures on Calvinism*, 78-80, 85. Kuyper's summary statement is: "Sin has, in the realm of politics, broken down the direct government of God, and therefore the exercise of authority, for the purpose of government has subsequently been invested in men, as a mechanical remedy." *Ibid.*, 85.

[13] Kuyper, *De Gemeene Gratie*, 3: 105.

[14] "If sin had not come to disturb the unity of the human race, then government would have been entirely unnecessary, and there would have been no dissolution needing to be bound up. There would have been no need of legal requirements where everyone walked in righteousness." Kuyper, *Pro Rege*, 3: 256-257.

[15] *Ibid.*, 271.

[16] Herman Dooyeweerd, *The Christian Idea of the State*, trans. J. Kraay (Nutley, NJ: The Craig Press, 1968), 4. See also, Dooyeweerd, "Kuyper's Wetenschapsleer," *Philosophia Reformata,* 4 (1939): 197.

[17] Dooyeweerd, "Kuyper's Wetenschapsleer," 200-204.

[18] *Ibid.*, 210-211.

[19] We noticed the dualism in Kuyper when discussing his doctrine of common grace. Zuidema uncovers the two directions which Kuyper tries to take in that regard, and he concludes, just as Dooyeweerd has done, that one must choose between the contradictory elements in Kuyper, since it is not possible to reconcile them even as Kuyper himself could not reconcile them. Zuidema, "Common Grace," 94-101.

[20] See H.G. Geertsema, "De actualiteit van 'De Souvereiniteit in eigen Kring'," in *Beweging* (Magazine of the Association for Reformed Philosophy in the Netherlands), April, 1985, 22ff. See also James W. Skillen, "Politics, Pluralism, and the Ordinances of God," in Henry Vander Goot, ed., *Life is Religion: Essays in Honor of H. Evan Runner* (St. Catharines, Ontario: Paideia Press, 1981), 201-205.

[21] For further exposition and criticism, see Herman Dooyeweerd, *A Christian Theory of Social Institutions*, trans. M. Verbrugge, ed. J. Witte (La Jolla, CA: The Herman Dooyeweerd Foundation, 1986); Skillen, "The Development of Calvinistic Political Theory in the Netherlands," 275-331, 378-383, and James W. Skillen, "Herman Dooyeweerd's Contribution to the Philosophy of the Social Sciences," *Journal of the American Scientific Affiliation*, 31 (March, 1979): 20-24. An excellent exposition and development of Dooyeweerd's modal theory in relation to the religious roots of all theory is Roy Clouser, *The Myth of Religious Neutrality: An Essay on the Hidden Role of Religious Belief in Theories* (Notre Dame, IN: Notre Dame University Press [forthcoming, 1991]).

[22] In addition to the brief selection from Dooyeweerd included above, see his longer discussion of Thomism and natural law in *Roots of Western Culture: Pagan, Secular, and Christian Options*, trans. J. Kraay, eds. M. Vander Vennen and B. Zylstra (Toronto: Wedge Publishing Foundation, 1979), 111-147, and Herman Dooyeweerd *A New Critique of Theoretical Thought*, trans. D. Freeman, H. de Jongste, and W. Young (Philadelphia: Presbyterian and Reformed Publishing Co., 1953-58), 1: 169-190. See also O.J.L. Albers, *Het Natuurrecht volgens de Wijsbegeerte der Wetsidee* (Nijmegen: Janssen, 1955).

[23] This is not to say that Dooyeweerd has not written in detail about the state. See Dooyeweerd, *A New Critique*, 3: 379-508. Yet most of that analysis and discussion is from the point of view of the modal functions of the state.

[24] H. Evan Runner, *Scriptural Religion and Political Task*, 5th rev. ed. (Toronto: Wedge Publishing Foundation, 1974 [1961]), 92-93.

[25] *Ibid.*, 65-66, and J.N. Figgis, *Political Thought from Gerson to Grotius: 1414-1625* (New York: Harper Torchbooks, 1960 [1916, 1907]), 241-250.

[26] Runner, *Scriptural Religion*, 67-76.

27 Bernard J. Zylstra, "Using the Constitution to Defend Religious Rights," in Lynn Buzzard, ed., *Freedom and Faith: The Impact of Law on Religious Liberty* (Westchester, IL: Crossway Books, 1981), 105.

28 *Ibid.*, 106.

29 *Ibid.*, 107.

30 *Ibid.*, 112.

31 Goudzwaard, "Sphere Sovereignty," from text above.

32 Goudzwaard, "Norms for the International Economic Order," in *Justice in the International Economic Order* (Grand Rapids: Calvin College, 1980), 237-238.

33 See e.g., James W. Skillen, *The Scattered Voice* (Grand Rapids: Zondervan, 1990), and James W. Skillen, "Toward a Comprehensive Science of Politics," *Philosophia Reformata*, 53 (1988): 33-58.

EPILOGUE

In this closing decade of the twentieth century the question of how best to structure complex societies in an interdependent world has become increasingly practical and urgent. The challenges confronting people in the United States and around the world are not simply specific problems requiring pragmatic solutions within the existing political and economic frameworks—problems such as prison reform, better health services, a fairer tax rate, or improved public transit. Many of the most urgent challenges have to do with the existing systems themselves—in their entirety. The Soviet empire with its centralized economy is the question that requires a radical, reconstructive answer. South Africa's race-based state must be replaced in its entirety. The very nature of welfare politics in America's federal system— touching everything from child care to health care, from education to social security—is the question. The future shape of the European Community's multinational structure is the practical test of the moment. Questions about entire systems abound. Can India transcend its caste system? Will the Philippines or El Salvador ever be able to outgrow its semi-feudal past? Will a genuinely open society, with religious freedom and democratic participation, ever be possible in the states of the Middle East?

Critics of collectivism are now in the ascendancy throughout much of the world because of the large-scale collapse of communist systems in Eastern Europe. But in the United States and other Western countries the criticism of individualism is also growing. For example, Christopher Lasch, who picks up the criticism of liberal progressive optimism where Reinhold Niebuhr and Robert Nisbet left off, is now seeking wisdom from a populist, petty-bourgeois tradition which respects "the natural limits on human power and freedom" and inspires realistic hope rather than shallow optimism.[1] The ideal of limitless individual freedom is a destructive myth, Lasch concludes. Elizabeth Fox-Genovese calls for a more mature and sophisticated feminist movement that will go beyond both individualism and a merely sentimental idea of community.[2] Leszek Kolakowski continues his relentless critique of modernity in his latest book *Modernity on Endless Trial*.[3] These and dozens of other learned contemporaries are probing for more solid ground on which to build and sustain socially complex, pluralistic societies. The individualist as well as the collectivist ideals of modern humanism are under attack as never before.

To these scholars as well as to public policy makers in Washington, Brussels, Moscow, Tokyo, and other capitals around the world, the wisdom of the pluralist traditions introduced in this volume has much to offer. The questions we face today are not just those concerning the *limits* to human freedom but those concerning the proper *norms* for human responsibility. The challenges of modernity are not those which face undifferentiated communities but those arising within complex societies made up of many communities and institutions. States and international organizations perform a legal integrating function, but they can do that with justice only by protecting all the differentiated institutions and communities of society.

Since there is no simple way to go about comparing and testing alternative views of society outside actual historical engagement, both argument about and experimentation with the structure of society must be carried on in the full heat of battle. One of the chief values of these readings, we believe, is the opportunity they afford both scholars and public policy makers to reflect on traditions of thought and experience that have long been engaged in challenging the underlying assumptions of both individualism and collectivism. These readings manifest a constructive and not simply a critical effort. They reveal attempts to understand and to shape society in ways quite different from the mainstream of modern humanism. This fact does not guarantee their correctness or superiority. In fact, to the extent that pluralist thinking has not had as much historical influence as individualist and collectivist philosophies have had, it undoubtedly lacks the kind of proof that can come only with further testing and trial. Sophisticated versions of pluralist thought and social ordering, such as we have introduced here, have not been subjected to "endless trial." Nevertheless, the tests now confronting humanity on both the largest and smallest scales call for new thinking and new directions in policy making that can lead to greater justice for our differentiating and integrating societies. A conception of social pluralism, grounded one way or another in a comprehensive and progressive Christian philosophy, demands consideration in this context.

NOTES

1 Christopher Lasch, *The True and Only Heaven: Progress and its Critics* (New York: W. W. Norton, 1991), 530.

2 Elizabeth Fox-Genovese, *Feminism without Illusions: A Critique of Individualism* (Chapel Hill: University of North Carolina Press, 1991).

3 Leszek Kolakowski, *Modernity on Endless Trial* (Chicago: University of Chicago Press, 1990).